WORKING IN THE GLOBAL ECONOMY

It is clear that, although the human resource management field has been drastically affected by global competition over the last twenty years, most of the research and publications in the field are geared to providing corporations with an understanding of their business environment. This book takes an entirely different approach by looking at the job and career markets from the point of view of individuals who are searching for new strategies to develop their careers in a global environment. This book offers readers the tools they need to evaluate and manage their career environment and personal career profiles, and, ultimately, to have a rewarding global career.

Roblyn Simeon is a Professor of International Business at San Francisco State University, USA.

WORKING IN THE GLOBAL ECONOMY

HOW TO DEVELOP AND MANAGE YOUR CAREER ACROSS BORDERS

ROBLYN SIMEON

Routledge
Taylor & Francis Group

NEW YORK AND LONDON

First published 2013
by Routledge
711 Third Avenue, New York, NY 10017

Simultaneously published in the UK
by Routledge
2 Park Square, Milton Park, Abingdon, Oxon OX14 4RN

Routledge is an imprint of the Taylor & Francis Group, an informa business

Library of Congress Cataloging in Publication Data
Simeon, Roblyn.
  Working in the global economy : how to develop and manage
  your career across borders / Roblyn Simeon.
    p. cm.
  Includes bibliographical references and index.
  1. Employment in foreign countries.
  2. International business enterprises–Employees.
  3. Career development. I. Title.
  HF5382.55.S55 2012
  650.14–dc23

ISBN: 978-0-415-89130-1
ISBN: 978-0-415-89131-8
ISBN: 978-0-203-10746-1

Typeset in Joanna
by Swales & Willis Ltd, Exeter, Devon

Printed and bound in the United States of America
by Edwards Brothers, Inc.

To the memory of my mother, Mavis Simeon, who taught me that overcoming challenges helps you grow, and learning and contributing puts you on the path to success.

Contents

Preface

There are numerous books and articles written about the strategies that corporations use to scan business environments before making decisions about which markets to enter and which business strategies to pursue. There are also many managers, academics, and consultants who have developed techniques for effectively managing a corporation's workforce across borders. The objective of most of these articles and business strategies is to either boost the coordination or productivity of employees or to enhance the general competitive strength of the organization. In most of these cases, international career development has generally been approached from the perspective of the needs of the firm. There has been very little written from the perspective of individuals trying to understand employment environments at home and abroad.

This book takes a new approach and examines work and careers from the perspective of the individual. This is extremely important since, in many employment environments, the burden of long-term career management has been placed squarely on the shoulders of employees. The risks, responsibility, and rewards of personal career management are now more closely tied to individuals' career objectives and their ability to develop and mobilize the specific capabilities that are in demand around the world. Moreover, because of the impact of globalization and the surge in demand for knowledge workers, employment opportunities can be found in a greater variety of national environments.

Since there are now many individuals who are passionate about working with, or in, foreign environments, there is clearly a need for a book which puts forth an entrepreneurial approach to skill and career development while, at the same time, providing strategies for scanning and evaluating foreign markets and employment opportunities. In various chapters, this book illustrates ways in which a focus on capability, mobility, and transferability can help to maximize an individual's employability and long-term career success in the international environment.

The book is divided into four sections. The chapters in the first section help you gain a better understanding of work environments and the personalized resource management perspective. The chapters in the second section explore the impact of capability, mobility, and transferability strategies on career management. Section three focuses on specific strategies for developing your international business career in different regions. Section four covers guidelines for working and managing your career across borders. Throughout the book, there are numerous discussions about regions, institutions, sectors, or organizations that can help you accelerate your entry into the international business arena. If you are passionate about working with, and in, foreign markets, and you need to have a deeper understanding of factors that affect your international career management, this book should provide you with ample resources. The target audience for this book includes consultants, recruiters, human resource managers, faculty, students, career advisors, counselors, or individuals who are re-evaluating their current careers.

Acknowledgments

I would like to thank Misha and Yumi Simeon, as well as Tarikua Feta, for their inspiration and assistance during the writing of this book. I hope that this book can help others discover their career goals and shine a light on their career path as they venture into the world of international business.

PART I

UNDERSTANDING WORK ENVIRONMENTS & THE PERSONALIZED RESOURCE MANAGEMENT PERSPECTIVE

1 UNDERSTANDING WORK, CAREER STRUCTURES & PERSONALIZED RESOURCE MANAGEMENT

LEARNING OBJECTIVES

- Understanding the nature of work and its impact on work attitudes & business practices

- Reviewing how employment arrangements & structures affect career patterns

- Exploring how the personalized resource management perspective can impact your career

THE ROADMAP

If you are passionate about working with, or in, foreign markets, you should adopt a perspective that maximizes your chances of developing a successful career in the international arena. This and other chapters of this book will illustrate how an entrepreneurial approach to the development of your capabilities, as well as a strong interest in, and knowledge of, different international regions and sectors can boost your long-term employability and career success. In the chapters to come, you will explore the personalized resource management perspective which puts you, the individual, at the center of career development and career management dynamics.

TOPIC FOCUS

The world economy and labor markets move in uncertain directions, the prospects of finding good work and rewarding careers seem even more daunting. It often appears that workers are trying to navigate unpredictable landscapes without a map or a compass to show them a clear direction. At times like these, some may wonder why we need a book on work or careers. One answer is that work continues to be important because of its economic and social consequence for individuals, organizations, communities, and society. Work is also important because of the amount of time it occupies in many of our lives and, for many of us, work is a central factor in our identify creation processes. Our attitude towards work often reflects our central values and reveals our desired or expected role in the community or society. [1, 2]

The continually changing employment landscapes make it imperative that individuals become more aware of how past and present developments are impacting job and career environments at home and abroad. The influx of women into the workforce, work-life issues, greater workplace diversity, and the shift from a manufacturing to a service economy are all developments which have posed serious challenges to individuals and organizations. Moreover, over the last 30 years, we have seen how a steady increase in the use of business strategies such as downsizing, restructuring, reengineering, mergers, acquisitions, outsourcing, and off-shoring have drastically altered the psychological contract between workers and organizations in many environments. More and more individuals are being pushed to take the primary responsibility for their own employability and career management. [3–5]

THE NEED FOR A PERSONALIZED RESOURCE MANAGEMENT PERSPECTIVE

The majority of employment and career management strategies that have been implemented as a response to the new challenges in the business environment have emerged from the dominant human resource management (HRM) perspectives. Since HRM is generally tasked with managing people in organizations, it should come as no surprise that the strategies developed and implemented are generally geared to managing workers in ways that make firms more productive, flexible, and efficient. This organization-centric approach has dominated the study of work and careers to date. One goal of this book is to shed more light on an often neglected perspective in human resource management. [6–9]

This book takes a new approach and will examine work and careers from the perspective of the individual. There is clearly a need for a more personalized resource management (PRM) approach to work and career management since the risks, responsibility, and rewards of career development and success are now more tightly tied to workers' decisions and actions. Understanding the dynamics of employment opportunity landscapes will be crucial. Employment opportunity landscapes consist of the rules, regulations, business practices, employment intermediaries, organizations, and institutions that influence the types of employment opportunities as well as the pathways to work, jobs, and careers. It goes without saying that employment opportunity landscapes (EOL) can vary across regions and national boundaries. Because of globalization influences, the boundaries of these employment opportunity landscapes are porous, and developments in one can significantly impact outcomes in another. This book takes the position that a personalized resource management approach is the best perspective for an individual to take when navigating these cross-border employment landscapes. [10, 11]

Although the PRM approach is one that has been developed for this book, the underlying concepts come from a variety of business perspectives. *Personalized resource management* sees the individual as a bundle of capabilities, resources, and strategic orientations. The four major components of a personalized resource management (PRM) approach would be (1) personal experience, skills, and capabilities; (2) personal friendships and information networks; (3) personal employability strategies; and (4) work transition management approaches. When all four components are utilized effectively, they work to build long-term career capabilities. There will be a more detailed discussion of the personalized resource management perspective later in this chapter. [12–14]

Numerous researchers and career consultants have written about work and careers over the years. The goal of this book is not to summarize or disregard their findings or conclusions. What this book does is define, explain, and re-conceptualize the essential insights, observations, and practices in the field from the personalized resource management (PRM) perspective. Whether you are entry level, mid-career, upper management, freelancer, contract professional, or a budding entrepreneur, you should be interested in developing a clear understanding of work-related concepts, career dynamics, and the employment landscapes in a variety of regions and nations. [15–17]

The key assertion of this book is that, with a better understanding of what motivates you, what the international employment landscapes looks like, and with a greater knowledge of which strategies can improve your employability, you should be better able to navigate around the constantly changing employment obstacles and achieve a desired level of career success.

A ROADMAP FOR PERSONAL CAREER MANAGEMENT SUCCESS

A lot of career management-related material is covered in this book and the figure below shows the various topics and strategies that are presented throughout. Although the chapters do not exactly follow the progression of the phases in the diagram, the chart illustrates the key career strategies that are covered. The personalized career strategy chart (Figure 1.1) separates international career management into three phases. In phase I, the bulk of your efforts should be concerned with the evaluation and development of your personal brand, experiences and skills as well as your knowledge of sectors and occupations. In phase II, your focus should shift to the targeting of specific locations, sectors, positions, or lifestyles that are related to the occupations you hold or the career you wish to pursue. In phase III, you take advantage of your capabilities, life experience, networks, and mobility to effectively manage your personal branding, personal career capital and long-term

Figure 1.1 Personalized career strategy chart

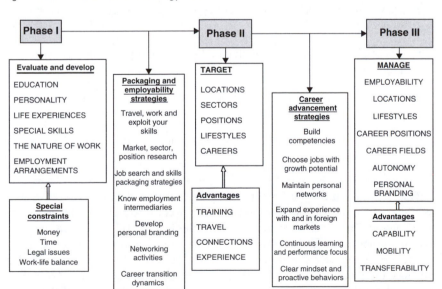

Developed by Roblyn Simeon

employability. Personal branding and personal career capital result from conscious image management strategies, the continuous accumulation of work-related capabilities and the effective use of networks to boost mobility and employability. For each phase, you need to figure out how to overcome your personal constraints and make use of any specific advantages you might have.

As you read the different chapters, you can refer to Figure 1.1 to see how the materials fit into the overall perspective and flow of activities. Throughout this book, you will be presented with strategies that help you *evaluate, develop, package, target, and manage* factors that impact your potential career success in the international business arena.

So what issues does the rest of Chapter 1 address? We will start by reviewing the nature of work and work attitudes, before examining how employment arrangements give shape to the career forms that we use to navigate employment experiences throughout our working life. Finally, you will be presented with a more detailed description of the personalized resource management perspective. The ideas covered in this chapter form the foundation for materials presented throughout the rest of this book. The international business arena is an exciting one, and understanding the fundamental aspects of work and career management can only boost your potential long-term international career success.

DEFINING WORK & UNDERSTANDING WORK GOALS & ATTITUDES

Is it important to define work? Don't we all know what work is when we see it? The short answers are yes and no. The nature of work, and which major dimensions get emphasized, can often depend on the socio-cultural and institutional environments in which work takes place. However, everyone generally agrees that work is important for most people because of the personal growth and satisfaction, as well as the potential social rewards and economic success, that can result from doing it. [1, 18, 19]

Various ways of using the concept of work

- Do you have the skills, training, and experience necessary to get this work done?

- Although he has a good reputation in the community, he doesn't have the required certifications to be working as a doctor in this area.

- The work I do for this organization is satisfying because I feel that I am giving back to the community.

- Since the work I do for this firm is valuable, I think I should be more highly compensated.

One explanation for much of the uncertainty that sometimes prevents a clear definition of work is the observation that the concept is *personal, contextual, metaphoric, and evolutionary*. The term "personal" refers to the feelings of attachment, growth, accomplishment, and satisfaction which individuals can derive from work. Contextual here refers to the technical activity, socio-cultural, and economic factors that influence the definition of work. Metaphoric refers to the range of work-related terms and associations, such as job, occupation, profession, and career that come to mind when using the word "work." Finally, evolutionary indicates that the meaning, application, status, and the scope of the activities related to the concept of work continue to change over time and across national boundaries. A detailed exploration of the context dimension of work can be found in the Appendix. [20–22]

Because of the richness and the complexity of the concept of work, it is essential that we clarify the definitions of a number of work-related terms we often hear associated with the concept. These basic definitions will serve as the departure points for more complex discussions of work and careers later in this chapter, and in other chapters of the book. [23–25]

Table 1.1 Definitions of work-related concepts

Terminology	Definitions
Work	It is an activity which requires physical or mental effort to do. A more goal-oriented view would say that work is effort directed at accomplishing a task.
Job	It is the regular or piece of work which a person does for a client or an organization, often to earn money or receive another form of compensation.
Occupation	It is a more formal way of referring to someone's regular work activity or job that is done for a client or organization. The term also indicates some level of personal identification with the work being carried out.
Profession	Any type of work or occupation which requires special experience, skills, education, training, or certification in order to be socially, institutionally, or technically recognized as being capable of accomplishing particular occupational assignments.
Career	The simplest definition would say that a career is a series of work or job situations that give shape to one's working life. Careers reflect an individual's or organization's strategy of combining personal capabilities, as well as work, educational, or life experiences over time, to project one or more occupational identities or professions.

Now that we have explored some of the factors behind the definition of work and associated work activities, we can focus on understanding the importance of work and associated work-related attitudes and goals. Research has shown that there is a link between individuals' subjective understanding of the importance of work and key job behaviors, and work outcomes such as job involvement and job performance. Three concepts that are crucial to understanding the "importance of work" are work centrality, work goals, and work attitudes.

TOPIC FOCUS

Work centrality refers to the general importance of work in an individual's life when compared to other significant life concerns, such as leisure, family, friends, community, or religion. In addition to personal preferences, the work centrality concept is embedded in specific organizational and societal conditions. In other words, work centrality is not only influenced by an individual's personality, it is also influenced by the national culture and social institutions which encourage the pursuit of some goals and discourage or sanction the pursuit of other goals. An understanding of work centrality and work goals can help to answer the question why, relative to other people at home or abroad, an individual or group might place a greater significance on work-related activities over other significant concerns. [26–29]

The importance given to understanding work centrality and work goals is directly related to the general experience worldwide of work being central among a range of life activities. The concept of work goals refers to the psychological needs, socio-economic outcomes, and work related factors that individuals identify as reasons for participating in work. Most of the research on work goals focuses on three major aspects:

1. Motivations to work

2. Job characteristics desired by workers

3. Working conditions that impact how work is done

It might seem apparent that the concept of work goals should be mainly related to the motivations for doing work. However, job characteristics and working conditions continue to be bundled with the concept of work goals. Based on this expanded scope of the work goals concept used in the literature, researchers found a lot of similarity in the importance and ranking of work goals for factors such as job challenge, job freedom, relations with supervisor, and advancement opportunities. However, there were significant differences with factors such as societal concerns, wage concerns, the profit motive, individual achievement, and autonomy. [1, 30, 31]

Another distinction which is often mentioned in the work goals literature is the difference between intrinsic and extrinsic motivations. Intrinsic motivation is related to the psychological factors that inspire workers to work harder or perform better than is obligated by the employment relationship. Extrinsic motivation is related to material or social structure factors that push workers to work harder than is obligated. A general observation across different research is that there is a limit to a complete focus on extrinsic rewards as motivators, since after a certain point, workers become satisfied with material compensation. At that point, intrinsic rewards become much more appealing and effective. Another observation is that job characteristics or working conditions that reinforce an individual's work motivations will boost employee performance for longer periods than those that conflict with work motivation and work goals. The wide range of organizational strategies developed over the years to respond to these varying internal and external motivators include job design, job enrichment, variable working hours, flextime, participative management strategies, and goal-setting strategies. The Appendix presents more detailed information on work attitudes that affect career management. [27, 30, 32]

TOPIC FOCUS

After understanding the importance of work centrality and work goals, why would an examination of employment structures and arrangements be necessary? The main reason is that this information is important because these structures and arrangements not only show how labor is distributed across the main productive segments of an economy, they also reflect the dominant work structures and employment agreements that impact career formation and career management. *Employment structures* refer to accepted categories for the main ways in which a country divides its labor force during different periods of economic development. These categories are directly linked to three key productive sectors in an economy: the primary, secondary, and tertiary sectors. On the other hand, *employment arrangements* refer to contractual or transactional agreements between individuals, clients, and organizations that center around the accomplishment of work-related goals and outcomes.

EMPLOYMENT STRUCTURES & ARRANGEMENTS

The *primary sector* of an economy is associated with activities that develop or extract materials from the natural environment (e.g. farming or fishing). The *secondary sector* refers to work activities that involve the manufacturing of things (e.g. making cars or trains). The *tertiary sector* is related to the development and deployment of service activities (e.g. teaching, financial). One can learn a lot about a country by examining the distribution of the employment structures. However, the distribution of employment structures change over time. In the early stages of development, countries usually have a high percentage of workers in the primary sector (e.g. agriculture). As a country industrializes, you usually see a growing secondary sector with more manufacturing activities and growing urban areas. As an economy develops and starts to mature, we tend to see a greater demand for services, in areas such as education, travel, financial, and healthcare. At this stage, we see significant growth in the tertiary sector. [33]

A second way of looking at how jobs are allocated in an economy comes from dual labor market theory. In this perspective, labor markets are divided into *primary and secondary markets*. The primary market has good high-skill jobs with better job security, higher pay, good working conditions, and many opportunities for promotion. The secondary market has low-skill jobs with little employment security, low pay, poor working conditions, and few opportunities for advancement. Depending on the national economic environment and dominant labor institutions, the size of the primary and secondary markets and the rate of movement between them can vary significantly.[34]

A third way of examining how jobs are divided up in an economy looks at ownership structures and separates the economy into three sectors: private, public, and non-profit. This approach may be the one most familiar to us today. The difference in this approach is that the employment distribution does not tell us the stage of industrial development or the quality of jobs. However, we do get a better idea of a country's approach to free market ideology and general economic management. The *public sector* refers to that part of the economy which is under total or partial state control. This occurs when the government, military, or bureaucracy controls the allocation and production of goods and services based on state-owned resources and organizations. Public sector activities can include such areas as national defense, manufacturing, and banking activities. The *private sector* refers to that part of the economy in which goods and services are produced by resources not owned by the government or the bureaucracy, but owned, rather, by individuals or organizations whose main objective is earning economic returns for the ownership of their resources (exception: non-profits). The *non-profit sector* can be considered part of the private sector, but its main goal is not profit generation, but using social activities, community support, and productive capabilities to accomplish morally and socially desired goals. [35, 36]

Employment Arrangements

As mentioned previously, employment arrangements refer to the types of employment contracts or task expectations that arise when individuals agree to carry out work-related duties for clients or organizations. Employment arrangements cover a wide range of cooperative situations, dependencies, and expectations among the participants. By examining how the skills, jobs, and careers are linked to the dominant employment arrangements, it is possible to gain insights into the nature of work-related social, technical, and economic change under way in different sectors, regions, and nations. Many different approaches have been taken to categorize these employment arrangements. The varying characteristics of these employment arrangements include the type of employing agent, permanency of employment, predictability of working hours, benefits expectations, and levels of compensation. This book consolidates these characteristics into four different employment arrangements that comprehensively cover the activities and roles of the various participants. The four employment arrangements are referred to as:

1. Traditional arrangements

2. Moderated traditional arrangements

3. Alternative arrangements

4. Contingent arrangements

Traditional employment arrangements refer to situations whereby individuals are directly hired by the organization on a full-time, part-time, or temporary basis. There is usually a salary and some short-term or long-term expectation of continued employment. The table below explains the factors linked to the traditional employment arrangements.

Table 1.2 Traditional employment arrangements

Employment arrangements	Explanations
Full-time permanent	Employees of organizationswho work for more than 30 hours a week on a regular basis, receive a salary, are eligible for a range of benefits, and have an expectation of long-term employment. They usually have one main occupational role at a time. The role changes as they move up or sideways in the organization.
Multiple-role full-time permanent	Employees who have two or more role positions in the organization. The jobs are usually divided up at the discretion of the manager. They are often full-time employees in small or medium-sized organizations that are trying to do more with fewer people. Workers have an expectation of continued longer-term employment and they also receive benefits.
Part-time permanent	Employees of an organization who work fewer hours than the full-time staff but do so on an ongoing basis, receive a salary, are eligible for prorata benefits, and have an expectation of long-term employment.
Full-time and part-time temporary	Employees are directly hired by the firm to work a full or partial work schedule for limited periods of time. Their salaries may be higher or lower than permanent workers, but benefits will usually be less. There is no expectation of continual long-term employment.

Moderated traditional employment arrangements can be short or long-term arrangements but continued employment, and the level of expected compensation, benefits, and training are more tightly linked to tasks or project performance objectives. Quite often, these arrangements are used so that the main organization can more closely evaluate an individual's potential or rely on a commission-based system. *Alternative employment arrangements* are generally more short-term or medium-term, in respect of the expectations for continued employment. There is also very little expectation of benefits, and the hiring agent is often an outside organization. *Contingent employment arrangements* occur when individuals are hired for very short-term or irregular periods of employment. They can be hired on a daily, hourly, or weekly basis. There is no expectation of ongoing work and the individuals are not required to be available for work. Moreover, worker protections and benefits are often non-existent. These types of arrangements can usually be found in the informal economy in most countries. The Appendix contains a more detailed description of all the non-traditional employment arrangements mentioned above. [37–42]

As corporations adjusted to a changing competitive landscape, they used some of the above-mentioned employment arrangements to enhance their strategic flexibility, lower costs, and shift career management responsibility to workers. Some individuals chose these employment arrangements to get more control over their working conditions, in order to have more autonomy or to better manage work-life issues. However, the search for flexibility on both sides did not end with the use of varied *external labor market intermediaries* and employment arrangements. Companies and workers agreed on a plethora of flexible *internal labor market* work arrangements that have significantly changed how work is done within firms. [17, 31, 43, 44]

Flexible work arrangements are usually a matter of agreement between the employer and the employee (or the employee's representative). A flexible work arrangement is an alternative to the traditional working hours in a company. This often includes different approaches to the 9 to 5 or 40-hour work week arrangements. Most of the changes in work arrangements occur in three areas:

1. Changes in working hours (e.g. starting times, number of hours worked)

2. Changes in working patterns (e.g. job sharing, shift splitting)

3. Changes in work location (e.g. working at home or elsewhere)

These flexible work arrangement include strategies such as flextime, reduced hours, compressed work week, telecommuting, job sharing, annualized hours (or the banking of hours), gradual retirement, leaves and sabbaticals. More detailed descriptions of many of these strategies can be found in the Appendix.

TOPIC FOCUS

When the concept of career was defined earlier, mention was made of how individuals or organizations are able to combine skills, capabilities, and experiences to project one or more occupational identities. What was not mentioned was how the nature of the *psychological contract* between individuals and organizations has undergone significant change. There used to be an implicit understanding that if individuals worked hard and sacrificed for the company, the company would, in turn, do its best to keep those individuals employed, create career paths, and compensate them for their loyalty and efforts. That psychological contract has been broken, and a number of factors have contributed to this shift in obligations and expectations for both individuals and organizations. Changes such as a surge in female participation in the workforce and the subsequent rise in the number of two-income families underscored the need for more flexible and family-friendly employment policies. Moreover, during the same period, corporate policies developed to respond to turbulent environments: increased competition and global sourcing possibilities appear to have done significant damage to the old psychological contract. Individuals now use a greater variety of employment arrangements to develop their careers, and participate in a wider array of career forms. The links between employment arrangements and career forms are discussed in greater detail below. [3, 10, 45, 46]

THE IMPORTANCE OF CAREER FORMS

Over the last 30 years, the steady increase in restructurings, downsizings, mergers, acquisitions, outsourcings, and off-shoring made workers and managers alike realize that the traditional career pattern was under siege. Moreover, corporations' greater use of business alliances and alternative employment arrangements intensified the externalization of employment relations and thereby gave them more strategic flexibility. During this period, it soon became apparent that there was a shift in the old psychological contract in which workers exchanged loyalty for job security to a new psychological contract in which workers exchanged performance for compensation and potential employability credentials. Although the traditional career form is still dominant in many environments, we can see varying degrees of a shift to alternative career forms around the world. This is occurring because, more and more, individuals are being forced to develop and manage their careers in environments full of economic and institutional uncertainty. [5, 8, 47]

Before discussing the major types of career forms that workers participate in around the world, we need to have a clear understanding of the concept of career form. A *career form* is a pattern of contractual or transactional relationships that link individuals, organizations, or clients, and also signals the expectations of, and obligations for, work and career creation and management. These expectations and obligations relate to decisions about continued employment, working hours, skill development, promotion possibilities, job transitions, and long-term career management. Career forms generally emerge from patterns of employment arrangements that have similar expectations and obligations. It is this interaction between expectations and obligations linked to employment arrangements that is at the heart of the structure of various career forms. In order to present a more dynamic view of careers, this book will often use the expression "participate in career forms." This refers to the possibility for individuals to vary the length, frequency, and intensity of their experience with different career forms. The five major career forms to be discussed below are the bureaucratic, boundary-switching, portfolio, entrepreneurial, and peripheral career forms.

Bureaucratic Career Form

This is often referred to as the traditional career form in the human resource management literature. The bureaucratic career form can be defined as a sequence of work roles in a formally defined organizational hierarchy of employment positions. Expectations are that, in exchange for satisfactory work role performances, employees get the opportunity to advance (be promoted) up the hierarchical ranks during their long-term association with the organization. Another expectation is that, in exchange for loyalty and job performance, workers can expect to stay within the same or affiliated organizations for the very long term or until retirement. Moreover, employees' authority, compensation, formal training, skill requirements, and responsibilities are expected to change as they move up the ranks of the organization. In essence, once individuals gain entry into the organization, they can move sideways or upward to occupy independent work roles for periods of time determined mostly by opportunities in the organization. In this career form, employees can take a longer-term career view of job assignments or job transitions, because it is the totality of positions they will hold that will characterize their careers with the organization. [4, 9, 48, 49]

Boundary-Switching Career Form

The main differences between the bureaucratic form and boundary-switching career form are the frequency of the employee's organizational changes, the lack of expectation of continued long-term employment and a stronger commitment by workers to maintain their personal view of a career trajectory. There is usually a focus on developing portable skills and knowledge as employees move sequentially across multiple firms and sectors during their working life. In effect, employees no longer have to depend on one main organizational hierarchy for promotions. They can take advantage of their capabilities and personal networks to move to firms that provide the best opportunities for career development. However, although the employees are changing organizations at a faster pace, they tend to do it sequentially. What tends to govern the manner in which these employees change jobs and firms is their personal view of how present and future tasks or jobs should match their view of a long-term career trajectory. [5, 50]

Other terms have been used to describe this particular career form. Discussions about the boundary-less career present similar descriptions. The literature focuses on the ability of workers to move easily across organizational boundaries and the shift to individual responsibility for career development and management. For the protean career types, the main focus is on developing and maintaining the skills, capabilities, and relationships that allow them to move quickly between jobs, organizations and sectors. The emphasis of both the boundary-less and protean career types is on independence, flexibility, and personal marketing, rather than on hierarchical reporting and promotion principles. This perspective also points out that an individual's career will generally unfold over multiple organizational settings. [51, 52][3, 53]

The professional career type is another concept which appears to be closely related to this book's concept of the boundary-switching career form. Professional careers are defined by the craft, skills, knowledge, social connection, or reputation factors that are linked to a specialized occupation. Although there may be frequent interactions or longer-term associations with a client or organization, an individual's career growth is linked to community or market reputation as well as the general capability to handle a range of tasks and projects. The importance of reputation or institutions for certifying a professional worker's competence is often crucial for career success. Although it is possible to have a professional career in one organization, these careers occur most often across multiple organizations or networks that rely on, support, legitimize, protect, or promote the individual's work activities and accomplishments. In essence, the psychological contract is with oneself, and there is a greater commitment to the occupation or profession than to the organization. [11, 13, 17]

Portfolio Career Form

The portfolio career is one based on a series of varied shorter-term job or projects that occur consecutively or concurrently. The portfolio career can be viewed as a collection of different pieces of work or projects from different clients. Very often, the individuals are self-employed and offer their services on a project basis to one or more employers at a time. This type of portfolio worker takes jobs and has occupations that may cross many organizations at one time. On paper it may often seem to an outsider that the various jobs or occupations indicate a lack of ambition or focus. However, this career form requires a strong personal approach to unifying the various work activities and performances as part of an overall career strategy. It is how individuals view the connections between their projects and occupations that determines the career trajectory or sense of career success. [16, 40, 54]

Although the situation whereby the portfolio worker has many jobs from different clients appears to be the most prevalent, it is also possible to have a portfolio career within one organization for long periods of time. As organizations and workers seek more flexibility, you can see more of these situations across the country. Some of these jobs are complementary, but there are situations where they are unrelated. It is not unusual in smaller dynamic organizations to have one individual who is the marketing manager and also the office manager. It is also possible to have someone work a few days a week as a receptionist and then work as an executive secretary for other days. Depending on the organization, these situations can continue for longer periods of time. From the individuals' point of view, they could see the different jobs as building different competencies, or as part of an overall strategy to move their career in a specific direction. [15, 55]

Entrepreneurial Career Form

The entrepreneurial career can occur over a single or several periods of an individual's working life. The entrepreneurial career can also cover a range of work and occupational activities that range from part-time participation in a single project to full-time major business developments that generate jobs and new organizations. In order to fully grasp the dynamic nature of this career form, it has to be examined by looking at four different areas of emphasis: behavioral style, arena of activity, goal orientation, and career management approach. Behavioral style refers to the personal characteristics and approach to work that entrepreneurial workers exhibit. In general, they tend to desire autonomy and are confident, resilient, flexible, and very goal-oriented risk takers. Their arena of activity indicates that they usually prefer to participate in or launch entrepreneurial activities. This can be in an established organization that has incorporated entrepreneurial structures or it can be a new venture. When firms incorporate work structures to allow for entrepreneurial behaviors, it is called intra-preneurship. This includes arrangements like corporate venturing, spin-offs, and entrepreneurs-in-residence, that allow employees to pursue more inspiring work-related goals. However, the intense desire for autonomy of most individuals that participate in entrepreneurial careers usually pushes them to be self-employed or to start a new organization, instead of working for an established one. [31, 37, 56]

The goal orientation of entrepreneurial careers is the focus on creating a new product, service, or work of art that can be marketed and/or provide entertainment to a range of customers. There is usually a strong focus on adapting something old or creating something new with the purpose of projecting a new experience into the market. Finally, the career management approach is based on individuals developing and managing their competence, reputation, and relationships in order to increase the chances of success of their projects, products, services, or organizations. There is an acceptance of the high risk-reward situations they choose and there is no expectation of a stable and constant revenue stream. For those participating in entrepreneurial careers, the lines between work, family, and community are not as clearly defined, since it is often important that they be able to quickly mobilize personal, professional, and community networks in order to initiate or complete projects.

Depending on the length and frequency of participation in this career form, we can identify four types of entrepreneurial careers: novice, serial, parallel, or portfolio. The *novice entrepreneur* would refer to those preparing for, or starting, their first entrepreneurial venture. This could occur on a part-time or full-time basis as they test the possibility of dedicating all their energy to the venture. The *serial entrepreneur* indicates those individuals whose main focus is to start new ventures and get them to reach a certain level of success before moving on to start another venture. The *parallel entrepreneur* would be those individuals who are participating in two different entrepreneurial ventures at the same time. This could also refer to individuals who have a full-time organizational career and a separate entrepreneurial career occurring at the same time. Finally, the *portfolio entrepreneur* concept would indicate individuals who are involved with multiple entrepreneurial ventures in a variety of locations or sectors. They would usually be leveraging their knowledge and contacts to become an important contributor to the various ventures. [11, 47, 53]

Peripheral Career Form

Peripheral careers can be stagnant, dynamic, diverse, simple or complex. There are two main approaches to defining peripheral careers: (a) the low living standards approach; and (b) the informal economy approach. In the first approach, peripheral careers can be defined as consisting of jobs that fail to generate income to reach minimally acceptable living standards. Individuals might hold these jobs for short or long periods of time, and the low quality job characterization could be due to insufficient working hours or extremely low wages. In the second approach, peripheral careers can be defined as participation in those jobs that are not recognized or protected under any national legal or regulatory framework. These are grey area or illegal jobs that all thrive outside formally developed regulatory systems. These jobs can range from own-account domestic workers to self-employed workers in microenterprises. The key characteristics of most jobs that constitute peripheral careers are the relative ease of entry and exit, self-employment or low wage work, low skill

levels, variable working hours, and no expectation of continued long-term employment. Because of structural economic issues, social stratification, or discriminatory
practices, many individuals are relegated to participating in this career form for
major periods of their life. [39, 57–59]

OBSERVATIONS ON JOBS & CAREER FORMS

Since a wide range of jobs populate the various career forms, some have attempted
to simplify the discussion by just focusing on the quality of jobs. The argument here
would be that it doesn't really matter what career form one chooses or is relegated
to, it simply comes down to whether the jobs are "good jobs, bad jobs, or dead-end
jobs." The remedy, then, would be that you should avoid bad jobs or dead-end jobs
at all cost and focus your efforts on getting good jobs. More detailed definitions of
good jobs, bad jobs, and dead-end jobs can be found in the Appendix. [34, 36, 41]

The problem with this "good jobs, bad jobs" classification approach to jobs is that
it ignores the subjective aspect of how individuals interpret the value of jobs. It also
ignores any long-term view an individual could have of how a job might fit into plans
for building a portfolio of skills and capabilities. There are four issues that should be
linked to any "good jobs, bad jobs" discussion: *the matching issue, the social comparison issue,
the job characteristics issue and the career-trajectory issue.* To evaluate a job, one has to decide
if skills and personal psychological needs match what the job offers or demands.
Compensation is not an absolute concept, but is often evaluated in comparison to
others in similar positions. The social respect given to a job position also impacts its
desirability. It is possible for society to respect individuals for doing a dangerous or
demanding job that most people would avoid. Job characteristics include the work
environment, employment demands for the position, relative wages, skill demands,
physical demands, and stress levels. Finally, it is possible for individuals to choose
jobs that place them in a trajectory toward longer-term career goals. Three of the four
issues above are very subjective, and only job characteristics can be evaluated objec-
tively (to a degree). Consequently, it appears that jobs are more varied and complex
concepts than the image of "good jobs, bad jobs" can capture. [56, 60, 61]

TOPIC FOCUS

The personalized resource management approach (PRM) will play a central
role throughout this book. Although there are varying levels of economic,
social, and institutional constraints in work environments, the PRM perspective sees employability strategies and the productive use of one's capabilities and resources as the central factors in career development and management. There is clearly a need for a personalized resource management (PRM)
approach to work and career development since the risks, responsibility,
and rewards of career development and success are now more tightly tied to
workers' decisions and actions. [13, 37, 52]

THE PERSONALIZED RESOURCE MANAGEMENT PERSPECTIVE

The personalized resource management perspective sees the individual as a bundle
of capabilities, resources, and strategic orientations. The four major components of

the personalized resource management (PRM) approach are (1) personal experience, skills and capabilities; (2) personal friendships and information networks; (3) personal employability strategies; and (4) effective job transition management. From the individual's point of view, a good personalized resource management approach would rely on effective strategies to develop and deploy all four abovementioned components over time. Figure 1.2 presents a micro level view of how the personalized resource management orientation plays a central role in career development behaviors.

Figure 1.2 Overview of the central position of the personalized resource management (PRM) orientation

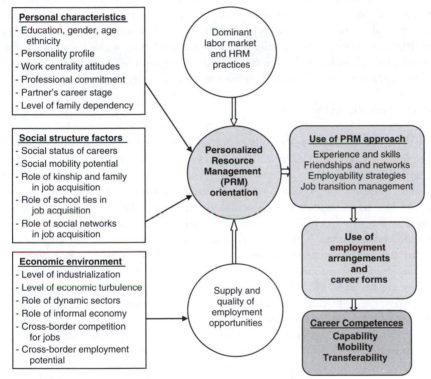

PRM orientation: powerless, passive, active, and pro-active behaviors
Employment arrangements: temporary, contract, part-time, full-time, self-employed etc.
Career forms: bureaucratic, boundary-switching, portfolio, entrepreneurial, peripheral

The overall model (Figure 1.2) shows that an individual's work and career-related attitudes and strategies are influenced by a number of personal, social, and economic factors. In other words, the individual's work and career- related behaviors and strategies are tempered by economic conditions as well as by personal characteristics and social structure factors. The strength of these factors varies depending on national environments, group demographics, and the nature of local economic conditions.

Personal Characteristics

Studies have shown that educational level, gender, age, and ethnicity all can play a significant role in how individuals approach the work environment. Because of the need to match skills to job tasks, the most direct link to certain jobs is one's level of education. Organizations can openly require various levels of educational achievement for employment positions. On the other hand, although there may be no overt explanations, certain jobs have consistently showed age and gender biases. In some national environments, there may even be open and legal age and gender restrictions placed upon certain jobs. Ethnicity is another area where we see subtle restrictions or self-selection for various occupations.

Personality profile and work centrality attitude also impact an individual's view of work and careers. Risk-taking individuals who are resilient and who like independence and autonomy will tend to favor or perform better in occupations that support those traits. The personality-occupation profile match can thus be very significant. The importance of work in one's life (work centrality) is an attitude which also impacts an individual's willingness to make sacrifices for the sake of work. Finally, professional commitment reflects how dedicated an individual is to maintaining a particular occupation even in difficult circumstances. It goes without saying that the extent to which individuals have family obligations and the stage of their ongoing career are factors that also strongly impact work and career decisions.

Social Structure Factors

The social status of careers can vary significantly across regions and national environments. Working as a police officer, a firefighter, or a soldier may seem equally appealing, but the local or national environment's view of these careers can impact an individual's desire to take on one of these professions. Occupations also vary by their ability to support upward social mobility. Becoming a doctor, lawyer, or engineer can significantly boosts one's social status and upward mobility potential in many environments. Another important social factor is the role of kinship and family ties in job and career acquisition. The impact of these ties can range from simple advice and support to strong and fixed traditions of providing access only to certain groups based on family and kinship ties. In a similar way, school ties are also important social structures that can disproportionately affect an individual's ability to enter certain organizations and occupations.

Social networks represent another important social structure. The concept of social networks refers to social interaction environments with multiple members that can provide advice, support, information, or access to individuals or groups. These networks can consist of family members, acquaintances, colleagues, or other individuals with similar interests. The social interaction can take place in formal or informal meetings or through an online community. Moreover, there are many published reports indicating that knowledge about, and access to, a vast majority of high profile jobs occur through social networks.

Economic Environment

This external factor is the one that is most beyond the individual's control. The level of industrialization and level of economic turbulence can dominate the employment characteristics of a region or nation. Nevertheless, knowledge about the dynamic sectors as well as cross-border employment opportunities can provide individuals with the information necessary for creating effective work and career development strategies even in uncertain economic environments. In many ways, the competition for jobs has become a global phenomenon. However, by focusing on mobility and employability, individuals can be mainly concerned about the location, supply, and quality of employment opportunities.

Dominant Labor Market & HRM Practices

The dominant labor market practices represent another external factor which greatly influences an individual's ability to rely on personal work and career development strategies. The extent to which there are strong and flexible internal or external labor markets impacts the tendency for an individual's career to occur within a few organizations or across multiple organizations. Human resource management policies that mainly focus on firm-specific or general and technical skills also influence the nature of career formation and development in many environments.

Personalized Resource Management Orientation

Taking into account the external social and economic constraints, this concept refers to the individual's attitude or action orientation in regards to job transition management and career development. A *powerless PRM orientation* indicates that the external constraints and employing organization are the dominant influence in the setting of strategies for job transition or career development. Even though the individuals might not be satisfied with their current position or occupation, external or organizational factors dominate and prevent them from personally initiating any significant change. A *passive PRM orientation* means that, although individuals may have the flexibility and the power to set job transition and career strategies, they tend to leave the decision up to the employing organization and react only after job transition conditions become clear. Aside from firm-specific skills, workers tend not to develop new general skills and capabilities unless absolutely necessary. An *active PRM orientation* occurs when individuals continue to develop relationships, skills, and capabilities so that they might be more successful within the employing organization. They will also periodically develop general and technical skills, but will only consider moving to other organizations when there is a clear sign that their current position is in danger. A *proactive PRM orientation* describes individuals who continually develop their skills, capabilities, and social networks in order to maximize their mobility and employability. Individuals regularly evaluate their career progress in relation to career objectives and will seek out employment opportunities within or across firms that get them to their stated career goals faster.

Participation in Employment Arrangements & Career Forms

Depending on the flexibility and strength of the external labor market, the manner in which individuals participate in employment arrangements and careers should generally reflect their status in the labor market, their job transition strategies, their employability focus, and their commitment to a particular occupation. We can say that employment arrangements are basically the vehicles individuals use to navigate the employment opportunity landscape. Career forms would then be the pathways they use to find or reach their planned or emergent career goals. Personalized resource management is about picking directions or destinations, gathering the necessary resources, choosing the right vehicles and then adjusting the pathways to match changing conditions in the employment opportunity landscape.

COMMENTARY ON THE PERSONALIZED RESOURCE MANAGEMENT PERSPECTIVE

It goes without saying that your freedom to enter, remain with, or leave employment arrangements and career forms is moderated by your personal characteristics,
occupational capabilities, employment opportunities, as well as the social and institutional labor-related practices in the region or national environment in which you
are located. Using the PRM perspective as just presented, it is possible to put forth a
clearer definition of the concept of a career. [13, 37, 52]

> **PRM Definition of Career:** A career is a planned or emergent subjective approach
> to linking personal, educational, or job-related experiences obtained by work-
> ing with or across organizations or clients in ways that boost employability,
> develops capabilities, and gives meaning to your work goals. Careers are also
> symbolic vehicles for navigating various employment opportunity landscapes
> that you encounter during your working life.

With this PRM-oriented definition of career, the focus shifts to the motivations, capabilities, and resources that you need to enter, remain with, or switch careers. Although
there are benefits and drawbacks to each employment arrangement or career option,
the crucial requirement is for you to be able to evaluate and package the work experiences and capabilities gained from jobs, clients, and organizations. The next step is
then for you to learn how to combine the past, present, and potential future experiences into a trajectory that projects a desired career path. This career path will most
likely not remain a fixed one, because of the dynamic nature of the employment
opportunity landscapes that you will have to navigate. [10, 12–15, 37, 47]

In essence, the personalized resource management perspective believes that
the following two paramount capabilities should drive your approach to career
management:

1. The ability to recognize, participate in, or change employment arrangements in
   order to maintain an active and rewarding career trajectory.

2. The ability to develop your work-related capabilities, as well as personal and
   formal network resources, in ways that boost employability and mobility in the
   international business arena.

In order to grasp the implications of the PRM perspective, the best metaphor that
comes to mind is that of using an extensive rail system in an area where is it the most
important mode of transportation. For someone going to a particular destination,
it is important to know which train to take, how long to stay on it, and when to
transfer to another train. If a particular train line breaks down, it might be necessary
to walk to get to another rail line. If one knows the rail system well, there may be
express trains or unique transfers that shorten the journey. Along the way, we can
get information and help from others that know the system better than we might.
However, without a clear idea of a general direction or a specific destination, one
can end up mindlessly traveling the rail system or giving up on the trip entirely. It
is also possible that a major event or realization could cause us to change direction,
or even our initial intended destination.

CHAPTER SUMMARY & OBSERVATIONS

This chapter explored some fundamental concepts about the nature of work, work attitudes, employment arrangements, and career forms. You were also introduced to the personalized resource management perspective. All the concepts mentioned above play a major role in how individuals develop and manage careers. We started out by showing that the concept of work is richer and more flexible than many people realize, because of its personal, contextual, metaphoric, and evolutionary attributes. Work continues to be important to individuals around the world because of the personal growth and satisfaction, as well as the potential social rewards and economic success, that can result from doing it. The importance given to understanding work centrality and work goals is directly related to the general experience worldwide of work being central among a range of life activities. Another concept that was helpful in illustrating the different ways in which work can shape careers was that of employment arrangements. Employment arrangements refer to contractual or transactional agreements between individuals, clients, and organizations that center around the accomplishment of work-related goals and outcomes.

We also came across the important concept of career form, which can be considered a symbolic vehicle for navigating employment landscapes. More specifically, a career form was defined as a pattern of contractual or transactional relationships that link individuals, organizations, or clients, and also signals the expectations of, and obligations for, work and career creation and management. Finally, the personalized resource management perspective was presented in detail. There were two paramount capabilities that appeared to be driving this approach to career management. One was individuals' abilities to recognize, participate in, or change employment arrangements in order to maintain an active and rewarding career trajectory. The other was individuals' abilities to develop work-related capabilities, as well as personal and network resources, in ways that boost employability and mobility in the international business arena.

The ideas and concepts presented above may seem too abstract or irrelevant for some individuals in the initial stages of their career development. However, if you wish to have greater insight into and control over your career development in the international business arena, a thorough understanding of how work, employment arrangements and career forms might differ across borders will be essential. This knowledge, along with the personalized resource management perspective, can become the foundation for your exploration of the international sectors, employment arenas, occupations, and business trends that can greatly influence your career development and management activities. Chapter 2 will continue the exploration of fundamental concepts and factors that influence career management dynamics. There will be a discussion of how career transition behaviors might be influenced by the personalized resource management perspective. That will be followed by an evaluation of the role of different types of employment intermediaries. Finally, you will be shown a model that represents the macro view of employment opportunity landscapes. These landscapes consist of the rules, regulations, business practices, employment intermediaries, organizations, and institutions that influence the types of employment opportunities as well as the nature of the pathways to work, jobs, and careers.

REFERENCES

1. Harpaz, I., *The importance of work goals: An international perspective.* Journal of International Business Studies, 1990. **21**(1): p. 75–93.
2. O'Toole, J. and E.E. Lawler III, *The new American workplace,* 2006, New York, NY: Palgrave Macmillan.
3. Briscoe, J. and L. Finkelstein, *The new career and organizational commitment.* Career Development International, 2009. **14**(3): p. 242.
4. Kanter, R.M., *From climbing to hopping: The contingent job and the post-entrepreneurial career.* Management Review, 1989. **78**(4): p. 22–27.
5. Orange, R.M., *The emerging mutable self: Gender dynamics and creative adaptations in defining work, family, and the future.* Social Forces, 2003. **82**(1): p. 1–34.
6. Garavan, T.N. and M. Coolahan, *Career mobility in organizations: Implications for career development - Part I.* Journal of European Industrial Training, 1996. **20**(4): p. 30.
7. Lundberg, C.D. and M.F. Peterson, *The meaning of working in U.S. and Japanese local governments at three hierarchical levels.* Human Relations, 1994. **47**(12): p. 1459–1487.
8. Sullivan, S., *The changing nature of careers: A review and research agenda.* Journal of Management 1999. **25**(3): p. 457–484.
9. Zaleska, K.J. and L. de Menezes, *Human resources development practices and their association with employee attitudes: Between traditional and new careers.* Human Relations, 2007. **60**(7): p. 987.
10. Ackah, C. and N. Heaton, *The reality of "new" careers for men and for women.* Journal of European Industrial Training, 2004. **28**(2/4): p. 141.
11. Dokko, G., S. Wilk and N. Rothbard, *Unpacking prior experience: How career history affects job performance.* Organization Science, 2009. **20**(1): p. 51.
12. Altman, Y., *Work and careers in the new millennium: a landscape.* Strategic Change, 2000. **9**(1): p. 67.
13. Clarke, M. and M. Patrickson, *The new covenant of employability.* Employee Relations, 2008. **30**(2): p. 121.
14. Ulrich, D., *Intellectual capital = competence x commitment.* Sloan Management Review, 1998. **39**(2): p. 15.
15. Kirpal, S., *Researching work identities in a European context.* Career Development International, 2004. **9**(3): p. 199.
16. Mallon, M. and S. Walton, *Career and learning: The ins and the outs of it.* Personnel Review, 2005. **34**(4): p. 468.
17. M'Hamed, D., *Vocational identities in change in the telecommunications sector.* Career Development International, 2004. **9**(3): p. 305.
18. MOW, *The meaning of work,*1987, London, UK: Academic Press.
19. Quintanilla, A.R., *Introduction: The meaning of work.* European Work and Organizational Psychologist, 1991. **1**(2/3): p. 81–89.
20. England, G. and I. Harpaz, *How working is defined: National contexts and demographic and organizational role influences.* Journal of Organizational Behavior (1986–1998), 1990. **3**(4): p. 253–266.
21. Levinson, D., *The seasons of a man's life,*1978, New York: Knopf.
22. Muna, F. and N. Mansour, *Balancing work and personal life: The leader as acrobat.* The Journal of Management Development, 2009. **28**(2): p. 121.
23. Merriam-Webster, *Comprehensive online English dictionary,* 2010, http://www.merriam-webster.com.
24. Mutlu, E.C. and O. Asik, *A look over the concepts of work and leisure throughout important historical periods.* Journal of American Academy of Business, 2002. **2**(1): p. 12.
25. Wengland, G. and I. Harpaz, *How working is defined: National contexts and demographic and organizational role influences.* Journal of Organizational Behavior (1986–1998), 1990. **3**(4): p. 253.
26. Harpaz, I. and R. Snir, *Workaholism: Its definition and nature.* Human Relations, 2003. **56**(3): p. 291.

27. Kunango, R., *Measurement of job and work involvement.* Journal of Applied Psychology, 1982. **67**: p. 341–349.

28. Parboteeah, P. and J. Cullen, *Social Institutions and work centrality: Explorations beyond national culture.* Organization Science 2003. **14**(2): p. 137–148.

29. Pryor, R. and R. Davies, *A Comparison of conceputalizations of work centrality.* Journal of Organizational Behavior, 1989. **10**(3): p. 283–289.

30. Herzberg, F. and D. Mausner, *The motivation to work,* 1959, New York, NY: Wiley.

31. Peel, S. and K. Inkson, *Contracting and careers: choosing between self and organizational employment.* Career Development International, 2004. **9**(67): p. 542.

32. Sladek, C. and E. Hollander, *Where is everyone? The rise of workplace flexibility.* Benefits Quarterly, 2009. **25**(2): p. 17.

33. Wright, E.O. and R. Dwyer, *The patterns of job expansions in the USA: A comparison of the 1960s and 1990s.* Socio-Economic Review, 2003. **1**(3): p. 289–325.

34. Doeringer, P.B. and M.J. Piore, *Internal labor markets and manpower analysis,* 1971, Lexington, MA: D.C. Heath and Company.

35. Litan, R., M. Pomerleano and V. Sundarajan, *Financial sector governance: The roles of the public and private sectors,* 2002, Washington DC: Brookings Institutions Press.

36. Tilly, C., *Half a job: Bad and good part-time jobs in a changing labor market,* 1996, Philadelphia, PA: Temple University Press.

37. Baruch, Y., *Transforming career: From linear to multidirectional career paths: Organizational and individual perspectives.* Career Development International, 2004. **9**(1): p. 58–73.

38. Duxbury, L., S. Lyons and C. Higgins, *Dual-income families in the new millennium: Reconceptualizing family type.* Advances in Developing Human Resources, 2007. **9**(4): p. 472.

39. Hennequin, E., *What "career success" means to blue-collar workers.* Career Development International, 2007. **12**(6): p. 565.

40. Mallon, M., *The Portfolio career: Pushed or pulled to it?* Personnel Review, 1998. **27**(5): p. 361.

41. Polivka, A. and T. Nardone, *On the definition of "contingent work."* Monthly Labor Review, 1989. **December**: p. 9–14.

42. Tsui, A.S., et al., *Alternative approaches to the employee-organization relationship: Does investment in employees pay off?* Academy of Management Journal, 1997. **40**: p. 1089–1121.

43. Cappelli, P. (Ed.), *Employment relations: New models of white collar work,* 2008, New York, NY: Cambridge University Press.

44. Segalla, M., D. Rouzies and M. Flory, *Culture and career advancement in Europe: Promoting team players vs fast trackers.* European Management Journal, 2001. **19**(1): p. 44.

45. Arndt, M., *Education and the masculinization of hospital administration.* Journal of Management History, 2010. **16**(1): p. 75.

46. Brislin, R., et al., *Evolving perceptions of Japanese workplace motivation: An employee-manager comparison.* International Journal of Cross Cultural Management : CCM, 2005. **5**(1): p. 87.

47. Kanter, R.M., *Careers and the wealth of nations,* in M.B. Arthur, D.T. Hall and B.S. Lawrence (Eds.), *Handbook of career theory,* 1989, New York, NY: Cambridge University Press. p. 506–522.

48. Sullivan, S., W. Carden and D. Martin, *Careers in the next millennium: Directions for future research.* Human Resource Management Review, 1998. **8**(2): p. 165.

49. Touomo, P., *Managerial career patterns in transnational corporations: An organizational capability approach.* European Management Journal, 1993. **11**(2): p. 248.

50. Raider, H.J. and R.S. Burt, *Boundaryless careers and social capital,* in M.B. Arthur and D.M. Rousseau (Eds.), *The boundaryless career,* 1996, New York, NY: Oxford University Press. p. 187–200.

51. Arthur, M.B. and D.M. Rousseau, *Introduction: The boundaryless career as a new employment principle,* in M.B. Arthur and D.M. Rousseau (Eds.), *The boundaryless career,* 1996, New York, NY: Oxford University Press.

52. Blau, G. and M. Lunz, *Testing the incremental effect of professional commitment on intent to leave one's profession behyond the effects of external, personal, and work-related variables.* Journal of Vocational Behavior, 1998. **52**: p. 260–269.

53. Inkson, K., *Understanding Careers: The Metaphors of Working Lives*, 2007, Thousand Oaks, CA: Sage.

54. Mallon, M., *Going "portfolio": Making sense of changing careers*. Career Development International, 1999. **4**(7): p. 358.

55. Duberley, J., M. Mallon and L. Cohen, *Exploring career transitions: Accounting for structure and agency*. Personnel Review, 2006. **35**(3): p. 281.

56. Carnoy, M., M. Castellsand C. Benner, *Labour markets and employment practices in the age of flexibility: A case study of Silicon Valley*. International Labour Review, 1997. **136**(1): p. 27–48.

57. Kalleberg, A.L., *Nonstandard employment relations: Part-time, temporary and contract work*. Annual Review of Sociology, 2000. **26**: p. 341–365.

58. Scully-Russ, E., *Agency versus structure: Path dependency and choice in low-wage labor markets*. Human Resource Development Review, 2005. **4**(3): p. 254.

59. Williams, C. and J. Round, *Beyond formalization: Rethinking the future of work*. Foresight : the Journal of Futures Studies, Strategic Thinking and Policy, 2007. **9**(3): p. 30.

60. Richardson, J. and J. Zikic, *The darker side of an international academic career*. Career Development International, 2007. **12**(2): p. 164.

61. Snir, R. and I. Harpaz, *Attitudinal and demographic antecedents of workaholism*. Journal of Organizational Change Management, 2004. **17**(5): p. 520.

2 WORK & CAREER INSTITUTIONS & ENVIRONMENTS

LEARNING OBJECTIVES

- Linking job transition dynamics and career management

- Introduction to the core concept of employability

- Evaluating the range and role of employment intermediaries

- Exploring the macro level view of an employment opportunity landscape

THE ROADMAP

In Chapter 1 you were presented with an overview of some fundamental aspects of work and career management. You were shown how the nature of work and work goals influence work centrality and other career-related attitudes. The subsequent exploration of employment arrangements and career forms highlighted their importance in understanding career management dynamics. Finally, you were given key reasons why there is a need for a personalized resource management (PRM) perspective. This perspective sees the individual as a bundle of capabilities, resources and strategic orientations. In Chapter 1, Figure 1.2 gave you an overview of the central position of PRM in career management. It was pointed out that, given the erosion of loyalty between workers and employees, the responsibility for career development and management has clearly shifted to the individual. The chapter explains why the personalized resource management perspective offers significant insights into how you go about identifying needed capabilities, developing network resources, and how charting a employment trajectory can lead to long-term career success.

Chapter 2 continues to examine work and career development from the perspective of the individual. However, you will also examine the economic, institutional and environmental factors that impact individuals' ability to find employment and mange their careers. One key to understanding the link between individual strategy and environmental factors is to explore how job transition dynamics work in a particular area. After explaining certain aspects of the job transition dynamics, the importance of employment intermediaries will be highlighted. With a growing focus on competitiveness and employability, the role of employment intermediaries has grown significantly in most national environments. The supply, diversity, and quality of employment intermediaries are often direct reflections of the career-creating capacity of regional and national work environments. Finally, this chapter also presents a macro perspective on work and career development. The model in the macro perspective focuses on the link between economic and environmental factors and the main functions that are needed to create a vibrant work and career development arena. In the macro perspective, external stakeholders also play an important role in moderating or accelerating crucial work and career development activities. Overall, the strategies and occupational paths that individuals use as they move from one position to another, within or across firms, can provide a lot of insight into the nature of the working environment and institutions that influence career development. [7–9]

TOPIC FOCUS

When comparing different national environments, we can expect significant diversity in the flexibility and strength of internal and external labor markets. In some environments, the economic, social, and cultural barriers to a proactive personalized human resource management approach are strong. In others, individuals are rapidly taking advantage of new resources and strategies to realize their career development objectives. However, since the forces of international competition and globalization continue to impact most countries and labor markets, the general direction of change has been towards the shifting of the responsibility for career development and management from the organization and government to the individual. Given these developments, there are many different ways to view the career development phenomenon. Some approaches consider a career as a series of vocational choices made over one's lifetime that reflect or support one's work-related self concept at particular periods in time. Other approaches which focus on change and equilibrium in employment status consider a career to be defined by alternating periods of stability and transition. During periods of stability, individuals focus on developing skills, capabilities, and relationships that can help them in their present or future job assignments. During periods of transition, individuals re-evaluate skills, capabilities and work goals as they boost their employability or change their views of career success. [1–4]

JOB TRANSITION DYNAMICS

This book takes the view that, no matter what your perspective on careers might be, an understanding of job transition dynamics will help significantly to explain the links between jobs, careers, and general employability trends in different regions and nations. "Job transition dynamics" refers to three possible work-related changes in an individual's career development:

1. The change from being unemployed to being employed, or vice versa.

2. The move from one job or position to another within the same or a different firm.

3. The change from one occupation to another within the same sector or to a different sector.

How should you go about exploring job transition dynamics in a particular environment and how can that help you better understand career management? You should start by examining the five major phases of job transition dynamics. Clarifying the major agents and activities supporting each phases will generally give a clearer picture. Figure 2.1 illustrates the process. The event that initiates the process is often the potential or actual loss of a job and the subsequent search for a new position. For those seeking their first job, the process also starts at this stage.

Figure 2.1 Job transition dynamics

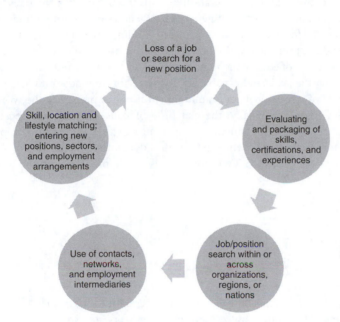

In many ways, "job transition dynamics" is a central career management process which has important implications for organizations, individuals, and nations. When individuals enter, leave, or move up in an organization, the change in personnel can impact knowledge transfer, workflow effectiveness, or even corporate culture. The extent to which this type of position change is usually initiated by the organization or the individual influences the nature of the firm's human resource management strategy. From the individual's perspective, a change in position or employment status provides challenges and opportunities. If individuals are usually the main initiator of this type of change, we would expect them to have a more proactive view of career management. We can also learn a lot about an employment environment by examining the key agents and decision-makers behind the various steps in the process. If we examine this process from an organization's viewpoint, we are faced with the issues that are normally considered in traditional human resource management.

According to Figure 2.1, the loss of a job or the need to find a new position should lead to the evaluation and packaging of skills and capabilities in ways that make it easier to carry out effective job searches. That search can take place within or across organizations or nations. The impact of a global marketplace for skilled employees expands the potential locations and sectors for finding a position. In terms of skill development, the job transition dynamics can reveal the individual's or organization's approach to capabilities diversification. Three approaches to the development of capabilities are non-diversification, related diversification, and unrelated diversification. Using this terminology, non-diversification would indicate that the individual would move to a position which required the same core skills and capabilities as the previous position. Related diversification would occur when the individual moves to a position that required an expansion or further development of the core capabilities of the previous position. Unrelated diversification would then refer to positions that required the individual to develop new skills and capabilities in order to be effective. [12–14]

After deciding on the configuration of skills that are needed for a new position, the use of personal contacts and networks, as well as employment intermediaries, becomes crucial for boosting the potential for finding a new position. By examining how individuals find and acquire new jobs, we can also gain a better understanding of the importance of employment intermediaries in the local and national economy. By evaluating the skills and capabilities required for new positions, we can ascertain the role of educational and training institutions in preparing the workforce in various environments. Finally, the matching of skills, lifestyle, and location with mutually beneficial employment arrangement signals a successful completion of the most important stage of the job transition dynamics. The personalized resource management perspective (PRM) looks at this whole process from the individual's perspective. [11, 12]

TOPIC FOCUS

Another factor closely related to job transition dynamics, which also gives an insight into an important characteristic of various employment environments, is the concept of the employability. Employability refers to the ability of individuals to find employment, maintain a position, or move to another position within or across organizations when necessary during their working life. Aside from the traditional focus on skills and labor shortages, interest in employability has generally been attributed to the changing nature of the psychological contract between employees and employers. Most of the blame for this shift in worker attitude and strategy has been placed on the erosion of job security and an increasingly competitive business environment. The new psychological contract has shifted the focus from employment security to an employability orientation. Two key assumptions behind this focus on employability is the view that (1) individuals have the capacity to manage their own work and career development; and (2) by stressing an employability orientation, individuals will manage to stay employed for much longer periods of their working life. With the focus on employability, it is clear that the timing and decision-making responsibilities for work and career development has shifted from the organization to the individual. Consequently, in environments with flexible external labor markets, personal employability management has begun to dominate work and career development strategies. [5–7]

Effective employability management requires that individuals be able to thoroughly evaluate their strengths and weaknesses. This kind of personal SWOT analysis can then become the starting point for a range of career development strategies. Employability management necessitates that individuals take advantage of friendship, informational and social networks, as well as work-related capabilities, to project their presence in potential employment arenas. Finally, individuals are expected to identify, target, and develop the skills and the capabilities necessary to give them access to current and potential employment opportunities. In essence, an employability focus demands that individuals focus on mobility, up-skilling, work experience, and networking strategies. In the relentless drive to maintain employability, one set of institutions continue to play a crucial role. Employment intermediaries provide individuals and organizations with a valuable service by matching employment opportunities with available and capable individuals. In many ways, employment intermediaries can help individuals maintain their employability. [10, 11]

EMPLOYMENT INTERMEDIARIES

Individuals and organizations have both been increasingly using third party intermediaries to help them manage various employment environments. Employment intermediaries (EMIs) or labor market intermediaries (LMIs) include employment agencies, recruiters, labor contractors, and temporary help service (THS) firms. The rapid growth and extensive use of EMIs has had a huge impact on labor market dynamics and the drive for flexibility from both organizations and individuals. Employment Intermediaries (EMIs) or labor market intermediaries (LMIs) function as brokers between workers and employers. There is, however, a wide range of differences among employment intermediaries. Nevertheless, these intermediaries all impact the speed of labor market adjustment, help build social and business networks, and reduce screening costs and risks. There are five main types of employment intermediaries: private sector, membership-based, public sector, web-based intermediaries, and social networks. You can find an extensive list of the various types of employment intermediaries in the appendix. [15–18]

Private Sector Intermediaries

Private sector intermediaries include temporary help service (THS) agencies, contract brokers, career consulting, professional employer organizations, and general labor brokerage firms. These for-profit organizations carry out a wide range of employment-related activities. These activities include recruiting, training, and finding employment for workers in many different sectors and at different skill levels. The temporary help agencies are the most numerous and well-known. They are generally active in areas such as shipping, assembly, industrial, clerical, and some administrative positions. Many of them also have access to highly skilled technicians, IT professionals, and engineers. In addition, some of the private sector intermediaries have strategies which link or integrate their activities into the human resource practices of many larger firms. [19, 20]

Example #1: Robert Half International (RHI)
This is a staffing and recruiting firm that is active in the United States and around the world. The company was founded in the late 1940s and is considered one of

the world's largest specialized staffing firms. The company handles temporary, temporary-to-hire, and full-time positions in fields such as accounting, finance, technology, office administration, legal, marketing, and design. The firm has over 350 locations worldwide. More information on the company can be found at rhi.com.

Example #2: European Recruitment Agency (ERA)

This is a UK-based recruitment agency which specializes in finding employment solutions throughout Europe. It is a highly ranked agency and is used frequently by European firms. They handle potential employees from Europe and around the world. The company is owned by seasoned professionals and they manage activities such as recruitment, payroll, regulations, visa issues, and skillsmatching. You can find out more about this organization at recruitment-agency.eu.

Member-Based Intermediaries

This type of intermediary is created from the membership of individual employees. This would include professional associations, guild-like associations, and certain union activities. The goal of these intermediaries is to enhance and protect the employment of their members. They do this by providing many services, one of which includes connecting their members to potential employers. These member-based intermediaries can provide training, networking opportunities, expanded learning situations, and strong employment links to specific types of potential employers. They have varying roles which range from providing information and skill development programs to advocating for their members through collective bargaining or legislative lobbying. [7, 15, 21]

Example #1: The CFA Institute

CFA stands for Chartered Financial Analyst. The CFA Institute is a global non-profit association of investment professionals. After you have successfully passed a series of exams, the organization awards the CFA and CIPM designations. The organization also offers a wide range of educational programs and other services for their members, investors, employers, and other institutions. Members can use the organization and its online resources to network about career opportunities and investment ideas. The CFA Institute also provides information on job openings in the financial sector around the world. You can find more details about the organization at cfainstitute.org

Example #2: Self-Employed Women's Association (SEWA)

SEWA is an Indian trade union whose goal is to help poor self-employed female workers. They organize poor women to help them achieve full employment. The organization believes in self-reliance and effective strategies to improve women's earning and bargaining power. The services that SEWA provides includes savings, credit, health care, child care, insurance, legal aid, capacity building, and communication services. The organization publishes various articles and books to help its members. In addition to its array of services, it generally teaches poor women how to network in order to start, improve, or expand business opportunities. It has many sister organizations, and some people even refer to SEWA as a movement. More information on the organization is available at sewa.org.

Public Sector Intermediaries

This group of intermediaries includes educational institutions and government-related programs that directly affect the training, career development and employment of job-seeking individuals. The three main types of public sector intermediaries are (1) training centers and workforce development institutions; (2) educational institution-related retraining activities and other training and skill development programs; (3) Publicly funded intermediaries which are usually community or non-profit organizations that focus on educating, training, and placing individuals in jobs. Funding for some of these organizations comes from both state and national level grants. [22, 23]

Example #1: The California Employment Development Department (EDD)

The California Employment Development Department is one of the largest state employment development departments in the USA. It has service locations throughout the State of California, and has been dedicated to connecting those seeking jobs with employers. The department has been in existence for over 70 years and plays an important role as an employment intermediary. The EDD website has links to an online job bank with thousands of job openings. The site also provides valuable information about training programs, unemployment insurance, family leave claims, payroll tax information, and numerous other issues.

Example #2: AmeriCorps

AmeriCorps is an organization established for state, national and community service. President Bill Clinton signed the National and Community Service Trust Act in 1993. This action established the Corporation for National and Community Service and brought the full range of domestic community service programs under the umbrella of one central organization. The goal of the organization is to encourage civic engagement at all levels and throughout the country. Each year, AmeriCorps offers over 70,000 jobs for young people and adults of all ages and backgrounds. The idea is to serve communities through a network of partnerships and non-profit organizations. AmeriCorps is able to help communities because many individuals share the ideals of helping others and giving back to communities around the nation. More information is available about AmeriCorps at americorps.gov.

Web-Based Intermediaries & Media Channels.

This is a special category of employment intermediaries, since it has only been over the last 20 years that this group of web-based organizations has become major players in the external labor market. Web-based intermediaries can be private, member, or public sector organizations. They can be linked to specific organizations or to associations. They can be stand alone organizations that only exist online or they can represent virtual web groups. The largest of this group are the international or nation-wide job sites that present employment information on most occupational categories. Some of the sites operate on a more regional level, often specializing in employment for specific occupations or providing career consulting services. Some web organizations are independent, while others are linked to a wide range of long-standing institutions or networks. As for media channels, the influence of this group's ability to disseminate information on potential jobs is often crucial in certain environments. In environments where the employment intermediary infrastructures are not extensive or not effectively open to all and where individuals might not have access to powerful friendship or social networks, we often see a dependency on newspapers, magazines, television, or radio announcements for information on employment opportunities. [18, 24]

Example #1: Career Builder

Career Builder is one of the largest employment online website in the US. The site has millions of visitors each month and has over a one-third market share of online employment websites. The organization provides many career services online and has partnered with numerous organizations and newspapers to deliver their extensive services. Individuals can post their résumé, track their job search history, and get access to education and training resources. This site covers employment opportunities in most sectors of the economy. More information about this website is available at careerbuilder.com.

Example #2: Global Career Company

Although its main offices are based in the UK, Global Career Company is an international recruitment organization that specializes in finding and posting candidates from Africa, Asia Pacific, Central and Eastern Europe back into positions in their home countries. They have recruited for hundreds of companies and frequently host recruitment summits, employment campaigns, and talent pool sourcing events. The organization states that it was founded out a desire to assist emerging markets attain their full potential by providing access to skilled and knowledgeable employees. More information about this organization can be found at globalcareercompany.com.

Social Networks

Unlike the other employment intermediaries, this type is not linked to specific organizations but rather to relationships across individuals and groups. These networks can provide the crucial information, advice, and support that might be needed for job referrals, recruitment, and promotion success. These networks usually emerge from links across occupations, communities, kinship groups, educational cliques, social class, personal friends, or web group memberships. For many individuals and groups, social networks are the first and most effective means of finding new jobs or new occupations. Finally, social networks often prove invaluable in identifying and developing the skills and knowledge needed to have successful careers. [25, 26]

Example #1: LinkedIn

LinkedIn is probably the largest professional networking site in the world. The organization states that over 120 million professionals around the world use LinkedIn to exchange information, ideas, and opportunities. The site continues to grow rapidly and is expanding into many countries. LinkedIn allows individuals and groups to stay informed about contacts and industries. Many firms reportedly use LinkedIn to recruit people with the knowledge and skills needed to achieve their goals. The site has built-in flexibility which allows individuals to control and project their professional identity online. More information about this organization can be found at LinkedIn.com.

Example #2: Latpro Network

Latpro is an organization that focuses on career social networking for bilingual and Hispanic jobs. The network was launched in 1997 to connect Hispanic or bilingual professionals with recruiters and business organizations. It is one of the largest networks of its kind and has filled an increasingly important niche. In addition to searching for positions, members can share ideas and solicit advice from others. The network has a presence in numerous countries and provides opportunities for job fairs, forums, and blogs. More information on this organization can be found at network.latpro.com.

TOPIC FOCUS

Many types of employment intermediaries are increasingly entering into long-term contracts and secondary sourcing arrangements with major organizations. These contracts take over a range of human resource services that used to be handled by the major firms. In addition to recruiting, training, and supplying qualified workers, many of these intermediaries have on-site management and sub-contractor management responsibilities. As the activities of these intermediaries become integrated into the overall human resource strategies of many firms, it has sometimes become harder to distinguish between the internal and external labor market, especially from the point a view of the individual employee. There are quite often issues of "joint employment" or "co-employment" to be resolved in order to clarify who is liable for certain workers. Those issues become all the more complicated when we realize that there is an ongoing practice of "temporary to permanent" conversions. Overall, the emergence of triangular employment relationships present challenges and opportunities to both employers and employees alike. [27, 28]

Part of the difficulty in understanding career development is that it is a phenomenon which is embedded in social, economic, and institutional environments which both constrain and support the work-related activities of individuals, organizations, communities and governments. In the sections below, we will take a look at the macro perspective which shows how work and career nurturing functions are at the core of the employment opportunity landscape (Figure 2.2).

THE EMPLOYMENT OPPORTUNITY LANDSCAPE

In this section, we will explore work and careers from a macro perspective. This involves an analysis of the roles and influence of the various factors such as institutions, intermediaries, social developments, and the media. These factors influence the specific employment environments and employment opportunity landscapes that individuals face around the world. "Employment environment" refers to the marketplace of jobs and job applicants in a region or national area. The employment opportunity arena encompasses more than just the immediate employment environment. The employment opportunity landscape consists of the rules, regulations, business practices, employment intermediaries, organizations, and institutions that influence the types of employment opportunities, as well as the nature of the pathways to work, jobs, and careers. Figure 2.2 shows the major components of the employment opportunity landscape.

Fundamental Environmental Factors

Fundamental factors are those that shape a labor market and provide opportunities for the development of dynamic career environments. The internal labor market refers to the internal boundaries of an organization within which skill development, promotion pathways, and coordination and control strategies dominate. The development of the internal labor market is linked to the need for organizations to maintain firm-specific skills and capabilities by controlling and managing its human resource base. Flexible internal labor markets provide employees with a wide range of training, education, and promotion opportunities within organizations. In some environments, internal labor market practices allow firms to manage and develop their workforce, not just within the focal organization and its subsidiaries, but across affiliates and alliances as well. The external labor market refers to human resource activities that take place outside the boundaries of a particular firm and usually involves employment intermediaries or direct cross-firm contacts. The larger and more flexible the external labor market, the more likely it is that recruitment, skill development, training, promotions, and career development will take place more frequently across several firms and involve a variety of employment intermediaries. The expansion of external labor markets worldwide support the view that organizations are externalizing many of their human resource management functions in order to cut costs and attain strategic flexibility in the management of their workforce.

The political economy factor is one of the key fundamental environmental factors. From the perspective of careers and general economic development, the political economy concept covers a number of important areas. It refers to the stability of the political system, the general openness of the economy, the level of the government's participation in the economy, and government's influence on workforce development. Stable, open, and resilient governments are usually more receptive to the idea of having their nation's firms compete in global markets. A government's participation in the economy and workforce development can have both positive and negative consequences on labor market flexibility and the quality of employment opportunities. However, what is important to evaluate is whether the government's activities boost, crowd out, or restrict the economic and labor strategies that are being used in the private sector.

The number and variety of education and training institutions in a national environment have a significant impact on workforce and career development. These institutions represent the backbone of human capital development activities in most societies. They not only preserve and develop skills and capabilities: they often can provide new opportunities for knowledge creation and entrepreneurship activities in a society. The greater the variety and scope of these education and training institutions, the more likely it is that a society has an innovative and capable workforce, managers, and entrepreneurs.

Although often underestimated, socio-cultural factors also represent important environmental factors. These factors influence a variety of work-related developments in a society. The main aspects of these socio-cultural factors include (1) cultural values orientations; (2) attitudes toward work (work centrality); (3) social mobility; (4) the role of kinship andsocial networks; and (5) the role of social movements. All these factors play a role in the attitude towards jobs and careers. Time and time again, we have seen grassroots movements take center stage and force a change in the preference for various business skills, strategies, occupations, and careers. Some socio-cultural factors work to maintain the status quo and slow the pace of change, while others challenge current paradigms, boost innovative thinking, and accelerate the pace of change.

Figure 2.2 Macro level view of the employment opportunity landscape

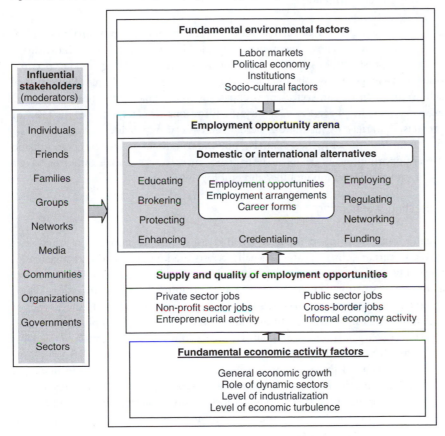

Employment Opportunity Arena

In the macro level model shown in Figure 2.2, the fundamental environmental and economic factors interact to form the foundation for an employment opportunity arena where essential work and career development functions, as well as employment opportunities and employment relationships, emerge. An employment opportunity arena refers to a regional, national, or international employment environment where skill development, employment opportunities, employment arrangements, and career forms are influenced and promoted by private, public, and non-profit organizations. In general, these organizations partially or completely support work and career development functions. The nine central nurturing and career development functions that promote the creation, development and expansion of work and careers are *educating, enhancing, protecting, regulating, funding, networking, brokering, credentialing,* and *employing.* The supply and quality of the organizations and stakeholders supporting these nurturing functions will usually impact the level and quality of workforce and career development activities in a particular environment. Overall, we can say that the presence and intensity of these main functional activities directly influence the work and career development capacity of an employment opportunity arena. Below is a more detailed description of these central functional activities. [8, 11, 15, 18, 29]

Educating & Credentialing

Educational activities can be carried out by private, public, and non-profit organizations. Their focus can be on theoretical or applied knowledge. From the individual's perspective, distinctions should be made between firm-specific, general or occupational knowledge. Many jobs and careers often require varying levels of educational achievement. In certain sectors or occupations, individuals often need to provide evidence that they have the necessary qualifications to carry out various tasks or projects. A variety of institutions across many sectors provide this credentialing function. With the proper credentials, individuals can get greater access to job and career opportunities. In flexible external labor markets, credentials can often have a significant impact on job mobility and employability.

Protecting & Enhancing

Having institutions that defend the qualifications, compensation, or task activities linked to certain jobs and careers usually boosts the longevity and attractiveness of those jobs and careers. Unions have played such a role for many jobs and careers across various national environments. Some institutions, such as professional associations, serve as strong gatekeepers for certain professions. Access to these types of jobs or careers can have a significant impact on an individual's employability.

The scope, qualifications, and status of many jobs and careers continue to evolve over time. It is often due to persistent institutional activity or new social developments that some of these jobs and careers rise in status. Unions and professional associations have often played a strong role in boosting the profile and exclusivity of certain jobs and professions. We can look at the evolution of jobs and careers related to the internet to see a concrete example of new and high profile jobs and professions that have emerged over time.

Regulating & Funding

Institutions and laws that regulate activities impacting jobs and careers tend to most directly impact employment arrangements and occupational qualifications. Although regulations about the terms of employment vary widely across national environments, their impact is to generally clarify or limit the actions of employers. Regulations concerning occupational qualifications also vary, but their impact on accessibility or demand for particular jobs or occupations can be both positive and negative. Overall, the more consistent and transparent the regulating functions in an environment, the more likely it is that jobs and careers can be protected and enhanced over the long run.

The funding function covers many activities, and is crucial in both the educational and economic development areas. We see that private, public, and non-profit institutions all play important roles in financing traditional education and training programs. The extent to which individuals receive funds or are provided with low-cost educational opportunities is usually correlated with the scope and participation of the educational sector. The funding of adult education and retraining programs is an example of a major policy issue in certain environments. Although funds for education are important long-term career development trends, it is the provision of capital for economic development and entrepreneurial activities which most directly boosts the job and career-creating potential of a particular environment.

Networking & Brokering

The networking function is often underestimated, but research has shown that, in some environments, it has the biggest impact on career development and long-term employability. The concept of networking covers many activities. Formal institutions that boost individual and group interaction within or across jobs and occupations are essential for the networking function. Many individuals also rely often on informal networks of relationships for advice and support as they manage their jobs and careers. Finally, social media has really expanded the importance of networking. Social media now provides formal and informal links across occupations, organizations, and individuals.

The brokering function reflects the ability of employment intermediaries to connect individuals to employment opportunities. The more extensive the activities of these intermediaries, the more likely it is that a particular environment depends on the external labor market to match employees to job opportunities. These intermediaries include organizations such as temporary help agencies, recruiting firms, public employment services, and career consulting firms. A flexible and efficient external labor market cannot develop without a range of organizations working to match the supply and demand of employment opportunities.

Employing

This is probably the most important functional activity of an employment opportunity arena. The capacity of organizations in an environment to provide wages for temporary or full-time employment is what drives economic growth and supports the expansion of jobs and careers. Depending on certain fundamentals in an economy, the volume and quality of jobs and careers will be distributed in various ways across the private, public, non-profit, or informal sectors. The biggest change for this functional activity is the role of the international demand for skilled workers. Individuals with the right skills and mindset can now seek employment beyond their borders for short or longer periods of time. The experiences and capabilities accumulated by working in foreign environments can sometimes be transferred back to the home country and boost an individual's employability.

Employment Opportunities, Employment Arrangements & Career Forms

The existence of, or emphasis placed on, the nine functional activities will depend greatly on the institutional and economic policies that make up the fundamental environment. However, it is the interaction of the nine functional activities and the organizational strategies of employers and individuals that allow for the emergence of, and preference for, certain employment opportunities, employment arrangements, and career forms. Although increasing international mobility has provided some alternatives to individuals, specific national environments continue to dominate the creation and use of employment opportunities, employment arrangements, and career forms.

Fundamental Economic Activity Factors

The level of industrialization has a major impact on the type of jobs that are dominant in a national economy. Specifically, the distribution of primary, secondary, or tertiary sector jobs will be greatly influenced by a country's stage of industrialization. However, another important factor is the role of dynamic sectors. The fastest growing, the most innovative, and the most competitive sectors tend to produce higher quality jobs in most environments. Beyond the level of industrialization, and despite the positive impact of dynamic sectors, economic development and employment trends are also greatly influenced by the level of economic turbulence. The uncertainty that accompanies most economic turbulence might be good for some sectors, but continued economic growth depends on some level of sustained economic stability.

The Supply & Quality of Employment Opportunities

The quantity and quality of jobs available in an economy are linked to the level of economic activity, the dynamism of companies and sectors, and the knowledge and skill level of potential workers in that environment. Policies that boost entrepreneurial activity and job creation directly affect the quantity of jobs. Policies that protect and expand the quality of education, skill formation, competence transferability, and worker protections generally enhance the quality of jobs in an economy. One new dimension to consider is the impact of globalization. Individuals can now search for position in different parts of the world. That expands the range for finding quality job opportunities. By expanding your search to beyond your national boundaries, you have, in effect, increased the supply and quality of employment opportunities available to you.

Influential Stakeholders

Stakeholders are individuals, groups, or organizational agents who can significantly influence the factors that impact work and career development in regional or national environments. The macro level view of the employment opportunity landscape shows how employment, political, and socio-economic factors interact to create an employment opportunity arena. Depending on the national environment, all these factors are moderated by stakeholders. In economic systems with flexible external labor markets, individual and organizational intermediaries play a significant role in work and career development. In economic systems with strong internal labor markets, institutions and employment organizations dominate the work and career development activities.

Commentary on the Employment Opportunity Landscape Model

Figure 2.2 shows that employment opportunities, employment arrangements, and career forms are influenced by a number of factors in the local and international environment. Fundamental economic and environmental factors generally drive the effectiveness of the nine functional activities that nurture the employment opportunities, employment arrangements, and career forms available to individuals. However, it is important to point out that there will be significant variations across national environments because of the comparative importance and strength of key influential stakeholders. Individual drive, as well as the power of friends, families, networks, and the government, can significantly moderate the impact of the nine functional activities in ways that boost one's chances for effective career development and success. The impact of influential stakeholders becomes even more crucial in areas where the fundamental economic and environmental factors are weak, disorganized, or uneven. Given these observations, it should be clear that understanding the dynamics in an employment opportunity landscape is an important step for individuals to map out any opportunities, challenges, and advantages they might have in developing and managing their careers. The personalized resource management (PRM) approach takes all of these factors into account and shows how individuals can develop up their capabilities and use their resources and networks to overcome challenges and take advantage of opportunities for career development and success.

CHAPTER SUMMARY & OBSERVATIONS

This chapter examined work and career institutions and environments. You were shown how some economic, institutional and environmental factors impact key functional activities that nurture employment opportunities, employment arrangements, and career forms. "Job transition dynamics" was presented as central to understanding potential career management strategies. A simple definition of job transition dynamics was a focus on strategies taken to coordinate or resolve major employment changes that influence an individual's career development or success. How the five major changes in job transition dynamics are managed reveals a lot about employment environments.

You were then introduced to the core concept of employability. This concept was defined as the ability of individuals to find employment, maintain a position, or move to another position, within or across organizations, when necessary during their working life. In order to accomplish this, individuals were expected to identify, target, and develop the skills and the capabilities necessary to give them access to current and potential employment opportunities. Effective use of employment intermediaries was seen as crucial for finding and matching employment opportunities to individuals' skill sets. The five main types of employment intermediaries discussed were private sector, membership-based, public sector, web-based intermediaries, and social networks.

Finally, there was an exploration of work and careers from the macro perspective. You were shown a model of the employment opportunity landscape that individuals have to navigate to develop and manage their careers. The employment opportunity landscape consists of the rules, regulations, business practices, employment intermediaries, organizations, and institutions that influence the types of employment opportunities as well as the nature of the pathways to work, jobs and careers. It was then pointed out that understanding the dynamics in an employment opportunity landscape is an important step for individuals to map out any opportunities, challenges, and advantages they might have in developing and managing their careers.

Chapter 3 will focus on the challenges and opportunities of working with, and in, foreign environments. There will be an examination of the obstacles to developing an international career and strategies for getting around some of them.

The chapter shows how the first step to having an effective international career development strategy is to understand how the modes of knowing are linked to self assessment. The second phase is exploring how the modes of doing support the personalized resource management perspective. Lastly, by discussing modes of entering different careers or national environments, you can clarify effective ways of participating in international career development and expansion. The modes of knowing, doing, and entering are then all combined in a model which shows how individuals can develop and accumulate their personal capital.

REFERENCES

1. Levinson, D., *The seasons of a man's life*, 1978, New York, NY: Knopf.
2. Levinson, D., *A conception of adult development*. Psychologist, 1986. **41**: p. 3–13.
3. O'Mahony, S. and B. Bechky, *Stretchwork: Managing the career progression paradox in external labor markets*. Academy of Management Journal, 2006. **49**(5): p. 918.
4. Super, D., A. Thompson and R. Lindeman, *Adult career concerns inventory: Manual for research and exploration use in counseling*, 1988, Palo Alto, CA.: Consulting Psychologists Press.
5. Clarke, M., *Understanding and managing employability in changing career contexts*. Journal of European Industrial Training, 2008. **32**(4): p. 258.
6. Fitzenberger, B. and A. Kunze, *Vocational training and gender: Wages and occupational mobility among young workers*. Oxford Review of Economic Policy, 2005. **21**(3): p. 392.
7. Gardner, T., *Human resource alliances: Defining the construct and exploring the antecedents*. The International Journal of Human Resource Management, 2005. **16**(6): p. 1049.
8. Hurley-Hanson, A., et al., *The changing role of education on managerial career attainment*. Personnel Review, 2005. **34**(5): p. 517.
9. Kirschenbaum, A. and J. Weisberg, *Employees' turnover intentions and job destination choices*. Journal of Organizational Behavior, 2002. **23**(1): p. 109.
10. Mano-Negrin, R. and S. Tzafrir, *Job search modes and turnover*. Career Development International, 2004. **9**(4/5): p. 442.
11. Clarke, M. and M. Patrickson, *The new convenant of employability*. Employee Relations, 2008. **30**(2): p. 121–141.
12. Drewes, T., *Internal and external labour mobility in Canada*. Applied Economics, 1993. **25**(10): p. 1355.
13. Lim, R. and W. Patton, *What do career counsellors think their clients expect from their services? Are they right?* Australian Journal of Career Development, 2006. **15**(2): p. 32.
14. McCormick, L., J. Dawley and E. Melendez, *The economic and workforce development activities of American business associations*. Economic Development Quarterly, 2008. **22**(3): p. 213–227.
15. Benner, C., *Labour flexibility and regional developments: The role of labour market intermediaries*. Regional Studies, 2003. **37**(6 & 7): p. 621–633.
16. Carnoy, M., M. Castells and C. Benner, *Labour markets and employment practices in the age of flexibility: A case study of Silicon Valley*. International Labour Review, 1997. **136**(1): p. 27–48.
17. Chapple, K., *Overcoming mismatch: Beyond dispersal, mobility, and development strategies*. Journal of the American Planning Association, 2006. **72**(3): p. 322.
18. Kalleberg, A. and P. Marsden, *Externalizing organizational activities: Where and how US establishments use employment intermediaries*. Socio-Economic Review, 2005. **3**: p. 389–416.
19. Garcia-Perez, J.I. and F. Munoz-Bullon, *Temporary help agencies and occupational mobility*. Oxford Bulletin of Economics and Statistics, 2005. **67**(2): p. 163.
20. Smith, V. and E. Neuwirth, *Temporary help agencies and the making of a new employment practice*. Academy of Management Perspective, 2008 (February): p. 56–72.
21. Kelley, E.H., *Strategies for a successful job search [2]*. Management Accounting, 1987. **69**(4): p. 32.
22. Balch, B.W. and B. Fayissa, *Declining government involvement in job search and the rise of self-placement: A macroeconomic explanation*. American Business Review, 1997. **15**(1): p. 43.

23. Blanton, B.L. and M. Larrabee, *High school and employment agency client views on career counseling.* Journal of Employment Counseling, 1999. **36**(3): p. 119.

24. Zeng, X. and Y. Cui, *Job search, labour market intermediaries and employment promotion: The evidence from China.* International Labour Review, 2008. **147**(2/3): p. 280–283.

25. Bosley, S., J. Arnold, and L. Cohen, *How other people shape our careers: A typology drawn from career narratives.* Human Relations, 2009. **62**(10): p. 1487.

26. Goodman, J. and S. Gillis, *Vocational guidance requests within the international scene.* The Career Development Quarterly, 2009. **57**(4): p. 335.

27. Kalleberg, A.L., *Nonstandard employment Relations: Part-time, temporary and contract work.* Annual Review of Sociology, 2000. **26**: p. 341–365.

28. King, Z., S. Burke and J. Pemberton, *The "bounded" career: An empirical study of human capital, career mobility and employment outcomes in a mediated labour market.* Human Relations, 2005. **58**(8): p. 981.

29. Kanter, R.M., *Careers and the wealth of nations,* in M.B. Arthur, D.T. Hall and B.S. Lawrence (Eds.), *Handbook of career theory,* 1989, New York, NY: Cambridge University Press. p. 506–522.

3 WORKING WITH & IN FOREIGN ENVIRONMENTS

LEARNING OBJECTIVES

- Using sector capabilities as a career path strategy

- Reviewing areas of international access and participation

- Understanding the barriers to international career mobility

- Linking the modes of knowing, entry, doing, and participation to the PRM perspective

THE ROADMAP

In Chapter 2 you were able to examine how economic, institutional, and environmental factors impact your ability to find employment and manage your career. You were shown how job transition dynamics reveal key underlying trends about career development strategies in various environments. You were then introduced to the concept of employability, which is at the heart of the personalized resource management perspective. Linked to the focus on employability was discussion of the variety and increasing importance of employment intermediaries around the world. Finally, you were able to explore a macro level view of an employment opportunity landscape (EOL). The EOL was defined as an arena consisting of the rules, regulations, business practices, employment intermediaries, organizations, and institutions that influence the types of employment opportunities, as well as the nature of the pathways to work, jobs, and careers. Understanding the dynamics of the employment opportunity landscape was seen as essential for individuals to map out opportunities, challenges, and advantages related to their career development and management.

Chapter 3 examines strategies for working with, and in, foreign environments. Despite the challenges of developing an international career, you will be shown how to use sector capabilities as a career path strategy. This will be followed by a review of positions and sectors that allow access and participation in the employment environment of different countries. In order to develop a strategy for working with, and in, foreign environments, it is important to understand the barriers to international career mobility. After an explanation of those barriers, you will be shown how the modes of knowing, doing, entering, and participation can boost career capabilities. Finally, a model linking these factors to the PRM perspective shows how you can develop your personal career capital and maintain long-term employability.

TOPIC FOCUS

In a global environment driven by the massive flow of goods and services across borders, corporations have long recognized the need to be mobile as they operate in multiple markets. Consequently, a lot of industry specialists, academics, and consultants have researched and presented effective entry and participation strategies for multinational firms. It is clear that firms operating in international markets see the benefits of entering, participating in, and expanding their presence in a variety of national environments. As for individuals entering and working in different foreign environments, most of the research and strategies focus on human resource management strategies that maximize the benefits to the organization. There is a vast literature on how expatriation, adjustment, and repatriation problems might impact the effectiveness of an organization. There is an equal volume of literature on the necessary preparation, training, evaluation, and promotion strategies for individuals who work for firms in foreign environments. In this literature, individual career development and career performance is significantly driven by organizational goals and strategies. [1–3]

Beyond the travel and study abroad literatures, there has been very little written on how individuals can take advantage of work with foreign environments in order to develop, manage, and expand their careers. The personalized resource management perspective presented in this book sees the need for a focus on a range of personal strategies to take advantage of learning, working, and career development opportunities derived from working with, and in, foreign environments. [4, 5]

A SECTOR CAPABILITY FOCUS AS A CAREER PATH STRATEGY

One way of accelerating your international business career is to get a position in a sector that is active globally. However, gaining entry and developing your career in a desired sector at home or abroad can be a very difficult task. It is even more difficult if you are focused on one specific position or location as a way of gaining entry into that field. However, experience shows that once you have gained entry into an international sector, it is then easier to navigate through different positions and build a long-term career. Moreover, it is easier to build a long-term career in a specific sector by developing expertise across different capabilities than it is to build a career by working frequently in unrelated sectors.

So how do you avoid the overly narrow focus on a specific position and, at the same time, increase your chances of entering a particular sector?

One approach is to explore sector employment activities from the capability perspective. This particular perspective has been conceptualized by this book to focus on the general capabilities required for most sectors to function effectively. This capability perspective holds the view that most sectors have to address, to some degree, eight key capabilities. All of these eight capabilities also represent key entry and career development opportunities for individuals. By focusing on these capabilities, you can find concrete pathways into a sector and expand your view of appropriate positions for developing your career. The eight key capabilities are *management, administrative, operations, technical, business development, financial, logistics,* and *regulatory activities.* Since there are numerous jobs, professions, and employment arrangements in every sector, the eight key sector capabilities represent a more targeted and manageable way of identifying employment opportunities.

The main suggestion here is that, since it is easier to move from one capability to another within a sector, the main goal should be to gain entry into a related area and then build the skills and experiences necessary to advance your career from the inside. This approach not only builds your competences but also builds transferable skills. A review of the eight main sector capabilities in Table 3.1 can provide insights into how you might target one or more of these capabilities to gain entry into a sector.

Table 3.1 Breakdown of typical sector capabilities and associated skills

Key sector capabilities	Associated activities and skills
Management	Leadership, negotiation, interpersonal, and business management skills.
Administrative	Human resource, information, and organizational coordination skills.
Operations	Core production, assembly, service, or distribution skills.
Technical	Core domain knowledge, technology development, and management skills.
Business development	Marketing, sales, client development, and alliance management.
Financial	Accounting, funding, cash flow, banking, and insurance relationships.
Logistics	Resource procurement and management, product or service delivery.
Regulatory	Intellectual property, compliance, legal, and government strategies.

Although most sectors have to address these eight capability factors, the importance and influence of these sector capabilities will vary by firm and by sector. It is up to you to understand the links and the priority given these capabilities in the sector and firm in which you are interested. Moreover, there are many positions, certifications, and educational fields associated with each of these capabilities. A full discussion of how certifications can boost entry, mobility, and capability is in the Appendix for Chapter 3. Figure 3.1 illustrates how the sector capability areas can be used to target your entry into the sector at different levels.

Based on this figure, we see that it is possible to enter a sector from either the lower, middle, or upper levels of the sector pyramid. You can also enter from a different foreign location. All eight sector capabilities have appropriate employment positions at every level. Individuals can make use of employment intermediaries, personal contacts, and other networks to get help with entry into the sector. It goes without saying that the higher up one tries to enter the sector, the more sector capability-related skills one has to have accumulated. The international environment presents an opportunity for sector-related skill development in a variety of locations. With barriers to skilled labor falling, it is not usual to find capable individuals who have entered a sector from different locations or similar positions abroad.

Figure 3.1 Sector pyramid and sector entry-point strategy model

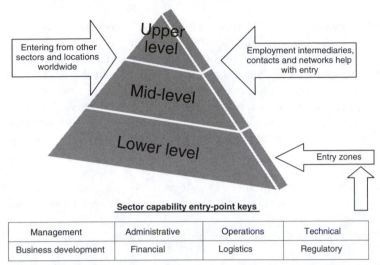

Sector capability entry-point keys			
Management	Administrative	Operations	Technical
Business development	Financial	Logistics	Regulatory

TOPIC FOCUS

Individuals who move to different countries to pursue or expand their career-sare often faced with cultural and institutional barriers that are difficult to overcome. Although they may adjust to the cultural differences, institutional barriers that impact the recognition of competences can be more difficult to overcome. Although individuals may have attained a high level of education and competence in their home country, they often need to get recognition in their new environment before they can proceed with their careers. The more expensive and long-term solution is often to enter educational institutions in the new environment and pursue degrees which are locally recognized and respected. Another approach, which can be equally effective, is to seek professional certifications in a chosen field. Detailed discussions of certifications are in the Appendix. Since some of these professional certifications are recognized internationally, they give the individuals the ability to move more freely across borders to find the new positions which allow them to transfer their competences. There are many different sectors and areas that allow individuals to access and participate in employment environments around the world. [6–10]

AREAS OF INTERNATIONAL ACCESS & PARTICIPATION

For individuals going to foreign environments for the purpose of career development, maintenance, or expansion, there is a wide range of fields that allows such access. In all of these fields there are entry level, mid-career and executive level positions available. In addition to organizations sending their employees to various locations around the world, it is possible for individuals to use employment intermediaries and local relationships and networks to gain access to these positions. Below is a description of five areas which cover most of the international employment opportunities. [11–14]

Teaching & Research

One of the easiest and most flexible ways of finding work in foreign countries is through language teaching. Although English teaching is the most dominant foreign language teaching activity, many other languages are in demand around the world. Language schools, colleges, and universities around the world continually recruit native speakers to teach a variety of languages. Another area with wide range of employment opportunities is being a professor. Academics can find short-term and long-term teaching and research opportunities in many different fields around the world. In most cases, local universities or research institutions will sponsor qualified professors to work in their countries. The main difficulty in getting these positions is that individuals usually need to have a recognized Ph.D. in their chosen field of specialization. Administrative positions in colleges, universities, and research institutes around the world are also available for individuals with the appropriate experience.

Business & Technology

The vast majority of non-teaching jobs in foreign environments tend to be found in the business and technology fields. There is a strong international dimension to jobs in sectors such as financial, logistics, wine, hospitality, energy, consulting, information technology, and retail. There are many entry level, mid-career, and executive level administrative, technical, and management positions in all of these sectors. The majority of these positions in foreign work environments are linked to expatriate assignments by business and technology companies. However, due to the expanding reach of global employment intermediaries, it is easier for individuals to search for and find business and IT positions abroad without waiting to be sent by an organization. Two business-related sectors that often go unnoticed when we think of international employment opportunities are the recreational and hospitality sectors. From working in summer camps to working in hotels around the world, individuals can find numerous employment opportunities if they know where to look.

Development, Non-Profit & Governmental

Local and international agencies and institutions around the world are involved in many economic development projects. Some of these projects are government sponsored, and some get their funding from other internal and external sources. These types of development projects tend to be found mostly in emerging markets and many require short-term or long-term participation by individuals in various aspects of economic and social development projects. Non-profit organizations that have a range of aid, investment, and educational goals operate widely in countries around the world. Most nations also carry out Foreign Service and other governmental activities around the globe. Many of these positions are linked to national civil service qualifications or appointments, but governments also hire individuals in the local environments to staff their local operations. Becoming a member of a branch of the military is another strategy for gaining military and non-military international experience.

Performing & Athletics

High level performing sports athletes represent a group that has been very mobile, as they transfer their acquired competencies across organizations and countries.

This is especially true for sports that are played in many countries, such as soccer, volleyball, basketball, tennis, and even baseball. Training and development could occur in one country and performance can take place for short-term or longer-term periods in other countries. Because of the strong demand for high performing athletes, the institutional barriers to mobility are greatly reduced. Although these individuals play for different teams, it is their acquired capabilities and cross-border mobility which boosts their personal career capital. We see similar patterns with highly capable performance artists in areas such as music, dance, and film. These performance artists go through a long developmental process in one or more countries and then can showcase their talents in many regions and countries. For both high level performing artists and athletes, their capability, mobility, and transferability factors drive their career management strategies.

Manufacturing and Services

In some countries, we find that immigrants provide cheap labor in sectors such manufacturing and services. Since some of these jobs do not usually require very high levels of skills or strong certifications, we often find that low-skilled self-initiated expatriates start out in these sectors. The service sector is especially attractive to new immigrants in urban areas. Jobs such as freelance language teaching, waiting tables, taxi driving, housekeeping, baby sitting, gardening, house repair worker or security guard represent areas where new immigrants can take advantage of their friendship or community networks to gain access to job opportunities. Although they may be low-skilled and low wage jobs, these jobs can also be categorized as springboard employment positions for some new immigrants. Many immigrants who had acquired employable skills in their home country will take these jobs while they go back to school, prepare to pass certifications, or build new networks to help them move into higher-skilled positions. It is clear that even low wage earning individuals in these sectors are concerned with capability development, job mobility, and the transferability of competences.

TOPIC FOCUS

It is not just trade barriers that have been coming down around the world. It appears that geographic barriers are increasingly incapable of deterring the movement of numerous groups and individuals in and out of various countries around the world. Many countries have experienced the influx of global travelers, skilled legal immigrants, refugees, and illegal immigrants. The motivation for going abroad, and some of the strategies used by these individuals and groups to enter and work in foreign environments, can be instructive for those wishing to use the international environment to develop, maintain, or expand their careers. Although firms will always play a significant role in managing the flow of skilled workers in and out of various countries, more and more individuals are deciding on work opportunities and career trajectories that take them outside their home countries. [15–18]

BARRIERS & OBSTACLES TO INTERNATIONAL CAREER MOBILITY

Although it is much easier now for individuals to travel across national boundaries, there are still many barriers preventing the effective development and management of personal careers in international environments. One barrier that is difficult to observe is the psychological barrier that individuals face when moving to, or working in, foreign environments. Individuals not only need to be resilient as they face a range of challenges, they must also be willing to accept much higher levels of uncertainty and stress. Cultural barriers can also take significant efforts to overcome. New entrants into a country often struggle with differences in language as well as differences in work behaviors, communication, and negotiation styles. New entrants need to navigate the new social, economic, and cultural contexts that underlie the foreign career environment. [18, 19]

Institutional barriers to international career development in foreign environments are far-reaching and complex. The national, regional, local, and organizational barriers to the free flow of human capital vary significantly across foreign environments. The immigration policies of many nations are linked to their evaluation of human capital and where they see the benefits to national competitive targets. However, even after gaining entry into a different national environment, the local institutional barriers can be difficult to overcome. Quite often, there is little recognition for degrees received in other countries and many credentialing and professional associations require the passing of local qualifying examinations. [17]

The technical barriers to developing and expanding a career across borders include language ability, general domain knowledge and capabilities, and firm-specific competences. Acquiring country-specific, company-specific and profession-specific competences requires the preparation and accumulation of a wide range of capabilities. However, in most cases, these developmental experiences are dominated by organizational goals and strategies. In other words, the hiring, expatriation, and repatriation experiences which underlie these capability-enhancing experiences are generally carried out from the perspective of the needs of the organization. [20]

The literature on self-initiated expatriates attempts to address some of the shortcomings of the traditional human resource perspective by focusing on the personal strategies that individuals use to overcome socio-cultural, institutional, and technical barriers to the development of international careers. Researchers rightly point out that, in addition to technical capabilities, motivation and psychological resilience are two characteristics that help qualified skilled immigrants overcome obstacles to the development or continuation of international careers. [18, 21, 22]

Although the physical barriers to the free flow of labor across environments are substantial, individuals can use a variety of strategies to enter and participate in different labor markets. However, the development of an international career involves a process which starts with self-assessment, followed by preparatory strategies that help to boost individual competence and mobility. In other words, self-assessment helps develop the proper mindset and awareness necessary to plan a career trajectory that involves working with, and in, foreign environments. The modes of knowing, doing, entering, and participation discussed below highlight concrete strategies that individuals can use to evaluate their potential for a successful international career.

MODES OF KNOWING & SELF-ASSESSMENT STRATEGIES

Modes of knowing refers to a typology of career-related competences and self-awareness factors which can boost the competitiveness and employability of individuals who take a proactive approach to career management. In the literature on the accumulation of personal competences, researchers have mainly talked about three modes of knowing: knowing why, how, and whom [15, 23]. However, in order to capture the full range of competences and self-assessment issues, this book supports expanding the range for the modes of knowing to six. The six modes of knowing introduced are knowing what, why, how, where, when, and whom. By exploring the extent of their own knowledge and awareness related to each mode of knowing, individuals can develop a clearer picture of potential jobs and career paths that matches their values, interests, and capabilities. [24]

Knowing What

This type of knowledge indicates that, after considering a variety of occupations and potential career trajectories, individuals have managed to narrow down their choices to a range of achievable options. "Knowing what" is especially important at the initial stages of career development or during periods of transition to new occupations. Developing an understanding of different sectors, job designs, job demands, and other characteristics of various occupations are crucial for individuals to be able to fully evaluate potential jobs and career paths.

Knowing Why

This is related to an individual's ability to understand the underlying motives, interests, and values linked to a particular occupation or career path. This type of knowledge relies on the self-awareness and motivation necessary to overcome a variety of obstacles in order to achieve one's career goals. "Knowing why" helps individuals align work-related decisions with their preferred identity and values. "Knowing why" is also a subjective dimension which has an impact on the processes of self-direction, self-reliance, self-evaluation, and self-satisfaction.

Knowing How

This type of knowledge shows that, after identifying a particular occupation or career path, individuals can focus on developing and accumulating the portable skills and knowledge that will allow them to work within or across organizations or national boundaries. This purposeful accumulation of portable skills can occur through education, certifications, training, work-experience, or life-experiences.

Although the "knowing how" competence may vary from job to job, it is the purposeful linking and accumulation of skills and experiences that creates a reservoir of capabilities that boost long-term employability.

Knowing Where

This reflects an individual's knowledge of which local, national, or foreign employment markets present the best opportunity to stay gainfully employed in order to build key capabilities and achieve career goals. Knowing which locations, sectors, and companies might provide the best opportunity to develop and support certain career trajectories underlies the "knowing where" competence. Moreover, since mobility is a crucial aspect of career management today, the willingness to learn about, work in, and benefit from cross-organizational and cross-border experiences is essential for long-term career success.

Knowing When

Since long-term employment within one organization or one region is fast becoming a rarity, the knowledge of when to change firms, locations, or positions can boost an individual's competitiveness and accelerate the accumulation of portable skills and capabilities. In addition, the awareness of opportunities and the timing of job transitions often depend on individuals' strategic insight into the direction of change in an occupation, sector, or business environment. However, there is a subjective dimension to "knowing when," since individuals often have subjective occupational or career goals. Knowing when to change can be a reflection of a sense of fulfillment, an attempt to get away from negative occupational experiences, or a move to build positive career opportunities

Knowing Whom

This type of knowledge emphasizes the building, development, and utilization of informal, professional, and friendship networks throughout one's working life. This type of competence emerges from an individual's connectedness to other individuals, groups, and organizations. However, the structure and types of networks have varying influences on an individual's ability to use them to enhance employability and mobility. "Knowing whom" is also a competence which gets accumulated as one's career extends across organizations and locations. It is not surprising, then, that intangible outcomes such as adaptability, mobility, reputation, and personal influence often depend on the effective mobilization of one's personal and professional networks.

MODES OF DOING, ENTERING, & PARTICIPATION

All the insights gained from the "modes of knowing" perspective have been useful for examining work with, and across, foreign environments. However, by linking these insights with the personalized resource management (PRM) perspective, it is possible to present an integrated view of how cross-border developmental activities can boost employability. An integrated view (Figure 3.2) is applicable for individuals whose careers occur across organizations within and across borders. In this regard, the two main propositions of this perspective are:

1. By working with, and in, foreign environments, individuals can explore alternative pathways to building career capabilities.

2. Working across borders provides the experiences necessary to enhance mobility and long-term employabilisty.

The main focus of the "modes of knowing" perspective is on awareness, mindset, and personal knowledge development. It is for this reasons that many researchers and consultants have stated that a global mindset is the precursor of the process of building global capabilities. With this in mind, the best way of linking the "modes of knowing" with the personalized resource management perspective is to incorporate the "modes of doing, entering, and participation" stages into one model (Figure 3.2). "Modes of doing" refers to the preparing, experiencing, executing, and adapting strategies that individuals use to build and apply work-related competences in a variety of work environments. So, after arriving at a certain level of self awareness, self-motivation, and knowledge of the elements needed to choose a career trajectory, individuals must then take action to build and apply career-related capabilities. "Modes of entry" refers to the range of strategies individuals can use to enter different employment environments around the world. Table 3.2 gives a list of the numerous entry strategies available for short, medium-term and long-term employment opportunities in various countries. "Modes of participation" refers to the different types of employment arrangements and career forms that are available for those working in international environments. The international environment provides extensive opportunities for continued employment and skill development. What this means is that, since careers have become fragmented in today's environment, it is generally up to individuals to link work experiences in ways that boost employability. [1, 20, 25]

Despite physical, institutional, and technical barriers, individuals continue to find ways to enter and participate in different work environments across the globe. In general, most of the HR and management literatures present strategies that organizations use for effective worker expatriation, adjustment, and repatriation. From that perspective, employee mobility is driven by organizational imperatives and cost-benefit analyses of foreign placements. In essence, individuals have to adjust their competence development and career management strategies to match the pathways made available by the firm. [26–29]

In contrast to the extensive research on long-term expatriation and repatriation activities, there is now a growing focus on alternative forms of international mobility for workers. Flexpatriates who travel frequently to foreign locations on short assignments to conduct business activities have received a lot of attention. Other alternative forms of international mobility in the business environment that have been examined include short-term placements, international commuting, and virtual teams. Most of these alternative forms of mobility are, however, still tied to the strategies of firms that are seeking flexibility, productivity, and cost benefits. [13, 30]

Despite the familiar patterns presented in the management literature, it is clear that the processes behind the modes of doing, entry, and participation of individuals in foreign work environments are more complex than the organizationally-driven expatriation, adjustment, and repatriation patterns usually examined. Refugees, self-initiated expats, and illegal immigrants all represent modes of entry and participation in new work environments. However, self-initiated expats most closely reflect the types of individuals who would choose a personalized resource management approach to career development. Self-initiated expats are not sent by companies, but go abroad of their own initiative to find work. The literature on self-initiated expats goes beyond a focus on people traveling abroad for pleasure to a wider focus on individuals from both developed and developing economies who move across borders to find longer-term employment This group includes both unskilled and skilled immigrants. The barriers that these individuals face often vary by skill levels, ethnicities, and regions of origin. [6, 31, 32]

Table 3.2 shows the wide range of entry strategies to foreign environments. Some allow individuals' short-term participation in the work environment, while others give longer-tem access to educational, living, and working situations. Since these access arrangements vary significantly from country to country, individuals need to choose the situations which give them the best opportunity to develop or expand career-related capabilities.

Table 3.2 Entry and access strategies for foreign environments

Limited period non-visa tourism	Special country work permits
Limited period visa-required tourism	Special exchange and researcher permits
Business purpose visit (visa and non-visa)	Special performance athletes and
Education studies (short & longer-term)	performers
Job training arrangements	Special knowledge consultants
Entrepreneur business venture visa	Special refugee or asylum status
Self-employment visa	Humanitarian entry permits
Working holiday permits	Family or spouse sponsorship
Temporary short-term work visas	Fiancé-sponsored visas
Long-term working visas	Special residency lotteries
	Foreign internships

LINKING MODES OF KNOWING, DOING, ENTERING, & PARTICIPATION WITH THE PERSONALIZED RESOURCE MANAGEMENT (PRM) PERSPECTIVE

In Figure 3.2, we see that the three main career outcomes from the interaction of the "modes of doing, entering, and participation" are capability, mobility, and transferability. "Capability" refers to the preparing, developing, and applying of competences across work environments. The full range of work and non-work activities that individuals undertake to build skills and competences would apply to the capability dimension. In addition to domain knowledge and technical skills, cross-cultural experiences and competences also count as key elements for building capabilities. [33–36]

"Mobility" refers to the preparing for, experiencing, and adapting to different work environments within and across borders. Mobility also refers to having strategies for gaining entry into different regional or national work environments through individual, organizational, or network efforts (Figure 3.2). However, it is important to mention that in the short-term, it is possible for moves across environments to have an upward, sideways or even downward impact. That is why mobility patterns need to be considered and managed from a long-term perspective. The ultimate goal of mobility should be the accumulation of experiences which build competences to achieve long-term goals. Besides a global mindset, one key characteristic that global managers often mentioned in the management literature is their ability to work in different environments as they strive to achieve organizational goals. [1, 12, 18]

The last outcome factor of the modes of doing, entering, and participation is transferability (Figure 3.2). Transferability, here, refers to the retention, adaptation, or expansion of competences acquired in previous work environments. In general, the transferability of personal competence is usually determined by the portability of the institutional, organizational, and technical knowledge acquired by

Figure 3.2 Linking the assessment and action modes with the PRM perspective

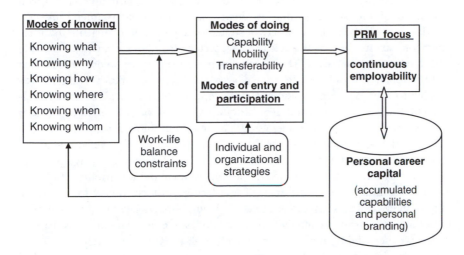

individuals in different regional or national environments. There are a wide range of personal, institutional, and organizational strategies that can be used by individuals to enhance the transferability of individual competences. These strategies can include using friendship networks, educational programs, company repatriation activities, and even professional certifications to signal to the markets and the work environments that you are capable of performing according to local or international standards and requirements.

The heart of the personalized resource management perspective is the emphasis on developing employability by accumulating capabilities and making effective use of personal and informational networks. In Figure 3.2, we see how the modes of knowing, doing, entering, and participation link up to boost the possibility of continuous employability. Employability is crucial because that is how individuals build personal career capital. "Personal career capital" can be defined as the privately accumulated resources, capabilities, and relationships that boost employability, recognition, and status in employment environments. Another way of understanding personal career capital is to see it as the combination of accumulated work-related capabilities and personal branding strategies. Based on these characterizations, it might even be possible to divide personal career capital into local, foreign, and global career capital dimensions. Finally, based on the model presented in Figure 3.2, we see that there is a feedback loop connecting personal career capital and the modes of knowing. This makes a lot of sense since our self-awareness, self-evaluation, and motivations are continually influenced by the work-related success or failures that we have experienced in previous situations. [9, 20, 21, 37, 38]

CHAPTER SUMMARY & OBSERVATIONS

In this chapter, you were presented with strategies for working with, and in, foreign environments. An important aspect of this career development strategy was to understand the barriers to international career mobility. The four main barriers to mobility were psychological, institutional, technical, and physical. You were shown that, although the barriers to the free flow of labor across environments are substantial, individuals can use a variety of strategies to enter and participate in different labor markets. One approach is to target sector capabilities as a way of entering and developing your career. This sector capability perspective holds the view that most sectors have to address, to some degree, eight key capabilities. The eight key capabilities are management, administrative, operations, technical, business development, financial, logistics, and regulatory activities. All of these eight capabilities also represent key entry and career development opportunities for individuals.

Using the personalized resource management (PRM) perspective, an integrated model was presented which incorporated the modes of knowing, doing, entering, and participation in ways which led to the enhancement of the capability, mobility, and transferability aspects of careers. These factors, in turn, boosted individuals' employability and personal career capital. In Figure 3.2, we saw that the three main career outcomes from the interaction of the modes of doing, entering, and participation were capability, mobility, and transferability. "Capability" referred to preparing, developing, and applying competences across work environments. "Mobility" referred to preparing for, experiencing, and adapting to different work environments within and across borders. Mobility was also defined as having strategies for gaining entry into different regional or national work environments through individual, organizational, or network efforts. Finally, "transferability" referred to the retention, adaptation, or expansion of competences acquired in previous work environments.

Chapter 4 will discuss strategies for maximizing employment mobility in international environments. You will be presented with a model that shows how a set of entry and participation strategies allows individuals to take advantage of a global mindset and cross-cultural capabilities to boost their international mobility. You will then have an exploration of the importance of gateway cities and worldwide dynamic regions in boosting the long-term success of your international business career. Globalization has not only increased the flow of goods and services around the world, it has also made it easier for skilled individuals to search out and take advantage of employment opportunities in different employment environments in many nations.

REFERENCES

1. Cappellen, T. and M. Janssens, *Global managers' career competencies*. Career Development International, 2008. **13**(6): p. 514.
2. Larsen, H.H., *Global career as dual dependency between the organization and the individual*. The Journal of Management Development, 2004. **23**(9): p. 860.
3. Linehan, M. and H. Scullion, *Selection, training, and development for female international executives*. Career Development International, 2001. **6**(6): p. 318.
4. Doherty, N. and M. Dickmann, *Exposing the symbolic capital of international assignments*. The International Journal of Human Resource Management, 2009. **20**(2): p. 301.
5. Fang, T., J. Zikic and M. Novicevic, *Crossing national boundaries: A typology of qualified immigrants' career orientations*. Journal of Organizational Behavior, 2009. **31**(5): p. 667.
6. Ariss, A.A., *Modes of engagement: Migration, self-initiated expatriation, and career development*. Career Development International, 2010. **15**(4): p. 338.
7. Beamish, P.W. and J.L. Calof, *International business education: A corporate view*. Journal of International Business Studies, 1989. **20**(3): p. 553.

8. Coulson-Thomas, C., *Developing and supporting information entrepreneurs.* Career Development International, 2001. **6**(4): p. 231.

9. Hannon, J., *AACE international "career capital" attainable at your nearest webbrowser.* Cost Engineering, 2007. **49**(5): p. 11.

10. Suutari, V. and M. Taka, *Career anchors of managers with global careers.* The Journal of Management Development, 2004. **23**(9): p. 833.

11. Chiaburu, D., V. Baker and A. Pitariu, *Beyond being proactive: What (else) matters for career self-management behaviors?* Career Development International, 2006. **11**(7): p. 619.

12. Clarke, M., *Plodders, pragmatists, visionaries and opportunists: Career patterns and employability.* Career Development International, 2009. **14**(1): p. 8.

13. Demel, B. and W. Mayrhofer, *Frequent business travelers across Europe: Career aspirations and implications.* Thunderbird International Business Review, 2010. **52**(4): p. 301.

14. Kirschbaum, C., *Careers in the right beat: US jazz musicians' typical and non-typical trajectories.* Career Development International, 2007. **12**(2): p. 187.

15. DeFillippi, R.J. and M.B. Arthur, *Boundaryless contexts and careers: A competency-based perspective,* in M.B. Arthur and D. Rousseau (Eds.), *The boundaryless career: A new employment principle for a new organization era,* 1996, New York, NY: Oxford University Press. p. 116–131.

16. Fish, A. and J. Wood, *A challenge to career management practice.* The International Journal of Career Management, 1993. **5**(2): p. 3.

17. Thorn, K., *The relative importance of motives for international self-initiated mobility.* Career Development International, 2009. **14**(5): p. 441.

18. Zikic, J., J. Bonache and J.-L. Cerdin, *Crossing national boundaries: A typology of qualified immigrants' career orientations.* Journal of Organizational Behavior, 2010. **31**(5): p. 667.

19. Osborn, D., *The international mobility of French managers.* European Management Journal, 1997. **15**(5): p. 584.

20. Jokinen, T., *Development of career capital through international assignments and its transferability to new contexts.* Thunderbird International Business Review, 2010. **52**(4): p. 325.

21. Myers, B. and J. Pringle, *Self-initiated foreign experience as accelerated development: Influences of gender.* Journal of World Business, 2005. **40**(4): p. 421.

22. Tung, R., *Brain circulation, diaspora, and international competitiveness.* European Management Journal, 2008. **26**(5): p. 298.

23. Tymon, W. and S. Stumpf, *Social capital in the success of knowledge workers.* Career Development International, 2003. **8**(1): p. 12.

24. Srinivas, S., *The impact of technological mobility on workers' careers.* Career Development International, 2009. **14**(2): p. 133.

25. Cerdin, J.-L. and M. LePargneux, *Career and international assignment fit: Toward an integrative model of success.* Human Resource Management, 2009. **48**(1): p. 5.

26. Guthrie, J., R. Ash and C. Stevens, *Are women "better" than men? Personality differences and expatriate selection.* Journal of Managerial Psychology, 2003. **18**(3): p. 229.

27. Haslberger, A. and C. Brewster, *Capital gains: expatriate adjustment and the psychological contract in international careers.* Human Resource Management, 2009. **48**(3): p. 379.

28. Mäkelä, K. and V. Suutari, *Global careers: a social capital paradox.* The International Journal of Human Resource Management, 2009. **20**(5): p. 992.

29. Stahl, G. and J.-L. Cerdin, *Global careers in French and German multinational corporations.* The Journal of Management Development, 2004. **23**(9): p. 885.

30. Wittig-Berman, U. and N. Beutell, *International assignments and the career management of repatriates: The boundaryless career concept.* International Journal of Management, 2009. **26**(1): p. 77.

31. Tharenou, P., *Women's self-initiated expatriation as a career option and its ethical issues.* Journal of Business Ethics, 2010. **95**(1): p. 73.

32. Tharmaseelan, N., K. Inkson and S. Carr, *Migration and career success: Testing a time-sequenced model.* Career Development International, 2010. **15**(3): p. 218.

33. Bonache, J., C. Brewster and V. Suutari, *Knowledge, international mobility, and careers.* International Studies of Management & Organization, 2007. **37**(3): p. 3.

34. Dickmann, M. and H. Harris, *Developing career capital for global careers: The role of international assignments*. Journal of World Business, 2005. **40**(4): p. 399.

35. Haines III, V. and T. Saba, *International mobility policies and practices: Are there gender differences in importance ratings?* Career Development International, 1999. **4**(4): p. 206.

36. Mahroum, S., *Highly skilled globetrotters: Mapping the international migration of human capital*. R & D Management, 2000. **30**(1): p. 23.

37. Lamb, M. and M. Sutherland, *The components of career capital for knowledge workers in the global economy*. The International Journal of Human Resource Management, 2010. **21**(3): p. 295.

38. McKenna, S. and J. Richardson, *The increasing complexity of the internationally mobile professional*. Cross Cultural Management, 2007. **14**(4): p. 307.

PART II

EXPLORING THE IMPACT OF CAPABILITY, MOBILITY, & TRANSFERABILITY STRATEGIES ON CAREER MANAGEMENT

4 MAXIMIZING MOBILITY & THE ROLE OF INTERNATIONAL GATEWAY CITIES

LEARNING OBJECTIVES

- Understand strategies for maximizing international career mobility

- Examine the role of international gateway cities

- Explore developments in key international gateway cities

- Review international study and work abroad activities

THE ROADMAP

In Chapter 3, you examined strategies for working with, and in, foreign environments. Overcoming barriers to international career mobility was seen as a crucial step in this area of career development. You saw that individuals can use a variety of strategies to deal with the psychological, institutional, technical, and physical barriers to career mobility. One strategy of focusing on sector capabilities for charting career development and career trajectory was clearly related to the personalized resource management perspective. The eight key sector capabilities discussed were management, administrative, operations, technical, business development, financial, logistics, and regulatory activities. All of these eight capabilities were shown to represent key entry and career development opportunities for individuals. Later in Chapter 3, an integrated model was presented which incorporated the modes of knowing, doing, entering, and participation in ways which led to the enhancement of the capability, mobility, and transferability aspects of careers. You were shown how the three main career outcomes from the interaction of the "modes of doing, entering, and participation" were capability, mobility, and transferability. These last three outcomes are at the core of the personalized resource management (PRM) perspective.

Chapter 4 will focus more closely on the mobility aspect of the PRM perspective. A model will be presented which highlight strategies for maximizing international career mobility. The two-stage model shows tangible and intangible activities that help individuals maximize their career mobility. The chapter then focuses on how accessing international gateway cities can help in this endeavor. This is because international gateway cities and regions are at the center of international demand for knowledge workers and business professionals. A review of significant developments in gateway cities in developed economies and emerging markets will show that employment opportunities for skilled workers have expanded significantly to more geographic regions and to a wider range of sectors. At the end of the chapter, a review of study and work abroad strategies shows how they aid significantly in maximizing international career mobility.

STRATEGIES FOR MAXIMIZING INTERNATIONAL CAREER MOBILITY

In previous discussions of the personalized resource management perspective, capability, mobility, and transferability were presented as crucial career outcomes for which you should strive. The more you are able to develop these factors, the closer you will get to maintaining continuous employability. In this chapter, we will explore some of the factors that enhance international career mobility. Figure 4.1 illustrates how some of these factors interact to boost mobility.

Figure 4.1 Maximizing your international career mobility

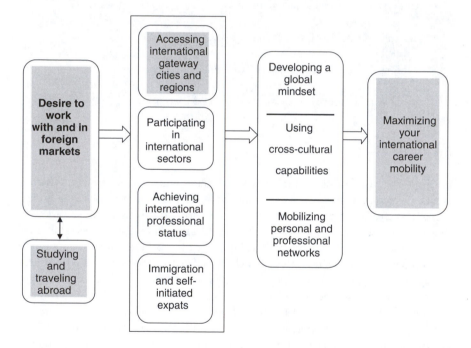

The whole process starts with your desire to work with, and in, foreign markets. The motivation to work in the international arena is what drives all other factors. This motivation can emerge for many reasons and from many sources. One experience that consistently tends to influence individuals to consider working internationally is studying or traveling abroad. In some circumstances, it is the desire to live and work abroad which drives individuals to study or travel in other countries. Once the motivation to work internationally is firmly established, there are a number of strategies and experiences that can lead to outcomes that increase mobility.

Although job opportunities exist in many places around the world, this book strongly believes that 'gateway cities' will provide the most dynamic employment opportunities. Gateway cities are usually connected to important economic regions and that enhances their importance as an employment opportunity landscape. The importance of the concept of gateway cities will be discussed more in detail later in this chapter. Gaining access to, and building up your experience with, sectors that have an exposure to global markets is another key strategy for boosting your mobility. This is especially true if you are able to develop your competences in some of the key sector capability areas mentioned in the previous chapter.

International professional status refers to individuals who have either obtained academic degrees or certifications that are recognized around the world or to individuals whose business, artistic, athletic, or professional achievements have enhanced their international reputation. These individuals create a pool of talented professionals and knowledge workers that are in strong demand in various sectors and for various projects. Having international professional status increases the likelihood that you will have access to employment positions in a variety of locations, thereby boosting your career mobility.

Immigration is probably the most drastic step a business professional can take to boost career mobility. Although individuals immigrate for a wide variety of reasons, they will generally do their utmost to have a viable career in their new location. Self-initiated expatriates represent one such category of individuals.

They voluntarily go to other countries to find employment or to expand their career opportunities. Some end up living permanently in the new location while others use the experience to build their professional portfolios in order to have a successful return to their home country. For both categories of individuals, career mobility is a matter of professional survival.

Using the strategies mentioned above is usually enough to improve one's short-term career mobility. However, in order to maximize your career mobility for the long-term, you need to incorporate the next set of strategies shown in Figure 4.1. Developing a global mind set is a crucial factor for those wishing to lead and interact effectively on an international level. A "global mind set" is a set of personal characteristics which enhances individuals' openness to different ideas, practices, and cultures as well as giving them the flexibility to adapt to uncertainty and the changing international environment. In essence, it is a way of thinking and managing which shows that individuals understand how to deal with the diversity and complexities of the international stage.

On the other hand, the term "cross-cultural capabilities" refers to the sensitivity towards different cultures, as well as the linguistic ability and psychological disposition, that make it easier for an individual to interact with people from different cultural backgrounds. Using this capability effectively can make it easier for individuals to perform in different business environments around the globe. Finally, the mobilization of personal and professional networks increases an individual's access to problem-solving advice and information on employment opportunities in different employment environments. Overall, individuals who are able to make use of strategies at both the tangible and intangible stages can more quickly maximize their long-term career mobility capability.

In the rest of this chapter, there will be an examination of one major aspect of the model shown in Figure 4.1. By focusing on international gateway cities and dynamic regions, you will be able to explore an increasingly important phenomenon in the growth of international employment opportunities. After explaining the phenomenon of "gateway cities," you will get more in-depth information on a selection of international cities around the world. The international cities discussed were not randomly chosen. There is a clear logic why these cities are, and will be, important players in present and future international employment patterns.

The cities presented later in this chapter can be separated into two groups: major international cities in developed economies, and dynamic cities in the increasingly important emerging markets. Tokyo, New York, and London were chosen as representatives of the industrialized economies. These cities all have well developed employment infrastructures and they have all played a major role in boosting the economic development of their country and surrounding regions. There are also well established expatriate communities that support the business activities of multinational firms in these international cities.

Shanghai, Mumbai, Sao Paulo, and Moscow represent key cities for the BRIC economies that are leading economic activities in the emerging markets. In many ways, emerging economies are growing faster than the developed economies and countries like Brazil, India, China, and Russia either have a tremendous resource base or large and growing consumer markets. Johannesburg and Dubai were added to the list of cities from emerging markets because they represent dynamic regions and the promise of accelerating development in Africa and the Middle East. Overall, the forces of globalization have played a major role in transforming these cities into dynamic economic engines.

There is strong evidence that globalization has not only increased the flow of goods, services, and ideas across borders, it has also boosted the importance of cities as key communication and interaction nodes worldwide. This is due to the fact that the economic success of nations in a global economy depends greatly on the integration of both internal and external trade, as well as transportation and communication routes. Consequently, cities now function more like hubs, with spokes leading inward to various domestic regions and outward to various international geographic areas. Moreover, as competition among nations intensifies, it appears that cities are becoming crucial to the effective development of urban environments that spur economic growth, innovation, and entrepreneurial activity. [8]

TOPIC FOCUS

Although technology now allows us to be more mobile and communicate across greater distances, there is still a need for the benefits of the clustering properties of cities. The vibrant social and business environment of cities directly impacts the cultural, economic, and political fabric of nations. It might not be an exaggeration to say that nations still matter but cities matter even more. This development can be highlighted by the growing competition among cities within, and across, nations. Some cities have gone as far to embark on location marketing campaigns and branding strategies to attract capital and talented people from around the world. [7]

With intensifying globalization and worldwide urban growth, the historical significance of cities has reached a new level. In 1900 there were only about 16 cities with populations of over 1 million. By the year 2000, there were over 417 cities with over 1 million residents. Recently, for the first time, over 50 percent of the world's population was living in cities. Although the levels of urbanization are higher in developed economies, the increasing rate of urbanization is higher in developing economies. Consequently, it is forecast that, by the year 2050, 70 percent of the word's population will live in urban areas. Cities are here to stay. [8, 13]

Another argument which supports the importance of cities in overall economic development is their relationship to surrounding regions. Regions that have a strong link to urban areas tend to be the most dynamic. The surrounding regions are not only a source of people and local resources, they also represent areas for the potential expansion of business and social activities developed in the cities. This relationship is the one that underlies the concept of a 'gateway city'. The reason for the interest in gateway cities in this book is due to their impact on employment growth and international career development opportunities. [1, 14]

THE ROLE OF GATEWAY CITIES

The concept of the "gateway city" has been used in different ways since the 1930s. In its most basic use, the term simply meant a city that served as an entry and exit point for the surrounding region. These types of gateway cities were characterized as being centers of economic power for the nearby regions. Over the years, the term has been used in social geography literature and urban studies. Recently the term has been revised and the concept expanded to account for some new urban developments. In the economic globalization literature, the "gateway city" is seen as an entry and exit arena for economic and socio-cultural activities that link it to the global economy. The expanded definition of gateway cities now reflects major institutional, economic, and communication concentration processes that are occurring around the world. More and more gateway cities are becoming the center of economic, socio-cultural, and political power in important international regions. This development also reflects the increasing importance of cities in general in the global economy. This book sees gateway cities as key employment environments that aid in the maximization of career mobility. [15–21]

This rich concept of gateway cities projects associations, such as entrance, port, doorway, portal, and hub. The expanded concept continues to be widely used by those in urban planning, healthcare, logistics, economic development, business strategy, and marketing. Gateway cities are seen as those cities that are open to world trade, travel, and business activity, because of the existence of significant seaports or airports. Since these cities serve as both arrival and departure points for people, goods, and services, they are really hubs or bridges to other geographic areas. It is important to note that there are many cities that qualify as international gateway cities, and much of their status depends on their ability to sustain worldwide attention and regional economic growth. [7, 22, 23]

The international gateway cities garner economic muscle from their links to global finance, trade, communication, and immigration flows. Since they are often job creation engines, they act as economic magnets attracting both domestic and foreign workers and immigrants. When these gateway cities become extremely large, we have seen terms such as "super-gateways," "mega-centers," "megacities" and "global cities" being used. The global city concept is the most complex, since it refers to cities which are not only gateway cities but those that have a disproportionate impact on international economic, financial, cultural, or political developments worldwide. [24–26]

In order to evaluate the impact of international gateway cities, key measures that are important for employment and career development are areas such as new company formation, venture capital financing, major infrastructure projects, competitive production or service firms, and active employment intermediaries. Another important measure of the status of a gateway city is the extent to which it energizes economic and employment activities in the surrounding regions. [27, 28]

TOPIC FOCUS

Most global economic activity can be attributed to the contribution of major distribution, production, and financial clusters around the world. The clusters that are found in developed economies have long played an important role as engines of growth for those nations, as well as for the global economy. However, as those large economies have matured, we have seen a shift in dynamic economic activities to other geographical regions. It is not an accident that many of the fastest growing regions of the world today are to be found in emerging markets. [1–3]

Many of these regions are rich in natural resources, have access to cheap labor, and are more aggressively pursuing open market strategies. Some of these regions have recovered much faster from the world financial crisis and consequently there has been a surge in production and investment activities. In these dynamic regions, cities are again taking center stage. There continues to be a steady flow of local and immigrant populations into the cities and foreign capital is providing opportunities for new economic development projects and business ventures. Despite serious institutional and economic imbalances, emerging markets continue to grow and create new business and employment opportunities. [4–6]

As individuals make plans to develop and manage their international careers, they will most likely have to consider opportunities in gateway cities and dynamic regions around the world. Understanding how to work with, enter, and navigate the business and social institutions in these environments could give individuals a competitive advantage in career mobility and employability. [8–12]

A FOCUS ON INTERNATIONAL GATEWAY CITIES

As indicated earlier, one way of maximizing your mobility is to become acquainted with the international gateway cities that could provide study, training, or employment opportunities as you build and maintain your international career. These international cities have been the focal point for social, economic and political developments around the world. This is partially due to the fact that globalization and liberalization have brought down many of the barriers to trade and foreign direct investments. Consequently, as business, research, and development activities expand rapidly in the international environment, the demand for skilled and knowledgeable individuals has spread beyond national boundaries.

In the rest of this chapter, you will be given an overview of some of the more important gateway cities in the global economy. The first three international gateway cities are good representatives of mature developed economies that continue to attract individuals seeking employment opportunities or entrepreneurial ventures. Tokyo, New York, and London all have numerous multinational firms operating within their borders and these cities also have a major impact on the surrounding region. The other six cities are excellent representatives of the increasingly important emerging market economies. These cities are major business centers in some of the fastest growing economies in the world. As such, they are now magnets for a whole range of domestic and international workers. The cities of Shanghai, Mumbai, Sao Paulo, Moscow, Dubai and Johannesburg are at the center of some of the most important economic and business developments in Asia, Latin America, emerging Europe, the Middle East and Africa. After each city is presented, there will be a chart with a list of specific organizations or sites that can be of help for those seeking employment opportunities. In the Appendix for Chapter 4, you will find detailed information on places to study in each of the international gateway cities.

Gateway City Tokyo

Tokyo is the capital of the third largest economy in the world. It is one of the top international gateway cities because of its economic, cultural, and political importance. With almost 13 million inhabitants in the city and up to about 36 million in the greater metropolitan area, Tokyo is the largest urban center in the world. Moreover, due to the extreme centralization of business and political activities in Japan, Tokyo is the key gateway city and a dominant economic engine in Japan. In addition to being one of the safest large cities anywhere, the vibrant food, fashion, media, and entertainment activities make this one of the most exciting and livable global cities in the world. Tokyo is a vital economic center for Japan and a majority of corporations from all sectors are headquartered there. Although slower growth has kept the level of job creation below what it used to be in the late 1980s, there are still job opportunities in a wide variety of sectors. Many foreigners can be found working in the education, service, hospitality management, IT, and financial sectors. The expatriate community is extensive, and there are many schools and networking institutions that help executives and their families adjust to life in Tokyo. Although lifetime employment practices and company loyalty are no longer the dominant situation, this is still an environment where individuals are expected to work very hard and for long hours. After-work socializing is still extensive and the Japanese networking and management style is still a challenge for foreigners. [29–31] [32–35]

Working in Tokyo	*Background information*
1. **Tokyo Connections** (tokyoconnections.com)	**Tokyo Connections** is job guide to Japan with reviews and links to over 200 employment sources.
2. **GaijinPot** (gaijinpot.com)	**Gaijinpot** has extensive information and links to jobs and resources for working and living in Japan.
3. **Jobs in Japan** (jobsinjapan.com)	**Jobs in Japan** is one of the largest English job sites in Japan. They have IT, bilingual, ESL, and many other positions.
4. **The Japan Exchangeand Teaching** (JET) **Program** (jetprogramme.org)	**The JET program**, which is government supported, promotes international exchange by recruiting ELS teachers and other staff from over 36 different countries to work in Japan.
5. **Daijob** (daijob.com) (also located at workinginjapan.com)	Daijob isone of the most comprehensive bilingual job sites. All types of jobs are listed in both English and Japanese.

Gateway City New York

With over 8 million inhabitants in New York City (NYC) and over 19 million in the greater metropolitan tri-state area, this is the largest urban area in the United States. The city is located along the Atlantic coast and has a large natural harbor and a major international airport. It is a dynamic international gateway city which continues to attract tourists, immigrants, and business people from all over the world. The city exerts tremendous influence on global trade, finance, media, culture, and entertainment. Having the United Nations Headquarters in the city also gives it a major role in international affairs. New York City supports the largest regional economy in the United States and is the second largest international city economy after Tokyo. New York is also considered by many to be the financial capital of the world. It has the world's largest stock exchange (the New York Stock Exchange) and corporations in the Wall Street and Mid-Town areas support major business activities in the financial, real estate, media, consulting, health care, and information technology sectors. New York City has more Fortune 500 corporations headquartered there than any other city. Although the financial crisis had a negative impact on the region's economy, the city has been resilient and still offers many employment opportunities in a variety of sectors. The workforce is very diverse and there is fierce competition for jobs at all levels. However, since job creation continues, and there is generally a significant turnover of positions, enterprising individuals can find opportunities for employment. [36–41]

Working in New York City	Background information
1. **NY City Works** (nycityworks.com)	**NY City Works** connects job seekers with NYC employers. The site covers a wide variety of sectors.
2. **Job Market NY Times** (jobmarketnytimes.com)	**JobMarketNYTimes.com**, in conjunction with Monster.com, list job positions across many sectors.
3. **Headhunters Directory** (headhuntersdirectory.com)	**Head Hunters Directory** provides extensive links to recruiters, headhunters, and employment agencies.
4. **Easy Expat NYC** (easyexpat.com)	**Easy Expat NYC** provides information on jobs, accommodation, and education in NYC and elsewhere.

Gateway City London

The city of London has a population of over 7 million in 32 boroughs. If we include the surrounding area, then the London metropolitan area has about 12 million inhabitants. This very multicultural city is the most populated metropolitan area in Europe. London is also one of the world's leading international gateway cities. It attracts people from all over the world because of activities in the arts, hospitality, commerce, finance, logistics, education, entertainment, fashion, media, research and development, and professional services. In terms of its economic clout, London is one of the world's largest and most influential financial centers. Having over 40 universities, and extensive research and development activities, London an important place for knowledge development. Most of Europe's largest companies have headquarters or major offices there. With five international airports, it is truly an international gateway city that serves as hub for various regions and countries nearby. London is a good place to work since there are many sectors and corporations in one place and job opportunities for skilled workers are usually good. Both domestic and foreign firms are very active employers in the city. The job market is more difficult for unskilled workers or for those with little English ability. However, there are many ethnic communities and networks that provide opportunities even for this segment of the population. In fact, people from all over Britain and all over the world continue to move to London to start over or to pursue their dreams. All these characteristics make London a true international gateway. [42–48]

Working in London	Background information
1. **London UK Jobs** (londonukjobs.com)	**London UK Jobs** is an extensive public online employment board that shows positions in London and the UK.
2. **London Office Jobs** (londonofficejobs.co.uk)	**London Office Jobs** is a key source for permanent, part-time or temporary positions in many sectors in London.
3. **London Careers** (londoncareers.net)	**London Careers** is a competitive recruitment website that posts positions for people in the UK and abroad.
4. **Internations** (internations.org/London-expats)	**Internations** is a network and guide for expats living and working in London and 250 other cities worldwide.
5. **Fish4Jobs** (fish4.co.uk)	**Fish4Jobs** is comprehensive site that provides career information and numerous job opportunities in the UK.

Gateway City Shanghai

With over 18 million people, Shanghai is the most populous city in China and has a significant impact on industrial activity, trade, finance, culture, fashion, research, and entertainment activities in the county. The city is located around the mid-point of the Chinese coastline and sits at the mouth of the Yangtze River. Shanghai now has the world's largest cargo port. It is also an important tourist destination because of the cosmopolitan lifestyle, the food, and landmarks such as the Bund, the Pudong skyline, the Oriental Pearl TV Tower, the Jin Mao Tower, and the World Financial Center. The massive infusion of foreign investment into various development zones has been one of the key factors in the emergence of Shanghai as an important international gateway city. As for industrial activities, steel, telecommunications, automobiles, power production equipment, petrochemicals, and electric appliances represent Shanghai's six major industries. In addition, with finance, insurance, commerce, real estate, and tourism all growing rapidly, the service sector is also contributing significantly to economic development in Shanghai. The city is a major participant in international business and has developed trade ties with more than 30,000 companies in about 170 countries. More significantly, Shanghai has become the first choice of foreigners who wish to work in China. However, competition for jobs is intense because of the highly educated Chinese students returning from abroad and the growing influx of foreigners from around the world. If you are not sent as expatriate by an established firm, it will be necessary to build connections (guanxi) and develop some proficiency in the language in order to be competitive in the local employment market. [49–55] [56–63]

Working in Shanghai	*Background information*
1. **eChinaCities** (echinacities.com/shanghai)	**eChinaCities** is a website with information on jobs and ideas for working and living in Shanghai.
2. **Locanto-China** (shanghai.locanto.cn)	**Locanto-China** has an extensive listing of jobs in many sectors in Shanghai and other cities in China.
3. **Enter Shanghai** (entershanghai.info)	**Enter Shanghai** is an excellent organization for expats with information on careers and living in Shanghai.
4. **Shanghai Expat** (jobs.shanghaiexpat.com)	**Shanghai Expat** has plenty of support information for careers and living in Shanghai and elsewhere in China.
5. **Job China** (jobchina.net)	**Job China** mainly provides information on English teaching positions throughout China.

Gateway City Mumbai

Mumbai lies on the west coast of India and has a deep natural harbor. With an estimated population of over 15 million, Mumbai is India's largest city. As India's most multicultural and richest city, Mumbai is generally liberal, and its business culture tends to be informal and friendly. However, the city also has India's largest slum population. Nevertheless, a fitting symbol of the cosmopolitan nature of Mumbai is the location of "Bollywood" within the city. Mumbai is clearly the primary center for the arts and entertainment industry, but is also the business and financial capital of India with most of the major financial institutions, banks, and stock exchanges being based in Mumbai. Most of India's large business houses and many foreign corporations have their corporate offices in the city. Although the Mumbai economy was once dominated by textiles, it has diversified to the point where petrochemicals, light manufacturing, metals, electronics, and food processing have gained a greater share of economic activity. Recently, there has been another shift whereby business process outsourcing (BPO), IT, and service activities are growing rapidly, as the city tries to become more internationally competitive. As for employment opportunities for skilled workers, good paying jobs can be found in BPO, IT, hospitality, software development, teaching, and government. There is a wide range of recruitment intermediaries that help with placement for the skilled individual. Overall, Mumbai is a dominant urban center in India because of its population, its cosmopolitan lifestyle, and its large share of employment in the industrial sectors, IT, professional services, and entertainment fields. [64–68] [69–73]

Working in Mumbai	*Background information*
1. **Easy Expat Mumbai** (easyexpat.com/en/Mumbai)	**Easy Expat Mumbai** provides information on living and working in Mumbai.
2. **Mumbai News (Mumbai Meri Jaan)** (mumbainews.wordpress.com)	**Mumbai News** has information on NGOs in the city and other information on jobs and living in Mumbai.
3. **Internations Mumbai** (internations.org/mumbai-expat)	**Internations Mumbai** is an expat guide with excellent information for living and working in Mumbai.
4. **Mumbai Craigslist** (mumbai.craigslist.co.in)	**Mumbai Craigslist** has extensive information on jobs, accommodation, and other activities in Mumbai.

Gateway City Sao Paulo

The capital of the state of Sao Paulo is the city of Sao Paulo. The city of Sao Paulo is Brazil's biggest center of commerce and is the largest city in South America. With over 11 million inhabitants in the city, and up to 19 million if the surrounding areas are included, Sao Paulo is one of the largest urban areas in the world. This exciting city is very ethnically ,with various levels of mixing across individuals with Portuguese, African, Indian, Italian, German, Spanish, Jewish, Arabic, Lebanese, Japanese, and other backgrounds. Although Sao Paulo is sometimes referred to as a concrete city because of its many skyscrapers and interesting landmarks, it also has many parks and nice beaches. The city has sometimes been compared to New York City. Over the years, immigrants from all over the world have gone to Sao Paulo and the communities and businesses they created have had a major impact on economic and social developments in the city. In addition, because of its importance in the Brazilian economy, most domestic and international companies have major offices in Sao Paulo. Overall, Sao Paulo exerts a strong influence in commerce, finance, the arts, and entertainment. The city is often referred to as the "locomotive of Brazil," since it has the highest share of GDP in the country. Foreign job seekers moving to Brazil need to depend on extensive social and professional networking strategies. Most job opportunities are found through friends, colleagues, business contacts, and some employment intermediaries. Despite these tendencies, it is becoming easier to search for and find employment opportunities through the internet. As Brazil's position in the global economy increases, Sao Paulo will also gain more recognition as a global city that is also a gateway to a vibrant economic region. [74–77] [78–82]

Working in Sao Paulo	Background information
1. **Go Abroad Sao Paulo** (goabroad.com/intern-abroad)	**Go Abroad Sao Paulo** offers information on internships in the city and elsewhere in Brazil.
2. **Overseas Digest** (overseasdigest.com)	**Overseas Digest** offers a complete guide to living and working in Brazil, for a small fee.
3. **Latpro** (brazil.jobs.latpro.com)	**Latpro** is a Hispanic job and networking site that has positions in Sao Paulo, Brazil, and elsewhere in Latin America.
4. **Brazzil** (brazzil.com)	**Brazzil** has information and articles on living and working in Sao Paulo and elsewhere in Brazil.

Gateway City Moscow

Moscow has a population of over 13 million and a significant proportion of Russian residents live in the metropolitan area. Moscow is not only the most populous city in Russia, it is also the most populous city on the European continent. The city is arranged into five major sections in a concentric pattern that has Red Square and the Kremlin right in the middle. This is significant, since the Kremlin is the administrative seat of power for the country. Moscow is clearly the main political, economic, cultural, financial, educational, and transportation center of Russia. The city has an extensive transit network and four international airports. After the collapse of communism, Russia started rebuilding its economy based on a freer market system. Subsequently, Russia became an economic force due to the sale of oil, gas, and other natural resources. A lot of that money has flowed into Moscow due to the influx of the newly rich, and, consequently, for a time, the city was named as one of the most expensive places for foreign employees to live. At the same time, there is an extremely large poor working class that struggles to benefit from the new economy. Nevertheless, the city is very active in international business and there are numerous large multinational firms operating there. Tourism is also increasing and many immigrants, expats, and Russians move there to work or find employment. Most expatriates working in Russia are employed by diplomatic missions, foreign companies, or English language schools. Nevertheless, since Moscow is a large and dynamic city, job opportunities exist in many sectors, especially if one has some working knowledge of the Russian language. As the Russian economy expands, Moscow's importance as an international gateway city will also grow. [83–87] [88–91]

Working in Moscow	Background information
1. **Moscow Portal** (moscow.ru/en)	**Moscow Portal** is a comprehensive site for information on living and working in Moscow.
2. **The Moscow Times** (themoscowtimes.com/careercenter)	**The Moscow Times** has a career center section which has information on jobs, business, and career development.
3. **Learn4Good** (learn4good.com)	**Learn4Good** has information on studying and working in Moscow and many other cities around the world.
4. **FLPersonnel** (flpersonnel.com)	**FLPersonnel** is a recruitment agency that handles Moscow and other regions in Russia, as well as the CIS countries.
5. **Craigslist Moscow** (moscow.craigslist.org)	**Craigslist Moscow** has a good section on jobs in Moscow and other cities in Russia.

Gateway City Dubai

In December 1971, Abu Dhabi and five other emirates formed the United Arab Emirates. Dubai joned the other emirates in 1973 and they all formed a unified currency. Dubai's population is about 1.8 million. However, it is said that during the day the population grows by almost another million as workers and business people from other emirates participate in various projects and business activities. About 71 percent of the population of Dubai consists of foreigners. Most of the foreigners are from Asian countries, such as India, Bangladesh, Pakistan, and the Philippines. About 3 percent of the foreigners are categorized as Westerners. Interestingly, only around 17 percent of the population of Dubai is made up of UAE nationals. Dubai has the largest population and is the second largest emirate by area. With this type of demographic, Dubai is, without question, the expat city of the world. Contrary to expectations, most of Dubai's revenues do not come from petroleum. Revenues from petroleum and natural gas contribute less than 6 percent of the economy. Most of the city's revenue results from activities in the Jebel Ali Free Economic Zone, as well as trade, tourism, financial services, real estate projects, and other service-related businesses. However, what has drawn the world's attention to Dubai is a series of astonishing multi-billion dollar infrastructure projects and a variety of international sporting events. Along with a range of stunning architectural developments, Dubai's attractive tax regime, modern telecommunications, and active business environment are factors creating a global city that effectively links the Middle East to the global economy. Although Dubai thrives on its ability to create big and new architectural experiences, its ultimate goal is the creation of a global hub of commerce, a tourism Mecca, and an international urban environment. It remains an attractive work environment for many foreigners because of the various projects underway, but also because there are no personal income tax obligations. [92–98] [99–105]

Working in Dubai	Background information
1. **Gulf Talent** (gulftalent.com/home)	**Gulf Talent** provides information on professional jobs in Dubai and the rest of the Middle East.
2. **Just Landed Dubai** (justlanded.com/english/Dubai)	**Just Landed Dubai** is a guide for entering, living, and working in Dubai.
3. **Work Getaways Dubai** (workgateways.com/dubai)	**Work Getaways Dubai** has a full array of links for working and living in Dubai and other regions.
4. **Dubai Job Spot** (dubaijobspot.com)	**Dubai Job Spot** has numerous links to job vacancies and recruiters in Dubai.
5. **Jobs in Dubai** (jobsindubai.com)	**Jobs in Dubai** is one of Dubai's largest recruitment services, with jobs in a wide range of sectors.

Gateway City Johannesburg

Johannesburg has the largest and busiest airport in Africa and serves as a gateway for much of southern Africa. The city is also colloquially referred to as Jozi or Jo'burg. The Greater Johannesburg Metropolitan Area has an estimated population of almost 10 million and is one of the larger urban areas in Africa. The growth of the Greater Johannesburg area was due mainly to the discovery of gold and other minerals. The city's economy is now the largest of any metropolitan region is sub-Saharan Africa. Johannesburg is a fascinating city, and is considered one of the greenest cities in the world, with over 6 million trees and a natural savannah landscape. The region and country has come a long way since the collapse of apartheid in 1994. Nelson Mandela has been succeeded by other democratically-elected presidents, and South Africa successfully hosted the soccer World Cup in 2010. These days, shiny modern skyscrapers are mixed in with nineteenth century architecture, Indian bazaars, and African traditional medicine shops. The streets of Johannesburg support a wide range of entrepreneurial activities. The city is an economic engine for the country and region. It is estimated that about 10 percent of sub-Saharan GDP is generated by activities in Johannesburg. Unfortunately, the distribution of income is very unequal, and many residents experience bottom-of-the-pyramid living conditions. Crime and the HIV epidemic are two major factors which affect the people and economy negatively. Despite these drawbacks, Johannesburg is a booming city with everyone putting much effort into making money at all levels of the economic ladder. The inner city, which was once abandoned by big businesses, is undergoing a transformation and urban rebirth. The success of the 2010 World Cup showed outside investors and visitors many opportunities in real estate and other areas. Overall, Johannesburg will continue to grow and provide employment opportunities for highly skilled domestic and foreign workers for many years to come. [106–110] [111–114]

Working in Johannesburg	Background information
1. **Career Jet South Africa** (careerjet.co.za)	**Career Jet South Africa** lists part-time, temporary, full- and internship positions in Johannesburg and other cities.
2. **Indeed South Africa** (indeed.co.za)	**Indeed South Africa** is a search engine for all kinds of jobs in Johannesburg and the rest of South Africa.
3. **Gumtree Johannesburg** (johannesburg.gumtree.co.za)	**Gumtree Johannesburg** covers classifieds and has a large jobs section for all sectors in Johannesburg.
4. **Hospitality Jobs Africa** (hospitalityjobsafrica.co.za)	**Hospitality Jobs Africa** is a leading hospitality recruitment service across South Africa, Africa and the Middle East.
5. **InfoHub South Africa** (infohub.co.za)	**Info Hub South Africa** has business and employment guides for Johannesburg and other cities in South Africa.

THE IMPACT OF STUDYING & WORKING IN INTERNATIONAL GATEWAY CITIES

In terms of the impact of studying in international gateway cities on career mobility, there are many dimensions that can be explored. The most frequent situation is the study abroad experience, which can be arranged in all the international gateway cities discussed. These study programs are generally set up or coordinated by academic institutions, non-profit organizations, business organizations, and governmental agencies. The programs range from short one-week study trips to semester or full-year programs. Students who have participated in these programs generally develop a more international view and will more likely consider working in an international sector as they develop their careers. As schools and colleges around the world participate more actively in recruiting international students, we see greater numbers of students who go abroad to complete a full undergraduate or graduate degree. These increasing numbers of international students are completing a crucial stage in the development of their future career mobility.

Another aspect of the study abroad situation involves families who are already working abroad. Those families with children need to place their children in schools abroad. Some opt for international schools and others place their children in the local schools of the country. In either case, these children are generally more exposed to the local culture, and often end up learning some of the local language. These children of expatriates also form a pool of individuals who are more disposed to seeking an international career in the future.

A third area which involves study abroad would be those individuals who go abroad for company or government sponsored internships or training programs. These individuals usually take part in programs that range from one week to up to a year or more. Although the focus of these programs is usually the development of specific skills, the participants often gain a greater appreciation for the foreign environments. For all the study abroad situations mentioned above, the most crucial outcome is that they allow the individuals to build friendship and information networks of which they can take advantage if they decide to work abroad in the future. These study abroad experiences also build up cultural sensitivity, and make it easier for these individuals to adjust to living and working in foreign environments.

The work abroad experience has a more direct effect on international career management. There are, however, many facets to this experience and individuals need to have clear strategies and career trajectories in mind when they rely on the international arena for career development. In general, the longer an individual works abroad, the better they are able to adjust to foreign environments. On the other hand, mobility is not always maximized by long stays in one location. It is sometimes possible for an individual's career to stagnate in a foreign environment. For this reason, it is crucial that individuals understand the full range of experiences and opportunities that can result from working abroad.

For many individuals, the most visible and sought-after situation is the firm-initiated expatriate experience. This occurs when an organization decides to send an individual to work for longer periods of time in its operations in a foreign country, in a capacity which benefits the sending firm. This foreign assignment usually comes with certain additional financial, housing, and family support benefits. These assignments are costly to the firm, but the individuals chosen generally can provide significant business benefits. This kind of assignment is also typically made after you have worked for the firm for a few years, since trust and competence evaluations take time. Another situation, which occurs more frequently than people realize, is getting a position as a local hire abroad. Many firms seek capable individuals already living abroad who are from their home country. Since these individual have the same language and cultural background, it is usually easier to integrate them into the firm's operations. Since these individuals are recruited as "local hires," they are generally paid local or slightly-more-than-local wages. The benefits of local hires are not the same as for the expatriates sent from home. This approach might be attractive for some individuals already living in a foreign location of their choice, because it might be easier to get an entry or lower level position in the firm than if they were home. Moreover, they still get to work for the firm in a foreign environment. Many individuals who are not willing to wait to move up the firm hierarchy have gone directly to foreign countries and then sought positions with firms originating in their home country.

Another approach to getting work experience abroad is through an internship or some medium-term business, research, or development project. These situations are usually project-oriented, and there is no expectation that your career will continue with the sending or receiving organization. However, this experience can provide significant skill development and chances to build connections in a foreign environment. Internships, business, research, and development projects can be found through private, non-profit, governmental, and intergovernmental organizations. The main goals for individuals who choose this approach is to build up their work experience, skills development, and knowledge of foreign environments.

There is yet another approach to actively working with foreign markets. This would be the frequent business traveler or "flexpatriates" who fly frequently, and work on many short-term projects in different business environments. These individuals are usually connected with an international business organization which has operations in different countries. Although this approach can reduce costs for the organization or give it more flexibility, it usually involves extensive travel and can be mentally and physically exhausting. Nevertheless, there are some individuals who enjoy the frequent travel and changing environments. This approach also can give individuals the opportunity to build an extensive international network in a particular field.

Finally, there is the drastic strategy of self-initiated expatriates who decide to emigrate to a different environment. This decision is usually a long-term one and it means that career development strategies will subsequently be dominated by the dynamics of the new environment. Some individuals make this choice because there is a strong international market for educators, performers, researchers, knowledge workers, or dynamic entrepreneurs. For many of these individuals, their nation of residence may not be as important as the opportunity to build and expand their international careers.

Overall, the ability and opportunity to study and work in different national environments are key aspects of building and maximizing your international career mobility. Major international gateway cities, such as Tokyo, New York, and London, have long been a beacon for those seeking career opportunities in an international environment. These cities continue to play an important role in the global economy and still provide employment opportunities for a wide range of occupations. However, as the mature economies slow and the emerging economies grow in influence and stature, cities such as Shanghai, Mumbai, Sao Paulo, Moscow, Dubai, and Johannesburg are becoming significant locations for career development. There are even signs of a "reverse brain drain," whereby some immigrants are leaving the mature economies and returning to the countries of their birth. We also see greater numbers of individuals from the industrialized economies going to emerging markets to find employment and career-building opportunities. In general, individuals who are able to adapt to, and work in, different international gateway cities are well on their way to maximizing their international career mobility.

CHAPTER SUMMARY & OBSERVATIONS

In this chapter, the focus was on the mobility aspect of career development. A two-stage model showed tangible and intangible activities that help with developing international career mobility. Beyond having a desire to work in foreign markets, the first stage stressed the importance of accessing international gateway cities, participating in international sectors, achieving international professional status, and choosing to be a self-initiated expatriate or immigrant. The second stage focused more on personal, psychological, and cultural factors. Developing a global mindset, using cross-cultural capabilities and mobilizing personal friendship networks were presented as key characteristics for those wishing to maximize their international career mobility. The rest of the chapter discussed the phenomenon of international gateway cities and their impact on global economic development and international employment opportunities. There was a contrast made between developments in the traditional global cities in the mature economies, and the rapidly growing international cities in emerging markets. Understanding the economic, political, and employment landscapes in these international gateway cities was seen as a key step in expanding your range of potential career development opportunities.

Chapter 5 will examine how key international sectors help individuals use or maximize their capabilities. These are sectors which can be found in many countries around the world, and sectors which have a strong demand for a clear set of capabilities. For each sector, you will examine the structure of the industry, the international dimension, and sector-related jobs and careers. Whether you are an entry level, mid-career or upper level worker, it is more important than ever to have a solid grasp of the major dynamics of the sector in which you work or plan to work. In the same way that international gateway cities play a key role in boosting the pool of employment opportunities, international sectors require a range of capabilities that can be targeted and developed by the individual seeking to boost their employability.

There will be an examination of the information technology, financial, and logistics sectors. These sectors contribute a significant amount to world economic activity and they represent some of the most dynamic sectors for building a long-term career that emphasizes capability, mobility, and transferability. Whether we are talking about mature or newly emerging economies, these sectors are in need of knowledge workers that can help them remain competitive, domestically and internationally. These are not the only sectors that have an international impact on international employment trends, but they are examples of exciting areas to build and maintain an international career.

REFERENCES

1. Altinbasak, I. and E. Yalçin, *City image and museums: The case of Istanbul*. International Journal of Culture, Tourism and Hospitality Research, 2010. **4**(3): p. 241.
2. Forrest, R., A. LaGrange and N.-M. Yip, *Hong Kong as a global city? Social distance and spatial differentiation*. Urban Studies, 2004. **41**(1): p. 207.
3. Lee, H. and D. Jain, *Dubai's brand assessment success and failure in brand management – Part 1*. Place Branding and Public Diplomacy, 2009. **5**(3): p. 234.
4. Panayiotopoulos, P.I., *Turkish immigrant entrepreneurs in the European Union: A political-institutional approach*. International Journal of Entrepreneurial Behaviour & Research, 2008. **14**(6): p. 395.
5. Simmie, J., *Trading Places: Competitive cities in the global economy*. European Planning Studies, 2002. **10**(2): p. 201.
6. Waibel, M., *Urban governance of economic upgrading processes in China: The case of Guangzhou Science City*. Internationales Asien Forum. International Quarterly for Asian Studies, 2010. **41**(1/2): p. 57.
7. Hanson, R., *US cities in transformation: Urban policy in an advanced economy*. Futures, 1985. **17**(3): p. 232.
8. Frost, M. and N. Spence, *Global city characteristics and central London's employment*. Urban Studies, 1993. **30**(3): p. 547.
9. Lightfoot, W., *London's challenge... staying a city slicker*. Financial World, 2008: p. 30.
10. Martin, N., S. Morales and N. Theodore, *Migrant worker centers: Contending with downgrading in the low-wage labor market*. Geo Journal, 2007. **68**(2–3): p. 155.
11. Wang, S. and Y. Zhang, *The new retail economy of Shanghai*. Growth and Change, 2005. **36**(1): p. 41.
12. Weiss, S., *Cities that sizzle: New Orleans*. Nation's Restaurant News, 2001. **35**(5): p. 118.
13. PRB. *Population Reference Bureau 2010*. Available from: http://www.prb.org/Educators/TeachersGuides/HumanPopulation/Urbanization.aspx.
14. Drennan, M.P., *Gateway cities: The metropolitan sources of US producer service exports*. Urban Studies, 1992. **29**(2): p. 217–235.
15. Burghardt, A.F., *A hypothesis about gateway cities*. Annals of the Association of American Geographers 1971. **61**: p. 269–285.
16. Drennan, M.P., *Gateway cities: The metropolitan sources of US producers service exports*. Urban Studies, 1992. **29**: p. 217–235.
17. Grant, R. and J. Nijman, *Globalization and the corporate geography of cities in the less-developed World*. Annals of Association of American Geographers, 2002. **92**: p. 320–340.
18. Rossi, E. and P. Taylor, *Gateway cities in economic globalisation: How banks areusing Brazilian cities*. Tijdschrift voor Economische en Sociale Geografie, 2006. **97**(5): p. 515–534.
19. Sassen, S., *Cities in a world economy*, 1994, Thousand Oaks, CA: Pine Forge.
20. Short, J.R., et al., *From world cities to gateway cities*. City, 2000. **4**: p. 317–340.
21. Taylor, P., G. Catalano, and D. Walker, *Measurement of the World City Network*. Urban Studies, 2002. **39**: p. 2367–2376.
22. Horrigan, J. and R. Wilson, *Telecommunications technologies and urban development: Strategies in US cities*. International Journal of Technology Policy and Management, 2002. **2**(3): p. 338.

23. Kamal-Chaoui, L. and A. Robert, *Competitive cities and climate change.* OECD Regional Development Working Papers, 2009. **2009**(2): p. 1.

24. Marlow, S., [review of] Struder, I. R., *Migrant self employment in a European global city: The importance of gendered power relations and performances of belonging for Turkish women in London.* International Small Business Journal, 2003. **21**(4): p. 485.

25. Mathews, J.S., *A counterpoint assessment of Vancouver International Airport as a gateway to North America.* Thunderbird International Business Review, 1999. **41**(3): p. 265.

26. Selko, A., *Global hot spots 2008: Revealing global manufacturing's best kept secrets.* Industry Week, 2008. **257**(6): p. 46.

27. Smallbone, D., J. Kitching and R. Athayde, *Ethnic diversity, entrepreneurship and competitiveness in a global city.* International Small Business Journal, 2010. **28**(2): p. 174.

28. Wagner, D., *Learning From global cities.* MIT Sloan Management Review, 2008. **49**(4): p. 10.

29. Bender, D. and T. Hornyak, *Lonely Planet Tokyo,* 2010, New York, NY: Lonely Planet.

30. Fujimoto, T., *Preferences for working hours over life course among Japanese manufacturing workers.* Career Development International, 2006. **11**(3): p. 204.

31. Pye, L., *Asia and Pacific: Securing Japan: Tokyo's grand strategy and the future of East Asia.* Foreign Affairs, 2008. **87**(1): p. 194.

32. DK_Publishing, *Tokyo: Eyewitness Travel Guide,* 2010, New York, NY: DK Publishing.

33. Fujita, K. and R. Hill, *The zero waste city: Tokyo's quest for a sustainable environment.* Journal of Comparative Policy Analysis, 2007. **9**(4): p. 405.

34. Kakihara, M. and C. Sorensen, *Practising mobile professional work: Tales of locational, operational, and interactional mobility.* Info: the Journal of Policy, Regulation and Strategy for Telecommunications, Information and Media, 2004. **6**(3): p. 180.

35. Scheier, R.L., *IS pros discover the ups and downs of working in Japan.* Computerworld, 1997. **31**(2): p. 28.

36. Bram, J., J. Orr and R. Rosen, *Employment in the New York-New Jersey region: 2008 review and outlook.* Current Issues in Economics and Finance, 2008. **14**(7): p. 1.

37. Currid, E., *How art and culture happen in New York: Implications for urban economic development.* American Planning Association. Journal of the American Planning Association, 2007. **73**(4): p. 454.

38. Silverman, B., K. Chauvin and R. Goodman, *Frommers New York City,* 2010, New York, NY: Frommers.

39. Gibberd, B. and K.B. Steckler, *Little Black Book of New York,* 2009, White Plains, NY: Peter Pauper Press.

40. Lee, B., "Edge" or "edgeless" cities? Urban spatial strucutres in US metropolitan areas 1980 to 2000. Journal of Regional Science, 2007. **47**(3): p. 479.

41. Walby, K., *Taxi! Cabs and capitalism in New York City.* Labour, 2007(60): p. 306.

42. McDowell, L., A. Batnitzky and S. Dyer, *Internationalization and the spaces of temporary labour: The global assembly of a local workforce.* British Journal of Industrial Relations, 2008. **46**(4): p. 750.

43. Steves, R. and G. Openshaw, *Rick Steves' London 2010,* 2010, Berkeley, CA: Avalon Travel Publishing.

44. Woods, A. and C. Dennis, *What do UK small and medium sized enterprises think about employing graduates?* Journal of Small Business and Enterprise Development, 2009. **16**(4): p. 642.

45. Caplan, A.S. and J. Gilham, *Included against the odds: Failure and success among minority ethnic built-environment professionals in Britain.* Construction Management and Economics, 2005. **23**(10): p. 1007.

46. Sisson, W., *Network your way through any recession.* Strategic HR Review, 2009. **8**(3): p. 36.

47. Turok, I., *Limits to the mega-city region: Conflicting local and regional needs.* Regional Studies, 2009. **43**(6): p. 845.

48. Williams, R. and M. Scott, *Top 10 London,* 2010, London, UK: DK Travel.

49. Alsop, R., *Career journal: MBA track: More Chinese graduates return home.* Wall Street Journal, 13 March 2007: p. B9.

50. Fram, E. H., L. Le and McHardy Reid, D., *Consumer behavior in China: An exploratory study of two cities.* Journal of Asia-Pacific Business, 2004. **5**(4): p. 25.

51. Goodall, K., N. Li and M. Warner, *Expatriate managers in China: The influence of Chinese culture on cross-cultural management.* Journal of General Management, 2006. **32**(2): p. 57.

52. Hutchings, K., *Koalas in the land of the pandas: Reviewing Australian expatriates' China preparation.* The International Journal of Human Resource Management, 2005. **16**(4): p. 553.

53. Hutchings, K. and D. Weir, *Understanding networking in China and the Arab World.* Journal of European Industrial Training, 2006. **30**(4): p. 272.

54. Lee, G. and M. Warner, *The management of human resources in Shanghai: A case study of policy responses to employment and unemployment in the People's Republic of China.* SSRN Working Paper Series, 2004.

55. Owyang, S., *Frommer's Shanghai* (6th edn.), 2010, New York, NY: Frommers.

56. Pitts, C., *Lonely Planet Shanghai encounter*(2nd edn.), 2010, New York, NY: Lonely Planet.

57. Shamdasani, A., *Sending expatriates into China's hinterland.* China Staff, 2009. **15**(4): p. 8.

58. Skapinker, M., *The importance of friends.* Financial Times, 30 April 2009: p. 2.

59. Skapinker, M., *China needs reform to become world class.* Financial Times, 14 April 2009: p. 7.

60. Wang, J. and S. Lau, *Forming foreign enclaves in Shanghai: State action in globalization.* Journal of Housing and the Built Environment, 2008. **23**(2): p. 103.

61. Xu, L. and L. Bennington, *Xiagang and re-employment policies in Shanghai.* Management Research News, 2008. **31**(12): p. 976.

62. Yang, Y., C. Chen and S. Hong, *Study on problems confronted with employment security in China - take foreign-invested enterprise in Shanghai city as example.* Journal of Information & Optimization Sciences, 2008. **29**(3): p. 423.

63. Zeng, X. and Y. Cui, *Job search, labour market intermediaries and employment promotion: The evidence from China.* International Labour Review, 2008. **147**(2/3): p. 280.

64. Bellman, E., *Moving up in Mumbai: Humble jobs at the mall are lifting legions of Indians out of poverty.* Wall Street Journal, 17 November 2007: p. A1.

65. Bhattacharya, S., *Mumbai expensive? You must be joking.* Business Today, 2008.

66. Chowdhury, A., *Air India appoints non-Indian executive.* Wall Street Journal (Online), 2010.

67. Dean, R., *Gulf Arabs primed to pour billions into Indian real estate sector.* Financial Times, 5 October 2006: p. 8.

68. Fodor's, *Fodor's India,*2008, New York, NY: Fodor's.

69. Gupta, R., *Fulfilling India's promise.* The McKinsey Quarterly, 2005: p. 4.

70. Hicks, R., *India's indomitable spirit surfaces post-attacks.* Campaign, 2009: p. 17.

71. Lublin, J., *India could provide unique opportunities for expat managers.* Wall Street Journal, 8 May 2007. p. B1.

72. Offbeat, *Mumbai Travel Guide, Kindle Edition,* 2009, San Francisco, CA: Offbeat Guides.

73. Rangnekar, S. and M. Sharma, *India's split personality.* Far Eastern Economic Review, 2006. **169**(1): p. 18.

74. Aguayo-Téllez, E., M. Muendlerand J. Poole, *Globalization and formal sector migration in Brazil.* World Development, 2010. **38**(6): p. 840.

75. Bei Editora, *Sao Paulo Guide,* 2007, Sao Paulo, Brazil: Bei Editora.

76. DeGraff, D., D. Levison and M. Robison, *Child labor and mothers' work in Brazil.* The International Journal of Sociology and Social Policy, 2009. **29**(3/4): p. 152.

77. Farrell, D., R. Jain and B. Pietracci, *Assessing Brazil's offshoring prospects.* The McKinsey Quarterly, 2007: p. 7.

78. Giovannetti, B. and N. Menezes-Filho, *Trade liberalization and the demand for skilled labor in Brazil/Comments.* Economia, 2006. **7**(1): p. 1.

79. GoingGlobal, *Country Career Guides: Brazil,* 2006, Going Global: Location unknown.

80. Henley, A., G. Arabsheibani and F. Carneiro, *On defining and measuring the informal sector: Evidence from Brazil.* World Development, 2009. **37**(5): p. 992.

81. Sommers, M., *Moon spotlight Sao Paulo,* 2009, Berkeley, CA: Avalon Travel Publishers.

82. Tanure, B., E. Barcellos and M. Fleury, *Psychic distance and the challenges of expatriation from Brazil.* The International Journal of Human Resource Management, 2009. **20**(5): p. 1039.

83. Anonymous, *Moscow tops list of costly expat locales*. The Moscow Times, 25 July 2008.

84. Engelhard, J. and J. Nagele, *Organizational learning in subsidiaries of multinational companies in Russia*. Journal of World Business, 2003. **38**(3): p. 262.

85. Jovanovic, B. and M. Lokshin, *Wage differentials between the state and private sectors in Moscow*. The Review of Income and Wealth, 2004. **50**(1): p. 107.

86. Linz, S.J., *Red executives in Russia's transition economy*. Post-Soviet Geography and Economics, 1996. **37**(10): p. 633.

87. Willis, M., *Top 10 Moscow*, 2010, New York, NY: DK Travel.

88. Morley, M., et al., *The Irish in Moscow: A question of adjustment*. Human Resource Management Journal, 1997. **7**(3): p. 53.

89. Richardson, B., *Women in Russia: The more things change, the more they stay the same*. Canadian Woman Studies, 1995. **16**(1): p. 48.

90. Richardson, D., *The rough guide to Moscow*, 2009, London, UK: Rough Guides.

91. Williams, C. and J. Round, *Beyond negative depictions of informal employment: So lessons from Moscow*. Urban Studies, 2007. **44**(12): p. 2321.

92. Al-Ali, J., *Emiratisation: Drawing UAE nationals into their surging economy*. The International Journal of Sociology and Social Policy, 2008. **28**(9/10): p. 365.

93. Coates, R. and C. Burns-Green, *What's happening in Dubai*. Benefits & Compensation International, 2007. **36**(7): p. 14.

94. Forde, N., *Group FD in Dubai*. Financial Management, 2008: p. 61.

95. Greene, C., *The call of the Middle East to lawyers*. Asia law, 2006: p. 1.

96. Kerr, S., *Exodus on hold as expats feel heat*. Financial Times, 10 August 2010: p. 4.

97. Kerr, S., *Dubai offered an alternative vision of the future*. Financial Times, 9 February 2010: p. 13.

98. Walsh, J., *UAE culture smart!*, 2008, London, UK: Kuperard.

99. Kerr, S. and M. Peel, *Good times end for Dubai's expats*. Financial Times, 17 March 2009: p. 14.

100. Mattioli, D., *Financial jitters spur interest in jobs abroad*. Wall Street Journal, 16 October 2008: p. D1.

101. Rahul, J., *Slowly going crazy in Dubai: Rahul Jacob findsthe city and its building boom ultimately exhausting*. Financial Times, 1 April 2006: p. 8.

102. Simeon, K., *Gulf jobs axed amid property gloom*. Financial Times, 2 December 2008. p. 5.

103. Time_Out, *Time Out Dubai*, 2009, London, UK: Time Out.

104. Wallis, W., *Rising cost of living dents Dubai's attraction for expatriates*. Financial Times, 19 June 2006: p. 8.

105. Wiggins, J., *Middle East identified as market with big potential*. Financial Times, 10 January 2006: p. 3.

106. Baumann, J., *Jo'burg gets cheaper for expatriates*. Business Day, 25 July 2008: p. 1.

107. Carroll, R., *South Africa hopes to reverse "chicken run": Big campaign to persuade expats to join homecoming revolution*. The Guardian, 7 January 2005: p. 16.

108. Dynes, M., *The whites go home to South Africa*. The Times, 3 April 2004: p. 24.

109. Edwards, L., *A firm level analysis of trade, technology and employment in South Africa*. Journal of International Development, 2004. **16**(1): p. 45.

110. Williams, L., *Johannesburg: The Bradt City Guide*, 2007, Buckinghamshire, UK: Bradt Travel Guides.

111. Haaruun, A., *Former South Side couple make new home: Life near Johannesburg*. Chicago Defender, 15 November 2007: p. 15.

112. Hirsch, B., *It is high time South Africans saw the positive side of our country*. Business Day, 29 March 2010.

113. Nuttall, S., A. Mbembeand A.M. Simone, *Johannesburg: The elusive metropolis*, 2008, Durham, NC: Duke University Press.

114. Vermeulen, S., A. Nawir and J. Mayers, *Rural poverty reduction through business partnerships? Examples of experience from the forestry sector*. Environment, Development and Sustainability, 2008. **10**(1): p. 1.

5 MAXIMIZING YOUR INTERNATIONAL CAREER CAPABILITIES BY FOCUSING ON INTERNATIONAL SECTORS

> **LEARNING OBJECTIVES**
>
> • Review strategies for maximizing your international career capabilities
>
> • Examine the role of international sectors
>
> • Understand key aspects of sector evaluation
>
> • Explore the IT, financial, wine, and logistic sectors

THE ROADMAP

In Chapter 4 you focused on the career mobility aspect of international career development. You were presented with a two-stage model which showed tangible and intangible activities that influence career mobility. You were then introduced to the concept of international gateway cities and shown how accessing these locations can help to maximize international career mobility. Since international gateway cities are usually engines for growth, as well as important areas which link to global economic development patterns, they play a key role in providing opportunities for building an international career. Basic background information was presented on the top international gateway cities in developed and emerging markets. In terms of individual strategies, developing a global mind set, using cross-cultural capabilities, and mobilizing personal and professional networks were presented as key characteristics for those wishing to maximize their international career mobility.

Chapter 5 will present strategies for maximizing your international career capabilities. A model similar to that shown in Chapter 4 will be presented. However, the focus will be on the career capabilities aspect of career development. Stage one of the two-stage model shows the basic academic, vocation, certifications, and training approach to building the fundamental skills needed to work internationally. Similar to the situation whereby firms learn more about working across borders by participating more in international business activities, stage two of the model points out that individuals can also build up their capabilities by finding different approaches to working with, and in, foreign environments. Although working as an academic, researcher, consultant, or entrepreneur represents a very good way of building international career capabilities, working for organizations in international sectors will be presented as the most achievable strategy for most individuals. There will be a discussion of the concept of international sectors followed by an examination of four key international sectors. Information technology, financial, wine, and logistics will be the sectors discussed, because of their importance in generating international employment opportunities around the world.

STRATEGIES FOR MAXIMIZING YOUR INTERNATIONAL CAREER CAPABILITIES

International career capabilities refer to the skills and competences needed to work with, and in, different international markets. As discussed in Chapter 3 and elsewhere in this book, these skills and competences have business, technical, cultural, and psychological dimensions. They take time to develop, and possibly longer to integrate them into a coherent career development strategy. This is because international career capabilities do not develop randomly. Individuals need to focus at different stages on developing, nurturing, and expanding these capabilities as they build an international career and boost long-term employability. Figure 5.1 illustrates a typical pattern of capability development for individuals who have launched their careers in international environments.

Figure 5.1 Maximizing your international career capabilities

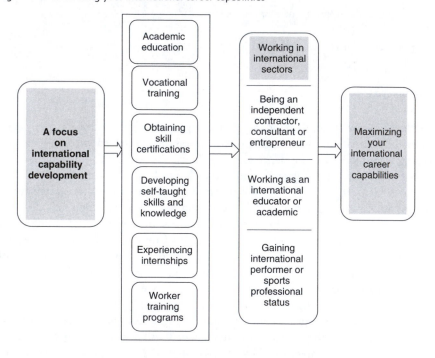

Similarly to the model for maximizing mobility shown in chapter 4, there is a two-stage perspective of the competence development process. The first stage shows the fundamental strategies for skill and competence development while the second stage focuses on applying those abilities in the international arena. The whole process starts with an individual's focus on developing international career capabilities. Academic education, vocational training, and skill certifications represent the traditional approaches to gaining some of the knowledge and skills needed to work internationally. There are also instances where individuals have worked to developed certain skills and knowledge on their own. Finally, experiencing internships or training programs at home or abroad give individuals more direct experience of working with, and in, foreign markets.

The second stage of international career development occurs when individuals find direct ways of working across borders. International performers and sports professionals are in a special category since reputation and well-connected talent agents can accelerate an individual's ability to work in different parts of the world. Teachers, professors, and researchers are another group of professionals who can take advantage of a network of research centers, schools, colleges, and universities around the world to gain access to the international arena. For those who wish to be self-employed, being an independent contractor, consultant, or entrepreneur gives individuals the opportunity to apply their expertise to solving problems, working with others, or developing a new business in different national environments.

Although all of the strategies above are direct approaches to working across borders, it is clear that working for firms operating in international sectors, or working in international areas of domestic-oriented firms, represent the most common way for individuals to develop and expand their international career capabilities. This book takes the view that understanding the concept of an "international sector" is crucial for understanding the increasingly global employment opportunities. Working in international sectors not only provides greater opportunities for developing international capabilities, it also boosts long-term mobility and employability, since individuals can access different employment environments around the world.

TOPIC FOCUS

For those wishing to develop an international business career, an important starting point is gaining entry into a sector that is active in international markets and plays an important role in international competitiveness. The next step is to determine which of those international sectors provides the best employment and career development opportunities to match one's long-term career goals. It is important to not only look at entry level positions, but also to look at possible career paths beyond initial employment. Many individuals become enamored with one type of position in an industry and often fail to explore how that position might, or might not, link to other positions in the sector. It is therefore crucial that individuals research and understand the sectors of interest. In addition to having a general understanding of the main operations of a sector, knowing the structure of the industry, the international dimension, and the nature of sector-related occupations and careers will make it easier to choose an occupation and career path that can lead to career success. In this chapter and throughout this book, you will be exposed to a number of sectors that provide individuals with extensive opportunities to work with, and in, a wide range of international markets.

A FOCUS ON INTERNATIONAL SECTORS

There are many sectors that carry out transactions across different national boundaries. However, the international sectors that are the focus of this chapter have a number of distinguishing characteristics. These international sectors generally have numerous business, production, or service operations overseas. The sectors are also active in foreign direct investment (FDI) activities around the world. Finally, these sectors make use of skilled employees in many different areas. These factors together make these international sectors a great place for mobile knowledge workers to seek employment opportunities. There are usually a variety of career development and career expansion opportunities throughout these sectors. [1, 2]

As globalization has intensified and international corporations have spread around the world, it has become easier for skilled individuals to gain access to different international jobs and sectors. The employment practices of the international sectors allow for a greater focus on the capability, mobility, and transferability of career competences. The box below shows a list of active international business sectors. All of these sectors have significant business activities in the economies of developed and emerging market countries around the world.

ACTIVE INTERNATIONAL BUSINESS SECTORS

1. The financial sector

2. The information technology sector

3. The logistics sector

4. The hospitality sector

5. The wine sector

6. The retail sector

7. The oil-energy sector

8. The consulting sector

9. The international development sector

In this chapter, we will focus on four of the sectors shown above. As you move to create or develop an international career, it is imperative that you know more about sectors that give you an opportunity to develop your international career capabilities. Before focusing on specific regions or companies, knowledge of a sector can help you plan your capability development and clarify the possible career paths that await you. In addition to general profitability and competitiveness, three aspects of a sector are important for determining its potential for international employment opportunities. These are *the structure of the sector, the international dimension*, and *sector-related jobs and careers*. The "structure of the sector" refers to how the leaders, challengers, and followers in a sector are linked to the major products, services, or business strategies in that sector. The "international dimension" reflects the extent to which that sector has major business activities or projects in different parts of the world.

"Sector-related jobs and careers" refers to the type skill-sets, employment opportunities and career paths possible in a particular sector.

The four sectors to be explored in the rest of the chapter are the information technology, financial, wine and logistics sectors. Although these sectors require different types of skillsets and knowledge workers, they all have a strong international presence and provide extensive opportunities for international career development and advancement. These sectors were chosen to illustrate different perspectives on international employment and career development. All of these sectors allow individuals to make the most of mobility and capability development. There are a number of key internet links, for each of the four sectors, in the Appendix.

Before reviewing the four international sectors, there are two concepts that should be mentioned. They are the concepts of "domain activities" and "domain knowledge." There are a wide variety of definitions in the literature regarding these two concepts. However, this book's definitions are mainly influenced by the personalized resource management perspective. *Domain activities* refer to the processes, activities and strategies that support the products and services of organizations in a sector. *Domain knowledge* refers to the skills, experiences and competences that allow individuals and organizations to create, manage, and expand domain activities. Being well acquainted with the domain knowledge and activities of a sector is crucial for recognizing the range of employment opportunities and career paths that the sector offers. [1, 3]

THE INFORMATION TECHNOLOGY SECTOR

General Overview

The information technology (IT) sector represents an innovative and high-growth sector for many economies around the world. With worldwide IT spending forecast to reach over 3 trillion dollars in the next few years, developments in the sector have far-reaching national and international ramifications for technological competitiveness. Since IT is used to refer to a wide array of activities, there is sometimes confusion over the scope of the sector. The definition below can illustrate why this sector's activities are so important to understanding innovation and business development. *Information technology* refers to any hardware or software technology that is used to study, acquire, develop, process, store, or distribute information to other individuals, clients, customers, or other technological agents. Since this information can take the form of sounds, visual images, texts, or numbers, we can see why IT is represented in some form or another in almost all industries. [4, 5]

One factor that has accelerated the widespread use of information technology is the cost of transmitting large volumes of information. The widespread use of fiber optics and other communication media, as well as the digitization of various types of data, means that large volumes of information can now be sent around the world for almost a few cents. The knowledge necessary to develop, use, maintain, and spread IT technologies has given tremendous importance to "knowledge workers" and IT-savvy organizations. Moreover, in many instances, the use of information technology has boosted blue and white collar worker productivity, as well as the overall effectiveness of many organizations. [6, 7]

A key distinguishing feature of information technology is its impact on multiple sectors and multiple knowledge domains. IT technologies are used in both established and emerging sectors in many innovative ways. Globalization has also accelerated because of the ability of information technology to connect to, and provide services for, individuals and groups around the world. As nations become more global and interconnected, so have IT jobs and IT careers everywhere. [8, 9]

Structure of the Industry

Given the widespread use of information technology, explaining the structure of the industry becomes a difficult task. As previously mentioned, IT activities range across numerous areas and require a wide variety of knowledge workers. The most logical approach to defining the sector would seem to be to focus on how widespread the use of information technology is within a sector or in the major products or services that sector produces. Size is not a major factor, since IT activities occur across firms of all sizes. From the perspective of an IT career, it makes more sense to focus on the main domain activity areas that characterize the firms that use or produce information technology. Table 5.1 breaks down information technology activities into four major activities: hardware, software, networks and systems, and services and support. This approach probably makes the most sense when trying to outline the structure of the information technology industry. [4, 7, 9]

Table 5.1 Main domain activities in information technology

Hardware	Software	Networks and systems	Services and support
Computers	Databases	World wide web	B2B services
Netbooks	File systems	Social networks	B2C services
Tablets	Operating systems	Communication networks	C2C services
Smart phones	Browsers	Logistics networks	Technical support
Game consoles	E-commerce	Business process management	Project management
Music devices	infrastructure	Risk management systems	Call centers
Photo and video devices	Business improvement	Quality control and security	Marketing
Storage devices	software	management systems	Distribution
Computer peripherals	Consumer-related	Etc . . .	Advertising
Semiconductors	software		Public relations
Integrated circuits	Programming languages		Financial activities
Memory chips	Etc . . .		Investor relations
Etc . . .			Etc . . .

Whether we are talking about hardware, software, systems, or services, information technology can help individuals, organizations, or even nations carry out activities in more effective and more productive ways. Information technology already plays a crucial role in established sectors such as financial services, healthcare, manufacturing, and logistics. However, there are many exciting new areas, such as the green sector, security, cloud computing, mobile communications, and bioinformatics, that are effectively incorporating IT.

Another dominant characteristic of firms whose competitiveness or profitability depends on information technology is the focus on core competences. Since there is a high degree of knowledge and experience needed to be competitive in any particular area of information technology, firms tend to focus on what they do best. This has made strategies such as outsourcing and off-shoring essential for large scale projects that involve many different domain knowledge areas. This sector has now become one of the most globalized, since it is possible to find knowledge workers in many different parts of the world and technology also allows the coordination of work across several geographical boundaries and knowledge specialists. [10–12]

The International Dimension

The information technology sector is one of the most international sectors because of the widespread use of its products and services across numerous business activities. The industrialized nations have been competing intensively for years in many areas of information technology. However, recent trends show that information technology is also playing a greater role in emerging markets. The BRIC countries (Brazil, Russia, India, and China) have been leading the charge. India has long been a leading recipient of outsourcing projects and the country's firms have begun to expand their IT activities internationally. China has poured billions into the IT sector and is very active in trying to expand its share of outsourcing activities. Russia has a large pool of educated and talented engineers and scientists and the country is trying hard to expand domestic IT activity. Finally, Brazil's rapid growth and increasing importance as a resource-rich nation has made development of its information technology sector a major priority. [6, 13, 14]

The main phenomenon driving the global expansion of information technology has been outsourcing and off-shoring activities. Since the skills required to participate in these activities vary, many countries, covering a range of economic development, have been chosen to support locations for IT activities. The low cost of data transmission and telecommunications has made it easier to open up call centers, technical support activities, programming projects, and research and development ventures, and even to operate virtual teams around the world. Information technology has helped to make the world more connected and interdependent and, consequently, it is a perfect example of an international sector that drives the development of numerous international careers in many different regions of the world. [12, 15]

Sector Related Jobs & Careers

Jobs and careers in the information technology sector have evolved dramatically over the years. Initially, it was mainly computer scientists and mathematical engineers who had a legitimate claim as professionals in the field. However, as the different technologies and services have been popularized and standardized, numerous new job titles and career paths have developed. Moreover, there are now many types of academic and vocational degrees which are tied to specific domain knowledge areas in information technology. [4, 7]

As the sector has expanded worldwide, there has been a concurrent increase in the demand for knowledge workers who can support the level of innovation and services needed to be a competitive organization or nation. Two different trends for getting access to these knowledge workers have emerged. One trend relies on the mobility of these workers by lowering immigration barriers and making exceptions for highly competent individuals to enter and work in different national environments with relative ease. The other trend is for organizations to move their development or support operations to areas where knowledge workers are plentiful and can be hired at relatively lower costs. [5, 15]

As you can see in Table 5.2, there are many different areas of domain knowledge that characterize this sector. This book breaks domain knowledge down into four areas: *core technical, supporting technical, supporting functional,* and *core strategic.* There are other ways to conceptualize jobs in this sector, but this approach is in line with the capabilities view of career development. The four different categories also represent the major career entry point for this sector. It is clear from this table that jobs in IT are widely varied, and people from many different types of educational backgrounds can find employment in the sector. It is also possible for individuals to use additional education or firm-level experiences to move from one position or domain knowledge area to another. Many individuals have started out in the core technical area and eventually moved to a core strategic position on a management team. Similarly, individuals have started out in a supporting functional area, moved to a supporting technical area, and then moved on to a core strategic area. Much of this cross-domain knowledge movement is determined by individuals' education and work experience as well as their drive to follow a chosen career path. [8, 10, 13]

Table 5.2 Areas of domain knowledge in information technology

Core technical	Supporting technical	Supporting functional	Core strategic
Engineers	Project management	Logistics	Management team
Programmers	Quality control	Financial	Funding and investors
Systems analysts	Localization	Marketing	HR management
Systems managers	Web management	Administrative	Knowledge management
Production managers	Tech support	Regulatory	Public relations

Whether individuals develop their capabilities with one firm or across many firms, those working in information technology have to commit to the work culture of the sector. Since speed, innovation, and competitiveness usually drive performance in information technology, individuals generally work under a lot of stress and often have continual deadlines and performance targets. However, those individuals who are capable generally find that the compensation, mobility, and transferability aspects of the career are highly rewarding. [11, 15]

THE FINANCIAL SECTOR

General Overview

The financial sector is one of the most important sectors in any economy. This sector includes a wide range of institutions and activities and can directly impact all other sectors in an economy. The financial sector can be defined as the set of institutions, activities, or financial instruments that allow for the funding, borrowing, lending, exchanging, protecting, or arbitrage of financial assets and transactions in an economy. Because its intermediary function and impact goes beyond the immediate activities of the sector, the financial sector operates like the central circulatory system of a business environment. In the US, the GDP share of the financial sector has gone up and down over time, but it has clearly moved from below 3 percent in the 1940s to around 8 percent in recent years. It is now widely recognized that there are strong positive links between the financial sector and economic growth and development. [16–19]

It is sometimes difficult to distinguish between the numerous types of financial institutions in the economy. However, by taking a functional approach, we can generally say that there are three types of financial institutions: (1) deposit taking institutions, such as banks that manage funds and make loans; (2) insurance companies and pension funds firms that accumulate, manage, and protect assets; and (3) brokers, underwriters and investment firms that support investor activity and market arbitrage opportunities. As any economy develops, the financial sector usually deepens, strengthens, and widens. If the financial sector is damaged in a crisis, its ability to circulate funds in an economy is usually impaired and most non-financial sectors would also experience negative outcomes. As global competition intensifies in the financial sector, the tendency in many countries is for financial institutions to get bigger. Nevertheless, medium-sized and smaller financial firms continue to play a very active role in specialized activities and regional business development. [16, 20, 21]

Structure of the Industry

The structure of the financial sector is determined by both the range of business activities and the regulatory limitations of various regional and national markets. Deposit taking institutions such as banks can vary significantly. In the US, the large "money center" banks operate across most of the country, and are involved in a wide range of lending and finance activities. Regional banks can operate in many of the same areas, but tend to focus on their local markets and clients. Most of the large and small deposit-taking banks are heavily involved in retail and commercial banking activities. However, most commercial banks focus mainly on doing business with business organizations. Retail banks, on the other hand, mainly focus on mass market products, such as checking and savings accounts, loans, mortgages, and credit cards. The retail banking category is very wide and covers many types of banks. Around the world, the institutions that would be considered retail banks include private banks, savings banks, postal savings banks, some commercial banks, mutually owned building societies, community banks, and credit unions.

Another type of financial institution is the insurance firm. Its main goals are risk management and protecting assets from damage, depreciation, or loss. Since risk is inherent in most transactions, insurance firms end up participating in many different market and asset management activities. Some of the more well-known insurance areas include auto, home, health, casualty, life, liability, and property insurance. Another type of asset management firm is the pension fund organization. Its main goal is to manage the retirement funds for individuals and a wide range of organizations. In so doing, these organizations often become important shareholders in many private and listed companies around the world. This gives them significant clout and, as activist shareholders, they can often spur change in corporate governance activities in many sectors. [22, 23]

The third group of financial organizations consists of brokers, investment banks and investment firms involved in activities that are supposed to benefit individual and corporate investors. These firms are generally involved in the sale, underwriting, managing, or arbitrage of various securities and assets in order to benefit their investors. In recent years, the most active of this type of institution were the investment banks and hedge funds. However, after the near collapse of the world financial system, the investment banks on Wall Street transformed themselves into bank holding companies. This subjected them to greater government regulation but provided them with more government support and protection. They are still involved in the same financial activities, and have recovered faster than other sectors of the American economy from the crisis. Another type of institution in this group is the hedge fund. Every hedge fund has its own investment strategy and that determines the type of investments it undertakes. These problematic firms are rapidly growing, and can provide high levels of profitability to investors and management. Since they are not as highly regulated as many other types of financial institutions, they tend to take more risks in order to achieve higher returns. Hedge funds often dominate certain specialty markets such as derivatives, some foreign exchange, and distressed assets. [22, 24, 25]

One type of financial institution that is hard to categorize is the universal bank. Universal banks participate in a wide range of financial activities that combine retail, wholesale, and investment banking services. They tend to be larger and operate in many international markets. However, there are usually certain restrictions on how some areas of this type of bank do business internally. The concept is more relevant in the US, where there have been historical restrictions separating commercial from investment banking activities. In many other countries, those restrictions do not exist and the universal bank structure is closer to the norm. [16, 23, 24]

The International Dimension

The financial sector is active worldwide at all levels of economic development. This easily makes the sector one of the most active international business areas. Whether we are dealing with advanced economies with large service or manufacturing activities, or with emerging markets that depend on smaller banking and micro-finance activities, the financial sector is often at the heart of most significant business strategies. Not only do financial firms compete across borders, the various stock markets also provide opportunities for domestic and foreign firms to raise funds for entrepreneurship and growth. For people wishing to work internationally, the financial sector provides many paths to working overseas. The financial sector tends to have some of the largest number of expatriates working in different foreign countries. [26–28]

Sector-Related Jobs & Careers

From the perspective of developing a career, the financial sector has numerous entry points because of the extensive range of business activities that the sector supports. Since it is also very possible to have a non-financial business sector position within a financial institution, the sector provides employment opportunities to many different kinds of employees. It is also important to point out that the salary levels tend to be higher in the financial sector than for similar positions elsewhere. For those wishing to have financial sector-related employment, jobs can be found in three different areas:

1.   Doing non-financial activities in financial institutions

2.   Doing financial activities in financial firms

3.   Doing financial activities in non-financial firms

Just like other organizations, financial firms have to be supported by various business activities. A list of business activities in financial firms includes sales, customer service, business development, market research, HR management, project management, legal services, information services, public relations, investor relations, and corporate governance. These types of business activities can also be found in IT, manufacturing, and service firms. Consequently, this presents opportunities for individuals to move into, and out of, the financial sector as they build a career. For those wishing to build a career around specific financial activities, there is a wide range of activities to choose from. Some of these financial activities can be considered complete sub-sectors of the financial industry. Table 5.3 shows an extensive list of such financial activities. Many of the jobs related to these financial sector activities can also be found in non-financial sector firms. This gives individuals with established financial sector experience and credentials a lot of flexibility to work within, or across, various sectors. [29–33]

Table 5.3 Financial sector activities

Accounting	Forex/money markets	Private banking
Asset management	Hedge funds	Wealth management services
Commercial banking	HR and recruitment	Private equity
Commodities	IT and information services	Venture capital
Compliance/legal	Insurance	Quantitative analytics
Consulting	Investment banking	Real estate
Corporate finance	Mergers and acquisitions	Market/equities research
CrediteEvaluation	Investment advisory	Retail banking
Debt/fixed income	Investor relations and PR	Risk management
Derivatives	Operations management	Financial sales
Equities	Corporate governance	Trading

THE WINE SECTOR

General Overview

The wine industry is no longer a cottage industry dominated by a few countries, but is now one that involves numerous countries competing for customer loyalty and market share. New world wines from countries such as the USA, Chile, Argentina, Australia, and South Africa are vigorously competing with old world wines from Italy, France, and Spain. As the wine industry has grown in its importance to economic development and growth, other countries are also developing their wine regions and are striving to improve their competitiveness. The US is the fourth largest wine producer and the fourth largest wine consumption market in the world. Although 95 percent of US wine exports originate in California, the wine industry is estimated of having a national economic impact of around $125 billion dollars. The industry accounts for about 309,000 full-time equivalent jobs in California and about 875,000 jobs in the US. [34–37]

Today, wine is an important cultural and economic activity in many countries, and the industry has created significant spill over effects into the hospitality, entertainment, and logistics sectors. Moreover, globalization and internet access have provided consumers and distributors worldwide with unprecedented level of information on wines, wineries, and wine regions everywhere. The economic impact of the wine industry should also include its impact on the transportation, tourism, entertainment, and hospitality sectors. As wine production, consumption, and distribution expand, so do the activities in these affected sectors. [38–41]

Recently, the wine sector has even become associated with the "green economy." There are significant programs under way in various regions around the world to develop sustainable growing and distribution practices in the sector. The environmental concern is an added dimension in the marketing of wines and wineries everywhere. The industry was successful in the past in promoting the health benefits of wine consumption and is now developing strategies to promote their sustainable and environmentally conscious practices. Beyond these developments, we should also point out that the wine sector has been successful in linking wine consumption with interesting lifestyles, and has boosted the participation of consumers to new levels. Consequently, wine sector-related occupations and careers can now develop across a wider spectrum of business and social activities domestically and internationally. [42–45]

Structure of the Industry

It is difficult to get a clear picture of the wine sector if we focus only on wineries. This is because there are wineries that produce grapes, wineries that do not produce grapes, and grape producers that do not produce wine. To get a comprehensive view of the structure of the wine industry, we need to consider all the core and supporting stakeholders who affect the value chain from grape production to wine consumption. Taking this more expansive view, we can identify six major activities that drive developments in the sector: [38, 46–48]

1. Vineyard and grower management

2. Production and bottling

3. Inventory and distribution

4. Wine tourism and direct sales

5. Marketing and finance

6. Hospitality and entertainment

"Vineyard and grower management" includes everything from soil preparation and planting to grape harvesting. Some of these activities are done in house, but others can be done in conjunction with other agricultural and environmental specialists. "Production and bottling" includes forecasting demand, product analysis, crushing, blending, fermenting, barreling, bottling, and cellar management activities. "Inventory and distribution" are crucial activities in the wine sector. These functions include warehouse and inventory management, sector allocations, and effective use of distribution channels. "Wine tourism and direct sales" involve many important activities. These include developing tasting room spaces and educational capabilities, customer tracking, point of sales technology, web-based platforms, wine club management, wine tourism activities, and order processing and delivery. Marketing and finance play crucial supporting roles in the wine sector. Marketing strategies range from product and location branding to the development of distribution channels and strategic alliances at home and abroad. The value of the finance function should also not be underestimated. Getting access to operating capital, as well as cash flow management and the forecasting of future financial needs, are essential strategies for maintaining a profitable enterprise. Finally, hospitality and entertainment strategies allow wine organizations to expand their range of income-generating activities while reinforcing their brand image.

One area that should receive special attention is the distribution strategy in the wine sector. How firms get their products to market and the proper mix of channels to support a brand image are crucial decisions. The four main distribution strategies involve the use of (1) agents and brokers; (2) distributors/importers (3) direct distribution; and (4) joint ventures. Based on a firm's desired level of control or their need to reach varied and distant markets, they may need to use one or a combination of the four strategies. Behind these strategies we can find a host of domestic and international business organizations. This is why the wine industry has the potential of impacting economic activities across many different sectors and regions. [49–51]

The International Dimension

Since developed economies and many emerging markets are now actively involved in the production, consumption, and distribution of wines, competition is truly occurring on a global scale. The demand for land, expertise, and workers in this sector has increased accordingly. There is not only growth in the need for expertise and labor in core wine related activities, there has also been a significant jump in the need for workers in wine sector-related hospitality, tourism, and entertainment. One phenomenon that captures much of this landscape is domestic and international wine tourism. As regions around the world become known for their wine-related activities, we are seeing a jump in tourism activities in those regions. Individuals and groups that travel and stay in different wine regions now participate in many different winery-related educational, leisure, and entertainment activities in those regions.

Other developments which have increased international business activity in the sector have been the increasing use of foreign direct investment and strategic alliance strategies by wine sector organizations. These cross-border alliances and production activities accelerate the interaction of markets around the world. Finally, in the area of wine business management, there are a growing number of educational institutions around the world offering certifications and graduate degrees to domestic and foreign students. These educational programs accelerate knowledge transfer and provide new pathways for the creation of many new occupations and careers in the wine sector. [45, 48, 52–54]

Sector-Related Jobs & Careers

Given the expanding reach of the wine sector, there are many entry points for individuals wishing to develop a career doing wine-related activities. The discussion above, on the structure of the wine sector, mentioned six areas that have significantly impacted developments in the industry. In addition to the supporting role of hospitality, all the major business functions such as sales, marketing, finance, and logistics play an important role in effective wine business management. In addition, supply side factors such as wineries, wine reps, distributors, wine shops, restaurants, retail stores, and hotels all play an important role in getting wine products to customers. [55–57]

A number of educational institutions in the US have large programs to teach wine growing or wine business management practices. Some examples include the University of California-Davis, the University of Missouri, Washington State University, California State University-Fresno, Oregon State University, Cornell University, and Sonoma State University. Similar programs exist in top institutions in many wine-producing countries worldwide. Getting a degree from one of these institutions in a field that supports international business, hospitality, wine production, or wine business management is a significant step toward developing a career in this sector. [56, 58–61]

Core wine sector occupations might include positions such as grape farmer, grape picker, vineyard manager, viticulturist, winemaker, enologists, wine market researchers, laboratory technicians, wine sales, tasting room manager, or marketing director. In addition to established university degree programs, certifications are also important in the wine sector. Some the certifications which can often help advance one's career in the industry include certified wine sommelier, certified wine merchant, certified chef of the wine arts, or certified cellar manager. Overall, there are many direct and indirect ways of finding employment in the domestic and international wine industry. This is a global industry where the need for expertise in a variety of related occupations is expected to rise substantially as the impact of the wine sector expands around the world. [56, 58, 61–63]

THE LOGISTICS SECTOR

General Overview

The term "logistics" was initially used to refer to military strategies for supplying troops with equipment and supplies. Logistics now refers to the strategies used to manage or transport goods, information, capital, or other resources from a point of origin to a point of usage or consumption. These inbound or outbound movements can often include the storage, packaging, or transformation of these items along a particular supply chain. Related activities which add significant value to logistics strategies are data collection, security enhancements, and plant and process management. From the modern business perspective, logistics also implies the management of increasingly complex information, communication, and control systems needed to operate in a wide range of infrastructures and geographical environments. [64–66]

Logistics plays a major role in the American economy, and its economic impact on GDP has been estimated at over 8 percent. The US logistics industry grew from $678 billion in 1990 to over $900 billion in 2005. That figure should be even higher now. A major reason for the central role of logistics is because it covers a broad array of functional areas. Activities such as land transportation, shipping, warehousing, import-export operations, purchasing, production planning, customer service, and inventory management fall within the scope of logistics. [67–69]

One area of logistics that is dominated by small and medium-sized firms is the import-export business. This area of international trade is a major commercial trend in many countries. The main operation of many small or medium-sized international business enterprises is the importing or the exporting of goods and services across national boundaries. This is especially true for niche markets or specialty products that are not distributed in bulk by large multinationals. Some of these smaller firms sometimes act as export management companies (EMCs) for larger organizations that don't know a particular environment. In addition to these developments, the internet revolution has significantly boosted the ability of individuals and smaller organizations to directly import or export their goods and services. This is especially true in the case of digitalized products or software sales, which can be managed directly by the website infrastructure. [70–72]

Since government agencies play a significant role in facilitating international trade, most governments will work aggressively to assist their organizations and entrepreneurs with strategies for entering foreign markets. Online government resources often provide extensive data and information on foreign markets. The US Small Business Administration (SBA) supports small international businesses through two major programs: business development assistance and financial assistance. Consequently, the SBA website (sba.gov/oit) is an excellent place for smaller organizations to go in order to gather information and get strategic advice for distributing to, or operating in, foreign markets. [68, 73–75]

Structure of the Industry

The structure of the logistics industry varies according to the dominant geographical characteristics and level of infrastructure development of a country or a region. However, the industry can be broken down generally into four main categories: surface transport, air transport, sea transport, and electronic or digital distribution. Fuel prices can have a significant impact on the first three categories, but companies usually mix distribution strategies to match the needs of the customer and minimize costs. [64, 76–79]

Due the size and complexity of operations, the American logistics sector can appear confusing. However, by examining the five fundamental characteristics of the sector, we get a clearer picture:

1. **Two major commercial orientations:** (a) the national and global distribution of goods and commodities; and (b) the NAFTA-influenced location of production facilities and distribution of inputs and outputs.

2. **Gateway cities and major ocean access areas:** cities such as Los Angeles, New York, Chicago, Miami, and Atlanta act as major international and domestic gateway cities; the Atlantic seaboard, the Pacific Coast, and the Gulf of Mexico are the key ocean access locations.

3. **Long distance inland freight distribution:** the use of rail corridors covering long distances and managed by privately owned companies.

4. **Economies of scale distribution:** the use of high capacity highways (trucking), logistic parks, and local rail corridors to match the needs of the region.

5. **Competitive major players:** express couriers (Fedex, UPS, USPS), third party logistic providers, freight forwarders, and in-house export departments are the major players in the sector.

In terms of the major players, one group that warrants a more detailed discussion is the third party logistics provider (3PL or TPL). Third party logistic providers are firms that provide a one stop service by specializing in integrated operations, warehousing, and transportation services that match the customer's needs. Overall, the key activities carried out by these 3PLs are transportation, warehousing, inventory management, information systems, and packaging. [72, 80–82]

Because of technological advancements, the growing importance of supply chain management, and the advancements in intercompany communications, there is now a focus on a new model of third party logistic operators. This is the non-asset-based logistics provider. These non-asset-based providers perform functions such as design, packaging, negotiations, consulting, freight quoting, financial settlement, auditing, tracking, customer services, and dispute resolution. They do all this although they do not own any physical freight distribution assets of their own. These organizations usually are run by a team of logistics experts and information technology specialists. They use their accumulated knowledge of the sector to significantly structure, guide, and evaluate distribution activities to match the strategic needs of customers. [69, 74, 79, 81]

The International Dimension

Since the 1970s, logistics companies have become more global. There are now more complex production and distribution networks spread around the world that guide the relentless flow of supplies and products to customers everywhere. Most international firms are not isolated entities but rather part of a supply network or a key player in a valuable supply chain. Due to the interdependent nature of globalization trends, effective logistics has become a key factor in international and domestic corporate strategy. [81, 83–85]

In recent years, a major economic development which has underscored the importance of international logistics is the rapid rise of emerging market nations. The meteoric rise of the BRICs (Brazil, Russia, India, and China), and a new emphasis on open market policies in other emerging market countries, has fueled international trade and changed the direction of traditional trade flows. There is now tremendous diversity in the demand for raw materials, parts, finished goods, and services, as firms and nations compete for larger shares of the economic pie. Moreover, demand and supply imbalances have placed tremendous pressure on logistic activities around the world. [64, 73, 77, 78, 86]

Sector-Related Jobs & Careers

Given the range of functions and organizations that fall under the umbrella of logistics, it should be considered an exciting area for occupation and career development. While it is relatively easy to enter and move up in the transportation, warehousing, and distribution areas of logistics, it is more difficult to gain entry and advance in supply chain management positions. For jobs in managerial or top executive positions, at least a bachelor's degree and sector experience are usually required. The types of foundation skills generally needed to succeed in logistics include the ability to pay attention to detail, as well as computer, reasoning, teamwork, organizational, writing, interpersonal, analytical skills, and project management skills. [2, 79, 87–90]

Although many universities do not have programs dedicated to logistics, there are a number of subjects and majors that can give individuals the foundation necessary to succeed in the logistic sector. Studies in foreign languages, English, marketing, accounting, international business, operations management, math, computers, and information systems can all impart significant knowledge that can be used in a career in logistics. Finally, a variety of industry organizations around the world offer certification programs which enhance the impact of academic credentials or work experience. These certifications also boost individuals' employment and promotion potential. Examples of two organizations that offer certifications in logistics are the American Society of Transportation and Logistics (AST & L) and the International Society of Logistics (SOLE). The three kinds of certifications offered by AST & L are (1) Certification in Transportation and Logistics (CTL); (2) Distinguished Logistics Professional (DLP); and (3) Professional Designation in Supply Chain Management (PLS). [83, 87, 88, 90]

With the rapid expansion of global trade, there will be continued growth in central and supporting occupations in logistics. Seaports, airports, railways, shipping companies, airlines, logistics parks, import-export firms, couriers, trucking companies, and even non-asset-based consulting firms will all need employees with the appropriate skills and experience. Table 5.4 shows examples of logistics jobs at the entry, mid-career, and executive levels. For those individuals who work across borders, foreign language proficiency will also give them a competitive advantage in the employment marketplace. [64, 81, 87, 90–92]

Table 5.4 Types of jobs in logistics

Entry level	Mid-career	Executive level
Forklift driver, truck driver, mail/ package delivery, service assistant, operator, warehouse stock clerk, capacity planner, call center traffic operator, scheduling analyst, logistics analyst, buyer or purchasing agent, transportation analyst, shipping-receiving clerk, customer service manager, logistics planner, logistics services salesperson, transportation coordinator, import-export clerk, translator, negotiator . . .	Supervisor, capacity planner, forecast analyst, supply chain analyst, supply chain manager, logistics manager, logistics consultant, distribution supervisor, warehouse manager inventory control manager client services supervisor, logistics engineer, purchasing manager, shipping-receiving supervisor, materials manager, area import-export manager, logistics software manager . . .	Chief Executive Officer (CEO), Chief Production Officer, Inventory Management Executive, Director of Operations, Vice President, International Logistics Manager . . .

CHAPTER SUMMARY & OBSERVATIONS

The background information provided above does not cover all aspects of the sectors, but you should be able to get some clear ideas on how activities in these sectors might affect your international career decisions. Having some idea of the domain activities of a sector can provide you with possible job or career entry points to the sector. Many of the domain activities themselves represent major sub-sectors that might have a different employment demand patterns from the overall sector. Another aspect of the domain activities is the regional or international distribution of those activities. Some domain activities might be more localized, while others could be more internationally dispersed. For individuals seeking to work abroad, such knowledge is important when it comes to choosing a particular career path. Another factor that should be clarified is the nature of the domain knowledge for the sector. An understanding of the domain knowledge will point out which capabilities you need to develop, maintain, or expand in order to be successful in that sector. Overall, for individuals wishing to maximize their international career capabilities, the first requirement should be a thorough understanding of the international sector of interest.

As discussed previously, the three most important outcomes of the personalized resource management approach to career development are mobility, capability, and transferability. Chapter 4 covered factors that influence career mobility, and this chapter covered strategies for maximizing your international career capabilities. There was a discussion of the concept of international sector. International sectors were defined as generally having numerous business, production, or service operations in different national environments. The sectors are also active in foreign direct investment (FDI) activities around the world. Finally, these sectors generate opportunities and make use of skilled employees in many different areas. A two-stage model focused on strategies to develop international career competences, as well as ways of increasing international work experience opportunities. The majority of the chapter then explored key characteristics of the information technology, financial, wine, and logistics sectors. For each sector, there was an examination of the structure of the industry, the international dimension, and sector-related jobs and careers. In the same way that international gateway cities play an important role in generating employment opportunities, international sectors provides opportunities for skilled individuals to develop, manage, and expand their international careers.

Chapter 6 will be about strategies for maximizing the transferability of career competences. You will be shown a model that highlights the main factors allowing the transferability of international career competences. The concept of cross-over sectors and cross-over skills will be introduced. You will then be presented with characteristics of the green and the international development sectors. These are two important cross-over sectors that provide opportunities for individuals from a wide variety of backgrounds to contribute and improve the performance of sector organizations. The chapter will then conclude with a description of programs and institutions around the world that provide education and training in fields that enhance the development and transferability of international business skills.

REFERENCES

1. Easterby-Smith, M. and I. Mikhailava, *Knowledge management: In perspective*. People Management, 2011: p. 34.
2. Field, A., *Raising the stakes*, Journal of Commerce, 26 January 2009.
3. Dalrymple, P., *Data, information, knowledge: The emerging field of health informatics*. Bulletin of the American Society for Information Science and Technology (Online), 2011. **37**(5): p. 41.
4. Allen, T. and M.S. Morton (Eds.), *Information technology and the corporation of the 1990s*, 1994, New York, NY: Oxford University Press.
5. Kim, J.M.M., *Technology jobs for physician leaders*. Physician Executive, 2011. **37**(4): p. 88.
6. Gartner Research. *Global IT spending forecasts*. 2011 [December 14, 2011]; Available from: http://www.gartner.com/technology/research/it-spending-forecast/.
7. Longley, D. and M. Shain, *Dictionary of information technology*, 1986, London, UK: Macmillan Press.
8. Fu, J., *Understanding career commitment of IT professionals: Perspectives of push-pull-mooring framework and investment model*. International Journal of Information Management, 2011. **31**(3): p. 279.
9. Hogan, P. and L. Li, *The perceptions of business students regarding management information systems (MIS) programs*. Journal of Technology Research, 2011. **2**: p. 1.

10. Berger, E., *Aging and working in the new economy: Changing career structures in small IT firms*. Canadian Journal on Aging, 2011. **30**(2): p. 304.

11. Vathsala, W. and J. Mayura, *Career management strategies among IT professionals in offshore outsourced IT firms in Sri Lanka*. The Journal of Management Development, 2011. **30**(9): p. 914.

12. Zimmermann, A. and M. Ravishankar, *Collaborative IT offshoring relationships and professional role identities: Reflections from a field study*. Journal of Vocational Behavior, 2011. **78**(3): p. 351.

13. Appelbaum, S., N. Asham and K. Argheyd, *Is the glass ceiling cracked in information technology? A qualitative analysis: Part 1*. Industrial and Commercial Training, 2011. **43**(6): p. 354.

14. O'Connor, F., *Hospitals compete for IT talent*. Computer world, 2011. **45**(14): p. 25.

15. Shamni, P., *Slowdown fears fail to hit global employee mobility*. Business Today, 16 October 2011.

16. Gowan, P., *Explaining the American boom: The roles of 'globalisation' and United States global power*. New Political Economy, 2001. **6**(3): p. 359.

17. Hwang, Y., H. Min and S. Han, *The influence of financial development on R & D activity: Cross-country evidence*. Review of Pacific Basin Financial Markets and Policies, 2010. **13**(3): p. 381.

18. Monal, A.-B., *The effects of bank reforms on the monetary transmission mechanism in emerging market economies: Evidence from Egypt*. African Development Review, 2010. **22**(4): p. 526.

19. Ramirez, C. and B. De Long, *Understanding America's hesitant steps toward financial capitalism: Politics, the Depression, and the separation of commercial and investment banking*. Public Choice, 2001. **106**(1–2): p. 93.

20. Bosworth, B. and A. Flaaen, *Financial crisis American style*. Asian Economic Papers, 2009. **8**(3): p. 146.

21. Wang, E., *A dynamic two-sector model for analyzing the interrelation between financial development and industrial growth*. International Review of Economics & Finance, 2000. **9**(3): p. 223.

22. Mertzanis, H., *The financial crisis and corporate governance reform*. International Journal of Business Governance and Ethics, 2011. **6**(1): p. 83.

23. Outreville, J., *Internationalization, performance and volatility: The world's largest financial groups*. Journal of Financial Services Research, 2010. **38**(2–3): p. 115.

24. Antinolfi, G. and E. Kawamura, *Banks and markets in a monetary economy*. Journal of Monetary Economics, 2008. **55**(2): p. 321–334.

25. Morrow, E., *A report on the life insurance sector*. Journal of Personal Finance, 2005. **4**(3): p. 29.

26. Quintyn, M. and G. Verdier, *African finance in the 21st century*, 2010, Basingstoke, UK and New York, NY: Palgrave Macmillan/International Monetary Fund. xvii, 320 p.

27. Tarr, J., *The regulation of insurance intermediaries in the Australian financial services market*. Australian Business Law Review, 2010. **38**(6): p. 332.

28. Torres, J., *China's leadership role during the global financial crisis*. Journal of American Academy of Business, Cambridge, 2011. **16**(2): p. 81.

29. Baron, L., *CPAs are a hot commodity*. Journal of Accountancy, 2006. **201**(2): p. 16.

30. Griffiths, S., *Financial careers services site sees huge increase in scope*. Professional Adviser, 2009: p. 23.

31. Maxwell, G., S. M. Ogden and D. McTavish, *Enabling the career development of female managers in finance and retail*. Women in Management Review, 2007. **22**(5): p. 353.

32. Rosenberg, D., C. Tomkins and P. Day, *A work role perspective of accountants in local government service departments*. Accounting, Organizations and Society, 1982. **7**(2): p. 123.

33. Sinacola, C., *Job fair hypes financial careers*, Telegram & Gazette, 17 July 1991: p. C2.

34. Bruwer, J. and R. Johnson, *Place-based marketing and regional branding strategy perspectives in the California wine industry*. The Journal of Consumer Marketing, 2010. **27**(1): p. 5–16.

35. Lee, J.-K., *A model for monitoring public sector web site strategy*. Internet Research, 2003. **14**(4): p. 259.

36. MKF Research, *Report on Economic Impact of California Wine*, 2006, St. Helena, CA: MKF Research LLC and The Wine Institute.

37. Shelton, T., *The global vs. domestic wine industry*. Paper from the Center for International Business Education and Research, University of Colorado. Available at: http://www.ucdenver.edu/academics/InternationalPrograms/CIBER/GlobalForumReports/Pages/GlobalForumReports.aspx

38. Aylward, D. and M. Zanko, *Reconfigured domains: Alternative pathways for the international wine indus-try*. International Journal of Technology Policy and Management, 2008. **8**(2): p. 148.

39. Brown, B. and J.E. Butler, *Competitors as allies: A study of entrepreneurial networks in the U.S. wine industry*. Journal of Small Business Management, 1995. **33**(3): p. 57.

40. Cox, J. and L. Bridwell, *Australian companies using globalization to disrupt the ancient wine industry*. Competitiveness Review, 2007. **17**(4): p. 209.

41. Harfield, T., *Competition and cooperation in an emerging industry*. Strategic Change, 1999. **8**(4): p. 227.

42. Alonso, A.D. and Y. Liu, *Wine tourism development in emerging Western Australian regions*. International Journal of Contemporary Hospitality Management, 2010. **22**(2): p. 245.

43. Aune, L., *The use of enchantment in wine and dining*. International Journal of Contemporary Hospitality Management, 2002. **14**(1): p. 34.

44. Houghton, M., *Classifying wine festival customers*. International Journal of Culture, Tourism and Hospitality Research, 2008. **2**(1): p. 67.

45. Marzo-Navarro, M. and M. Pedraja-Iglesias, *Wine tourism development from the perspective of the potential tourist in Spain*. International Journal of Contemporary Hospitality Management, 2009. **21**(7): p. 816.

46. Aylward, D. and G. Carey, *High-value niche production: What Australian wineries might learn from a Bordeaux first growth*. International Journal of Technology Policy and Management, 2009. **9**(4): p. 342.

47. Bernetti, I., L. Casini and N. Marinelli, *Wine and globalisation: Changes in the international market structure and the position of Italy*. British Food Journal, 2006. **108**(4): p. 306.

48. Insel, B., *The U.S. wine industry*. Business Economics, 2008. **43**(1): p. 68.

49. Marshall, R., et al., *Environmental practices in the wine industry: An empirical application of the theory of reasoned action and stakeholder theory in the United States and New Zealand*. Journal of World Business, 2010. **45**(4): p. 405.

50. Ryan, M. and K. Mizerski, *Place branding for sustainable futures: A case study*. Place Branding and Public Diplomacy, 2010. **6**(1): p. 49.

51. Swaminathan, A., *Resource partitioning and the evolution of specialist organizations: The role of location and identity in the U.S. wine industry*. Academy of Management Journal, 2001. **44**(6): p. 1169.

52. Kolyesnikova, N. and T. Dodd, *Effects of winery visitor group size on gratitude and obligation*. Journal of Travel Research, 2008. **47**(1): p. 104.

53. Sainz Ochoa, A., *Analysis of the explanatory factors of the firm success: An application to the Spanish wine industry within the Appellation d'Origine Rioja*, 2001, Spain: Universidad de la Rioja.

54. Spawton, A.L., *Grapes and wine seminar – Prospering in the 1990s: Changing your view of the consumer*. International Marketing Review, 1991. **8**(4): p. 32.

55. Alleyne, S. and K. Carter, *Sweet success in South Africa*. Black Enterprise, 2008. **38**(11): p. 200.

56. Davis, H., *Work: Graduate: Becoming a master's chef: MBA courses fair: Now MBAs are no longer limited to the world of finance. Hazel Davis looks at specialist food courses*. The Guardian, 17 January 2009: p. 6.

57. Velluzzi, N., *Community colleges, clusters, and competition: A case from Washington wine country*. Regional Studies, 2010. **44**(2): p. 201.

58. Damitio, J.W. and R.S. Schmidgall, *Hospitality professionals' responses to ethical situations*. Cornell Hotel and Restaurant Administration Quarterly, 1993. **34**(4): p. 40.

59. Hanagriff, R., M. Beverly and C. Robinson, *Texas wine marketing assistance program and the impacts to the Texas economy*. The Business Review, Cambridge, 2005. **4**(1): p. 104.

60. O'Neill, M. and S. Charters, *Service quality at the cellar door: Implications for Western Australia's developing wine tourism industry*. Managing Service Quality, 2000. **10**(2): p. 112.

61. Srivastava, P., *Wine industry promises a rewarding career*. Business Today, 2008.

62. Barber, N., *Wine consumers information search: Gender differences and implications for the hospitality industry*. Tourism and Hospitality Research, 2009. **9**(3): p. 250.

63. Cordano, M., R. Marshall and M. Silverman, *How do small and medium enterprises go "green"?*

A study of environmental management programs in the U.S. wine industry. Journal of Business Ethics, 2010. **92**(3): p. 463.

64. Bowersox, D.J. and R.J. Calantone, *Global logistics.* Journal of International Marketing, 1998. **6**(4): p. 83–93.

65. Jon Tetsuro, S., *British naval operational logistics, 1914–1918.* The Journal of Military History, 1993. **57**(3): p. 447–480.

66. Schrady, D. and D. Wadsworth, *Naval combat logistics support system.* The Journal of the Operational Research Society, 1991. **42**(11): p. 941–948.

67. Bandyopadhyay, T., J. Varghese and S. Raghunathan, *Information security in networked supply chains: Impact of network vulnerability and supply chain integration on incentives to invest.* Information Technology & Management, 2010. **11**(1): p. 7–23.

68. Bonar, M., *The Railways Act 2005 – The new structure.* Logistics and Transport Focus, 2005. **7**(4): p. 14.

69. Jaffee, D., *Industry structure, organizational forms, and labor dynamics in the intermodal logistics supply chain.* SSRN Working Paper Series, 2010.

70. Freathy, P. and F. O'Connell, *Supply chain relationships within airport retailing.* International Journal of Physical Distribution & Logistics Management, 1998. **28**(6): p. 451.

71. Jennifer Baljko, S., *International trade standards define buyer/seller responsibilities.* EBN, 2002(1317): p. 42.

72. Marlow, M., *The role of the aggregator: Using third-party suppliers to reach the market.* Learned Publishing, 2010. **23**(4): p. 357–361.

73. Bury, L., *Designed to cross continents.* Bookseller, 2010: p. 15–15.

74. Strachan, A., *Beyond investment: Engaging the private sector in trade faciliatation.* International Trade Forum, 2009(4): p. 32.

75. White Jr., C., *Future challenges for private sector railroads.* Journal of Transportation Law, Logistics, and Policy, 2005. **72**(2): p. 226.

76. Boisvert, H., *Integrating the internet.* CMA Management, 2003. **77**(3): p. 20.

77. Hickey, R., *Postal privatization and the transformation of the global logistics industry.* Management International, 2008. **12**: p. 39.

78. Keane, M.P. and S.E. Feinberg, *Advances in logistics and the growth of intra-firm rrade: The case of Canadian affiliates of U.S. multinationals, 1984–1995.* The Journal of Industrial Economics, 2007. **55**(4): p. 571–632.

79. Wassenhove, L.N.V., *Humanitarian aid logistics: Supply chain management in high gear.* The Journal of the Operational Research Society, 2006. **57**(5): p. 475–489.

80. Khanam, B.R., *Highway infrastructure capital and productivity growth: Evidence from the Canadian goods-producing sector.* Logistics and Transportation Review, 1996. **32**(3): p. 251.

81. Liu, H. and P.J. McGoldrick, *International retail sourcing: Trend, nature, and process.* Journal of International Marketing, 1996. **4**(4): p. 9–33.

82. MacCarthy, B. and A. Jayarathne, *Fast fashion: Achieving global quick response (GQR) in the internationally dispersed clothing industry.* SSRN Working Paper Series, 2009.

83. Markides, V. and M. Holweg, *On the diversification of international freight forwarders.* International Journal of Physical Distribution & Logistics Management, 2006. **36**(5): p. 336.

84. Oliver, G., *Value chain of information sharing: Information seeking and information providing.* Proceedings of the European Conference on Knowledge Management, 2009: p. 587–597.

85. Visser, A., *Best practices for implementing business process management.* Infonomics, 2009. **23**(6): p. 22–24.

86. Brooks, M. and K. Button, *Market structures and shipping security.* Maritime Economics & Logistics, 2006. **8**(1): p. 100.

87. Cassidy, W., *Teaching hands-on logistics,* Journal of Commerce, 22 February 2010.

88. Keller, S. and J. Ozment, *Research on personnel issues published in leading logistics journals.* International Journal of Logistics Management, 2009. **20**(3): p. 378.

89. McCrea, B., *Supply chain education: Bracing for the future.* Supply Chain Management Review, 2009. **13**(1): p. S.1.

90. Roberts, J., *Great career opportunities within the supply chain world.* Logistics and Transport Focus, 2008. **10**(10): p. 60.

91. Agg, S., *Women in logistics and transport and more.* Logistics and Transport Focus, 2009. **11**(8): p. 6.

92. Blesius, D., U. Hug and L. Woelk, *Career planning for graduates: It is multichannel!* Logistics and Transport Focus, 2009. **11**(10): p. 28.

6 MAXIMIZING THE TRANSFERABILITY OF YOUR CAPABILITIES & THE ROLE OF FOREIGN INSTITUTIONS & CROSSOVER SECTORS

LEARNING OBJECTIVES

- Clarify the concept of transferability

- Examine strategies to maximize transferability

- Review the role of foreign educational institutions

- Explore the impact of crossover sectors on careers

THE ROADMAP

In Chapter 5 you explored strategies for maximizing your international career capabilities. A two-stage model was presented which looked at academic, vocational, and worker training activities as well as specific approaches for working with, and in, foreign environments. After a clarification of the concept of the international sector, you were shown how these sectors generate the kinds of jobs that help to build strong international careers. To further illustrate the role of international sectors, there was an in-depth review of the characteristics of four key sectors: information technology, financial, wine, and logistics. For each sector there was an examination of the structure of the industry, the international dimension, and sector-related jobs and careers. The general conclusion was that these sectors provide significant opportunities for skilled and mobile employees to develop, manage, and expand their international careers.

Chapter 6 will examine the concept of transferability and then provide a framework for exploring strategies to maximize the transferability of your capabilities. As with Chapter 5, another two-stage model will focus on the transferability aspect of the personalized resource management perspective. The first stage will show academic and vocational development activities that help individuals retool their capabilities. The second stage will show direct-action strategies for moving your capabilities to other sectors or working environments. The role of foreign educational institutions in developing and expanding international career capabilities will be highlighted. You will also be given background information on a selection of international programs and institutions around the world.

The last section of Chapter 6 will look at the process of capability transfer and suggest ways individuals can accelerate this transformation process. The concept of a "crossover sector" will be defined, and you will then examine the characteristics of these internationally-oriented sectors. To fully illustrate the role of crossover sectors, you will be presented with information on the international development and green sectors. For both of these sectors, there will be a review the structure of the sector, the international dimension, and sector-related jobs and careers. Finally, you will be shown how the wide scope of domain activities and the use of a range of domain knowledge experts make these sectors attractive arenas for transferring your capabilities.

TOPIC FOCUS

The ultimate goal of personalized resource management (PRM) is long-term employability. As covered in earlier chapters, the three PRM strategies which enhance the possibility of long-term employability are capability, mobility, and transferability. Chapters 4 and 5 elaborated on strategies for maximizing mobility and capability. Since most of the discussions in this chapter will highlight strategies for maximizing transferability, a clear definition is indispensible. *This book defines transferability as using a set of skills, competences, and experiences developed in one business sector or business environment to adapt to a new position or career in an alternative sector or business environment.* In essence, transferability is the ability to adapt and mobilize business, technical, psychological, and cross-cultural skills in different regional and national environments. This ability is especially important for managing career transitions across sectors or national boundaries.

There are many different approaches to successfully transferring one's capabilities to new sectors or new regions, and individuals need to find the most suitable strategies to fit their situation. There several reasons why individuals might need to transfer their capabilities during their working life. The unfortunate reality is that most individuals will not be able to keep the same job or stay in the same sector for their entire career. The intense globalization of competition, significant changes in the economy, and the periodic restructuring of sectors are developments which often force individuals to change professions. Finally, global trade, networks of international corporate alliances, and the growing demand for knowledge workers have accelerated the necessity of working with different business environments, and created new employment opportunities at the same time.

STRATEGIES FOR MAXIMIZING THE TRANSFERABILITY OF YOUR CAPABILITIES

Just as organizations sometimes have to transform or reinvent themselves to stay competitive, individuals sometimes need to reconfigure or transfer their capabilities to new positions or careers after periods of crisis in order to maintain their employability. When individuals are faced with the necessity of changing locations or sectors in order to stay employed, they need to evaluate their current capabilities and devise strategies for making a successful transition. Figure 6.1 illustrates the process individuals might go through to increase the chances of successfully transferring their capabilities to a new sector or new environment.

The whole process starts with the motivation and the commitment to change location or sector in order to maintain employability. The position you gave up or were forced to vacate required a particular set of capabilities. If you were moving to a similar position in the same sector or environment, transferability would not be an issue. However, if the change requires a different set or different configuration of capabilities, then you will need to develop strategies to acquire the needed capabilities. Figure 6.1 shows a set of retooling and a set of direct action strategies to maximize the transferability of your capabilities.

There are various approaches that you can use to transform your capabilities. One simple and direct strategy is to participate in either a public or private sector retraining program. Some corporations provide retraining opportunities for people who are about to be laid off. There are also some private sector organizations that specialize in worker retraining programs. However, the public sector retraining programs are extensive and are sponsored by local level and national governments in many countries. Retraining has been presented by many economists and consultants as the fastest way of getting segments of the workforce to learn the new skills needed to work in new sectors. Another option, which is often used by individuals during economic downturns, is going back to school to acquire new degrees that will bolster their capabilities and make them more attractive employees to a variety of firms.

For individuals who might not have the time to return to school for a new degree, there is always the option of acquiring new certifications that can signal new competences in areas that are in demand. Most sectors have certifications that signal a higher level of competence for carrying out different types of domain activities. Some of these certifications have been mentioned in different sections of this book. Certifications alone are not usually enough to guarantee a new position but, coupled

Figure 6.1 Transferring your capabilities to new sectors or new locations

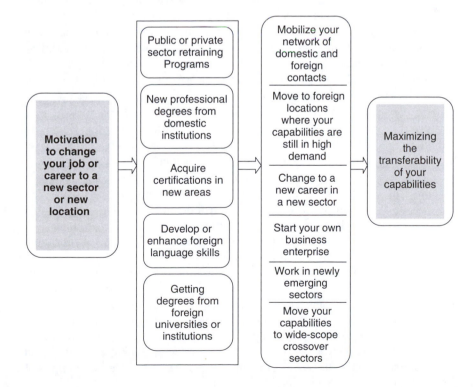

with capabilities from your previous positions, they can make you a more attractive candidate. Depending on your linguistic ability, another strategy that might pay dividends is to develop or enhance your foreign language skills. This is important, since many of the capabilities you have acquired in your local environment are quite often in high demand in other countries. You do not necessarily have to be fluent in that foreign language but a working knowledge increases your chances of finding a new position abroad.

For those who are considering a longer-term relocation to a foreign environment, one significant strategy is to get a degree from an institution in the country where you plan to work. This strategy is usually used at the initial stage of career development but it can also be used by those who have had an established career elsewhere. For many foreign environments, if you are not an expatriate, having a degree from a local institution connects you to the local network of employment intermediaries and gives your package of capabilities more legitimacy. Other benefits of attending the foreign institution include a better understanding of local business practices as well as creating a legitimate pathway for obtaining working visas or establishing permanent residency. There are also instances where a foreign institution may offer degrees in areas that are not offered in your home country. Getting that degree can then create employment opportunities abroad, as well as back in your home country.

The next set of strategies for maximizing transferability can be referred to as direct action strategies. Once you have repackaged or reconfigured your set of capabilities, there are a number of direct actions you can take to increase your chances of staying employed. The first strategy is mobilizing your network of domestic and foreign contacts. Personal and professional networks can alert you to employment opportunities that best fit your set of career capabilities. If you are willing to change countries, one increasingly popular strategy is to move to foreign locations where your capabilities are in high demand. This is especially true for knowledge workers who have clearly recognized competences that are in demand. In this case, the main challenge is not so much the packaging of your technical capabilities as it is adapting to the new environment.

Individuals who have seen employment in their chosen sector collapse can also choose to change to a new career in a new sector. They may be able to use some of their previous competences but, for the most part, these individuals have to start over in a new area. This move could be psychologically rewarding if they are fulfilling a long-held ambition, or it could be a chance for individuals to start over by reinventing themselves. One of the more courageous strategies for individuals who want to start over and gain more autonomy in the process is to start their own business. This is usually a difficult decision, because starting a business involves not only the use of your previously accumulated capabilities, but also requires the rapid development and application of new capabilities in a competitive environment.

The final two direct action strategies involve the active reworking of your capabilities to match new opportunities in new sectors. Finding work in newly-emerging sectors is an attractive option for those wanting to experience new competitive environments. The concept of "emerging sectors" can refer to many business activities, but there are some characteristics that are most salient. Firstly, emerging sectors represent business opportunities in a rapidly growing domain activity area. These sectors are considered emerging because they are driven by new technologies or significantly new applications of old technologies. Finally, innovation and network relations help the sectors grow in competitive environments. Examples of emerging sectors include sectors based on new medical, green, mobile location, or automotive technologies, as well as activities based on digital creative industries, social entrepreneurship, or social networking. Some newly emerging sectors can also be considered crossover sectors. This concept of the crossover sector is a new one that has been developed for this book, in order to explain some important sector characteristics.

Crossover sectors represent a viable alternative for transferring capabilities for individuals who are willing to adapt their competences and working styles. *The term "crossover sector" is used here to refer to those sectors that have a wide scope of domain activities and that make active use of a wide variety of domain technologies.* These sectors also tend to be open to using individuals from diverse careers and diverse technical backgrounds, since the main focus is on generating a wide range of solutions to a wide range of problems. Examples of some of these crossover sectors include consulting, government, the military, non-profit, international development, and the green sector. Later in this chapter, there will be a lengthier discussion of crossover sectors and an examination of the green and international development sectors. [1, 2]

TOPIC FOCUS

Foreign study has become an important development due, in part, to the globalization of educational institutions. As countries become major players in the global economy, they often seek to establish domestic institutions to educate their population and develop greatly needed knowledge workers. Consequently, there has been an expansion of colleges and universities in many countries around the world. Many of these institutions have set up undergraduate and graduate programs which focus on internationally-oriented educational degrees. A large percentage of these programs are organized to serve both domestic and foreign students.

A FOCUS ON EDUCATION & DEGREES FROM FOREIGN INSTITUTIONS

In many industrialized nations, educational institutions are competing with each other and other countries for students. The economic benefit of foreign students paying high tuition fees and bringing money into the country is clearly recognized by institutions and governments alike. These educational institutions have started to aggressively market the benefits of attending their institutions, and they often set up offices in foreign locations to facilitate recruitment. In rapidly-emerging economies, educational institutions are also establishing new programs and expanding their reach to other nations. This has created an international education market in many fields of study.

One result of these developments is a convergence toward recognizable educational standards and similar educational approaches for certain degrees. Language schools, colleges, and universities are all learning from successful programs elsewhere. To boost the quality of their instruction, many of these institutions around the world have actively invited foreign educators and professors into their organizations in order to bring in new knowledge and boost their reputation. Many of these institutions now operate with a mixture of domestic and foreign scholars and educators as they expand their educational programs. What has also helped many of these programs is the general international acceptance of certain degrees and certifications. More and more individuals with degrees from a wide range of international institutions are able to find employment based on these professional degrees. Individuals can now find a variety of reputable institutions worldwide that will offer degrees in fields such as international affairs, area studies, international development, international economics, international business, international management, sustainability, linguistics, languages, finance, logistics, hospitality, and even the liberal arts.

In addition to the goal of developing the knowledge and skills of individuals, what many of these internationally-oriented programs have in common is the goal of nurturing global citizens who can interact effectively with people in other parts of the world. With these goals in mind, many of these programs are taught in English as well as the local language. Some even push students to develop a proficiency in a third language. Another feature of many of these programs is that they participate in an international network of educational exchange programs. This makes it possible for students to spend as little as a few weeks to a year or more at one of these international institutions. In some nations, these international programs have strong local support because they boost the international reputation of the country. Sometimes local agencies or governments provide scholarships and other support systems for foreign students, since this is part of a national strategy to share the cultural or intellectual perspectives of the country. This type of strategy can be considered part of the national soft power approach that has been mentioned so frequently of late.

For individuals seeking to develop the capability, mobility, and transferability aspects of their career, studying at, or completing a degree at, a foreign educational institutional has a number of obvious benefits. It is potentially the most important step in developing a global mindset. By increasing their interaction with, and awareness of, foreign environments, individuals learn to deal effectively with global diversity. From a career perspective, this experience also makes it easier for individuals to work in a wider range of foreign environments. Another clear benefit is the opportunity to build up a network of friends, supporters, and advisers in a foreign environment. This network can be used later to support career development strategies or help with problem-solving issues in the foreign work environment. However, for many individuals who have used this strategy of studying at, or acquiring degrees from, foreign institutions, the main benefit is usually the opportunity to establish a pathway to gain a working visa or permanent residency status. Overall, it is much easier to gain entry into the foreign employment network if you have received a degree or have support from a reputable local educational institution.

As discussed in earlier chapters, the vast majority of individuals get access to work abroad experiences by way of expatriate assignments from international corporations. Nevertheless, we are increasingly seeing individuals develop their own strategy for finding employment overseas. For this reason, the study abroad strategy can be helpful at the initial or later stages of career management. For individuals who had a well established career or profession in their home country, getting a degree from a foreign institution is a way of gaining recognition for their capabilities as well making it easier to transfer their profession from one environment to another. In the next section, there will be a review of some international programs and institutions that are actively providing opportunities for individuals from different countries to gain valuable experience and degrees.

TOPIC FOCUS

As the importance of doing business across borders has grown, so too has the number of academic programs around the world that promise to develop and educate future employees and business leaders. For many years, the US was the best place to study some of the internationally-oriented disciplines, such as international business, international management, and international affairs. However, there has been a tremendous increase worldwide in the number of quality academic programs that have an international business, management, or international relations focus. This has given individuals in the US and elsewhere tremendous flexibility in choosing where and how they want to gain important international competences. Although these types of programs around the world are too numerous to present here, in the section below you will find a sample of some of the more interesting programs that individuals might consider. A longer list and description of American and foreign institutions offering good international programs is provided in the Appendix.

A SELECTION OF FOREIGN EDUCATIONAL PROGRAMS & INSTITUTIONS

Country: **Canada**
Program: The University of British Columbia: Bachelor of Commerce (BCom) in
International Business (source: ubc.ca)

International Business is one of the other nine options available through the BCom program. International Business students study abroad and must take at least 12 credits of a language other than English. In combining business, language, and international studies with study abroad, students are expected to enter the workforce with an excellent understanding of the international environment. This program also offers commerce-specific exchange programs and summer programs in Shanghai and Europe.

Country: **Mexico**
Program: Egade Business School; Tecnologico de Monterrey: MIB in International Business (source: egade.mx)

EGADE Business School offers a Masters in International Business. EGADE is located in Monterrey and it has various alliances with prestigious business schools in Europe and the USA. This gives their students a more international experience, by allowing them to go abroad as part of their program. The Master in International Business (MIB) is an 18 month, full-time program that begins annually in June or September. The program is oriented towards the mastering of international business and administrative methods. The courses are given in a face-to-face format in EGADE Business School, Monterrey.

Country: **Columbia**
Program: Universidad Del Norte: M.B.A in International Business (source: uninorte.edu.co)

Universidad Del Norte is located in Barranquilla, Colombia. This university offers undergraduate and graduate programs in International Business. The general goal is to develop highly qualified professionals and executives that understand, interact, and take advantage of the businesses opportunities that the new globalized world offers.

Country: **Japan**
Program: Waseda University, School of International Liberal Studies: BA. (source: waseda.jp)

Newly launched in 2004, the School of International Liberal Studies (SILS) at Waseda University has gained recognition and established a foothold as a unique educational and research organization. It has a multilingual focus, but English is the main language of instruction. SILS has graduated many excellent students that have gone on to very good positions in business and research. One year of study abroad is required for native Japanese students. SILS has focused its efforts toward the unprecedented, ambitious, aim of nurturing students who will excel in international organizations and businesses or continue their studies in graduate school. SILS also accepts a very high number of students from countries around the world either for short-term study or for the full four-year program.

Country: **Japan**
Program: Hitotsubashi University, Tokyo: MBA. Strategy (source: ics.hit-u. ac.jp)

The Graduate School of International Corporate Strategy (ICS) offers students the opportunity to earn an MBA degree in International Business Strategy at Hitotsubashi University. Students in the two year program have the option of custom-building their second year curriculum. Students consult with faculty members in choosing from a wide array of options, such as participating in a company internship program, spending a semester overseas in a student exchange program, developing a business plan for starting up a new venture, conducting an individual research project, or searching for post-MBA job opportunities. The classes are offered in English, and many of the teachers and advisors have worked in well-known Japanese and American businesses.

Country: China
Program: Shanghai University of Finance and Economics: International
            Business.
(source: shufe.edu.cn)

Designed for students interested in international business and economics, this program offers undergraduates the opportunity to study Chinese language, international business, and economic development. Students participate in carefully-designed activities and experiential study trips that provide a first-hand encounter with China's rapidly changing business environment. Classes are based at the International Cultural Exchange School (ICES) of the Shanghai University of Finance and Economics. ICES is devoted to training students with a background in international economics or management.

Country: India
Program: Amity International Business School: BBA, MBA (source: amity.
            edu)

Priding themselves as being "India's no. 1 ranked private university," Amity International Business School has a full-time three year bachelor's program which builds professionals for the future. Students are taught communication skills, how to conduct business internationally, and how to understand management concepts. Amity International Business School claims to offer a definite edge over other local international business programs because it provides a concentrated focus of study. This program is also beneficial for any student who wishes to gain better knowledge of India.

Country: Thailand
Program: Institute of International Studies (IIS-RU), Ramkhamhaeng University, Bangkok: BBA in International Business in English & Chinese. (source: iis.ru.ac.th)

This university offers a BBA in International Business in English and Chinese. The goal of the program is to prepare quality students who will graduate with advanced knowledge of business administration and technology. Students in the program are exposed to the use of new technology and new business strategies, so that they will be able to find positions in the public and private sectors. One part of the course deals with contract dynamics and commercial communications. Another part of the course focuses on trade fair exhibitions and good participations techniques with an emphasis on Thailand's multilateral and bilateral trade agreements.

Country: **France**
Program: INSEAD: MBA Program (source: mba.insead.edu)

INSEAD has two fully-integrated campuses in Europe and Asia. It offers an accelerated 10 month curriculum, in which the MBA Program runs on campuses in France and Singapore. Students also have the opportunity to take an elective course at the campus in Abu Dhabi or take advantage of an alliance with the Wharton School at the University of Pennsylvania. The program is designed to prepare students for a career in international business with an emphasis on group work and on international markets and settings.

Country: **Germany**
Program: European University, Munich: MBA (source: munich.euruni.edu)

This International Business Program's goal is to extend students' knowledge of theory and practice in the international business field. The program focuses on theory, business practice, law, analysis, and strategy. The school states that the international business program responds to the needs of business professionals who recognize that their skills and knowledge are going to be required in a diversity of organizational situations determined by the international nature of business transactions today. This covers the comprehensive knowledge needed to run many different areas of a business, while specializing in the specific skills needed to deal with the complexity of doing business across borders.

Country: **United Kingdom**
Program: Manchester Business School, University of Manchester: IBFE. (source: mbs.ac.uk)

The International Business, Finance and Economics (IBFE) Program takes an interdisciplinary approach to the study of business that is strongly informed by leading contemporary research. It offers competing and complementary perspectives on international business issues, largely from a social science perspective. The program's primary aim is to provide students with a knowledge and understanding of the international context of core business issues, whilst at the same time providing sufficient latitude to allow them to specialize in particular disciplines relevant to international business. Students also have the opportunity to learn a foreign language as part of their degree and can also apply to the exchange program in Singapore or Sweden in the second year.

Country: **United Kingdom**
Program: University of Sussex: BSc International Business. (source: sussex.
ac.uk)

The University of Sussex is located in southern England, about 70 miles south of London. It has been around since the early 1960s and, since then, has gained a significant amount of recognition for being a leading university in Europe. The International Business Program covers general business requirements alongside global business classes such as International Marketing and International HR Management. Since it is considered by some to be one of the best schools in Europe, graduates from the University of Sussex can often have a competitive advantage over others upon entering the professional world.

Country: **Netherlands**
Program: Arnhem Business School at HAN University in Arnhem: ABS.
(source: han.nl)

The ABS bachelor programs prepare students for an international career. Graduates are expected to have a sound understanding of business and managerial skills, both in theory and practice. To accomplish this, students have to study in English and choose a language in which they have not been educated, such as Dutch, French, German, or Spanish. ABS employs several international lecturers, mainly for the programs that are internationally-oriented. Foreign guest lecturers are frequently invited to lecture on specialist or topical subjects. Students take five to six modules per semester, and are also involved in interactive group projects which enable them to develop their practical skills.

Country: **UAE Dubai**
Program: University of Dubai: MBA in International Business (source:
ud.ac.ae)

The University of Dubai is located in Dubai, United Arab Emirates. This university offers an MBA in International Business and Marketing. The objective of this program is to develop an international leadership mindset and a strong foundation of management skills to in order to excel throughout one's career. The University of Dubai's MBA Program is designed to prepare business leaders and professionals for successful careers in organizations around the world. It focuses on critical thinking, oral and written communication skills, an appreciation for diverse cultural perspectives, and effective decision-making in a rapidly changing global environment. Ethics and corporate social responsibility are woven throughout the curriculum.

> **Country:**   **South Africa**
> Program: University of Cape Town, Graduate School of Business: MBA
> (source: gsb.uct.ac.za)
>
> The Graduate School of Business (GBS) wields a reputation for innovation and excellence. In 2009 it was voted by Ed universal as the top business school in Africa, in terms of influence. The GSB is one of just two business schools in South Africa to be accredited by the European Foundation for Management Development as a recognized centre of excellence in its field. The school's full-time MBA Program is also the only one in Africa to be ranked by the prestigious Financial Times Global Top 100 MBAs. With its roots in Africa, the GSB's goal is a leading emerging market business school that is both relevant and excellent.

TOPIC FOCUS

Transferring your capabilities from one position to a similar position in the same sector is the easiest type of job transition. However, it is a very different process when individuals try to move from a position in one sector to a new position in a new sector. Yet, transferability is a crucial strategy for those wishing to maintain their long-term employability. When a sector is facing difficulties and employment opportunities start to disappear, the best strategy for those not averse to moving is to go to a different domestic or international location where their particular set of competences are still in high demand. Although it is a much more difficult task to change from one sector to another, there are proven strategies, and long-term employability depends on effectively using these strategies.

A FOCUS ON CROSSOVER SECTORS & THE TRANSFERABILITY OF CAPABILITIES

If individuals must absolutely leave one sector to find employment in another, this book suggests one approach which can be very effective for those who have already accumulated some capabilities. That strategy is moving to a crossover sector. Moving one's capabilities to a crossover sector is achievable and has clear benefits. As mentioned earlier, crossover sectors are those that have a widescope of domain activities and also require a widerange of domain knowledge experts. The wider scope of activities provides individuals with the opportunity to reconfigure their capabilities to match a new position in the new sector. These crossover sectors are also more open to accepting individuals with differing educational background and technical expertise, since the focus is on finding solutions to a wide range of problems. As stated earlier, examples of some of these crossover sectors include consulting, government, the military, non-profit, international development, and the green sector. After identifying a target crossover sector, the next step is developing the strategy for reconfiguring your capabilities to transfer to a new position in a new sector. Figure 6.2 illustrates what the process of capability transfer to a new sector might look like.

Figure 6.2 The process of sector capability transfer

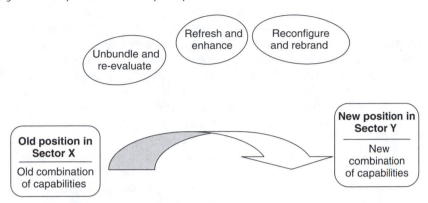

The whole process starts from the old position in the old sector. As is generally understood, each position is a combination of a set of capabilities which allows an individual to perform a range of duties and tasks. In order to take the serious step of moving to a new position in new sector, individuals need to have a clear process that increases their chances of finding a new fit. This usually starts with an unbundling and re-evaluation of old capabilities. Individuals need to find out which capabilities are lacking and which capabilities would best fit a new employment environment. The next step is to refresh old capabilities that might still be useful and then find ways to enhance or add new capabilities to the existing ones. This could be done through new certifications, new educational degrees, or some type of retraining program. Finally, the expanded range of capabilities needs to be reconfigured or rebranded in ways which signal that the individual is a good fit for the new demands of the new position in another sector. This process is not necessarily a one-time event. It might take place a number of times during the entire working life of an individual. In the next section, we will review various aspects of two crossover sectors.

TOPIC FOCUS

The two crossover sectors to be discussed below are both very important in the international business arena. The international development and green sectors not only have a global reach, but the strategies being used in them are changing business practices in fundamental ways. Both of them reflect the situation whereby the major domain activities are linked to different types of domain knowledge and also involve a wide range of stakeholders. Both sectors also benefit from strong grassroots movements around the world and both have benefited from the increasing importance of corporate social responsibility. Consequently, we see extensive participation in sector activities by individuals, non-profits, intergovernmental organizations, corporations, communities, and governments. [3–6]

Because of the wide range of activities and stakeholders in both sectors, it is difficult to quickly define and evaluate the core activities and major strategies. In both sectors, we see that, just by focusing on the profit motive, we are not able to justify the range of strategies and outcomes. Effective strategies in both sectors often have to balance the seemingly competing demands of people, planet and profits. In both cases, the developed world and the developing world have to work together to achieve meaningful long-term goals. Both sectors also have interesting and challenging job opportunities for individuals who wish to have strong international careers. There are many skill sets and knowledge-driven competencies that are in strong demand in both areas. Moreover, there are many entry points at the lower, mid and upper management levels in both sectors. However, since career paths are not as clear, it will require that individuals become proactive and goal-oriented as they map out successful career trajectories. However, more than most other sectors, careers in either international development or the green economy can bring personal satisfaction and rewards far beyond financial compensation. [7–10]

THE INTERNATIONAL DEVELOPMENT SECTOR

General Overview

The area of international development covers a wide range of activities and institutions around the world. Part of the difficulty in clearly evaluating this sector is its association with seemingly unrelated concepts, such as gender equality, disaster preparedness, water and sanitation, humanitarian aid, human rights, environmental protection, foreign aid, healthcare, education, economics, infrastructure, and institutional governance. However, one way of reconciling these activities is to realize that they are all linked by the goal of improving the quality of life through the development of the appropriate infrastructure and the building of effective economic, socio-cultural, health, and governance institutions. For the most part, development activities are aimed at alleviating poverty and improving living conditions in the developing world. Longer-term goals generally include the building of civil society, as well as sustainable economic, educational, and healthcare policies. [1, 2, 5, 6]

Though related to some foreign aid activities, international development differentiates itself by focusing on long-term growth and development issues in emerging and under-developed economies around the world. For that reason, these activities can often be found in many areas of Asia, Latin America, Africa, Eurasia, and emerging Europe. Over the years, the economic and infrastructure aspects of development were the ones that garnered the most attention. For many years, the focus was squarely on the impact of foreign aid and debt forgiveness. However, in recent years, there has been a strong debate over the effectiveness of the aid versus the investment model for developing emerging economies. In fact, many developing countries have begun to take advantage of the increasing competition for energy and raw materials. These countries have engaged in alliances and signed special development deals with private companies in return for a substantial infusion of development funds and infrastructure projects. There has also been a lot of effort put into expanding micro-finance activities in these areas so that entrepreneurship and basic business institutions can rapidly develop. [11–13]

International institutions play a very significant role in the development sector. If we examine the Millennium Development Goals supported by the United Nations, we get a clearer picture of the range of concerns. Below is the declaration of eight Millennium Development Goals that are to be accomplished between 2015 and 2020 (source: un.org/millenniumgoals):

Goal 1: Eradicate extreme poverty and hunger

Goal 2: Achieve universal primary education

Goal 3: Promote gender equality and empower women

Goal 4: Reduce child mortality rate

Goal 5: Improve maternal health

Goal 6: Combat HIV/AIDS, malaria, and other diseases

Goal 7: Ensure environmental sustainability

Goal 8: Develop a global partnership for development

Structure of the Sector

It is not easy to get a clear understanding of the structure of the international development sector. As indicated above, it is a sector defined by the common goals that a wide range of institutions and stakeholders undertake in a particular environment. When we consider that private companies, non-profits, intergovernmental, and governmental organizations represent the various types of institutions actively involved in development activities, we realize the tremendous scope of sector domain activities (Table 6.1). The best approach to understanding the underlying structure might be to consider the major activity areas of the international development sector. The economic, humanitarian, educational, socio-cultural, healthcare,

Table 6.1 Institutions and activities in the international development sector

Economic and humanitarian	Education and socio-cultural	Healthcare and infrastructure
IMF, World Bank, the Red Cross, Center for Global Development (CGD), International Service for Human Rights (ISHR), Grameen Bank, micro-finance firms, FINCA, USAID, IDB, WBCSD, ICT, Accion International, Amnesty International, HRW, CARE . . . etc.	UN, WHO, ISHR, Peace Corps, the Academy for Educational Development (AED), Teach for America, World Neighbors, UNESCO, UNICEF, WBCSD, ICT programs, World Learning, RAN, civil society programs: CSSP, CSPP . . . etc	UN, WHO, Doctors without Borders, CGD, Partners in Health (PIH), the Red Cross, UNICEF, ICT4 Dev (ICT) programs, Overseas Development Institute (ODI), CHF International, Water Partners International, ACDI/VOCA, AAH . . . etc

and infrastructure arenas represent the dominant areas of the sector (Table 6.1). In development projects, these six activity areas are not always separate, and we often find major projects that span a number of the arenas. In fact, it is often argued that effective development strategies need to address a number of arenas at the same time. These characteristics make international development an exemplary crossover sector. [11, 12, 14]

In international development, some of the major players include the IMF, World Bank, and the UN. Many smaller development and aid agencies often follow their lead. The UN can be considered a leader in this area, since it has set the above mentioned Millennium Goals to be reached by 2025. Although the IMF is a central player in the economic sphere, many other institutions are involved in a wide array of projects to provide financing and economic development support to nations in need. One of the newest trends is the increasing role played by micro-finance institutions that provide micro-credit to individuals and groups. Micro-credit is the extension of small loans for the purpose of spurring entrepreneurship and self-reliance in developing communities. Micro-finance institutions now provide a wide range of financial services to the very poor. As if to highlight the success of this development model, the 2006 Nobel Peace Prize was awarded jointly to Muhammad Yunus and the Grameen Bank for their pioneering work in providing micro-finance. [3, 13, 15]

Since the lack of access to education is a major obstacle to human development, most development projects usually include an educational component. The development of reliable healthcare systems involves infrastructure, technology, and educational and training issues that impact many stakeholders. The World Health Organization (WHO) is a leading organization in this area, but other institutions, such as the United Nations (UN), the Center for Global Development (CDG), Partners in Health (PIH), UNICEF, the Red Cross and Doctors without Borders all play major roles in healthcare. [2, 16, 17]

Development activities occur in organizations of all sizes. There are many large, medium-sized and smaller non-profit, intergovernmental agencies and private firms supporting various projects and initiatives. Since the general focus is not on the profitability or competitiveness of the sector, as in most business environments, different approaches need to be taken to evaluate the effectiveness of these organizations. The general impact on stakeholders is usually the first thing that should be considered in evaluating these development organizations and programs. An outcome perspective could look at the improvement in infrastructure, healthcare, and general living standards to gauge sector effectiveness in various regions. However, because of the need for alliances that incorporate many organizational types and objectives, the international development sector remains a difficult one in which to clearly gauge competitiveness. [17–19]

The International Dimension

The international development sector's activities involve the international community. However, the vast majority of development activities are mainly concentrated in underdeveloped or emerging markets around the world. The global nature of the field, and the complexity of the goals, often cause non-profits, intergovernmental, and private agencies and firms to work together in shifting alliances. The temporal aspect of their activities can be separated into emergency, short-term, medium and long-term projects and goals. The IMF, for example, has from time to time extended emergency loans to countries in Asia, Latin America, and Africa, to help them deal with sudden economic shocks or natural disasters. Another example is that of the Inter-American Development Bank (IDB) that has provided loans, grants, and investments to fund development projects throughout Latin America and the Caribbean. [4, 20, 21]

The global CSR (corporate social responsibility) movement has given a tremendous boost to development activities in different parts of the world. There is a growing belief by many corporations that "they can do well by doing good" around the world. Many private corporations are becoming more actively involved in creating and funding development projects so that they can position themselves as socially responsible. Other firms have also developed "bottom-of-the-pyramid" (BOP) strategies to cultivate and expand business activities to the poor in many countries. With some emerging market economies growing rapidly and, consequently, expanding their middle class, firms are also seeing new market opportunities in the developing world. [3, 22, 23]

Another important international activity in the development arena is the expanded use of the digital economy, and digital strategies, to tackle developmental problems. Creating, accessing, and disseminating information has become a crucial aspect to many international development projects. Organizations, governments, and regions are able to interact more freely and share solutions to similar problems. Open-source software and the "one-laptop per child" projects, for example, have gained serious traction and have become an important part of the digital strategies to boost development efforts around the world. These and other factors demonstrate that overall, the international development sector provides many strategies for the improvement of global living standards. [24–26]

Sector-Related Jobs & Careers

As stated earlier, there are numerous institutions, corporations and governments that are actively involved in the international development sector. We also can see that there are a wide range of activities and projects that are constantly being undertaken in this sector. Consequently, the scope of careers within the international development sector is as extensive as the varied regions and domain activities around the world. Despite the variety of organizations involved in international development, there is a general impression that non-profit institutions dominate most of the development activities. The reality is that most projects involve numerous stakeholders and non-profits are increasingly working with private firms, governmental, and intergovernmental organizations at all stages of development activities. [18, 27, 28]

Because of the global nature of the sector and the extensive scope of development activities, it is now possible to start, develop, and finish one's career in the international development sector. Yet, since it is a crossover sector, we often see people from many different backgrounds and professions finding new careers in various areas of international development. One of the main attractions of this sector is the numerous points of entry and numerous strategies for participating in international development. In effect, work in international development is supported by many types of careers in many sub-sectors. One can choose to be a generalist or a specialist, in areas such as human rights, education, healthcare, micro-finance, economics, information technology, water and sanitation, governance assistance, or general infrastructure development. There are also many entry level, mid-career, and upper management jobs in all of the various sub-sectors of international development. [10, 20, 29]

International development is also a great sector for exploring internships, since many non-profits and other institutions offer opportunities to students and recent college graduates to work in different regions and areas of development. Some of the organizations that are known to offer internships or entry level positions include the Peace Corps, World Learning, International Development Exchange, USAID, the World Bank Group and many others. Mid-career jobs in international development consist of technical or management jobs in a variety of fields. Top level positions usually entail running, managing, or providing consulting or high-level technical support for development projects. There are five main career areas that are central to most international development activities: project manager, technical expert, researcher, field work, and consultant. The required capabilities linked to each position will vary depending on the development activity and the nature of the organizations involved. Due to the nature of the sector, all of these positions require adaptability, dedication, and competence. In the Appendix you can find key links to important development organizations and activities. [9, 19, 30–33]

THE GREEN SECTOR

General Overview

The "green sector" is more a unifying concept across production and service activities than a clearly delineated description of one specific set of domain activities. In many ways, it can even be considered a transformational movement that is impacting the way business is carried out around the world. The various ideas and activities associated with the green sector are so numerous that a simple definition would misrepresent its true scope. This makes it another great example of a crossover sector. Along with the concept of the green sector, we often hear the concepts of the "green economy" and "green jobs." Underlying all these "green concepts" is the belief that it is possible to foster economic growth while at the same time ensuring that there are (1) no long-term negative environmental impacts; (2) improved health, social and working conditions; and (3) more effective use of renewable energy and other productive resources. Given this definition, one approach to measuring success in the green sector is to evaluate its impact on the triple bottom line: people, planet, and profit. The assumption is that, by focusing on the triple bottom line, it is possible to achieve success at the social, ecological, and economic levels simultaneously. [34–38].

It is important to point out that just making a few green products and services does not automatically make a company entirely green. In essence, we might say that there are different stages of green for companies, from a partial to full participation in producing green products and services. For a company to be considered "fully green," it must commit to continually incorporating environmentally friendly and sustainable business practices. [39–42]. The green sector is so broad that it includes domain activities in areas such as renewable energy, energy systems installations and storage, energy efficient buildings, transportation, alternative fuels, water management, waste management, and farming. The concept of "green" has grown over the years, and now includes both sustainable and environmentally friendly practices and strategies. This is also a sector where actions by individuals can also have a significant impact over time. Environmentally friendly and sustainable practices are the most common ways that individuals can contribute. Simple practices such as recycling, buying more locally grown products, and energy conservation, all help to reduce our "carbon footprint" on the planet. [7, 36, 43, 44]

For many countries, the "greening of industries" has become a significant strategy in their drive for economic competitiveness and sustainable economic development. Greening strategies not only bring down long term costs, they can revitalize many older sectors, create new jobs, and open new market opportunities. More and more each day, companies around the world are participating in the act of "going green" as a way of reducing their negative impact on the environment as well as generating a positive brand image through corporate social responsibility (CSR) practices. [6, 45–47]

Structure of the Sector

A number of researchers have explained the structure of the green sector by focusing on six major activity areas: renewable energy, green building, clean transportation, water management, waste management, and land management. This is a good categorization, since we can include both the type of technologies used as well as the main production or service activity areas. Another approach to understanding the green sector is to look at the major stakeholders that are impacted by its objectives and strategies. In addition to interest groups in each of the areas mentioned above, there are private companies, governmental, intergovernmental and non-governmental organizations (NGOs) that are key influencers in the investing and promoting of the green sector. [48–51]

Many local and international organizations dedicate themselves to improving the environment for people and communities all around the world. These organizations often work in collaboration with businesses, development agencies, labor departments, and governmental agencies to develop and execute projects that boost sustainability and reduce negative impacts on the environment. International organizations such as the United Nations Environment Program (UNEP) work with businesses to fund green development projects. [52–55]

In the United States, a key stakeholder and governmental organization is the Environmental Protection Agency (EPA). In its mission statement, the EPA states that its goal is to protect human health and the environment. The agency accomplishes this by the developing and enforcing of environmental regulations. On its website, the EPA lists five strategic goals that guide the agency's work: [42, 56]

1. Taking action on climate change and improving air quality

2. Protecting America's waters

3. Cleaning up communities and advancing sustainable development

4. Ensuring the safety of chemicals and preventing pollution

5. Enforcing environmental laws

Beyond the impact of regulations, innovation is a driving force for most green companies. It goes without saying that new ideas, strategies, business models, and technologies are what allow green companies to be competitive with firms that do not have similar environmental and sustainability restraints. The green sector is not limited to new and relatively unknown firms. Large companies like PG & E, Wal-Mart and Starbucks are beginning to be influenced by the green movement. Recently, the online magazine Inc. put together a list of 50 of the most intriguing companies driving the green revolution in the US. Table 6.2 shows that these innovative companies participate in wide variety of domain activities. [48, 57, 58]

The International Dimension

As global consciousness has moved in the direction of creating sustainable business practices, we see major efforts underway in developing the green sector worldwide. The global economic impact of the green sector is now huge and growing. Over the years, the sector has received numerous grants from governments trying to support environmentally friendly and sustainable business practices. This continues to be the case and, in 2011, the United Nations called for 2 percent of worldwide income to be invested in the green economy. There are several large intergovernmental organizations that advocate for the adoption of environmentally friendly policies and regulations. The United Nations Industrial Development Organization (UNIDO), the United Nations Environment Program (UNEP), the European Environment Agency (EEA), and the Intergovernmental Panel on Climate Change (IPCC) are all intergovernmental organizations that lobby for the positive impact of green regulations and policies. In fact, many economists now say that the only path to sustainable long-term economic growth is through investment in the green economy. [5, 51, 55, 59, 60]

Table 6.2 The "Green 50"

The industrialist	The recyclers	The pioneers
Interface	ReCellular	Eden Foods
	Excellent Packaging	Clif Bar
The road crew	& Supply	Seventh Generation
Tesla Motors	TerraCycle	Stonyfield Farm
Extengine Transport Systems	Recycline	Collins Cos.
IdleAire		
Prometheus Energy	**The integrators**	**The builders**
Zipcar	Frog's Leap Winery	AFM
	Comet Skateboards	Michelle Kaufmann
The futurists	New Belgium Brewery	Designs
Gridpoint	NaturaLawn of America	American Clay
Cilion	Konarka Technologies	Teragren
CoalTek	Memorial Ecosystems	IceStone
EnerTech Environmental	Seahorse Power	IBC Engineering Services
Energy Innovations	Southwest Windpower	
Verdant Power	Affordable Internet	**The converts**
Nanosolar	Services Online	Burgerville
GreenFuel Technologies	Teko Socks	Hayward Corp.
GreatPoint Energy	Vivavi	GreenOrder
BlackLight Power	Voltaic Systems	Pantheon Chemical
	Zoots	Ryzex Group
		New Leaf Paper

Source: Adapted from *Inc.* online magazine (2011): inc.com/green/

Brazil's production of biofuels represents one of the largest transformations any area in the green sector. Currently, renewable resources account for 43.8 percent of Brazil's total energy consumption and this is the highest percentage in the world. Brazil is clearly one of the leaders in the production of biofuels, and the phenomenon has the potential of significantly affecting the people's way of life. In a similar way, countries like India and China are expected to put over a trillion dollars into the green sector over the next decade. However, the industry is still fairly young and we still do not see dominant monopolies in most regions. Nevertheless, there are companies that have begun to separate themselves from the pack and are becoming more dominant. Some of the top producers in the renewable energy sector in the world include First Solar, Suntech, Sharp Solar, Siemens, Q-cell, Yingli, JA Solar, Kyocera, Trina Solar, SunPower, Gintech, SunOpta, and Vestas. In addition, many organic farming and sustainable environment-oriented companies are also spreading worldwide. There is also increasing activity in green consulting. International consulting groups like Blue Skye are becoming more common as the sector becomes more advanced. [40, 61–64].

It is significant that international competition to obtain green business is at an all-time high. Many countries increasingly see the green economy as an important component of their GDP. Although the companies that develop the new green technologies are mostly in developed nations, we are seeing a strong push to make green products and technologies more affordable for developing nations. Some people see the green sector as playing a critical role in poverty alleviation, by promoting energy security, improving health conditions, creating green jobs, and making business operations more sustainable. Overall, the green sector has become a transformational movement and a major factor in economic development strategies for both developing and developed countries. [43, 46, 47, 52, 65, 66]

Sector-Related Jobs & Careers

As the green sector expands, employment in the green economy has been increasing. In 2008, the wind industry surpassed the coal industry in the US for total people employed. Wind jobs increased to 85,000 while coal industry jobs remained at around 81,000. All expectations are that green jobs will continue expanding while old technology sectors will continue to lose jobs. It is estimated that, as of 2006, there were just more than 750,000 green jobs in the US economy. The numbers have since increased significantly. Green jobs are generally distributed across the country. However, about 85 percent are located in metropolitan areas, with the remaining 15 percent in non-metropolitan areas. Recently, the top 10 areas for green jobs are New York, Washington DC, Houston, Los Angeles, Boston, Chicago, Philadelphia, San Francisco, San Diego, and Pittsburgh. [8, 45, 58, 67, 68]

The wide range of green jobs include electricians, plumbers, solar panel installers, construction, financial, engineers, green architects, secretaries, accountants, building inspectors, researchers, and farmers. In terms of top management, some of the occupations connected to the green sector include warehouse recycling manager, environmental health and safety managers, alternative fuel vehicle infrastructure engineers, and transportation program specialists. Based on the observations above, we can see that the green economy has caused significant shifts in the demand for certain occupations, as well as the skills, knowledge, and credentials necessary to be a successful worker in the field. [40, 53]

In terms of the educational requirements for the different occupations in the field, they vary by the level of skill and technology needed. Some technical and scientific occupations require significant post-secondary education. On the other hand, some less-skilled occupations require certifications or short-term training. Despite the skill levels, most individuals who want to be qualified to work long-term in the green sector will need some kind of certification in a core area of activity. Some of the main certifications include LEED-AP (Leadership in Energy and Environmental Design), PE (Professional Engineer), PMP (Project Management Professional), CCM (Certified Construction Manager), CPEA (Certified Environmental Auditor) and CWO (Certified Water Treatment Plant Operator). [7, 8, 39, 50, 69, 70]

The current distribution of green jobs shows that Brazil, the US, China, and Germany are home to the greatest number of green jobs. The findings of the UNEP 2008 report identify six key areas that will provide the majority of green jobs around the world. These areas are energy, transportation, industry, buildings, agriculture, and forestry. Clearly, the green economy is global. Countries such as Denmark, Germany, Spain, and Japan are already busy investing in wind and solar research as well as construction and manufacturing related to green activities. According to some sources, the European Union and China are investing considerably more than the US in the sector. The 2008 United Nations Environment Program (UNEP) report projects that the global market for green goods and services will more than double, moving from $1.37 billion per year to $2.74 billion by 2020. The report estimates total green jobs employment of about 20 million by 2030. [35, 51, 55, 56, 58]

Investing in business activities that create green jobs is one important strategy in developing careers in the green sector. Training, skill development, and certification options are also as important in getting new green careers established. In terms of searching for jobs locally, many people are using websites such as greenjobsearch. org and greencollarblog.org to find out about green jobs. Sites like these not only display an array of green collar jobs, but also share knowledge on how one can practice green collar job tactics in current jobs. In terms of the international geographic distribution of these new jobs and careers, they will most likely be in the countries following aggressive green strategies. However, it is important to point out that major non-profit and public works projects will also impact the trajectory of green jobs and careers in developing countries. These green sector-related development activities should provide significant local employment opportunities in regions such as Africa, Asia and South America, while simultaneously bringing in health and infrastructure benefits. Whatever the approach, the best way for the green sector to grow is through education. Whether it is educating the public, educating consumers, or educating potentially new workers about green jobs, the more people are aware of the economic, social, and health benefits of the green economy, the more central a role the sector will play in economic competitiveness. [6, 8, 35, 67, 70, 71]

CHAPTER SUMMARY & OBSERVATIONS

The goal of this chapter was to present strategies for maximizing the transferability of your capabilities. This is extremely important for individuals who are facing the loss of continued employment in their sector or local area. In order to maintain their employability, individuals have to re-evaluate their capabilities and devise methods for transferring them to an area or sector where they might be in greater demand. With that in mind, transferability was defined as the ability to adapt and mobilize business, technical, psychological, and cross-cultural skills in ways that boosts one's employability in different sectors, regions, and national environments. Subsequently, a two-stage model highlighted the transferability aspect of the personalized resource management perspective. The first stage showed academic and vocational development activities that can help you retool your capabilities. The second stage presented direct action strategies for moving your capabilities to other sectors or working environments.

Later in the chapter, two strategies for increasing the transferability of capabilities were explored. The use of foreign educational institutions and crossover sectors were shown to be key adaptation strategies for boosting transferability. An important observation from the point of view of international career development is that individuals can now find a variety of reputable institutions worldwide that will offer degrees in fields such as international affairs, area studies, international development, international economics, international business, international management, sustainability, linguistics, languages, finance, logistics, hospitality, and even the liberal arts. Foreign institutions not only provide legal access to a new employment environment, they also expose individuals to the new skills, business practices, and professional networks that increase the chances of finding employment in that area.

The concept of the "crossover sector" was also introduced, in order to point out certain sector characteristics that could make it easier to transfer capabilities. Crossover sectors were defined as those that have a wide scope of domain activities and also require a wide range of domain knowledge experts. This wider scope of activities provides individuals with the opportunity to reconfigure their capabilities to match a new position in a new sector. These crossover sectors were also characterized as more open to accepting individuals with different educational background and technical expertise, since the focus is on finding solutions to a wide range of problems. Finally, in-depth analyses of the international development and green sectors showed why they are now the source of different types of jobs and career paths.

Chapter 7 will explore international business capabilities in ways that show how individuals can build a successful international career. The chapter will also present the personal capability pyramid that shows how a hierarchy of skills can support different careers in international business. The chapter will clarify the distinctions between concepts such as skill, knowledge, competence, and capability that are often used to discuss careers in international business. The second half of Chapter 7 will re-introduce the personalized resource management approach from a more practical point of view. A model will show the six practical strategies that will help an individual build, target, and apply their capabilities in the employment arena in ways that enhance their long-term employability. Overall, the chapter will provide clear analytical insights into which competencies can give individuals a competitive advantage in different employment arenas around the world.

REFERENCES

1. Alexander, D., *Beyond aid: The future of international development.* Public Policy Research, 2008. **15**(1): p. 48.
2. Chibba, M., *Poverty reduction in developing countries.* World Economics, 2008. **9**(1): p. 197.
3. Goldsmith, A., *Is governance reform a catalyst for development?* Governance, 2007. **20**(2): p. 165.
4. Luiz, J., *Institutions and economic performance: Implications for African development.* Journal of International Development, 2009. **21**(1): p. 58.

5. Chapple, K., et al., *Innovation in the green economy: An extension of the regional innovation system model?* Economic Development Quarterly, 2011. **25**(1): p. 5.

6. Cruz, L.B. and E.A. Pedrozo, *Corporate social responsibility and green management.* Management Decision, 2009. **47**(7): p. 1174.

7. Braun, P., *Going green: Women entrepreneurs and the environment.* International Journal of Gender and Entrepreneurship, 2010. **2**(3): p. 245.

8. Waits, J.P., J.P. Wallace, and S. Smith, *Green jobs don't grow on trees.* Business Perspectives, 2010. **20**(3): p. 29.

9. Stanton, M., *Work around the world.* Occupational Outlook Quarterly, 1986. **30**(2): p. 20.

10. Welch, C., D. Welch and M. Tahvanainen, *Managing the HR dimension of international project operations.* The International Journal of Human Resource Management, 2008. **19**(2): p. 205.

11. Ball, R., *Cultural values and public policy: The case of international development aid.* Quarterly Review of Economics and Finance, 2010. **50**(1): p. 3.

12. Decker, J. and J. Lim, *What fundamentally drives growth? Revisiting the institutions and economic performance debate.* Journal of International Development, 2008. **20**(5): p. 698.

13. Dessy, S. and D. Vencatachellum, *Debt relief and social services expenditure: The African experience, 1989–2003.* African Development Review, 2007. **19**(1): p. 200.

14. Bowden, S., B. Chiripanhura and P. Mosley, *Measuring and explaining poverty in six African countries: A long-period approach.* Journal of International Development, 2008. **20**(8): p. 1049.

15. Hudon, M., *Management of microfinance institutions: Do subsidies matter?* Journal of International Development, 2010. **22**(7): p. 890.

16. Chari-wagh, A., *Raising citizenship rights for women through microcredit programmes: An analysis of MASUM, Maharashtra, India.* Community Development Journal, 2009. **44**(3): p. 403.

17. Zingerli, C., *A Sociology of international research partnerships for sustainable development.* The European Journal of Development Research, 2010. **22**(2): p. 217.

18. Presbitero, A., *Institutions and geography as sources of economic development.* Journal of International Development, 2006. **18**(3): p. 351.

19. Stallings, B., *Globalization and labor in four developing regions: An institutional approach.* Studies in Comparative International Development, 2010. **45**(2): p. 127.

20. Moore, K., *Development through business: What do American business students know about emerging markets and opportunities in Africa?* Journal of Teaching in International Business, 2010. **21**(3): p. 200.

21. Shellenbarger, S., *The job that follows you wherever you may roam,* Wall Street Journal, 26 July 2007: p. D1.

22. Barkemeyer, R., *Beyond compliance – Below expectations? CSR in the context of international development.* Business Ethics, 2009. **18**(3): p. 273.

23. Kaja, A. and E. Werker, *Corporate governance at the World Bank and the dilemma of global governance.* The World Bank Economic Review, 2010. **24**(2): p. 171.

24. Kay, S., *IS abroad: It's not just a job.* Computerworld, 1989. **23**(31): p. 74.

25. Simons, J., *Adventurous IS folk wanted.* Computerworld, 1990. **24**(37): p. 104.

26. Thompson, M., *ICT and development studies: Towards development 2.0.* Journal of International Development, 2008. **20**(6): p. 821.

27. Jordan, S. and T. Bird, *The evolving links between business and international development agencies in PPPs.* International Trade Forum, 2009(4): p. 24.

28. Sherraden, M.S., et al., *The forms and structure of international voluntary service.* Voluntas, 2006. **17**(2): p. 156.

29. Heeks, R., *Emerging markets development 2.0: The IT-enabled transformation of international development.* Association for Computing Machinery. Communications of the ACM, 2010. **53**(4): p. 22.

30. Bach, J. and D. Stark, *Innovative ambiguities: NGOs' use of interactive technology in eastern Europe.* Studies in Comparative International Development, 2002. **37**(2): p. 3.

31. Callaghan, P. and E. Walmann, *Meeting new learning challenges: How IDI and OLACEFS delivered the*

first regional e-learning workshop. International Journal of Government Auditing, 2006. **33**(3): p. 17.

32. Leftwich, A. and K. Sen, *"Don't mourn: organize" institutions and organizations in the politics and economics of growth and poverty-reduction.* Journal of International Development, 2011. **23**(3): p. 319.

33. Logue, A., *Trainer: Will travel.* Training & Development, 2001. **55**(4): p. 46.

34. Dart, R. and S. Hill, *Green matters?: An exploration of environmental performance in the nonprofit sector.* Nonprofit Management and Leadership, 2010. **20**(3): p. 295.

35. Hamdouch, A. and M. Depret, *Policy integration strategy and the development of the "green economy": Foundations and implementation patterns.* Journal of Environmental Planning and Management, 2010. **53**(4): p. 473.

36. Harvey, F. *Green economy needs 2% of every nation's income says UN.* 2011 [cited 2011, Feb. 24]. Available from: http://www.guardian.co.uk/environment/2011/feb/20/green-economy-energy.

37. Ong, P. and R. Patraporn, *The economic development potential of the green sector,* 2006, Los Angeles, CA: Ralph and Goldy Lewis Center for Regional Policy Studies. p. 30.

38. Triple_Bottom. *Triple bottom line: Sustainable business strategies,* 2011. Available from: http://www.getsustainable.net/.

39. Fine, J., *When the rubber hits the high road: Labor and community complexities in the greening of the garden state.* Labor Studies Journal, 2011. **36**(1): p. 122.

40. McDonald, S., et al., *Comparing sustainable consumption patterns across product sectors.* International Journal of Consumer Studies, 2009. **33**(2): p. 137.

41. BLS. *Overview of the BLS green jobs initiative.* 2011 [cited 2011, Feb.20]. Available from: http://www.bls.gov/green/.

42. EPA. *Our Mission and What We Do.* 2011 [cited 2011 Feb. 10]. Available from: http://www.epa.gov/aboutepa/whatwedo.html.

43. Albino, V., A. Balice and R. Dangelico, *Environmental strategies and green product development: An overview on sustainability-driven companies.* Business Strategy and the Environment, 2009. **18**(2): p. 83.

44. Energy_Race. *Who's winning the clean energy race?* 2011 [cited 2011, Feb. 12]. Available from: http://www.pewtrusts.org/uploadedFiles/wwwpewtrustsorg/Reports/Global_warming/G-20%20Report.pdf.

45. PEW. *Pew findsclean energy economy generages significant job growth.* 2009 [cited 2011, Feb. 20]. Available from: http://www.pewtrusts.org/news_room_detail.aspx?id=53254.

46. Watts, J. *China plots course for green growth amid a boom built on dirty industry.* 2011 [cited 2011, Feb. 16]. Available from: http://www.guardian.co.uk/world/2011/feb/04/china-green-growth-boom-industry?INTCMP=SRCH.

47. Whitlock, C. *Cloudy Germany a powerhouse in solar energy.* 2007 [cited 2011, Feb. 24]. Available from: http://www.washingtonpost.com/wp-dyn/content/article/2007/05/04/AR2007050402466.html.

48. Plumb, I. and A.-I. Zamfir, *A comparative analysis of green certificates markets in the European Union.* Management of Environmental Quality, 2009. **20**(6): p. 684.

49. Rivera-Camino, J., *Re-evaluating green marketing strategy: A stakeholder perspective.* European Journal of Marketing, 2007. **41**(11/12): p. 1328.

50. Jackson, J. and K. Rogers. *A green economy will keep growing.* 2010 [cited 2011, Feb. 12]. Available from: http://www.cnn.com/2010/OPINION/08/24/jackson.rogers.green.jobs/index.html.

51. Lindstrom, E. *Green industries and jobs in California.* 2009 [cited 2011, Feb. 10]. Available from: http://www.coeccc.net/green/.

52. Shukla, A.C., S. Deshmukh and A. Kanda, *Environmentally responsive supply chains.* Journal of Advances in Management Research, 2009. **6**(2): p. 154.

53. Zhang, Z., *Asian energy and environmental policy: Promoting growth while preserving the environment.* Energy Policy, 2008. **36**(10): p. 3905.

54. Bradsher, K. *China leading global race to make clean energy.* 2010 [cited 2011, Feb. 21]. Available

from:http://www.nytimes.com/2010/01/31/business/energy-environment/31renew.html.

55. UNEP. *UNEP background paper on green jobs.* 2008 [cited 2011, Feb. 26]. Available from: http://www.unep.org/labour_environment/pdfs/green-jobs-background-paper-18–01–08.pdf.

56. Richardson, B., *Climate finance: Regulatory and funding strategies for climate change and global development.* Carbon & Climate Law Review: CCLR, 2010. **4**(1): p. 116.

57. Stankeviciute, L. and P. Criqui, *Energy and climate policies to 2020: The impacts of the European "20/20/20" approach.* International Journal of Energy Sector Management, 2008. **2**(2): p. 252.

58. Ucci, M., *Sustainable buildings, pro-environmental behaviour and building occupants: A challenge or an opportunity?* Journal of Retail & Leisure Property, 2010. **9**(3): p. 175.

59. Chan, E., Q. Qian and P. Lam, *The market for green building in developed Asian cities: The perspectives of building designers.* Energy Policy, 2009. **37**(8): p. 3061.

60. IEA. *About IEA.* 2011 [cited 2011, March 29]. Available from: http://www.iea.org/about/index.asp.

61. Horwitch, M. and B. Mulloth, *The interlinking of entrepreneurs, grassroots movements, public policy and hubs of innovation: The rise of Cleantech in New York City.* Journal of High Technology Management Research, 2010. **21**(1): p. 23.

62. Windsor, S., *Understanding green.* The Journal for Quality and Participation, 2011. **33**(4): p. 26.

63. Pollin, R. *Building the green economy: Employment effects of green investments for Ontario.* 2010 [cited 2011, Feb. 12]. Available from: www.greenenergyact.ca.

64. Richtel, M. and J. Markoff. *A green energy industry takes root in California,* The New York Times, 2008 [cited 2011, Feb. 14]. Available from: http://www.nytimes.com/2008/02/01/technology/01solar.html.

65. Aizawa, M. and C. Yang, *Green credit, green stimulus, green revolution? China's mobilization of banks for environmental cleanup.* Journal of Environment & Development, 2010. **19**(2): p. 119.

66. El Dief, M. and X. Font, *The determinants of hotels' marketing managers' green marketing behaviour.* Journal of Sustainable Tourism, 2010. **18**(2): p. 157.

67. Green, M., *Government workforce of the future: Four key trends.* Public Manager, 2010. **39**(2): p. 13.

68. Hasler, J., *Are green jobs for real?* . Popular Mechanics, 2009. **186**(12): p. 98–102.

69. Hintons, A. *Job certifications and licenses you will need in the green economy.* 2009. Available from: http://www.usgbc.org/

70. Renner, M., S. Sweeney and S. Kubit, *Job prospects in a low-carbon world.* Environment & Poverty Times, 2009(6).

71. Rodriguez, J.-P. and C. Comtois. *Transportation and energy: The geography of transport systems.* 2011 [cited 2011, Feb. 10]. Available from: http://people.hofstra.edu/geotrans/eng/ch8en/conc8en/ch8c2en.html.

PART III

A FOCUS ON STRATEGIES FOR DEVELOPING YOUR INTERNATIONAL BUSINESS CAREER

7 EXPLORING STRATEGIES FOR ESTABLISHING YOUR INTERNATIONAL BUSINESS CAREER

LEARNING OBJECTIVES

- Understand strategies for establishing an international business career

- Examine the role of the business capability pyramid

- Explore the fundamental competencies of international business

- Review skill assessment options

- Initiate the proactive career management cycle

THE ROADMAP

In Chapter 6 you were presented with strategies for maximizing the transferability of your international career capabilities. Transferability was defined as the ability to adapt and mobilize business, technical, psychological, and cross-cultural skills in ways which boost one's employability in different sectors, regions, or national environments. A two-stage model was presented which focused on the transferability aspect of the personalized resource management perspective. The first stage showed how academic and vocational development activities could help individuals retool their capabilities. The second stage emphasized direct action strategies for moving your capabilities to other sectors and working environments. The importance of foreign educational institutions in developing and expanding international career capabilities was also highlighted. Finally, Chapter 6 examined the process of capability transfer and showed how crossover sectors provided opportunities for individuals to transfer their accumulated capabilities. The chapter ended with an in-depth review of the green and international development sectors as good examples of crossover sectors.

In Chapter 7 you will explore the steps for establishing an international business career. This will start with an examination of role of the business capability pyramid. This concept, which was developed for this book, divides business capabilities into a number of hierarchical competencies. This pyramid will allow you to examine in detail the skills and competencies that support the fundamental capabilities in international business. The business capability pyramid can be used to evaluate most business professions. However, its application in international business will provide insights into how you might go about fixing your weaknesses and shoring up your strengths. As for establishing an international business career, the three main steps suggested in this chapter are to (1) clarify the fundamentals international business capabilities you need to succeed; (2) evaluate your personal skills and competencies; and (3) activate your career management cycle.

Chapter 7 will also clarify the definition of terms such as skill, knowledge, competence, and capability which are often used interchangeably in the human resource management literature. Using these definitions in conjunction with an understanding of the business capability pyramid should make it easier to evaluate your current competencies. The chapter also provides information on a number of popular assessment tools to help with this endeavor. The last section of the chapter highlights the six action verbs that drive the proactive career management cycle: develop, evaluate, strategize, configure, network, and execute. This cycle is based on a continuous focus on developing and adapting your skills and competencies in ways that maximize employability within and across borders.

RESEARCH ON INTERNATIONAL SKILLS & CAREER DEVELOPMENT

In order to fully understand how individual skill and competence development might impact career management strategies, it is important to first examine how these factors have been treated in the human resource management literature. The human resource management literature on international skills and career development has approached the topic from many different perspectives. However, despite the fact that the perspectives have changed over the years, there is universal agreement that skills and career development are as important to organizations as they are to individuals. After surveying the literature, this author decided to separate the various approaches covering international skills and career development into three perspectives: the *competence development and matching focus*, the *internationalization and knowledge migration focus*, and the *global manager focus*. The names of the categories chosen come from the author's analysis of the literature and do not reflect previously established categories in the field. It should also be mentioned that the three approaches might occur sequentially, or at the same time in some environments. [1–4]

In the *competence development and matching focus*, the literature emphasizes how technological changes and the more competitive business environments challenge competence development for both individuals and corporations. In other words, the information technology revolution and the new organizational structures and processes that have emerged worldwide severely challenge old approaches to skill development and training. Moreover, the increased mobility of workers and the changing makeup of the necessary industry-specific skills have created competence gaps that individuals, educational institutions and other organizations are constantly trying to close. These developments have increased the need for effective employer and employee profiling and evaluation. Consequently, the role of employment intermediaries and professional networks is crucial for both individual career development and effective organizational human resource matching. [5–8]

Globalization is the major force behind developments in the *internationalization and knowledge migration focus*. Educational institutions, governmental agencies, and private organizations now work harder to change individuals' attitudes and perceptions about working abroad. This is because, as organizations expand their activities abroad, they meet new management challenges that require new approaches to recruitment, training, and career development. The required competencies for working effectively in different international environments now include multicultural, negotiation, leadership, and problem-solving skills. In this perspective, there is a lot of emphasis placed on developing flexible and effective expatriate training and adjustment programs in order to improve employee and company success. Another aspect of this view of human resource management is the role of mobile knowledge workers. As competence gaps widen because of increased international business opportunities, companies and countries have started to compete for the highly-skilled and technically competent workers needed to boost competitiveness. Knowledge workers can migrate to areas where they are most needed, if those environments have the institutional and economic policies in place to easily accept them. [9–12]

The third perspective focuses on the development of a *global mindset* and the *global manager focus*. In this approach, there is a lot of emphasis placed on the motivations and profiles of those who desire to excel at international work. There is also the recognition that global companies need global managers to compete effectively. Many researchers point out that, beyond technical skills and mobility capabilities, global managers need to first and foremost have a global mindset. In addition, individuals and organizations both need to nurture international leadership skills by working to understanding how different leadership styles function in various regions of the world. To fulfill this growing need for global managers, we have seen a surge in global MBA programs around the world. In essence, from the international career development point of view, it is important that capable individuals become more comfortable with international boundary-spanning or boundary-less career strategies. [13–17]

Unfortunately, in most of the human resource management literature, the skill and competence development strategies examined were presented as ways of making organizations more competitive. Most of the international human resource challenges mentioned are those that organizations face as they grow and expand their activities across boundaries. Even in cases when researchers examine individual behavior, the solutions to they suggest are most often geared at making the situation better for the organizations individuals work in. In the sections below, you will explore international capability development issues from the individual's viewpoint, as is suggested by the personalized resource management approach (PRM). You will explore ways of understanding, developing, and utilizing international business skills that maximize your capability, mobility, and transferability as you strive for international career success.

TOPIC FOCUS

The concept of international business is very broad, and brings to mind many different business activities. Some definitions focus on the nature of the transactions, others focus on the range of environments, and some even stress the types of organizations and stakeholders involved. This book combines all three and *sees international business as commercial, investment or logistical activities carried out by individuals and private, public, or governmental organizations across national boundaries*. Moreover, the scope and scale of international business activities vary significantly across countries, because these activities are influenced by political developments, international treaties, regulations, economic development, cross-cultural differences and human resources capabilities.

ESTABLISHING YOUR INTERNATIONAL BUSINESS CAREER

The human resource capability aspect in international business is the one that is the most important for the personalized resource management perspective presented in this book. This factor is also crucial for international business in general, since the continued expansion of the global business arena has increased the need for internationally-savvy individuals and firms that can generate a competitive advantage. The competitive international business environment has made an international business education an imperative for all who participate in the global economy. This has clearly put the spotlight on international business education. Academic institutions worldwide realize that they must educate individuals and organizations about the psychological, cross-cultural, technical, and business capabilities that are needed to be successful in international environments.

There are many different approaches for individuals who desire to establish a career in international business. There are now numerous international business programs in the US and abroad, and companies are increasingly seeking individuals with good capabilities in the field. However, because the international business arena covers so many activities, it is sometimes a daunting task for individuals to have a clear sense of the capabilities needed establish a career. Figure 7.1 shows three important steps for starting an international business career.

The first step is to clarify the fundamental capabilities that are needed for those who wish to work in the international business arena. By finding out the necessary capabilities, individuals can devise strategies for developing or enhancing them to match the demands of the business environment. By mapping out the vast array of competencies, individual can target those areas in which they might have a competitive advantage over other individuals. Later in this chapter, you will see that international business capabilities can be separated into different levels and different competencies. This knowledge is key to be able to compare different international business programs in order to find the ones that help you best maximize your business capabilities.

Figure 7.1 Initial steps for establishing an international business career

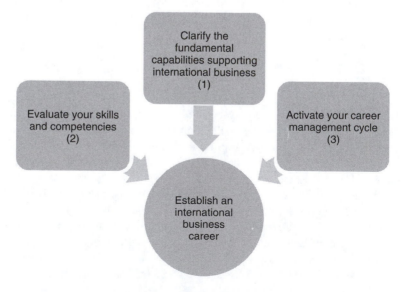

A second, and equally important, step is to find ways of evaluating your set of skills and competencies. There are many assessment programs that can help you evaluate your skills and competencies. The assumption behind all of them is that by understanding your work attitudes, work environment preferences, and general capabilities, you are better able to choose a potential profession or career path. Another assumption for competence-matching assessment programs is that there is no ideal set of attitudes and skills for all individuals. Depending on your educational background, psychological makeup, and goal orientation, you will find that certain situations are a better match than others.

The third step in establishing your international business career is to activate your career management cycle. It is called a career management cycle because *it is an ongoing process which individuals use to build, expand, and manage their careers throughout their work-ing life.* The six actions which drive this career cycle call on individuals to develop, evaluate, strategize, configure, network, and execute in ways which maximize their long-term employability. The career management cycle, which will be discussed in greater detail later in this chapter, focuses on active strategies you can take to estab-lish and maintain your career. In the remaining sections of this chapter, you will be presented with an in-depth exploration of factors that drive each of the three steps mentioned above.

THE BUSINESS CAPABILITY PYRAMID

In order to discuss international business capabilities in detail, this book will introduce the concept of the business capability pyramid. This is another concept which was developed in this book to allow you to examine your capabilities and their link to career development. *The business capability pyramid shows the hierarchical arrangement of a range of skills and competencies which an individual should have if they wish to maximize their career capabilities.* After showing you how this pyramid can be used to examine the capability arrangements of different business fields, it will be used to explore international business capabilities. In order to better understand the business capability pyramid, it is essential that you understand how this book uses the terms skills, competencies, and capabilities.

In the human resource management literature, the terms 'skills', 'competencies' and 'capabilities' are often used interchangeably. At times, this can be confusing, since the terms are sometimes referring to employees and at other times referring to com-panies or firm-level strategies. Since this chapter will be examining those terms from the individual's perspective, it is important to clarify how they relate to each other in the business capability pyramid. The definitions in Table 7.1 not only clarify the con-cepts but link them to the personalized resource management approach. [18–20]

Table 7.1 Factors that are linked to capabilities

Skill:	A skill can be defined as an individual's proficiency or facility to accomplish certain task(s), most often arising from training, education, inherent ability, or general experience.
Knowledge:	The theoretical or practical expertise that is gained by an individual through training, education, or general experience.
Competence:	A competence is the development and mastery of knowledge and skills to the point where an individual is able to reliably and consistently perform tasks and accomplish intended goals.
Capability:	A capability is that which results from the ability to effectively use or mobilize one or more competencies to achieve strategic goals.

Based on these definitions, it is easier to introduce the concept of the business capability pyramid. The business capability pyramid shown in Figure 7.2 illustrates the hierarchical arrangement of skills and competencies that an individual working in business should possess. It goes without saying that all individuals will not possess the same number and level of expertise for all the skills and competencies. However, this capability pyramid can also serve as a diagnostic tool to help individuals clarify the gaps in their skills and competencies. [21–23].

Figure 7.2 The business capability pyramid

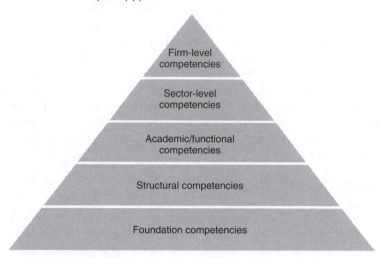

The business capability pyramid can show how individuals preparing for a career, or those already employed, might go about examining the various aspects of the skills and knowledge that support the core competencies of the profession. After going into more detail below, you will see how the business capability pyramid accomplishes three main tasks:

1. It illustrates how skills and competencies combine to create business capabilities.

2. It breaks down the major business competencies into the key skill components.

3. It allows individuals to map out skill and competence gaps in their academic or employment experiences.

The main idea behind the capability pyramid is that it is possible to evaluate any business profession more effectively if you can break down the overall required capabilities into key hierarchical components. The skills behind these components will usually arise from a mixture of personal, vocational, academic, and on-the-job experiences. As will be demonstrated, without good fundamental or structural competencies, it becomes more difficult develop into a fully capable professional in a particular field. In Table 7.2, there are definitions for the key competencies that make up the business capability pyramid.

Table 7.2 The hierarchy of competencies in the business capability pyramid

Foundation competencies:	Fundamental knowledge, skills and experiences that should form the base of a developing business specialist.
Structural competencies:	Higher level knowledge, skills and experiences that can be more directly used to add value to the success of an entrepreneurial venture or a company's products, processes and strategies.
Academic or functional competence:	Professional knowledge and skills that are attained through the completion of an organized training or educational program that is institutionally recognized as a qualified source.
Sector competence:	The knowledge, skills, or experience that are gained by working in an industry and being recognized by sector organizations, professional institutions, or one's peers as being qualified to successfully complete or manage a range of tasks.
Firm-level competence:	The knowledge, skills, or experiences that are gained within a firm and that allow employees to understand a firm's unique approach to management, production, service, or business strategy.

APPLYING THE BUSINESS CAPABILITY PYRAMID TO THE INTERNATIONAL BUSINESS ARENA

Now that you have familiarized yourself with the definitions of the various competencies, it is easier to understand how the business capability pyramid can be used to explain what is required to become a good international business professional. In the next section, you will be shown how various skills support the key competencies at all the hierarchical levels. One useful aspect of this approach is that it allows individuals to compare their personal capability pyramid with the general business capability pyramid for the profession. Individuals can rate their skills and competencies and focus on developing weak or absent areas of their pyramids.

Foundation Competencies in International Business

The skills that make up each of the competencies were derived from extensive reviews of the literature on fundamental international business skills. In Table 7.3 you can see the four key competencies are that considered international business foundation competencies: communication, networking, quantitative, and cross-cultural. In Tables 7.3 and 7.4, the competencies are at the top of the grid and in bold, while the supporting skills are below each competence category. [1, 24, 25]

For the communication competence, there are four main skills: oral and presentation, editing and writing, negotiation, and conflict management. Oral and presentation skills cover many activities that are crucial for a business professional. The ability to express oneself and discuss a variety of topics clearly is important for ongoing interpersonal relationships. Another dimension, which takes more practice to develop, is the ability to do effective presentations in front of small or large groups. With the overabundance of information at our fingertips, the ability to edit and organize information can easily make us more effective communicators. Writing is a skill that covers a wide range of activities from emails and short memos to in-depth reports and published proposals. An often-overlooked skill is the ability to negotiate. This can range from small issues to a full-blown project or contract. If the negotiation takes place across borders, it then requires an additional awareness of cross-cultural differences and varied institutional constraints. Finally, conflict management is presented as an important communication skill because as firms operate in a wider variety of regions, conflicts inevitably arise. Some research has shown that a large part of managing those conflicts has to do with the communication styles of the parties involved.

Table 7.3 International business foundation competencies

Communication	Networking	Quantitative	Cross-cultural
Oral and presentation	Teamwork	General math	Multicultural awareness
Editing and writing	Organizing	Problem-solving	Foreign language
Negotiation	Socializing	Statistics	Global mindset
Conflict management	Political	Survey research	Diversity management

The networking competence is one that is one that is not easily quantified but, in many ways, has the potential of having the biggest impact on one's career performance. We have indicated four key skills that make up this competence: teamwork, organizing, socializing, and political. The ability to work in, or with, teams is fast becoming a standard requirement of most jobs. In some sectors, the need to work with virtual teams requires individuals to work with groups across different time zones and occupational groups. The organizing skill enhances one's ability to work with groups and group-related activities. The interpersonal nature of this skill generally boosts an individual's ability to manage or lead groups. The socializing skill is often underrated, but in some international environments a lot of time is spent interacting with fellow employees after work. Quite often, individuals can get a lot of feedback about their image at work or can get key information about new developments at work by participating in after-work socializing activities. Political skills are rarely mentioned as important but, as individuals get closer to the top of an organization, the ability to influence or persuade others is crucial for building support or getting projects completed.

For the typical business professional, the quantitative competence at the foundation level is composed of four general skills: general math, problem-solving, statistics, and survey research. General math skills are important for a wide range of activities. From working with spreadsheets to reading charts and graphs, basic math is important for handling many business activities. Problem-solving skills take general math skills to another level. Here the individual must know how to use reasoning and math skills to come up with solutions for a range of situations where numbers are telling an important story. The ability to use statistics takes more training, but it should be considered a fundamental business skill which helps individuals manipulate and evaluate large amounts of data. Survey research ability is another skill which takes some training to develop, but is essential for gathering and understanding customer or supplier feedback. Survey writing and evaluating skills are also important tools for understanding employee attitudes and behaviors.

For the typical international business professional, the *cross-cultural competence* may be the most interesting and the most difficult competence to develop. The cross-cultural competence is considered to be composed of four skills: multicultural awareness, foreign language, a global mindset, and diversity management. Multicultural awareness comes from having experience interacting with individuals or groups from other cultural or national environments. This skill can be developed by engaging in study/travel abroad, or by extensive interactions with people from other cultural backgrounds. The awareness of other cultures and ways of thinking can form the basis of a more flexible approach to communication and leadership. Foreign language fluency is not absolutely necessary, but multi-lingual individuals can more quickly break through a variety of barriers that often lead to misunderstandings. A global mindset develops when individuals start incorporating their knowledge of different cultural and social perspectives into their approach to interacting with, and managing, people. This is especially pertinent for managers who work in, or across national boundaries. Diversity management skills are applicable on both a domestic and international level. Since the workforce is increasingly made up of individuals from different ethnic, socio-economic, and national backgrounds, workers and managers need to develop methods of managing their interactions in ways that reduce conflict and maximize communication.

Structural Competencies in International Business

As mentioned earlier, structural competencies are higher level business skills, knowledge and experiences that an individual can use to add value to an organization's strategy or operations. In the international business arena, we have suggested four main structural competencies: business development, market research, project management, and information technology. Table 7.4 shows a breakdown of the key skills that make up these important competencies. [20, 26, 27]

Table 7.4 International business structural competencies

Business development	Market research	Project management	Information technology
Interpersonal and selling	Marketing knowledge	Time management	Software applications
Creativity and pro-activity	Industry analysis	Process management	Internet management
Entrepreneurial behavior	Product analysis	Interpersonal skills	Basic programming
Business planning/strategy	Quantitative analysis	Problem-solving	Mobile communications

Business development is an essential competence and refers to a wide range of activities that are necessary for a business organization's success. The central skills supporting this competence are interpersonal and selling, creativity and pro-activity, entrepreneurial behavior, and business planning and strategy skills. Interpersonal and selling skills lead the interaction with the wholesale and retail customer. Individuals who are able to personally connect with customers and communicate the benefits of the firm's products or services are invaluable. Creativity and pro-activity are personal skills that aid greatly in problem-solving and the development of innovative outcomes. Individuals with these abilities can bring energy and vitality to a firm and boost their personal brands at the same time. Entrepreneurial skills are helpful for both self-employed individuals as well as those working in larger organizations. These individuals have the ability to work in fast-changing environments that are characterized by a lot of uncertainty. Finally, the ability to have an effective approach to business planning and strategy is a highly sought-after skill. All organizations need individuals who can develop, manage, and execute the short and long-term plans needed to be competitive. The above mentioned four skill areas are all crucial for successful business development activities.

The market research competence is a major aspect of competitive advantage in a wide range of organizations. The four skills that support this competence are marketing knowledge, industry analysis, product analysis, and quantitative analysis. Knowledge of marketing and the ability to evaluate industry and product dynamics are often the first requirements for the development of a competitive business model. Individuals who possess these skills often also need to have good quantitative skills, so that they can make sense of the data collected at the national, sector, and product levels. On the individual level, most of these skills are gained from a combination of academic training and employment experiences.

The project management competence encompasses four areas: time management, process management, interpersonal skills, and problem solving. This competence is used, here, in a wider sense than just the activities of a project manager. Time and process management are skills that all project managers have, but they are also skills that individuals in a variety of other positions can acquire and use effectively. Since any businesses activity with a clear beginning and a process for getting to a clear end can be considered a project, these skills fit properly under this competence. Interpersonal and problem-solving skills are also very important for the accomplishment of project-related activities. Since most project-related activities in firms involve other individuals and groups, these four skills should boost one's effectiveness in organizations.

In a globalized world where the internet and mobile technology impact many business processes and modes of interaction, the information technology competence is an important one for individuals to acquire. The main skills of this competence are software applications, internet management, basic programming, and mobile communications. Developing the skills in order to use a variety of standard software packages, such as word processing, spreadsheets, and databases management, is an absolute necessity for individuals in international business. The ability to use the internet for research or marketing purposes is also becoming an expected business skill. Finally, the ability to do basic programming and the ability to use mobile communications effectively are important skills which can give business professionals significant competitive advantages.

Academic Competencies in International Business

In the field of business in general, there is a wide range of study majors or functional business competencies which individuals can choose as an area of specialization. Some of these general business competencies include accounting, finance, logistics, information systems, management, marketing, and hospitality management. There are business programs around the world that teach all these specialties. For many years, except for finance and logistics, most of these academic programs had a domestic focus. However, in recent years, most business-related academic programs have had to incorporate international components in order to be responsive to the reality of the globalization of business competition. [28–30]

The academic field of international business has been around a long time. Some universities have had an established department for over 40 years. However, it has been over the last 20 years that the discipline has really got the attention it deserves. Given the broad nature of this business area, it is not surprising that there are a vast number of business topics which can be included in an international business major. Table 7.5 shows a list of courses or study areas that a comprehensive international business program might offer.

Table 7.5 General academic competencies in international business

International trade	International development strategies	International e-commerce
International marketing	International human resource management	Multinational management
International finance	Doing business in emerging markets	Diversity management
International economics	Comparative management	International negotiation
Export-import management	Global leadership development	International legal issues
Business logistics	International market research	International institutions
International entrepreneurship	International business theory	Interntational project management
Global strategic management	International business development	Doing business in world regions

A number of these topics are often taught in conjunction with other majors or are rearranged to include an international perspective. Consequently, it is not unusual to have international business courses cross-listed with courses in marketing, finance, economics, international relations, hospitality management, and logistics. The advantage of the international business or international management major is that it gives individuals the flexibility of developing a pattern of courses that highlight areas of greatest interest and expected expertise. [2, 3, 31, 32]

Sector Level Competencies in International Business

These competencies are those that arise from either long-term working experience in a sector or a firm. In addition, at the sector level, we often find that there are specific certifications or training programs that individuals have to complete to be allowed to work in a particular area. Some of these certifications have to be renewed or kept up to date through training or actual work experience. Sector level competencies are often reflected in the range of career titles in the sector. Table 7.6 gives a list of some of the career titles that can found in the international business arena.

Table 7.6 International business-related career titles

International Account Executive	International Media Planner	International Restaurant Manager
International Bank Manager	International Stock Broker	International Job Analyst
International Consultant	International Purchasing Agent	International Travel Agent
International Real Estate Broker	International Financial Analyst	International Quality Control Auditor
International Commodities Trader	International Bookkeeper	International Economist
International Finance Writer	International CEO	International Appraiser
International Loan Officer	International Sales Analyst	Foreign Exchange Trader
International Account Representative	International Advertising Executive	International Marketing Specialist
International Financial Planner	International Buyer	International Product Manager

Source: uncw.edu/career/internationalbusiness.html (University of North Carolina, Wilmington)

Firm Level Competencies in International Business

Firm level competencies are the most peculiar, since only long-term exposure to the way work is done in an organization can really give an individual the chance to master those competencies. Firms often have specific processes, technical expertise, or approaches to strategy and decision-making, that differentiates them from other firms. Individuals who have mastered these competencies are very valuable to the firm. The main drawback is that some of these competencies may not be easily transferable to other organizations and, therefore, may not enhance career mobility across firms. Nevertheless, it is often the case that individuals who have worked for highly successful organizations tend to benefit from the reputation of those firms. It is also possible that firms wishing to capture some of the competitive capabilities of successful firms may attempt to do so by hiring away certain employees. In these cases, the firm level competencies represent valuable process or product knowledge that the individuals might be able to take to other organizations. [15, 27, 33, 34]

STRATEGIES FOR EVALUATING YOUR SKILLS & COMPETENCIES

Getting a clear picture of your work preferences, as well as your present and potential skills and competencies, is crucial for putting yourself on the right career path. For most people at the initial stages of career development, that task is not as easy as it might seem. In general, there are four different approaches that individuals can take to choose a particular career path. The four approaches involve benefitting from feedback, counselors, passion for something, and assessment tools. Getting feedback from friends, colleagues, or former employers can be extremely helpful for those who have worked at different jobs but are still not clear which direction to take. Friends, colleagues, or employers can give you feedback about which skills you excel at, and which activities you tend to gravitate towards. It often happens that they can spot a pattern in your performance or behavior that you might miss. This view from the outside can sometimes help you pinpoint the skills that can help you succeed.

Another approach is getting help from counselors who spend time examining your motivation, work habits, education, and long-term goals. These counselors can be from a university or they can be professionals in public or private sector organizations. Sometimes these services can be obtained free of charge, and other times you might need to pay an individual or organization that specializes in career development analysis. The advantage of this approach is that counselors often go beyond pointing out your key skills and competencies. They will sometimes help you package and market yourself in the job market. The third approach to evaluating your competencies is to rely solely on your passion for a certain activity or sector. Your drive and skills may not be apparent to outsiders but, if you are passionate about an activity and work tirelessly to develop your abilities, it often works out that others will eventually recognize your capabilities. We often see this situation with writers, musicians, artists, performers, and athletes who did not get much support initially but managed to persevere and become successful at something they were passionate about. There are many individuals who have succeeded in the business world because they had the passion to pursue a dream that others thought was unattainable.

The final approach is taking advantage of the numerous assessment tests and survey instruments that are available online and elsewhere. In general, these assessment tests examine an individual's attitudes, preferences, skills, and capabilities. These tests have become more sophisticated over the years, but there are generally a set of standard psychological and statistical techniques supporting the validity of the results. These tests do not guarantee that all individuals will succeed or excel in predicted areas. They are most effective if used to guide individuals who wish to verify if their interests match up with the skills and capabilities they have acquired. These tests can also be helpful for those individuals who are at a complete loss about the nature of their capabilities and how they might apply to a range of career choices. Some of the assessment tests go as far as to suggest specific professions that might be the best fit for different individuals.

Overall, these tests are good for giving you a profile of your abilities and preferences and suggesting careers that would make the most sense based on your profile. Sometimes the results of the assessment test are surprising in that individuals find themselves already engaged in professions that they are not supposed to be good at. However, this occurs more often than you would expect since, in order to just get a career established, some individuals have to make the choice between doing what they love and doing what they are good at. Nevertheless, if motivations are properly aligned, the best situation would be for individuals to love what they are actually good at doing. Such a situation would bode well for a long and successful career. Below, you will find a list of some of some of the more actively-used assessment tests. A more extensive list of assessment tests can be found in the Appendix. It is a good idea to try out a few so that you can evaluate if your predicted capabilities are a match for the career path that you have chosen.

Name:	**Strengths Finder Assessment Test**
Source:	strengthsfinder.com
Description:	This personal assessment test was developed to examine an individual's strengths. Much of the test is based on a self-help book by by Marcus Buckingham and Donald O. Clifton. The Clifton Strengths Finder test measures the presence of 34 talent themes. Talents are considered an individual's naturally recurring patterns of thought, feeling, or behavior that can be productively applied. The key idea is that the more dominant a theme is in a person, the greater the theme's impact on that person's behavior and performance. The authors advocate focusing on building strengths, rather than focusing on weaknesses.

Name:	**Myers–Briggs Assessment Tests**
Source:	myersbriggsreports.com
Description:	These assessment tests can help you figure out your personality type, job preferences and in turn help with career planning. The Myers-Briggs assessment tools are some of the most frequently used by many well-known companies around the world. The Myers-Briggs Type Indicator assessment takes about 20 minutes to complete online. The site claims that, once completed, a report will be mailed to you within 90 minutes. There are a variety of tests available at the site, but they are not free of charge.

Name:	**Self-Directed Search**
Source:	Self-directed-search.com
Description:	The SDS was developed by Dr. John Holland. Dr. Holland's theory states that most people can be loosely categorized into six types—*realistic, investigative, artistic, social, enterprising, and conventional*—and that occupations and work environments also can be classified by these categories. The assertion is that people who choose careers that match their own type are most likely to be both satisfied and successful. The SDS can help with career decisions, and it has been used around the world. The test takes about 20–30 minutes and costs about five dollars.

Name:	**Career Directions Inventory (CDI)**
Source:	Livecareer.com
Description:	The careers center at this site offers careers advice, information about new careers, pay scale, a salary calculator, and continuing education information. The CDI survey measures career interests and contains an overview assessment of interests, administrative scores, personality, workplace fit graph, values, knowledge, skills, and abilities. The tests appear to be free of charge.

Name:	**Future-Proof Your Career**
Source:	Futureproofyourcareer.com
Description:	This career test aims at figuring out your temperament, talents, weaknesses, and career situation preferences. This free self-assessment questionnaire take around 12 minutes and the results are shown online. The site claims that the assessment reveals how your individual mix of intelligences, abilities, temperament, learning style, and skills can be used for optimum performance in the ever-changing knowledge workplace.

ACTIVATING YOUR CAREER MANAGEMENT CYCLE

There are many different ways to define careers. However, one perspective, that might be the most helpful for the perspective taken in this book, is to see a career as a long employment cycle composed of three different states which vary across individuals and employment environments. The three states are the stable, proactive, and survival states. Depending on the individual or employment environment, those states can vary in frequency or duration. During the stable state, individuals are mainly concerned with developing their skills, expanding their networks, and performing their main job requirements. During the proactive state, individuals are actively seeking out promotions or new employment opportunities while still performing their current job duties. During the survival state, individuals have to deal with drastic changes in their employment conditions. These changes could include the loss of a job, company restructurings, sector down sizing, or the loss of motivation to continue in the same profession. How individuals handle these different states ultimately impacts how effectively they can maintain their employability over their working life. Ideally, individuals should build their resources and networks during stable periods. During proactive and survival periods, individuals should take advantage of their accumulated skills and networks to set new goals and maximize their chances of successful job transitions.

It is this book's position that the best career management posture is one that remains proactive throughout your working life. To illustrate that approach, you will be introduced to the proactive career management cycle. By taking advantage of the strategies in this cycle, you can more effectively respond to the challenges your career might face. This career management cycle is defined by the use of strategies that enable the development, management, and transformation of your professional career during your working life. Since the proactive approach is action-oriented, it is characterized by six action verbs which highlight the core activities that reinforce each other (Figure 7.3).

Figure 7.3 The proactive career management cycle

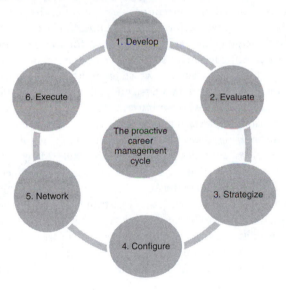

This author's view is that, although some of the core career management activities are continually being carried out, the emphasis placed on certain activities will vary according to the career phase and current career goals of the individual. The implications of each strategy (action verb) are explored below.

Develop: Building Goals, Skills, & Experiences

At this point in your work experience, the focus is on the motivation to pick a path or direction for achieving certain goals. Motivation is the fuel that is necessary to start and maintain the process of career development. Having goals makes it easier to focus learning and experiential activities at this stage. The process of development is especially important at the initial stage of one's career, as well as for later transition periods. Most of your effort at this point is aimed at selecting the skills and experiences that fit certain goals or boosts a particular self image. Development can occur continuously or in spurts, depending on the nature of the skills or experiences being acquired. For university students, you generally have about four years to build a set of skills and expand your work and non-work experiences. For others, there are certification programs, on-the-job training, graduate degrees, or informal learning that can take place once a career is under way. The objective during this phase is the accumulation of capabilities and experiences which can be used immediately, or at some later date. [35–42]

Evaluate: Assessing Skills, Preferences, Aptitudes, & Attitudes

We often see a situation where individuals have accumulated valuable skills and experiences but are unclear about their real capabilities and aptitudes. That is why assessing your skills, preferences, aptitudes, and attitudes are so important. Careers do not take place in a vacuum. Careers occur in certain work environments, demand particular abilities, require interaction with some individuals, and have a variety of performance measures to be considered successful. Broadly speaking, assessments are mainly helpful at three points during your career: before starting a position, while fulfilling the duties of the current position, and after the position has ended. Firms usually have their own performance measures in place for examining work performance, and the guidelines are generally clear for workers. However, assessment is much more difficult before starting a major endeavor, when you are not clear about which direction to take and which capabilities to depend on. The assessment activity should be focused on understanding factors that can affect your future performance. For individuals who are uncertain about their motivation and many aspects of their capabilities, assessment exercises can be very helpful. [43–47]

There are many reliable survey instruments that have been used over the years to assess people's attitudes, aptitudes, preferences, and skills. Many of them are available online, and some are carried out by well known career management organizations. Earlier in this chapter and in the Appendix, you can find information on some of the more frequently-used sites and survey instruments. For the majority of these sites and surveys, the goal is to find out which type of work environment is the best fit, and how your skills and work attitudes might match particular professions. The general assumption is that, if your aptitudes and attitudes fit a certain occupation, you are more likely to be successful at building a career around that occupation. [48–51]

Strategize: Visualizing & Picking Performance Goals & Career Paths

From the proactive career management perspective, "strategize" can be defined as a combination of visualization and planning activities that help you clarify a potentially successful career path in a chosen business environment. The power of visualization has often been highlighted in certain types of performances. Many athletes routinely use visualization techniques in training and competition to achieve new levels of performance. Some people have referred to visualization as mental rehearsal or guided imagery. However, the key process behind this practice is the creation and rehearsal of an image or series of actions that you want to accomplish at a future date. The assumption is that, the more detailed and committed that individuals are to these series of imagined actions, the more likely they will carry them out when necessary in the future. The proactive career management approach strong believes that visualization can be used to guide occupational choices and help to establish medium and long-term career paths. In the Appendix, you will find two examples of career path visualization. [52–55]. Some suggested visualization and planning strategies that can help in career management include:

- Narrowing down occupational choices to achievable alternatives.

- Imagining alternative career paths that might accomplish certain occupational goals.

- Writing down a 10-year career biography that lays out the path to your goals.

- Creating a list of potential jobs that link up and support your long-term occupational goals.

By forcing yourself to make choices and map out career trajectories, you can become more aware of your employment opportunities and also can guide your actions in a particular direction. Since establishing achievable career goals can play a huge role in how effectively you perform, visualization and planning are important aspects of long-term career management. [56–59]

Configure: Packaging & Projecting Your Personal Brand & Capabilities

The concept of "configuration" refers to the periodic reshaping or repackaging of your skills, competencies and experiences so as to project a particular professional image or to signal your willingness to take on a new career challenge. This configuring activity is often necessary for those who have accumulated a variety of work-related capabilities that could be potentially used in different employment arenas. During periods of transition, you may need to emphasize certain skills and experiences while down playing or de-emphasizing others that may not be relevant to the new sought-after position. Configuring then becomes a strategy for presenting yourself in ways that increase your employability in different work environments.

This configuration strategy is also tightly linked to the concept of self-branding or personal branding. In terms of career management, personal branding is a process whereby individuals market their personality, skills, achievements, and experiences in ways that consistently project their professional image and capabilities. Some of the ideas behind self-branding emerged from the marketing literature and others from the use of impression and reputation management strategies. In the same manner as product brands, your personal brand can project capability, credibility, and promise. Your résumé, cover letter, and online profile are concrete techniques for packaging and projecting your image in ways that might make it appealing to employing organizations. Consequently, tremendous care should be given in the organization and production of these projection mechanisms. [60–65][66–70].

Network: Link Personal Connections & Social Groups

The reality, in most employment environments around the world, is that most employment positions first become available through family, friendship, professional, or social networks. In some countries, school cliques dominate the hiring practice in influential firms. In other countries, family ties and social status can have a huge impact on successful position acquisition. Since there are many types of networks, it is essential that you activate and build a variety of networks over your entire working life. Why is networking so crucial to career management success? The main reason is that networking is a kind of personal social capital that can be accumulated and used in times of need. This is especially true in the challenging and traumatic periods of your career. Generally speaking, individuals with better social networks have more resilient careers that can withstand the changes and disruptions that characterize the working environment today. [71–74]

It is important to understand the variety of networks and networking strategies available to you. The personal network consists of family, friends, and community associates. This network is probably the easiest to cultivate and generally has your strongest supporters. The school or academic network consists of classmates, school associations, and alumni. The best school network is actively developed while attending an educational institution. This is because there are usually many opportunities to work with classmates, join school clubs, and interact with alumni while attending your school. Those students who are proactive and who maintain a consistent and positive image can generally build very good school networks. Some educational institutions make it easy by setting up online school networks to keep in touch with school activities, classmates, and alumni. Finally, informational and social networks can help you build professional networks at any phase of your career development. Facebook is good for keeping in touch with friends in general, but LinkedIn (linkedin.com) has a much clearer professional focus. There are many other trade and occupational networks that are good for working individuals. Whichever network you choose to participate in, it is important to consistently project a certain level of professionalism and commitment. [75–77]

Execute: Cultivate the Proper Mindset & Be Proactive

In the context of the proactive career management cycle, "execute" refers to your ability to first understand your strengths and weaknesses and then take decisive actions to accomplish strategic career goals. With that in mind, the focus will often be on your mindset and proactive behaviors once your career goals have been established. Stolz & Reed (2011) wrote about the importance of mindset and the three Gs (global, good, grit) in boosting career success. The personalized resource management (PRM) perspective presented throughout this book incorporates some of these ideas, but extends the range of suggested behaviors. The core PRM characteristics behind the ability to execute consistently are *self-knowledge, global view, persistence, action-oriented,* and being *adaptable.* Individuals having these characteristics should be more successful in maintaining their employability and long-term career success. [78–82].

Self-knowledge implies that you have a clear understanding of your preferences, capabilities, limitations, and potential as they related to career goals. *A global view* indicates that you take the time to gather information on business and career activities around the world, as well as developing your career with global opportunities in mind. *Persistence* means that once you have established certain goals you do your best to overcome obstacles that might prevent you from arriving at those goals. *Action-oriented* implies that take a proactive view in regards to your career management strategy. This means that, while you are continuously aware of challenges, threats, and opportunities, you also can be decisive once a course of action is in place. Finally, *adaptable* refers to the ability to adjust to changes in the work environment by shifting career strategies in order to be responsive to new realities in the environment. [83–86]

CHAPTER SUMMARY & OBSERVATIONS

In this chapter, you explored the skills and competencies that support the main capabilities needed to become an international business professional. In order to illustrate this, you were introduced to the business capability pyramid which divides business professions into capabilities arranged in hierarchical levels. This pyramid was used to look at the foundation, structural, academic, sector, and firmlevel competencies which support international business activities. *Foundation competencies* were defined as fundamental knowledge, skills, and experiences that should form the base of a developing business specialist. *Structural competencies* were defined as higher level knowledge, skills, and experiences that can be more directly used to add value to the success of a company's products, processes, and strategies. *Academic or functional competencies* were explained as the professional knowledge and skills that are attained through the completion of an organized training or educational program that is institutionally recognized as a qualified source. *Sector competencies* refer to knowledge, skills, or experience that is gained by working in an industry, as well as being recognized by sector organizations, professional institutions, or one's peers, as being qualified to successfully complete or manage a range of tasks. *Firm-level competencies* refer to knowledge, skills, or experiences that are gained within a firm that allow employees to understand a firm's unique approach to management, production, service, or business strategy.

The main idea behind the business capability pyramid is that it makes it possible to evaluate any business profession more effectively if you can break down the overall required capabilities into key hierarchical components. These components will be tightly linked to a mixture of personal, vocational, academic, and on-the-job experiences and competencies. As for establishing an international business career, the three main steps suggested in this chapter were to (1) clarify the fundamental international business capabilities you need to succeed; (2) evaluate your personal skills and competencies in comparison to the business capability pyramid; and (3) initiate your proactive career management cycle. This chapter also provided information on a number of popular assessment tests that can give you effective feedback on how your capabilities and interests match up with a range of professions. Finally, the chapter introduced the proactive career management cycle, which highlights an ongoing process supported by six strategies (action verbs). The six action verbs that drive the career management cycle were develop, evaluate, strategize, configure, network, and execute. This cycle is based on a continuous focus on developing and adapting your skills and competencies in ways that maximize employability within, and across, borders.

Chapter 8 will present practical guidelines for launching your international business career. The chapter will use some of the insights gained from the discussions in this chapter to present concrete steps to improve your chances of gaining employment in the international arena. You will be shown the value of carrying out effective market research in order to find the most fitting environment, sector, or firm for the skills and experiences you have accumulated. Chapter 8 will also provide you with examples of some of the most effective methods for evaluating company performance. You will learn the importance of distinguishing between evaluation factors, evaluation tools and evaluation measures. You will also get concrete advice on how to carry out job searches as well as how to structure cover letters and résumés. The ultimate goal of Chapter 8 will be to give you the tools to research, evaluate, and choose your next position or career path, based on a good understanding of international business environments and international employment trends.

REFERENCES

1. Ayranci, E. and E. Oge, *A study of the relationship between students' views toward a career management class and their future careers.* International Business Research, 2011. **4**(1): p. 198.
2. Beamish, P.W. and J.L. Calof, *International business education: A corporate view.* Journal of International Business Studies, 1989. **20**(3): p. 553.
3. Bloch, B., *Career enhancement through foreign language skills.* The International Journal of Career Management, 1995. **7**(6): p. 15.
4. Cappellen, T. and M. Janssens, *Global managers' career competencies.* Career Development International, 2008. **13**(6): p. 514.
5. Gray, F., *Specific oral communication skills desired in new accountancy graduates.* Business Communication Quarterly, 2010. **73**(1): p. 40.
6. Greene, S. and R. Zimmer, *An international internet research assignment: Assessment of value added.* Journal of Education for Business, 2003. **78**(3): p. 158.
7. Hague, D., *The development of managers' knowledge and skills.* International Journal of Technology Management, 1987. **2**(5–6): p. 699.
8. Hollmann, J. and B. Elliott, *Core competencies, expectations and career path for an estimating professional.* AACE International Transactions, 2006: p. DE11.
9. Fish, A. and J. Wood, *A challenge to career management practice.* The International Journal of Career Management, 1993. **5**(2): p. 3.
10. Fitzgerald, B., *Identifying career routes and key skills at Atkins.* Strategic HR Review, 2006. **5**(4): p. 32.
11. Furuya, N., et al., *Managing the learning and transfer of global management competence: Antecedents and outcomes of Japanese repatriation effectiveness.* Journal of International Business Studies, 2009. **40**(2): p. 200.
12. Hudson, S. and K. Inkson, *Volunteer overseas development workers: The hero's adventure and personal transformation.* Career Development International, 2006. **11**(4): p. 304.
13. Fluck, U., S. Clouse and N. Shooshtari, *Reducing ethnocentrism in international business students with an online multicultural supplement.* Journal of Teaching in International Business, 2007. **18**(2/3): p. 133.
14. Hanson, D. and C. Lackman, *Managing through cultural differences.* Competitiveness Review, 1998. **8**(2): p. 46.
15. Hurn, B., *The selection of international business managers: Part 1.* Industrial and Commercial Training, 2006. **38**(6): p. 279.
16. Irving, J., *Educating global leaders: Exploring intercultural competence in leadership education.* Journal of International Business and Cultural Studies, 2010. **3**: p. 1.
17. Sami, M., *Highly skilled globetrotters: Mapping the international migration of human capital.* R & D Management, 2000. **30**(1): p. 23.
18. Agarwala, T., *Factors influencing career choice of management students in India.* Career Development International, 2008. **13**(4): p. 362.
19. Palmer, K., D. Ziegenfuss and R. Pinsker, *International knowledge, skills, and abilities of auditors/accountants: Evidence from recent competency studies.* Managerial Auditing Journal, 2004. **19**(7): p. 889.
20. Stevens, P., *Career planning for the individual.* The International Journal of Career Management, 1992. **4**(1): p. 30.
21. MacLean, D., R. Paton and E. de Vries, *Personal competences and outdoor development for managers.* Career Development International, 1996. **1**(1): p. 23.

22. Parham, A., T. Noland and J. Kelly, *Skills that students perceive as important.* Allied Academies International Conference. Academy of Educational Leadership. Proceedings, 2010. **15**(1): p. 43.

23. Suutari, V., *Global leader development: An emerging research agenda.* Career Development International, 2002. **7**(4): p. 218.

24. Moravec, M., *A new view of employee development.* The International Journal of Career Management, 1994. **6**(1): p. I.

25. Newburry, W., L. Belkin and P. Ansari, *Perceived career opportunities from globalization: Globalization capabilities and attitudes towards women in Iran and the US.* Journal of International Business Studies, 2008. **39**(5): p. 814.

26. Lawrence, C.L., *Integrating writing and negotiation skills.* Business Communication Quarterly, 2002. **65**(2): p. 54.

27. Whybark, D.C., *Education and global logistics.* Logistics and Transportation Review, 1990. **26**(3): p. 261.

28. Smith, R., A. Terry and A. Vibhakar, *Increasingly global: Combining an international business degree with a post-degree designation.* Journal of Teaching in International Business, 2006. **18**(1): p. 53.

29. Suutari, V. and M. Taka, *Career anchors of managers with global careers.* The Journal of Management Development, 2004. **23**(9): p. 833.

30. Woodbury, D., W. Neal and L. Addams, *The career portfolio: Teaching students to market themselves.* Allied Academies International Conference. Academy of Educational Leadership. Proceedings, 2008. **13**(1): p. 49.

31. Mihail, D. and K.A. Elefterie, *Perceived effects of an MBA degree on employability and career advancement.* Career Development International, 2006. **11**(4): p. 352.

32. Milhauser, K. and T. Rahschulte, *Meeting the needs of global companies through improved international business curriculum.* Journal of Teaching in International Business, 2010. **21**(2): p. 78.

33. Coe, M. and J. Delaney, *The impact of certifications on accounting education.* Strategic Finance, 2008. **90**(1): p. 47.

34. Lertwannawit, A., S. Serirat and S. Pholpantin, *Career competencies and career success of Thai employees in tourism and hospitality sector.* The International Business & Economics Research Journal, 2009. **8**(11): p. 65.

35. Chivers, G., *Professional competence enhancement via postgraduate post-experience learning and development.* Journal of European Industrial Training, 2007. **31**(8): p. 639.

36. Hart, C., et al., *Retailer and student perceptions of competence development.* International Journal of Retail & Distribution Management, 1999. **27**(9): p. 362.

37. Hunt, V. and E. Rasmussen, *Patterns and motivations of successful women pursuing their careers in New Zealand call centres.* Asia-Pacific Journal of Business Administration, 2010. **2**(2): p. 167.

38. Katz, R., *Motivating technical professionals today.* Research Technology Management, 2005. **48**(6): p. 19.

39. Lantz, A. and K. Andersson, *Personal initiative at work and when facing unemployment.* Journal of Workplace Learning, 2009. **21**(2): p. 88.

40. Pinnington, A., *Competence development and career advancement in professional service firms.* Personnel Review, 2011. **40**(4): p. 443.

41. Van der Heijden, B. and A. Bakker, *Toward a mediation model of employability enhancement: A study of employee-supervisor pairs in the building sector.* The Career Development Quarterly, 2011. **59**(3): p. 232.

42. Van der Sluis, L., *Learning behaviour and learning opportunities as career stimuli.* Journal of Workplace Learning, 2002. **14**(1/2): p. 19.

43. Armstrong, P. and J. Rounds, *Integrating individual differences in career assessment: The Atlas model of individual differences and the strong ring.* The Career Development Quarterly, 2010. **59**(2): p. 143.

44. Babio, N.C. and R.G. Rodriguez, *Talent management in professional services firms: A HR issue?* International Journal of Organizational Analysis, 2010. **18**(4): p. 392.

45. Hirschi, A. and F. Vondracek, *Adaptation of career goals to self and opportunities in early adolescence.* Journal of Vocational Behavior, 2009. **75**(2): p. 120.

46. Iqbal, M.Z. and R.A. Khan, *The growing concept and uses of training needs assessment.* Journal of European Industrial Training, 2011. **35**(5): p. 439.

47. Park, Y., *An integrative empirical approach to the predictors of self-directed career management.* Career Development International, 2009. **14**(7): p. 636.

48. Rehfuss, M., S. Cosio and J. Del Corso, *Counselors' perspectives on using the career style interview with clients.* The Career Development Quarterly, 2011. **59**(3): p. 208.

49. Stumpf, S., *Stakeholder competency assessments as predictors of career success.* Career Development International, 2010. **15**(5): p. 459.

50. Thompson, E. and D. Feldman, *Let your life speak: Assessing the effectiveness of a program to explore meaning, purpose, and calling with college students.* Journal of Employment Counseling, 2010. **47**(1): p. 12.

51. Wagner, J., *Personalize your career development plan.* Strategic Finance, 2010. **91**(9): p. 17.

52. Albinsson, P. and D. Andersson, *Extending the attribute explorer to support professional team-sport analysis.* Information Visualization, 2008. **7**(2): p. 163.

53. Blochinger, W., M. Kaufmann and M. Siebenhaller, *Visualization aided performance tuning of irregular task-parallel computations.* Information Visualization, 2006. **5**(2): p. 81.

54. Huang, W., P. Eades and S. Hong, *Measuring effectiveness of graph visualizations: A cognitive load perspective.* Information Visualization, 2009. **8**(3): p. 139.

55. Pettersson, L., et al., *On the role of visual references in collaborative visualization.* Information Visualization, 2010. **9**(2): p. 98.

56. Prieto, G. and A. Velasco, *Does spatial visualization ability improve after studying technical drawing?* Quality and Quantity, 2010. **44**(5): p. 1015.

57. Skerlavaj, M., V. Dimovski and K. Desouza, *Patterns and structures of intra-organizational learning networks within a knowledge-intensive organization.* Journal of Information Technology, 2010. **25**(2): p. 189.

58. Thi Lam, L. and S. Kirby, *Is emotional intelligence an advantage? An exploration of the impact of emotional and general intelligence on individual performance.* The Journal of Social Psychology, 2002. **142**(1): p. 133.

59. Vermeulen, P. and J. Benders, *A reverse side of the team medal.* Team Performance Management, 2003. **9**(5/6): p. 107.

60. Labrecque, L., E. Markos and G. Milne, *Online personal branding: Processes, challenges, and implications.* Journal of Interactive Marketing, 2011. **25**(1): p. 37.

61. Lair, D., K. Sullivan, and G. Cheney, *Marketization and the recasting of the professional self: The rhetoric and ethics of personal branding.* Management Communication Quarterly: McQ, 2005. **18**(3): p. 307.

62. Locander, W. and D. Luechauer, *Building equity.* Marketing Management, 2005. **14**(3): p. 45.

63. Marques, J., *Self-renewal: The space between our steps.* Interbeing, 2007. **1**(1): p. 13.

64. Morgan, M., *Leveraging self-awareness.* Strategic Finance, 2011. **92**(9): p. 21.

65. Rampersad, H., *Aligning personal branding with corporate branding.* Singapore Management Review, 2010. **32**(2): p. 1.

66. Rampersad, H., *Matching your personal brand to that of your employer.* Training & Management Development Methods, 2011. **25**(2): p. 413.

67. Rigopoulou, I. and J. Kehagias, *Personal development planning under the scope of self-brand orientation.* The International Journal of Educational Management, 2008. **22**(4): p. 300.

68. Vitberg, A., *Developing your personal brand equity.* Journal of Accountancy, 2010. **210**(1): p. 42.

69. Williams, A., *Authentic personal branding: A new blueprint for building and aligning a powerful leadership brand.* Journal of Applied Management and Entrepreneurship, 2010. **15**(2): p. 156.

70. Young, C., *Brain waves, picture sorts, and branding moments.* Journal of Advertising Research, 2002. **42**(4): p. 42.

71. Donelan, H., et al., *Patterns of online networking for women's career development.* Gender in Management, 2009. **24**(2): p. 92.

72. Hatala, J., *Assessing individual social capital capacity: The development and validation of a network accessibility scale.* Performance Improvement Quarterly, 2009. **22**(1): p. 53.

73. Kim, S.-K. and M.-J. Kim, *Mentoring network and self-monitoring personality*. Management Review, 2007. **18**(1): p. 42.

74. Pittenger, K., *Networking strategies for minority managers*. The Academy of Management Executive, 1996. **10**(3): p. 62.

75. Shortland, S., *Networking: A valuable career intervention for women expatriates?* Career Development International, 2011. **16**(3): p. 271.

76. Williams, T., *Networking as a way of gaining business for training consultants*. Industrial and Commercial Training, 2000. **32**(5): p. 169.

77. Yang, E. and N. Gysbers, *Career transitions of college seniors*. The Career Development Quarterly, 2007. **56**(2): p. 157.

78. Clarke, M., *Plodders, pragmatists, visionaries and opportunists: Career patterns and employability*. Career Development International, 2009. **14**(1): p. 8.

79. Enache, M., et al., *Career attitudes and subjective career success: Tackling gender differences*. Gender in Management, 2011. **26**(3): p. 234.

80. Harvey, M., *Dual-career expatriates: Expectations, adjustment and satisfaction with international relocation*. Journal of International Business Studies, 1997. **28**(3): p. 627.

81. Newman, B., *Career change for those over 40: Critical issues and insights*. The Career Development Quarterly, 1995. **44**(1): p. 64.

82. Reed, J. and P. Stoltz, *Put your mindset to work: The one asset you really need to win and keep the job you love*, 2011, New York, NY: Portfolio Trade.

83. O'Leary, J., *Developing a new mindset: The "career ambitious" individual*. Women in Management Review, 1997. **12**(3): p. 91.

84. O'Sullivan, S.L., *The protean approach to managing repatriation transitions*. International Journal of Manpower, 2002. **23**(7): p. 597.

85. Priola, V. and M. Brannan, *Between a rock and a hard place*. Equal Opportunities International, 2009. **28**(5): p. 378.

86. Zikic, J., et al., *Repatriate career exploration: A path to career growth and success*. Career Development International, 2006. **11**(7): p. 633.

8 PRACTICAL GUIDELINES FOR LAUNCHING YOUR INTERNATIONAL BUSINESS CAREER

LEARNING OBJECTIVES

• Explore market research strategies that support career development

• Use networking to boost your personal brand and job search efforts

• Implement strategies to improve job searches across regions and nations

• Maximize your competence projection factors

THE ROADMAP

In Chapter 7, you were presented with strategies for establishing an international business career. The business capability pyramid was shown to be important for understanding the hierarchical arrangement of capabilities that support international business professionals. The pyramid was used to look at the foundation, structural, academic, sector, and firm level competencies that support most international business activities. The key capabilities of the pyramid were shown to be composed of a mixture of personal, vocational, academic, and on-the-job-experiences and competencies. The chapter also presented three steps for establishing an international business career: (1) clarify the fundamental international business capabilities you need to succeed; (2) evaluate your skills and competencies in relation to the business capability pyramid in your field; and (3) initiate your proactive career management cycle. This proactive career cycle highlights an ongoing process of career asset management supported by imperatives that should drive your career over time: develop, evaluate, strategize, configure, network, and execute. The main assertion was that, if individuals keep this career asset management cycle going, they will boost their long-term employability across different regions and sectors. Finally, Chapter 7 provided information on a number of popular self-assessment tests that can give you effective feedback on how your values, interests, and capabilities might point you in the direction of a particular profession or work environment.

In Chapter 8, you will be given practical guidelines for launching your international business career. The chapter will illustrate that, in addition to carrying out some form of self-assessment to clarify your values, motivations, and capabilities, you should start by doing some market research. This chapter will show that market research can be done on countries, sectors (industries), companies, and even occupations. You will be introduced to the market research grid which separates out evaluation factors, evaluation tools, and evaluation measures. There will also be a discussion on how traditional market research can help you do better career market research, which looks at employment trends and career opportunities around the world. Networking strategies will be broken down into different types of networks and tailored approaches be presented for each. Chapter 8 will identify friendship, academic, professional, and social networks as the major network categories. As for a job-search strategy, the chapter breaks it down into the preparation, targeting, and search phases. You will examine the activities that should support each stage and find ways to link them to your market research, networking, and competence projection strategies. The last section of Chapter 8 will present competence projection strategies that not only support your personal brand but can help you find employment quickly. This section will give you ideas on how to effectively use business cards, résumés, cover letters, recommendations, portfolios, and interviews to project your competence and personal brand into employment arenas at home and abroad. Throughout the chapter, you will be given suggestions about organizations and websites that can aid you with your strategies to launch your international business career.

REVIEWING STRATEGIES FOR LAUNCHING YOUR INTERNATIONAL BUSINESS CAREER

Getting your international career started can be a daunting task if you do not have clear strategies in place for developing your career and scanning the different employment environments around the world. Many individuals are only focused on finding a job, and they tend to neglect the necessary preparation and employment perspective necessary to build a viable career. When firms plan on entering new markets, they usually scan the environment in order to understand the fundamental competitive forces and strategic opportunities with which they are faced. Individuals need to take the same approach to the finding employment in different environments. Figure 8.1 shows some of the key strategies that can help you launch your domestic or international business career.

Figure 8.1 Key strategies for launching your international business career

Carrying out good market research is one of the most important steps in getting your career off the ground. Traditional market research generally examines economic and social trends to find market opportunities for firms. Traditional market research

also investigates developments at the sector and company level to find which firms, products, or services are the most competitive. As you can imagine, there are many ways to define market research. However, for the purpose of this book, the focus should be on the link to individual employment opportunities and business dynamics in different career markets. Given that condition, *we can define career market research as the gathering and utilizing of information on nations, sectors, companies, and occupations for the purpose of discerning employment trends and giving individuals a better view of career opportunities in different regions and organizations.* At every stage of a search for employment, good market research can provide you with information and insights that make choosing a position or an occupation much easier. There are many standardized measures, tools, and strategies that you can use to carry out market research. Later in the chapter, you will be exposed to some of the key market research analytical techniques that are often used by researchers, academics, and consultants. [1, 2]

Another essential factor in launching your career is your ability to network across many individuals and groups to gain support, advice, and referrals to potential employment positions. Networking is especially important at the initial and transition phases of your career. *Networking, here, can be defined as the use of virtual and real interaction situations to build relationships with individuals, groups, or organizations that can provide information, support, advice, or even problem-solving strategies, as we manage our careers.* In a more detailed discussion of networks later in this chapter, you will see that there are many different types of networks and each has certain advantages and shortcomings. The four main types are the friendship, academic, professional, and social networks. [3, 4]

The job search strategy covers a wide range of search activities that could ultimately help you secure employment. It also has different phases which require specific approaches in order to ensure the success of later activities. Depending on the individual and the circumstance, the main focus of the search could be a country, a particular sector, an occupation, or a specific job. It is, therefore, essential that you clarify and prioritize the main goals of your search strategy. *Job search can be defined as strategies for identifying career goals and potential locations for employment, as well as sectors, companies, and specific employment positions that can give individuals the chance to use or develop their capabilities or experience.* In later discussions, the search strategy will be broken down into three stages: preparation, targeting, and search. [5, 6]

The final key strategy for launching your career can be referred to as the concept of competence projection. *This can be defined as the use of techniques for clarifying, summarizing, enhancing, and projecting your work-related capabilities and attitudes in ways that signal you might be a productive and motivated employee, manager, or business partner.* The key techniques for competence projection are usually related to ways in which you use résumés, cover letters, recommendations, personal portfolios, and interviews to project your capabilities and image into the employment environment. There will be a more detailed discussion of all of these techniques later in the chapter. [6–8]

TOPIC FOCUS

The ultimate goal of personalized resource management (PRM) is long-term employability. As covered in earlier chapters, the three PRM strategies which enhance the possibility of long-term employability are capability, mobility, and transferability. Chapters 4 and 5 elaborated on strategies for maximizing mobility and capability. Since most of the discussions in this chapter will highlight strategies for maximizing transferability, a clear definition is indispensible. *This book defines transferability as using a set of skills, competences, and experiences developed in one business sector or business environment to adapt to a new position or career in an alternative sector or business environment.* In essence, transferability is the ability to adapt and mobilize business, technical, psychological, and cross-cultural skills in different regional and national environments. This ability is especially important for managing career transitions across sectors or national boundaries.

There are many different approaches to successfully transferring one's capabilities to new sectors or new regions, and individuals need to find the most suitable strategies to fit their situation. There several reasons why individuals might need to transfer their capabilities during their working life. The unfortunate reality is that most individuals will not be able to keep the same job or stay in the same sector for their entire career. The intense globalization of competition, significant changes in the economy, and the periodic restructuring of sectors are developments which often force individuals to change professions. Finally, global trade, networks of international corporate alliances, and the growing demand for knowledge workers have accelerated the necessity of working with different business environments, and created new employment opportunities at the same time.

GUIDELINES FOR DOING MARKET RESEARCH

Whether you are at the initial stages of your career or in transition between employment positions, knowing how to do market research is an essential skill that can increase your chances of staying on your desired career path. This is especially true if your career has to cross different sectors, regions, or national boundaries. In addition to giving you ideas on where your capabilities and experiences might be in greatest demand, market research can help you avoid areas and positions that will not significantly advance your career. The market research concept, as used in this book, includes strategies for evaluating business markets in general, as well as strategies for evaluating the employment potential of different sectors and environments. This is clearly because business activities and developments have a major impact on certain employment trends and the related demand for a wide range of capabilities. Having a greater understanding of both the business and career markets can increase your chances of finding the right fit for your package of capabilities.

Much of the uncertainty with how to carry out this type of market research has to do with the variety of factors and measures that could be used to evaluate environments and markets. Quite often, individuals mix up research levels and confuse evaluation tools with evaluation measures. To reduce some of this confusion, this chapter will present a market research grid which should help you get a clearer picture of the various levels and aspects of market research that can be carried out. The first thing to be clear about is the market evaluation level. This refers to the level of focus for the research being carried out. In Table 8.1, you will find three different evaluation levels across the top column: country, sector, and company. This approach allows you to identify the context for particular developments. The left column of the table separates the strategies into evaluation factors, tools, and measures. "*Evaluation factors*" refers to major concepts or qualitative items to consider at each market evaluation level. "*Evaluation tools*" refers to well-known evaluation frameworks used by analysts, consultants, and researchers when they examine developments at each market evaluation level. Finally, *evaluation measures* refer to specific numbers, statistics, ratios, or trends that can be used to evaluate developments at all the research levels. In the Appendix, you will also find strategies for evaluating occupations, products, and services. Table 8.1 also shows exemplary evaluative items at each evaluation level. [11, 14, 15]

Table 8.1 Market research grid and sample factors for evaluating countries, sectors, and companies

	Country	Sector	Company
Evaluation factors (describes general factors to consider that provide good insights)	Taxation policy Trade policy Corruption Political stability	Regulations, M & A trends Industry structure Alliance behavior Industry trends	Corporate governance Brand equity Foreign market entry Organizational structure
Evaluation tools (refers to well-known evaluation ideas/tools that are used by consultants/researchers)	Stakeholder analysis PEST, PESTLE five cultural dimensions Ease of doing business	Porter's five forces analysis SWOT analysis Benchmarking strategies Economies of scale	Balance sheet analysis Porter's generic strategies The BCG matrix SWOT analysis
Evaluation measures (refers to statistics, ratios, or trends used to evaluate present/future situations)	Country credit rating GDP, GDP per capita Economic growth rate; GINI coefficient	Firm concentration ratio Sector GDP distribution Import-export ratios Industry profitability	Price/earnings ratio Market share Return on investment Return on equity

In the sections below, you will find discussions on exemplary market research factors, tools, and measures that are appropriate for each market evaluation level. This is not a comprehensive list, but it should give you a good idea of which approaches have been used for each level of market research. As mentioned earlier, whether you are about to interview for an entry level position or engage in a mid-career move, good market research will provide you with the information needed to improve your understanding of the environments and markets in which your target firm operates. [16]

Doing Country Research

When firms operate in the international business arena, it is important for them to develop an understanding of the countries in which they do business. Knowledge of developments in those environments can help to explain the behavior and strategies of firms in foreign markets. Researching foreign countries also gives firms an insight into the obstacles and advantages of entering and doing business in those markets. In general, there are numerous institutional, cultural, economic, and business developments to consider. Overall, country research focuses on a number of key areas in order to gain significant insights into the competitive aspects of foreign environments. [13, 17–19]

Traditional country research generally examines how political, economic, social, technological, legal, and environmental factors impact business activity and the dynamics of competition among firms. Analysts and consultants are generally interested in areas such as the level of political stability, the attitude towards free markets, and a range of demand and supply factors that could influence a firm's operations. Career market research should take all these traditional areas into account, but should focus even more on factors that impact employment trends and the attitude towards foreign workers. In addition to finding out which industries generate the most employment and which ones are most open to hiring foreign workers, you should also investigate the dynamics in the existing expatriate communities. Below, you will find examples of traditional country-related market research factors. These traditional country factors can often help you put together a profile of what career development or career expansion opportunities might look like.

National taxation policy (evaluation factor)

An evaluation of the individual and corporate taxes of a country can provide much information about that environment. Tax policies are tightly linked to the four Rs: revenue, redistribution, re-pricing, and representation. *Revenue* refers to how a particular government used the money from taxes collected. *Redistribution* is related to how progressive a tax policy might be, or how a government might use funds received from some segments to help other segments of the population. *Re-pricing* is linked to the impact of tax policy on the pricing of products or services and the direct impact that might have on the incentive to use or produce those items. *Representation* implies that citizens will get some services in return for their tax payments and that the government will consider their input in deciding certain tax policies. Overall, both individual and corporate taxes are important factors impacting the cost of doing business or having a career in a particular region or country. [20]

Credit rating and country risk (evaluation measures)

The credit rating of a country is a reflection of its fundamental economic strength, the stability of the political system, and the likelihood that it can repay any debts it might incur. This rating also has an impact on the borrowing costs for each country. The worse the credit rating, the higher the premium that a government has to pay to get access to loans. Credit ratings also reflect the risk profile of a country, to some degree. The country risk rating signals the degree of risk possible in doing business in a particular country and, often, the cost of insurance for operations there. Other factors are also used to compile a country risk profile.

Trade policies (evaluation factor)

A trade policy is a collection of rules and regulations which a country's government uses to control international trade. The general purpose of trade policies is to regulate the flow of trade into and out of the country in ways that are supposed to benefit that particular country. Groups of nations sometimes coordinate or make special agreements as to how to handle trade among themselves. The trade practices range from being highly protectionist to almost a free trade orientation. Knowing how to work with or around trade policies can often have a significant impact on international business strategies. [21]

PEST (evaluation tool)

PEST is an evaluation tool that can be used to evaluate the nature of the environment and overall developments in a country. PEST stands for the political, economic, social, and technological aspects of a country. PEST is a tool that researchers and analysts can use to scan and evaluate the macro environment of a country. This is done by evaluating the key trends and developments for a country in each category. Insights from this type of analysis can help firms, agencies, and governments devise the most responsive strategies. Table 8.2 gives more detailed information on each of the four categories. [22]

Table 8.2 PEST categories

Political/legal	Economic	Social	Technological
Environmental regulation and protection	Economic growth (By industry sector)	Change in disposable income distribution	Government spending on research
Corporate and consumer taxation	Monetary policy (interest rates)	Demographics	Government and industry focus on technology
International trade regulation	Government spending	Labor/social mobility	New discoveries and developments
Consumer protection	Policy towards unemployment	Lifestyle changes (single households, etc.)	Speed of technology transfer
Employment law	Taxation	Attitudes towards work and leisure	Rates of technological obsolescence
Government/organization attitudes	Exchange rates, inflation	Education, fashion, fads	Energy use and costs
Regulation and competition	Business cycle, consumer confidence	Health and welfare	Internet use

GDP and GDP per capita (evaluation measures)

The Gross Domestic Product (GDP) indicates the market value of the goods and services produced within a country in a given period. Many analyst use the number as a measure of the productivity of a country, as well as a indirect reflection of that country's standard of living. This figure might also give potential entrants into a country some idea of the possibility of generating profits from a business venture. Despite the prominence of the GDP measure, direct comparisons of certain countries can be misleading. It is hard to compare the relative productivity of large and smaller countries using this measure. GDP per capita takes the GDP measure and divides it by the population of the country. This is a more accurate way to view the comparative productivity and general standard of living of countries. [23]

Corruption perception index (evaluation measure)

Knowing the level of corruption in a country provides various external and internal stakeholders with information on how easy or difficult it might be to do business in a particular country. A helpful evaluation measure called the Corruptions Perceptions Index has been developed by Transparency International (transparency.org). The index assigns a number between zero and ten, zero being the most corrupt and ten being the least corrupt. With an understanding of the level of corruption, it is possible to evaluate the type of local or governmental challenges one might face. [24]

Hofestede's five cultural dimensions (evaluation tool)

Hofstede's Cultural Dimensions were developed to help us better understand the way that cultures might affect management styles and business practices in different national environments. A wide variety of cultural and work-related behaviors have been grouped into five value dimensions. Countries can be grouped together, or contrasted, based on how these dimensions stack up. A wide range of business practices and management approaches have been linked to the five cultural value dimensions, which are set out below:

1. Power distance index: the extent to which the unequal distribution of power in a society is accepted.

2. Individualism: the extent to which a culture values individual goals over collective objectives.

3. Masculinity: refers to gender role distribution and masculine gender attitudes.

4. Uncertainty avoidance: a society's tolerance for uncertainty and ambiguity.

5. Long-term orientation: the amount that a society values long-standing traditions and will plan for long-term outcomes. (source: geert-hofstede.com)

Doing Sector (Industry) Research

If we understand the structural dynamics of a sector, it is easier to understand why some firms are leaders and others followers. Sector research also gives us insights into how attractive an industry might be for new entrants or how firms might go about protecting their position in the industry. Based on the knowledge of how the average firms are behaving and performing in their sector, it is then easier to evaluate the performance and strategic effectiveness of a target firm. Traditional sector research looks at factors that influence the competitive dynamics in an industry (e.g. Porter's five forces), as well as the nature of regulation and its participation in the global economy. [14, 15, 25–27]

Sector research from a career management perspective would not only take into account most of the traditional measures of industry activity, but would also try to evaluate how conditions impact general employment and career development opportunities. Determining whether the sector's performance is greatly influenced by the contribution of knowledge workers is a first step. Finding out the level of inward foreign direct activity can also tell you how much foreign firms are participating in the sector. Finally, ascertaining whether there is strong demand in that sector for individuals with your bundle of capabilities would make it easier for you to consider a position in the new environment. Below is a list of some sector level evaluating factors, tools, and measures that could be used to develop a good profile of the business and employment conditions in a sector.

Level of regulation (evaluation factor)
Regulations are government rules that constrain social or market behavior in a country or region. In the business arena, there are mainly two types of regulations that matter: legal governmental restrictions or requirements, and self-regulation carried out by industry or trade associations. Regulations can include restrictions on industry participation, prices, wages, employment, and environmental standards. Regulations very often impact the costs of doing business in a particular sector. A good analyst should not only know the regulations, but understand their contrasting impact on various sectors. [28]

The four-firm concentration ratio (evaluation measure)

The four-firm concentration ratio was developed to measure industry concentration. It is calculated by measuring the market share of the top four firms in an industry. Ratios of over 90 percent are a clear sign of an oligopoly, indicating that the top firms have a significant degree of market power. On the other hand, ratios between 0 and 50% generally mean a low degree of industry concentration. The ratios also signal varying degrees of industry competition.

Sector (industry) distribution or sector (industry) GDP composition (evaluation measure)

This measure indicates how big a particular sector is in a nation's economy. The measure is arrived at by calculating the percentage of total GDP for which that the sector accounts. Although there are many different sectors in an economy, the main way of comparing economic structure across countries is to look at the GDP share of four main sector categories: the primary sector (natural resources, agriculture etc), the secondary sector (manufacturing, construction etc), the tertiary sector (services and distribution etc) and the quaternary sector (the knowledge-based part of the economy). [23, 29]

Porter's five forces model (evaluation tool)

The five forces is a model developed by Michael E. Porter around 1980, and refers to five market forces that shape the competitive intensity of industries. This tool is often used for industry analysis and strategy development. One of benefits of using this model is to give companies and analysts some indication of the profit potential, as well as how attractive a sector might be in the short and long run. The five forces are intensity of rivalry, threat of new entrants, threat of substitutes, bargaining power of suppliers, and bargaining power of buyers. [30, 31]

Doing Company Research

Company research, from the career management perspective, would focus squarely on such areas as employee recruitment strategies, international compensating policies, expatriate support levels, training activities, and the full range of international business activities. You are trying to find out if a particular firm is competitive in their sector, if they are active in overseas markets, if they recruit individuals from diverse backgrounds and regions, if they provide quality training, if they compensate well, and if they provide opportunities for advancement in the domestic and foreign operations. Another aspect of company research is using the information gathered to prepare for interviews with the target company. In both cases, doing some traditional market research will be extremely helpful.

Traditional market research at the company level is usually more about the internal behavior and capability development strategies of a firm. However, their position in the sector and their alliances are also important aspects determining their competitive advantage. Consequently, good company research should point out the firm level factors that enable the organization to adjust to changes in their external environment. In addition, the manner in which the firm interacts with customers and other stakeholders often shows how effectively they are organized. Although we might not have complete access to what is going on inside a firm, there are many indicators and signals that can provide great insights into a company's competitive strategy. Below are some relatively easy-to-observe factors and measures that can show the reasons for a company's success or failure. [13, 16, 32, 33]

Market share (evaluation measure)

This is calculated by dividing a company's total sales in a sector by the total sales of the sector overall. A company may have a presence in different sectors and, consequently, the market share comparisons are only for the specific sectors being compared. Quite often, the market share measures will indicate who the leaders, followers, challengers, or niche firms are in an industry. By examining the comparative market share figures over many years, we can also get a dynamic view of the extent to which a firm is maintaining or expanding its competitive position in a sector. [2, 11, 34]

Balance sheet analysis (evaluation tool)

A balance sheet is a financial statement which reports the state of a company's assets, liabilities, and owner's equity accounts at a specific point in time. A typical balance sheet contains eight primary categories. [35]

Balance sheet categories	Balance sheet analysis
• Current assets • Current liabilities • Long-term investments • Property, plant, and equipment • Other long-term assets • Liabilities • Working capital • Stockholders' equity	The primary purpose of a balance sheet analysis is to reveal the strength, stability, or earnings potential of a stability, or earnings company's financial condition. There are many financial ratios that can be calculated by looking at the components of the balance sheet categories. These ratios provide a snapshot of the company's financial health. By examining these ratios over several years, an analyst can better explain the firm's present condition and point to expected performance in the future. [32, 36]

Return on equity (ROE) (evaluation measure)

This is one measure of a company's profitability. It reveals how well a company generates a profit from the money shareholders have invested in it (ROE = net income/shareholder equity). This figure can be used to compare the profitability of companies in the same sector, or compare the firm's profitability performance over many years. Companies with high ROE generally attract more investors and also tend to have higher stock prices. [37]

Brand image (evaluation factor)

The brand image is an important aspect of a company's reputation and potential market value. The brand refers to the image or perception of a company in the minds of consumers and other stakeholders. Usually, the brand image is tightly linked to expectations about the company's products, services, or overall strategy. Brands can develop from planned marketing campaigns or emerge from the continued interaction and feedback from consumers. Other terms linked to the concept of brand that should be examined are brand extensions, brand equity, and brand loyalty. Positive brand image over time tends to be associated with more highly valued companies that have competitive positions in their sectors. [38]

Generic competitive strategies (evaluation factor)

A major assumption behind this view of strategy is the idea that, even in an unattractive industry, a firm improves its competitiveness by focusing its core competence behind one of three generic strategies. They are called generic strategies because they are not dependent on the type of firm or the type of industry. Michael Porter's three suggested generic strategies are cost leadership, differentiation, or focus (niche) strategies. Competitive advantage goes to the firm that commits its resources to become a cost leader, a significant differentiator, or a stand out niche player. The differentiation and cost leadership strategies seek competitive advantage in a broad range of market or industry segments. In contrast, the niche differentiation focus strategies are adopted in a narrow market or industry. [1, 15, 17, 26, 39]

The BCG (Boston Consulting Group) growth-share matrix (evaluation tool)

The BCG matrix is a portfolio planning tool developed by the Boston Consulting Group. It is a way of evaluating business units in a company by examining their growth rate and relative market shares. A unit's position in the matrix has implications about future profitability and cash flow, as well as general competitiveness. Based on a unit's position in the matrix, executives can make decisions about supporting, milking, or divesting the operations. [40]

Table 8.3 Outcomes and strategies for the BCG growth share matrix

Low growth and high market share	High growth and high market share	High growth and low market share	Low growth and low market share
Cash cows: Cash cows have a leading market share in a mature market. However, they generate more cash than they consume. This type of unit should be "milked" to support other firm strategies.	**Stars**: Stars generate large amounts of cash because of their strong growth and relative market share. If a star can maintain its position, it can become a cash cow in later years	**Question marks**: Question marks are growing rapidly but have low market share. Yet, they have the potential of becoming a star. Extensive analysis needed to decide whether to keep supporting them.	**Dogs**: Dogs have low market share and a low growth rate and should eventually be divested.

SWOT analysis (evaluation tool)

The SWOT (strengths, weaknesses, opportunities, threats) tool can be used effectively at the company level. It can help a firm clarify the issues behind problems or point the way to future business strategies. The SWOT tool is used for scanning and evaluating the external and internal environment and resources that impact a firm's ability to achieve its goals. Strengths and weaknesses are used to evaluate all internal capabilities and resource factors of the company. Opportunities and threats are used for analyzing the external factors that might impact the company. [39, 41]

The General Importance of Market Research

The market research factors, tools, and measures presented throughout this section are not exhaustive by any means. However, they do give a clear idea how one might proceed in evaluating a nation, sector, or company. The advantage of separating the market research into different market evaluation levels is that that we get a better picture of the conditions impacting a firm's strategy and performance. It is even possible to prioritize and give weights to the impact of each level of analysis in order to highlight the key success factors for an organization. For some strategies and some organizations, the sector level developments will dominate and constrain the strategic objectives of the firm. However, in some markets, it will be the quality and innovativeness of the management team, as well as the company's available resources, that determine success or failure. Finally, we can imagine situations in which developments in the external environment, links to governments, and the firm's other external networks become the dominant factors behind an organization's success. [13, 33, 42, 43]

In essence, good market research requires good judgment, flexibility, and the ability to integrate a wide range of factors and measures. The analytical frameworks and tools presented do make it easier to evaluate qualitative and quantitative information but, in the end, the goal of market research is to use the insights gained from past actions and conditions to better predict future behavior and performance. This approach could also be applied to career management strategies. Proactive individuals should have an excellent grasp of the relative performance of those organization for which they work or which they wish to enter. They should also understand the external and internal environments that affect their occupations and their career trajectories. [10, 44–47]

In the same way that corporations scan different environments to determine the most effective strategy for entering and competing, individuals can use market research to locate and evaluate different potential employment environments. There are simple and complex concepts in market research, and some require practice in order to use them effectively. There is also the distinction between traditional market research and career market research, which might affect the area of focus. As mentioned previously, the goal of traditional market research is to evaluate factors in an environment that impact the level of business competition and strategies for delivering products or services. The aim of career market research is to investigate how social and business developments are impacting employment opportunities and career development strategies. The view of this book is that it is important to know how to do both. Traditional market research strategies represent the foundation and departure point for the more targeted career market research strategies. Once you have a clear idea how the political, social, economic, and technological factors are influencing a certain business environment, it becomes easier to evaluate the labor markets, as well as sector and corporate employment practices. In the box below, you can see some evaluation factors and evaluation measures which could be used for more targeted career market research.

Career market research evaluation factors	Career market research evaluation measures
Flexibility of the external labor market	Level of incoming FDI activity
Attitude towards foreign workers	The GINI index and gender wage gap
Expatriate networks in the region	Expatriates as a percentage of the workforce
Ease of obtaining work permits and visas	Compensation levels for foreign and local hires
Migrant worker conditions	International sales a percentage of total sales
Work centrality attitudes	The level of unionization across sectors
International orientation of different sectors	The number of employment intermediaries
The role of corruption in business practices	Number and types of foreign companies operating

NETWORKING STRATEGIES TO LAUNCH YOUR CAREER

For many individuals, networking is often the secret weapon to their success in finding a job or generally being effective at managing job transitions throughout their working life. As mentioned earlier, networking can be defined as the use of virtual and real interaction situations to build relationships with individuals, groups, or organizations that can provide information, support, advice, or even problem-solving strategies as we manage our careers. In essence, networking is a process of exchanging or sharing information, resources, or access in ways that create beneficial relationships. In the context of career management, there are several benefits to networking. It is not only a good way of publicizing your skills and preferences, it is an effective way of getting feedback, drawing support, and tapping into the hidden job market. Incredibly, over 70 percent of current jobs are not first advertised online. Employers generally go to their employees and their networks or to specialized job pools before taking the final step of posting them on the major job sites. The best way of breaking into this hidden job market is through your networking strategies. [48, 49]

The first step in building your network is recognizing that there are different types of networks and using the appropriate strategies for building and managing them. This chapter will discuss four major types of networks: friendship, academic, professional, and social. There may be situations where relationships overlap across networks but, generally speaking, it is helpful to manage them differently. *A friendship network* is usually composed of family, friends, neighbors, and individuals from the community who know you personally. *An academic network* is one that is linked to educational institutions, functional specialties, university clubs, alumni organizations, university events, and job fairs. For faculty in universities, there are also a number of academic networks which can link them by areas of specialization or by affiliation to educational institutions. *A professional network* is one in which individuals are linked by business associations, professional activities, or a common experiences with, or interest in, certain functional specialties. *A social network* is the most general, since individuals can be linked by hobbies, general interests, and types of social activities where the interaction is either virtual or personal. Although many people use social networks to refer to all the networks mentioned above, this approach can unfortunately cause you to use the same network management strategies for all of them. [50–53]

Friendship Networks

Friendship networks are probably the longest lasting and the most trusted, since they often go back many years and tend to be populated by the people who know your general personality and attitudes best. This is where you can get honest feedback on your general weaknesses and strengths, because these are the people who know you best. Unfortunately, many individuals do not actively cultivate or take advantage of their friendship network. When it comes to job search or launching your career, the friendship network is a good place to start. You should begin by listing all the people you know for the full range of your personal activities over the years. This should include family, neighbors, long-time friends, community organizations, and activity friends. Figure out the best way of getting in touch with them directly or indirectly to let them know you are job hunting or seeking a career change. Recommendations or referrals by friends generally have the highest trust factor, and companies can often avoid recruiting and screening costs. Another advantage is that referrals from friends can often get you inside the hidden job market and reduce the level of competition you face for a particular position.

Academic Networks

Academic networks are generally most important at the initial stages of your career development. These academic networks can take many forms, but they are all centered on activities at an educational institution you attended. The highest level of interaction is usually with your classmates and professors that you encounter in a variety of circumstances. Since you are never sure which of your classmates or professors might be the most helpful in the future, treat them all with respect and try to keep friendly ties even after you no longer share classes or after you have left the school. Some of your classmates will go on to be successful in firms you might wish to join at some point. Many firms also ask for a recommendation from a professor or former employer. Another proactive strategy is to join a university club which shares your interest in a particular field. Becoming an officer of that club and actively taking part in its running is also one way of signaling your interests and capabilities to potential employers. Be sure to go to many job fairs and attend informational sessions hosted by firms, since it gives you an opportunity to get a better understanding of various organizations and might even give you an idea for a potential career path. Finally, take advantage of your university career center and alumni network since they are a rich source of internship, part-time, and full-time employment opportunities. It is important to keep this network active even after you have graduated from an institution. Many universities now have local chapters around the country for alumni to meet and share information.

One type of academic network which is rarely discussed is the one that links professors, scientists, and researchers. These types of networks may also be considered professional networks, but they are included here as part of the academic network section of the chapter. Many academics already use Linked In (linkedin.com) to connect with colleagues around the world. However, there are other networks that are specifically tailored for academics to talk about their research, share ideas, and find employment opportunities in different regions and nations. Organizations such as academia.edu or epernicus.com give academics a place to network and keep up with the accomplishments of others. Since academics actively attend conferences in different countries, and often work for short or longer periods in other nations, they have benefited from the global market for knowledge specialists. In addition to presenting research, a lot of networking is done at conferences such as those of the Academy of Management (aomonline.org) and the Academy of International Business (AIB: aib.msu.edu). Other organizations, such as akadeus.com (Europe-centered) and academickeys.com (USA and elsewhere), regularly send out notices on employment opportunities around the world. Finally, academics can go directly to the website of educational institutions around the world to find out about short-term or long-term employment opportunities.

Professional Networks

There are numerous professional networks that link individuals across a wide range of specialties. Some of these networks are active on the internet, and others involve more direct interaction in business and social settings. By becoming members in business associations, regularly attending certain conferences, and joining organizations for different professions, you are building your professional network. In terms of internet strategy, the easiest place to start is, again, LinkedIn. Your first move should be to connect to individuals you have met who might remember you. College connections and colleagues from former jobs are obvious choices for building your presence on LinkedIn. Moreover, some people use LinkedIn in the same way that they use business cards. You can try the same strategy. If you have interacted with someone in a business setting and if you wish to keep in touch, inviting them to connect on LinkedIn is a good way to stay connected even if they later change their jobs. Joining business or country groups on LinkedIn and being active on LinkedIn Answers are other ways getting others in the network to notice your presence and expertise. The most important strategy, however, is to have a complete professional profile on your LinkedIn space (and keep it updated), since many recruiters and some firms now use the network to find capable individuals.

Attending networking events, trade shows, professional certification programs, and special topics conferences is a direct way of building relationships and reaching out to many different professionals. This should be an ongoing occurrence during your career, since you are never certain when those relationships might become helpful in employment transitions or problem-solving situations. The internet now has many sites that not only let you build your network, but also allow you to actively market yourself. Sites such as slideshare.com and viadeo.com allow you to network, post your portfolio, or present your expertise online. Xing.com, ecademy.com, and wisestep.com are other social networks for business professionals and entrepreneurs here and around the world. As you get active on a variety of different sites, the important thing to remember is to present a consistent and positive image of your personal and professional background. This is one area in which image management counts tremendously and, just as you can develop a bad reputation in real interactions, you can do the same with virtual ones. Table 8.4 is a sample list of professional networking sites operating domestically and internationally.

Table 8.4 Domestic and international professional networking sites

Country	Name	Link	Comments
CFA Institute of CFA members	USA	cfainstitute.org/Pages/index.aspx	Global association
Intermediary Network	USA	intermediarynetwork.org/	Youth and workforce development group
United Association of Plumbers	USA	ua.org	Training programs & apprenticeships for members
Amer. Society of Training & Development	USA	astd.org	Training & development activities nationwide
Latinos for Hire	USA	latinosforhire.com/	Networking & career advice organization
AIGA (Design Focus)	USA	aiga.org	Professional association for the design field

NAPO (Organizers)	USA	napo.net/	National association for professional organizers
ASIS (Security Professionals)	USA	asisonline.org/	National association of security professionals
The International Bar Association	UK/ Global	ibanet.org/Default.aspx	International legal practitioners' group
Recruitment and Employment Confederation	UK	rec.uk.com	Recruitment industry professionals
The Art Workers Guild	UK	artworkersguild.org	Training & support for members
ViewCreatives.com	UK	viewcreatives.com/	Networking for the creative industry
RENGO	Japan	jtuc-rengo.org/about/index.html	Trade union-based members' site
SBI Business Japan	Japan	sbibusiness.com/	Social networking for entrepreneurs
The Irish Congress of Trade Unions	Ireland	ictu.ie/	Governmental union-related organization
Self Employed Women's Association	India	sewa.org/	Member-based union
Euro CHRIE Hospitality	Europe	eurochrie.org/	Hospitality career advice & membership site
ACFTU (China Trade Union Federation)	China	acftu.org.cn/template/10002/index.jsp	Working class trade union members' organization
Airports Council International (ACI)	Belgium/ Europe	aci-europe.org/	Worldwide airport professionals' association
European Projects Association	Belgium/ Europe	europeanprojects.org	Projects and training assistance for members

Social Networks

A social network is a very broad category, and refers to networks that link individuals across hobbies, interest groups, regular social gatherings, or a wide range of services that have a membership component. Most of them are online services, platforms, or websites based on social relations between individuals and groups. Meetup.com is a domestic site that specializes in group participation in a wide range of activities and interests. The site's motto is "do something, learn something, share something, and change something." Although this network exists on the internet, the focus is on real interactions based on mutual interest. Facebook, Google+, and Twitter are well known social networks that have tremendous international reach. Although most of these sites are used for social interaction and information sharing, more and more we see individuals using them for job search or career management purposes. You can now sign up on Facebook to career development organizations such as wisestep.com. Business organizations now have Twitter followings, Facebook pages, and groups on LinkedIn. Many university alumni groups also use Facebook to share information on school developments and career opportunities. [8, 50, 54, 55]

What all these social networks allow you to do is to interact with others and expand your connections and the flow of information coming back to you from the world around you. Some individuals focus a lot on the size of their network, which is usually measured by the number of connections to others. However, you should also strive to have a diverse network. Having people from different professions, backgrounds, locations, ages, and genders will allow you to tap into a wider range of activities and information sources. If everyone in your network is pretty similar, you will generally get similar advice and viewpoints. That may be good in some cases but, for the most part, a greater range of connections will give you a more productive network, as far as your long-term career management is concerned. It is also important to reach out periodically to the people in your network with updates or questions. Many people just push to get connected and then they just ignore the interaction aspect of a network. Connections are not trophies. They are links to others who may have the solutions to the social or career problems you might encounter over the years. You can find an extensive list of all kinds of social networks at Wikipedia (en.wikipedia.org). Table 8.5 is a list of social networking sites in different regions of the world. [4, 48, 51]

Table 8.5 Domestic and international social networking sites

Name	Country	Link	Comments
LinkedIn	USA/Gobal	linkedin.com	Professional networking site
Latpro Network	USA/Gobal	network.latpro.com/	Multi-country hispanic career networking site
Doostang.com	USA	doostang.com	High earning jobs & social networking site
Bebo	USA	bebo.com/	Social networking site
Hub Culture	USA	hubculture.com/	Sharing business-related expertise & advice
Twitter	USA/Gobal	twitter.com	Social networking medium
Tuenti	Spain	tuenti.com/?m=login	A Spanish social networking site
MIXI	Japan	mixi.jp/about.pl	Social networking site in Japan
Hong Kong Discussion Forum	Hong Kong	careers.discuss.com.hk	Personal & career-related discussions
Skyrock	Global	skyrock.com/	Social networking site in many languages
TwoLingos	Global	twolingos.com/jobs/index.php	Social networking for multi-lingual job seekers
XING	Germany/Global	xing.com	Professional networking & career Site
StudiVZ	Germany	studivz.net	Student-oriented German social networking site

Viadeo	France/Global	viadeo.com	Business-oriented social networking site
QQ (ICQ)	China/Asia	qq.com/	China & Asia social networking site
Italki.com	China	italki.com/static/about.htm	Language learning & social networking site
Renren (Xiaonei Network)	China	renren.com/	Chinese university social networking site
kaixin001.com	China	kaixin001.com	Social networking site in China
Orkut	Brazil/Global	orkut.com	Social networking site in Brazil, India, & elsewhere

JOB SEARCH STRATEGIES TO LAUNCH YOUR CAREER

Many individuals approach job search as a simple straight forward process of trying to find a job. Nothing could be farther from the truth. Job search has many layers and can even be broken down into different stages. Earlier in the chapter, job search was defined as strategies for identifying career goals, potential locations for employment, and the specific employment positions that can give individuals the chance to use or develop their capabilities or experience. In order to fully explore the job search concept, this chapter breaks it down into three distinct stages: preparation, targeting, and search. *Preparation* refers to self-assessment activities, as well as getting feedback from diverse sources about the likely direction your job search should take. *Targeting* is concerned with making clear whether your main focus should be about locations, sectors, companies, or specific jobs, as you explore employment opportunities. *Search* refers to the mobilization of your resources, connections, and strategies to get you closer to your desired position and career path. [5, 51, 56–60]

The Preparation Stage

Whether it is done by you, by acquaintances, or by professionals, some form of skills, resources, and attitude assessment is absolutely necessary in order to carry out an effective job search. As discussed in Chapter 7, there are several self-assessment tools and websites that can help you clarify your preferences, work attitudes, skills, and capabilities. These tools not only point out your potential strengths, they also indicate limitations or areas which need to be developed. This type of information, self-knowledge, or self-awareness is very important because it helps you narrow your target and also makes it easier to justify your choices in interviews and elsewhere. For those with access to a professional career advisor, use them to get a more objective view of your resources, skills, and potential career path. During the preparation stage, make use of acquaintances and career professionals to get external reviews of your résumés and cover letters. Take into consideration their advice on how best to use your resources and connections to maximize your presence in the job market. Your personal preferences and assessment activities should also be used to clarify your short-term and long-term career goals. On the practical side, use a binder or a digital folder to keep track of important career-related information. Your preparation should include general market research on countries, regions, sectors, companies, and professions that might play a role in your future career.

The Targeting Stage

Targeting activities occur after you have narrowed down your universe of choices to areas that are most suitable or achievable for developing or expanding your career. For those individuals who choose to focus on a specific country for employment, their approach to information gathering will be somewhat different. In some cases, the job or the sector is not as important as finding some form of employment in a desired country. In this case, information on work permits, visas, the working environment for foreigners, and different strategies for gaining access to that country should be thoroughly researched. For those whose main focus is on gaining access to a particular sector, research should be done on the structure of the sector, its long-term economic potential, and the full range of occupations in the sector. For some individuals and in some countries, job hunting is mainly about getting hired by a particular company. In many of those countries, once individuals are hired, it is the company that will decide the type of training, the main area of work, and the best career path to match their capabilities. However, even in environments with very flexible external labor markets, there are individuals who see getting into a specific company as crucial to their career success. In both of the cases above, individuals need to do extensive company research to support such a crucial decision. Finally, the most typical situation is when individuals target a specific job or occupation. That also requires knowledge of the required skills, compensation levels, and importance of the occupation across various sectors. Career management-related internet sites, such as insidejobs.com and glassdoor.com, provide a wealth of information on a wide range of career groups, occupations, and, sometimes, even give a range of expected salaries for different regions of the country.

In the first part of this chapter, you were presented with several market research strategies for evaluating countries, sectors, and companies. Those strategies can be used to narrow your choices and give you the insights you need to make informed job search decisions. However, there are also a number of practical strategies you can take get a better understanding of your employment environment. One such strategy is using informational interviews. This is usually much easier to do while you are a student, since you can tell executives that you are just gathering information on their sector and various career paths in that sector. If you manage to talk to a number of executives, you can then follow up later to thank them and ask them to let you know if good job prospects become available, since you are now extremely interested in their firm or their sector. It is also possible to use your networks to set up informational interviews. Speaking with employment agencies is another way of gathering information on prospects in the job market. A more direct strategy is to somehow use volunteer work, internships, or temporary positions within a firm, to find out more about potential long-term positions while getting others to notice you at the same time. Although you should try to narrow your target, you should still focus on employers of all sizes. It is a good idea to even look at startups. You will probably get more responsibilities and a greater exposure to a wider range of business activities in smaller firms. Overall, the key thing you need to do at the targeting stage is locate the areas and sectors that are actively hiring and also try to understand the full range of job responsibilities that go with different occupations.

The Search Stage

The active search stage should take place after you have narrowed down your options and have become committed to finding a position in a particular country, sector, or company. This is also the stage at which you should rely on personal and professional networks for advice, suggestions, and referrals. Through your connections and other resources, you should push hard to get access to the hidden job market. One internet resource is appropriately called the hidden jobs report (hiddenjobsreport.com). It is a newsletter that was founded by Jim Stroud and is now edited by Chris Russell. The newsletter gives timely information on companies and sectors that are about to hire. Another helpful site is rileyguide.com, which introduces you to the online job search arena, listing many online sites and services that can help you land a job.Smartbrief.com is another site that publishes industry newsletters and reports that can be very helpful to the job seeker. In addition to using your networks, this is the stage where you should also take full advantage of the job placement potential of professional associations, job fairs, career forums, and career centers.

In terms of practical search strategies, make sure you prioritize your internet sources and use reliable high impact ones. Create a recording and tracking system for your job searches, since you are never sure when certain leads can result in an interview opportunity or, possibly, a job offer. One important strategy you can use is to take advantage of RSS feeds. You can sign up for feeds from a host of different sources and companies. RSS feeds automatically deliver updated information to your computer or mobile device. This strategy allows you to keep track of news, blogs, employment listing, and company announcements. However, to properly read and use RSS feeds, it is helpful to use an RSS feed reader. You can get a stand-alone RSS reader software or plug-in application for free, for a short-term trial, or for immediate purchase. Overall, using RSS feeds is an effective way of keeping track of many different sources of information that get updated regularly.

Review and update your résumés and cover letters regularly, since your skills and applicable experiences may have to be tailored to improve your fit for a particular position. Be persistent in your search and remember to not to take rejections personally. Learn from the rejections by trying to understand if it was due to a faulty presentation on your part. You may have to expand your search geographically, and so you should be open to opportunities in other sectors, regions, and countries. If you are open to learning new languages and living in foreign environments, your search arena will expand dramatically. It is even possible to start out with an internship or a work holiday situation abroad before deciding on a long-term commitment to the country. Having connections in foreign countries can help significantly with your job search. However, there are now many job search sites that are global or have multi-lingual interfaces. These sites often offer a wide array of job opportunities. In some cases, it might be possible to complete the screening process by phone or skype, but in many cases you will have to take a trip to that country for the final interviews. Table 8.6 is a list of some of the top job search websites. Become acquainted with those that match your field of interest.

COMPETENCE PROJECTION STRATEGIES TO LAUNCH YOUR CAREER

Before, during, and after the periods you worked on your market research, networking, and job search strategies, you should not forget the importance of

Table 8.6 Popular job search sites and their areas of focus

Job search sites	Link	Comments
Beyond	Beyond.com	One of the largest network of niche career communities.
Career Builder	Careerbuilder.com	One of the oldest and biggest job sites.
Craigslist	Craigslist.org	Has an extensive listing of local job opportunities nationwide.
Execu Search	Execu-search.com	Focuses on higher tier job search opportunities.
Hound	Hound.com	A search engine showing jobs from employer websites only.
Indeed	Indeed.com	Is an aggregator from other job sites and company sites.
Job Central	Jobcentral.com	Is a service formed by a consortiums of US companies.
Job Serve	Jobserve.com	Claims to be the first internet recruitment service across many sectors.
Jobster	Jobster.com	Uses social recruiting to find candidates for various organizations.
Linked in	Linkedin.com	A social networking site for professionals, and has many job listing.
Monster	Monster.com	A well-known global job listing site which offers many other services.
Oodle	Oodle.com	Specializes in online classifieds and has jobs listed by many categories.
On Target Jobs	Ontargetjobs.com	Owns many smaller niche search sites with more targeted jobs.
Simply Hired	Simplyhired.com	An aggregator listing for websites, newspapers, and companies.
Snag A Job	Snagajob.com	Focuses mainly on hourly employment listings for many firms.
The Ladders	Theladders.com	Has a reputation for listing only jobs paying over $100,000.
Trovix	Trovix.com	Uses templates and mapping software to match you with job listings.
Tweet My jobs	Tweetmyjobs.com	Delivers job listings instantaneously to twitter users.
USA Jobs	USAjobs.gov	The official job site for the US government.
Yahoo Hot jobs	Hotjobs.yahoo.com	One of the largest jobs sites on the internet.

competence projection. *Competence projection can be defined as the use of strategies to project your skills, capabilities, and personal brand in all aspects of your career management and to a wide range of personal and professional stakeholders.* In order to do this, you need to not only communicate to others your key competencies: you need to manage your reputation and your image on a regular basis. To manage your image and reputation, you need to organize, coordinate, and monitor online and real life activities that can impact your expected behavior and performance over long periods of your working life. It is important to remember that your reputation is not only built from your capabilities, and things that you have said about yourself, but, quite often, from your actions and from what others say about you. It would help if you could verify whether or not you have a personal brand, and if it is recognizable and viewed in similar ways by others. The key requirement in handling your personal brand is to know whether others are clear about who you are and for what you want to be known. [6, 7, 61]

The first step you can take to review your personal brand is to ask yourself honestly what your general emotional impact is on others. Do you have a positive and uplifting impact on others, or do you generate controversy and distrust? One way of answering this question is to figure out how others describe you. If you are not sure, feel free to ask a variety of friends and colleagues how they would describe you in a few words. The next step is to figure out how you would describe yourself. If there is a large gap between those impressions, then you might not be managing your personal brand correctly. If you are at the initial phase of building your personal brand, you should start by focusing on the core capabilities for which you wish to be known. Communicate to others your desire to work in a field that allows you to fully explore those capabilities. If you can think of a career title that links to those capabilities, it is then easier to get the image across. You can show your interest in being a graphic designer, a project manager, a sales professional, a market researcher, or a consultant. Getting some volunteer, internship, part-time, or full-time experience in fields that allow you to explore those capabilities makes it much easier to project your competence. The next step is to decide on what your core emotional appeal might be to others. Remember that it is the combination of your visual presence, your attitude, and your behavior in a variety of situations that drive these aspects of your personal brand. The key factor in developing and maintaining and your emotional appeal is to behave consistently and project an interest in others and the world around you. [4, 62, 63]

Overall, the key drivers of your career-related personal brand are your self-awareness, active interaction with others, your task performance, and the effective use of strategies to package and project your competencies and work-related attitudes. By actively joining and participating in the appropriate organizations, you can get the opportunity to showcase your talent and interpersonal skills. By making sure you do your best whenever you take on a work-related task or other challenges, you send a signal that you good performance is important to you. By being aware of how your reputation is developing and changing, you can take action to correct misconceptions and get others to focus on your accomplishments. All of the above long-term strategies are crucial for maintaining a positive personal brand. There are, however, short-term strategies that are just as important and, quite often, they may be the difference in you in getting the employment opportunity you seek. These short-term strategies include the manner in which you handle business cards, résumés, cover letters, recommendation letters, work-related portfolios, and interviews. In the rest of this chapter, you will find some helpful techniques for each of these factors. [3, 48, 56, 64–66]

Using Business Cards

It may seem, after the advent of LinkedIn and Facebook, that business cards might be going out of fashion and losing their importance. That is absolutely not the case, and in many ways they continue to represent an essential component of business interaction. The prevalence and importance of business cards will, of course, vary by region and national environment. There may also be specific protocols as to how and when you exchange business cards as you travel around the globe. Although LinkedIn is important for keeping in touch over the long-term with colleagues and other business professional, there is no substitute for the personal nature of the business card exchange. Quite often, the exchange is preceded by extended conversation about different topics, or by your participation in a unique event which connects you to others at that event. The business card takes the interaction to the next level and signals that you are open for continued interaction in the future.

Whether you are unemployed, at the initial stages of your career or making the transition to a new career, you should carry some type of business card. Companies such as vistaprint.com or overnightprints.com make it affordable for anyone to create their own business card. It is even advisable to have at least two types of business cards. You should, of course, have one that connects you with your current place of employment or current educational institution. You can also have one that highlights your core competencies and desired occupation goals. You can probably do a lot more customization with the latter type, and it can serve as a mini introduction to your résumé, if done properly. The main points are that you should have your contact information on your card and the style and content of card should make it easier for others to recall their interaction with you. Since some of you will exchange numerous business cards over time, one smart thing to do is to request that individuals with whom you have made some sort of connection and exchanged business cards join you on LinkedIn. The business card then serves as a means of expanding your professional network, and LinkedIn helps you keep in touch even after your contacts have changed jobs.

Résumé Strategy

Even for those who have managed to develop an extensive network of contacts, it is important to have a good résumé handy when seeking employment. In many countries, the résumé or curriculum vitae is the most important document you can hand to your contacts or prospective employers. In addition to sharing information about your skills and capabilities, your résumé should tell a story or project a particular image. A résumé should organize, highlight, emphasize, and signal the type of person or employee you will be if hired by a firm. Remember that the résumé is also a visual space and how you use that space is also a reflection of your personal brand. Organizing your visual space in a high impact manner may be difficult for electronic résumés, but it is still possible to organize your work and experiences in ways which differentiate you from others. However, be careful not to let the page design and organization overwhelm the story you are trying to communicate. Visual design issues aside, there are basically two types of résumés: chronological and functional.

A chronological résumé is the most typical résumé for individuals who have had a number of jobs or a medium to long work history. The most recent position is generally listed first, and the rest in reverse chronological order. This type of résumé clearly shows what tasks and accomplishments you have had at each position, and when those employment positions occurred. Some employers might prefer this type of résumé because they can easily link your job task to places of employment and quickly see the types of employment gaps you might have experienced. Consequently, this type of résumé might work best for those who have had uninterrupted employment with significant jobs at all times. However, if you have had more jobs than those you want to highlight, or some of the jobs are completely insignificant or unrelated to the type of position you are seeking, you might want to consider using a functional résumé.

A functional résumé highlights the skills, capabilities, and experiences that you consider important to project a certain level of professionalism. The typical approach is to separate out your experiences and accomplishments into major work-related functions. You can list areas such as leadership, management, organizational, project management, analytical, software programming, sales, customer service, business development, market research, design, editing, or communication skills. This modular approach now allows you to pull your capabilities from a wide variety of experiences and put them under the functions you which to highlight. This type of résumé is excellent for those at the initial stage of their career development, those trying to change to a new sector, those changing their careers, or those who have significant employment gaps they wish to de-emphasize. The main advantage of the functional résumé is that it gives you more freedom to tell a particular kind of story and highlight areas you think are best for getting you a new position. You can find examples of both the chronological and the functional résumés below.

Whichever you type of résumé you choose to use, there are a number of strategies that can help your résumé stand out. Choose the best font to help you visually organize your content in an appealing way. Make sure the format you choose is a good fit for the kind of position you are seeking. Include important keywords throughout the résumé. It is often helpful to revisit the specific job advertisement, or find similar ones, so that you can become familiar with the keywords that the firm has used to describe the position. Carefully studying the language of job offers can give you important clues on how to describe your accomplishments. This is the first step in customizing your résumé to match the kind of position for which you are applying. Don't forget to choose a specific career objective that shows why you might be interested in an employment position and make sure that your résumé supports your career objective. Finally, use action words in your résumé wherever possible. This will generally make your comments more dynamic and signal your proactive work attitudes. Table 8.7 is a list of action words you might consider using. You will also find two sample résumés provided.

Table 8.7 Sample of action words for your résumé

Accomplished	Conducted	Energized	Influenced
Achieved	Controlled	Established	Implemented
Adapted	Coordinated	Evaluated	Improved
Administered	Delegated	Expanded	Initiated
Analyzed	Designed	Facilitated	Instituted
Arranged	Developed	Gained	Interviewed
Communicated	Directed	Generated	Issued
Compiled	Distributed	Handled	Launched
Conceived	Earned	Increased	Led
Maintained	Performed	Referred	Supervised
Managed	Planned	Researched	Supported
Modernized	Prepared	Reviewed	Taught
Motivated	Presented	Revitalized	Trained
Negotiated	Produced	Scheduled	Translated
Operated	Provided	Simplified	Updated
Originated	Published	Sold	Used
Ordered	Purchased	Solved	Won
Organized	Recommended	Spearheaded	Wrote

(Chronological Résumé Sample)

Gisela Johnson
San Francisco, California
Email: gjohnson@mymail.com
Cell: 011–777–7878

GENERAL SKILLS

I have excellent leadership, communication, financial and marketing skills. I am very proficient in Microsoft Office (Excel, PowerPoint, Outlook, Word, and Access), in addition to a very good knowledge of accounting, statistical analysis, business forecasting, sampling, and network modeling software. I am also fluent in Spanish (read/write).

EDUCATION

Frisco University, California: B.S. in Business Administration; Minor: Spanish (May 2012)
Universidad de Madrid, Spain: study-abroad program (2010–2011)
Sidesaddle Community College, California: Associate Degree, Business Administration (May 2009)

WORK EXPERIENCE

All Country Insurance, Monterey, California: Agency Staff   2008–2010
- Provided exceptional customer service to a wide range of clients
- Generated new policies and wrote auto and home insurance quotes
- Controlled busy phones and responsible for opening and closing duties
- Coordinated front desk operations

Bank of the East, Monterey, California: Teller   2007
- Responsible for thousands of dollars on a daily basis
- Handled cash transactions
- Provided guidance and customer service for bank customers
- Maintained daily operational procedures

St. Royals, Monarch Beach, California: Spa Attendant   2006
- Managed daily operations of the Spa
- Coordinated opening and closing duties for this 5-star resort and spa
- Applied strong customer service skills to high profile clients

STUDENT LEADERSHIP ACTIVITIES

Women's Soccer, Valley Athletics: *Team Player and Co-Captain*
- Motivated team of up to eighteen girls to play to their full potential
- Directed team during practice and warm-ups
- Liaised between head coach, assistant coaches and athletic director

Delta Sigma Pi, Co-ed Professional Business Fraternity: *Vice President of Financial Development* (Rated #1 Professional Business Fraternity in the Nation)
- Organize creative events to raise funds
- Responsible for soliciting sponsors and coordinating various committee efforts

AmeriCorps, Corporation for National & Community Service: *Member/Volunteer*
- Served on specific projects at nonprofit organizations and public agencies.
- Assisted low-income communities in building the organizational, administrative, and financial capacity of the community

(Functional Résumé Sample)

James Franco
9K 400th Ave. San Francisco,
CA 94121 Phone: (015) 777–8888
E-mail: james@yourmail.com

CAREER OBJECTIVE

A position in business development in which my sales and organizational skills may be utilized in an enterprising environment.

SUMMARY OF QUALIFICATIONS

I have developed excellent management, communication, marketing and computer skills. I have been a productive employee and worked well with clients and staff at all my places of employment. I have a passion for international business and I am bilingual in Spanish and English. I have used my technical and organizational skills in a variety of settings and I am dedicated to getting the job done well.

ORGANIZATIONAL AND MANAGEMENT SKILLS

- Accountable for department while manager was on vacation
- Filled out time sheets and expense reports
- Coped with deadlines and prioritized work
- Coordinated off-site events
- Managed a small team of employees on several projects

COMMUNICATION AND COMPUTER SKILLS

- Managed client/customer database
- Interacted with people at different levels
- Participated in the adaptation of new POS systems
- Maintained contacts and gave bi-weekly feedback to company buyers
- Updated real estate loan data input
- Communicated with virtual teams across company network

SALES AND MARKETING

- Was ranked as one of top 20 bankers in the region
- Consistently top sales performer in the department
- Managed the highest year to date volume in the department
- Exceeded departmental goals every quarter

EDUCATION

B.S. in Business Administration at California State University (May 2011)
Major Concentration: International Business
CSU GPA: 3.7 Dean's List: Fall 2009 and 2010
Related courses: Business Communications, Marketing, Management, and Market Research

EMPLOYMENT

Major Commerce Bank, San Francisco: Feb. 2008–July 2008
Bloomington, San Diego: Oct. 2006–Sept. 2007
North Star Financial, San Diego: Dec. 2004–Oct. 2006

Cover Letter Strategy

Your cover letter is usually a half-to-one-page document you send or attach to a résumé in order to introduce yourself and highlight your key accomplishments. Since résumés include many different tasks, positions and experiences, they can take a lot of time to get through. Often, if the résumé is not properly organized, an employer might not even be sure why you are applying for a position and what makes you a good fit. Consequently, each cover letter must be tailored to each job and each company. Your cover letter should explain things your résumé can't do equally well. In addition to communicating your capabilities and your strong desire for the position, cover letters can explain gaps in your employment, why you might be seeking a career change, or why you might be an excellent fit for the job. Despite the customization of content and perspective, cover letters generally have certain formal factors in common. In the cover letter sample below you will see the formal aspects on the right and the sample text on the left.

Sample Cover Letter

John DoSomething
East Success Ave. # 7 Cotati, CA 90001
(070) 600–7100. ijohndsome@yuhoo.com

Your Contact Information

January 10, 2012

Date

Mr. David Palomine
President
Natural Systems, Total Recovery Division
1700 Lostheway Lane, Buffalo Pasture,
IL 60089

Employer Contact Information
Name
Title
Company

Dear Mr. Palomine,

Salutation
Dear Mr./Ms. Last Name

Body of Cover Letter
The body of your cover letter lets the employer know what position you are applying for. Give reasons why the employer should select you for an interview and indicate how you will follow-up.

I was referred to you by Mr. James Dolittle who thought your company might be a good fit for me. After reviewing your company and available positions, I am extremely interested in the Sales Account Executive position. I have wanted to work in the bio-health field for a long time and was very happy that your firm is expanding in this area. My educational background and previous experiences have

First Paragraph
The first paragraph of your letter should include information on why you are writing. Talk about the position you are applying for and how you were referred or how you found the job listing.

prepared me to be a productive contributor in this area of your business.

As you will see on my attached résumé, I have more than seven years' experience in the bio-health field and just completed an internship in a related area while completing my recent degree. I am generally well acquainted with the technologies that your firm uses, and I feel that I can enthusiastically develop new customers for your expanding operations.

Middle Paragraph(s)
The next section should describe what you have to offer the employer. Talk about how your qualifications match the job you are applying for. Summarize your best skills and experiences.

Overall, I have proven multi-tasking capabilities and work well with colleagues and clients. Moreover, I am a self-directed professional with excellent communications and management skills. If you are open to discussing the position in person, please contact me by email or telephone at your convenience. I will also contact you again in a few weeks to check the status of my application for the position. Thanks in advance for your kind consideration.

Final Paragraph
One final comment on your overall abilities, and then conclude your cover letter by thanking the employer for considering you for the position. Include information on how you will follow-up.

Respectfully Yours,

John DoSomething

Complimentary Close

Respectfully yours,
Signature

References & Letters of Recommendation Strategy

Letters of recommendations can be very helpful in your job search. They are usually most helpful after you are in the final interview phases for a particular position. They can help an employer get a better idea of your past performance and support your claims for being a good fit for the position. In many situations, firms will ask for someone to whom they can talk or write, instead of relying on just a letter of recommendation. For this reason, it is a good idea to advise two or three people that you will be using them as references. Make sure to update your references on the status of your interviews and briefly discuss the kinds of firms you are considering. A good reference from a teacher or former employer can often be the difference in you getting the position you are after. While you are student, it is generally a good idea to get to know your professors. If you have done very well in certain courses, you might ask the instructor for a general letter of recommendation. This approach will help you to avoid having to track down instructors who may no longer remember your performance in their class. For those who are already working, it is a good idea to stay on good terms with your colleagues. Make sure to stay in touch with a few of them even after you have left your place of employment. Your new employer might ask to speak to a former colleague or boss.

If you have been involved in any significant university, non-profit, professional association, or community projects outside of work, it is a good idea to ask for a letter of appreciation. Letters of appreciation represent one way of documenting your activities and performance in a wide variety of situations. They also serve to show you as a well-rounded person who has significant ties to others and the community. Another approach, which is becoming increasingly popular on sites such as LinkedIn, is the use of endorsements. This is really an online recommendation which you have place on your LinkedIn profile. It can come from friends, instructors, colleagues, or former employers. What this kind of endorsement does is to highlight your work attitudes, capabilities, and previous achievements. It can be a powerful tool to build your personal brand and attract potential employers. One key suggestion is that you try to use people whose opinions will be valued, or people with whom you have actually worked. If you are using a professional site, such as LinkedIn, stay away from having friends or family saying what a nice person you are. Associations, former employers, and colleagues make the most sense. Overall, you should use references and letters of recommendations to build and maintain your personal brand. As much as possible, make sure that a consistent message about your capabilities and attitudes is being projected.

Career Portfolio Strategy

Career portfolios are a good way of organizing and documenting your skills, capabilities, and experiences in ways that boost your image and employability. Although most career portfolios are being created and used by students about to enter or graduate college, they can be used by individuals at any stage of their career. A good portfolio can help to boost the capability, mobility, and transferability aspects of your career. Career portfolios go much farther than a résumé, because they not only document skills and achievements, they can provide powerful visual support for your personal brand. If used effectively, career portfolios can speed the time to finding employment and possibly boost your potential salary.

Career portfolios should tell your personal story, as well as explain and document your achievements. It is a good idea to include evaluations, letters of appreciation, recommendations, writing samples, awards, special projects, and general acknowledgments for your performance. Generally, individuals keep these portfolios in binders or folders. However, increasingly, individuals are now using electronic portfolios since it is easier to manage and update them over time. It is also much easier to share electronic portfolios with potential employers in many different employment environments. You can use sites such as slideshare.com and collegecentral.com to upload your portfolios and share them with others. Remember that a career portfolio is a marketing tool that can be used to build your personal brand and project your presence into many different employment arenas.

There are many different approaches you can use to develop a systematic inventory of your skills, capabilities, and experiences. One approach is to use the business capability pyramid presented in Chapter 7 to explore and document all the skills and competencies needed in your field. The matrix shown in Table 8.8 gives a range of activities that might be used to document the skills and competencies in the various areas of the business capability pyramid. The example provided shows the foundation and structural competencies for international business. You could use an excel sheet to get started, but some of the online portfolio sites will allow you to customize your matrix to show how you attained your skills and capabilities. One very good aspect of this matrix is that it shows how you attribute skills and capabilities to a wide range of activities.

Table 8.8 Example of a career portfolio matrix based on the business capability pyramid

Foundation and structural competencies for international business (Chapter 7)	Internships	Jobs	Service/volunteer	Memberships	Education	Experience
Communication						
Networking						
Quantitative						
Cross-cultural						
Business						
development						
Market research						
Project management						
Information technology						

Interviewing Strategy

This is generally the final stage of your job search. You have been successful in getting the attention of a prospective employer, and now you need to complete the process successfully. However, always be aware that there are times when an interview tells you that this is not the right organization for you and at that stage you should see the experience as preparation for the interview that will really count. The worst thing you can do if you are offered an interview is to just show up at your appointed time to have a casual chat and to let them know why they should hire you. Successful interviews generally have three main phases: the preparation, the interaction, and the follow-up. If you do each stage well, that should increase your chances of being made a job offer.

In the preparation stage you should do extensive research on the sector, the company, the main executives, and the position for which you are applying. Many individuals just focus on the position and fail to see the importance of connecting the position to developments in the company and the sector. Knowing the company's products and services, as well as how competitive they are in their sector, can show that you understand the organization's needs in the marketplace. Knowing about the firm's executive team will help you to determine the kind of leadership style that is dominant at that firm. If you can find any information on the individuals who will be interviewing you, that will also help you interpret the types of questions they might ask. Using sites such as glassdoor.com and payscale.com can help you find information about the corporate culture, the pay scale for various titles, and the required skills and duties for different positions. Finally, review the position announcement thoroughly. You want to completely understand the various skill requirements and work conditions associated with the position for which you are applying. Make sure your résumé has been adjusted to highlight you as one of the best candidates for the job.

It is usually during the interaction stage when you efforts signal you as one of the best candidates for the position. Doing thorough research on the sector, company, and the job can be very helpful, but effective interviewing will also require good interpersonal and communication skills. One final preparatory strategy you might use is to take advantage of informational interviews. It is usually easier for university students to use this strategy because they can tell executives that they are researching a sector or range of companies, and they are just trying to get feedback from various professionals. The informational interview can give you a chance to meet many different individuals, find out good information about the company and sector, and verify if this is really the kind of profession you should pursue. It is usually harder to get access to these executives if you are unemployed or already working for another firm. For those who can set up informational interviews, it is a great way of getting others to know you while you expand your network of contacts. You can usually contact the executives later to tell them how impressed you were with their organization, and how interested you are in pursuing a career with their organization. Since the executives might even ask for a copy of your report, you should plan on doing some write-up of your view of the sector. Another preparatory strategy for the interaction stage is to do mock interviews with friends or career advisors. This type of interaction preparation should help you be more relaxed during the actual interview.

Remember that, during the interaction stage, it is a combination of how you visually present yourself, how you interact with the interviewer, and how you project your competence and confidence, that will help to make it a successful interview. Make sure that you are dressed properly, and it is always better to take the more conservative route in terms of fashion. Having a professional look is the most significant thing you can do to make a good first impression. Your posture, and the clarity and the tone of your voice are also important elements of your interview. In addition to the variety of typical interview questions, you should be prepared to give good answers to the following four questions:

1. How you contributed to organizations in your previous jobs or experiences.

2. How your previous jobs or experiences prepared you for the position you are seeking.

3. How your personality and work attitudes make you a good fit for the organization.

4. How you might be able to add value to the organization going forward, if hired.

In most interviews, they are mainly seeking to verify your capability, your motivation, and fit. In addition to finding out your key competencies and capabilities, the interviewer usually wants to see if you have the energy, the drive, and the passion for the position you are seeking. The trickiest part of the interview, over which you often have no control, is "seeing if you fit the organization." Sometimes, it is good enough to get along well with the interviewers and other times they are looking for a certain type of individual beyond specific capabilities. Although you want to communicate you competence and confidence, it is very important to be sensitive to the flow of the interview. If the interviewer is very talkative, you might want to ask more questions and follow his or her lead. If the interviewer is very quiet, you might want to get your energy level up and try to get the interviewer engaged. However, in either situation, always maintain a positive attitude and never dwell on negative or unpleasant experiences at previous organizations. If you have a writing sample or a portfolio of your achievements, this might be a good time to present it or mention it to the interviewer. It is your goal to convince the interviewers that you will not only add value, but also be committed to always doing an excellent job even if you don't plan on staying at that firm for the rest of your career.

The final stage, which many individuals often neglect, is the follow-up stage. You should remember that the organization may have interviewed many other individuals and they may not be clear on who is really committed to joining the firm if made an offer. You should usually follow up by sending a letter or an email to all you interviewers to thank them for taking the time to see you. You should also reiterate your interest in the organization and why you think you might be a good fit for the position and the firm. Always include your most recent contact information in any follow up messages. The simple gesture of sending a thank you message can often put you in the final group of potential hires. Although you may not get all the jobs for which you have interviewed, if you have done your best at all three stages of the interview phase you should greatly increase your chances of getting that elusive job offer.

Overall, effective competence projection results from an integrated approach to using résumés, cover letters, recommendations, portfolios, and interviews. Each of these elements gives you an opportunity to signal your professionalism and project your personal brand. It is important to be consistent for each element and at all stages. Take advantage of online storage and presentation technologies to give the organization a chance to review your capabilities beyond just the interview or résumé. Your presence on LinkedIn or other social networks should also be consistent with the image you are projecting to prospective employers. If you are persistent, motivated, and adaptable, you will stand out and will eventually be given the chance to create value for yourself and for interested organizations.

CHAPTER SUMMARY & OBSERVATIONS

In this chapter, you were presented with many activities and strategies that can be used to launch your international business career. The chapter stressed the importance of carrying out good market research before making a final decision on which direction to take your career. Market research covers many levels and, to be thorough, the chapter suggested that you do country, sector, company, and occupation level research. Depending on the level you are researching, you should know the key factors that help you figure out the direction of change or performance. You were also introduced to the market research grid which separated out market research activities into evaluation factors, evaluation tools, and evaluation measures. The chapter also pointed out that having a good grasp of traditional market research is important for doing more targeted career market research. In career market research, you are trying to understand how factors such as economic conditions, employment trends, regulatory practices, and expatriate dynamics might impact employment opportunities and career trajectories within and across borders. The chapter suggests that, after completing your market research and a thorough self-assessment of your values, motivations, and capabilities, you should then turn to more concrete strategies for launching your career.

You were shown in this chapter how having a good networking strategy can boost your personal brand and help support your job search activities. The chapter discussed how your networking can be viewed from the friendship, academic, professional, and social networking perspectives. You examined how each networking approach has certain advantages and how they might help you with career development. Your actual job search was broken down into three phases: preparation, targeting, and search. The chapter showed how each phase can be helped by a range of activities that boost your chances for finding employment. Competence projection was the final strategy presented to help you launch your career. This strategy is not only linked to how you manage your personal brand over time, it is most often connected with how you effectively use business cards, résumés, cover letters, recommendations, portfolios, and interviews, in the short-term, to present yourself as a desirable employee to a range of prospective employers. Throughout the chapter, it was stressed that employers are generally seeking individuals who are capable, motivated, and adaptable. If all your preparations are carried out well, the only question remaining should be whether or not you and your potential employer see the situation as a good fit.

Chapter 9 will present practical guidelines for working in Asia and Europe. You will be given general background information on Asia and Europe, followed by more specific work-related information for both regions. There will also be more detailed information on four countries in each region. In Asia, the four countries discussed are China, Japan, India, and South Korea. Although there are many other important countries in Asia, these four either have actively developing employment arenas or a longer history of working with different expatriate communities. For each nation in the list, you will get information on the general working conditions and the general attitude towards foreign workers. That will be followed by legal and visa related guidelines for gaining entry into that country. Countries vary significantly in their attitude towards foreign workers. Some countries are more proactive in their attempts to attract knowledge workers to their shores. Overall, Chapter 9 should give you a good idea on how welcoming some of these countries are, and what employment opportunities might look like.

REFERENCES

1. Day, G.S. and R. Wensley, *Marketing theory with a strategic orientation.* Journal of Marketing, 1983. **47**(4): p. 79.
2. Hughes, P., R. Morgan and Y. Kouropalatis, *Market knowledge diffusion and business performance.* European Journal of Marketing, 2008. **42**(11/12): p. 1372.
3. Grant, A., *Latest in career networking: Network roulette.* US News & World Report, November 2010: p. 1.
4. Van Hoye, G., E. Van Hooft and F. Lievens, *Networking as a job search behaviour: A social network perspective.* Journal of Occupational and Organizational Psychology, 2009. **82**(3): p. 661.
5. Brown, D.W. and A. Konrad, *Job-seeking in a turbulent economy: Social networks and the importance of cross-industry ties to an industry change.* Human Relations, 2001. **54**(8): p. 1015.
6. Diaz, A., *Informal referrals, employment, and wages: Seeking causal relationships.* Labour, 2012.**26**(1): p. 1.
7. Caldwell, D. and J. Burger, *Personality characteristics of job applicants and success in screening interviews.* Personnel Psychology, 1998. **51**(1): p. 119.
8. Light, J., *Managing and careers: Start-ups tag Facebook for career networking,* Wall Street Journal, 31 May 2011: p. B11.
9. Carrillat, F., F. Jaramillo and W. Locander, *Market-driving organizations: A framework.* Academy of Marketing Science Review, 2004. **2004**: p. 1.
10. Bell, J., B. Gray and R. McNaughton, *Developing an undergraduate international business program: Context, rationale, process and focus.* Journal of Teaching in International Business, 2003. **15**(1): p. 61.
11. Eilon, S., *A methodology for analysis of corporate performance.* Omega, 1993. **21**(5): p. 551.
12. Key, M., H. Thompson, and J. McCann, *Knowledge management: A glass half full.* People and Strategy, 2009. **32**(4): p. 42.
13. Parnell, J., *Strategic clarity, business strategy and performance.* Journal of Strategy and Management, 2010. **3**(4): p. 304.

14. Klepic, Z., *The influence of business intelligence on the business success of medium and large companies. An Enterprise Odyssey.* International Conference Proceedings, 2004: p. 705.
15. Kolk, A., *Evaluating corporate environmental reporting.* Business Strategy and the Environment, 1999. **8**(4): p. 225.
16. Market_Research. *Doing market research.* 2011 [cited 2011, Feb. 12]. Available from: http://www.euromonitor.com/.
17. Shih, T., *Comparative analysis of marketing strategies for manufacturers' and retailers' brands.* International Journal of Electronic Business Management, 2010. **8**(1): p. 56.
18. Udechukwu, O., M. Stuart and G. Shuting, *Global operations management during major change.* Business Process Management Journal, 2009. **15**(5): p. 816.
19. Richardson, T. *Country evaluation and selection.* 2011 [cited 2011, Feb. 20]. Available from: http://www.witiger.com/internationalbusiness/countryevaluation.htm.
20. Taxation. *Taxation: The four "Rs."* 2011 [cited 2011, Feb. 18]. Available from: http://www.taxplaza.org/the-four-r%27s.asp.
21. Trade. *What is trade policy?* 2011 [cited 2011, Feb. 21]. Available from: http://www.wise-geek.com/what-is-trade-policy.htm.
22. PEST. *PEST analysis explained.* 2011 [cited 2011, Feb. 21]. Available from: http://marketingteacher.com/lesson-store/lesson-pest.html.
23. GDP. *What is GDP and why is it so important?* 2011 [cited 2011, Feb. 18]. Available from: http://www.investopedia.com/ask/answers/199.asp.
24. Corruption. *Corruption perceptions index 2010 results.* 2011 [cited 2011, Feb. 21]. Available from: http://www.transparency.org/policy_research/surveys_indices/cpi/2010/results.
25. Industry. *Industry analysis.* 2011 [cited 2011, Feb. 21]. Available from: http://www.referenceforbusiness.com/small/Inc-Mail/Industry-Analysis.
26. USBLS2. *Industries at a glance: Industry at a glance home.* 2011 [cited 2011, Feb. 14]. Available from: <http://www.bls.gov/iag/home.htm>.
27. Whipple, W., III, *Evaluating alternative strategies using scenarios.* Long Range Planning, 1989. **22**(3): p. 82.
28. Bagley, A., *The Sarbanes-Oxley Act leap of faith: Why investors should trust corporate executives and accountants.* The Suffolk Law Review 2004.
29. Johnson, P. *A glossary of political economy terms.* 2011 [cited 2011, Feb. 13]. Available from: http://www.auburn.edu/~johnspm/gloss/GNP.
30. Five_Forces. *Porter's five forces.* 2011 [cited 2011, Feb. 22]. Available from: http://www.quickmba.com/strategy/porter.shtml.
31. USBLS. *Databases, tables and calculators by subject.* 2011 [cited 2011, Feb. 13]. Available from: <http://www.bls.gov/data/#productivity>.
32. Tipton, R. and K.-N. Au. *Company research guide.* 2011 [cited 2011, Feb. 21]. Available from: http://www.libraries.rutgers.edu/rul/rr_gateway/research_guides/busi/company.shtml#A.
33. Ryals, L., *Making customer relationship management work: The measurement and profitable management of customer relationships.* Journal of Marketing, 2005. **69**(4): p. 252.
34. Weidenbaum, M. and L. Rockwood, *Corporate planning versus government planning.* Public Interest, 1976(46): p. 59.
35. Financial_Analysis. *Financial statement analysis.* 2011 [cited 2011, Feb. 14]. Available from: http://www.accountingformanagement.com/accounting_ratios.htm.
36. Peavler, R. *Profitability ratios: Finance for small business owners and entrepreneurs.* 2011 [cited 2011, Feb. 15]. Available from: http://bizfinance.about.com/od/financialratios/a/Profitability_Ratios.htm.
37. ROE. *Return on equity.* 2011 [cited 2011, Feb. 21]. Available from: http://www.investopedia.com/terms/r/returnonequity.asp.
38. Brand_Loyalty. *Brand loyalty.* 2011 [cited 2011, Feb. 20]. Available from: http://www.businessdictionary.com/definition/brand-loyalty.html.
39. SWOT. *SWOT analysis.* 2011 [cited 2011, Feb. 20]. Available from: http://www.quickmba.com/strategy/swot/.

40. BCG. *BCG matrix explained: Management methods, management models, and management theories.* 2011 [cited 2011, Feb. 21]. Available from: http://www.valuebasedmanagement.net/methods_bcgmatrix.html.

41. Piercy, N. and W. Giles, *Making SWOT analysis work.* Marketing Intelligence & Planning, 1989. **7**(5/6): p. 5–7.

42. Taylor, D.E., *Strategic planning as an organizational change process: Some guidelines from practice.* Long Range Planning, 1979. **12**(5): p. 43.

43. Yau, O., et al., *Developing a scale for stakeholder orientation.* European Journal of Marketing, 2007. **41**(11/12): p. 1306.

44. Fernández, J., A. Cala and C. Domecq, *Critical external factors behind hotels' investments in innovation and technology in emerging urban destinations.* Tourism Economics, 2011. **17**(2): p. 339.

45. Fugate, B., J. Mentzer, and D. Flint, *The role of logistics in market orientation.* Journal of Business Logistics, 2008. **29**(2): p. 1.

46. Jenkins, M. and G. Johnson, *Entrepreneurial intentions and outcomes: A comparative causal mapping study.* The Journal of Management Studies, 1997. **34**(6): p. 895.

47. Kinra, A. and H. Kotzab, *Understanding and measuring macro-institutional complexity of logistics systems environment.* Journal of Business Logistics, 2008. **29**(1): p. 327.

48. Lublin, J., *Career journal: Managing your careers: Networking? Here's how to stand out,* Wall Street Journal, 4 November 2008: p. D4.

49. Pryor, C., *Put career networking on your priority list.* Internet Week, 1998(728): p. 20.

50. Cole, N., *Expatriate spouses eager for career networking help.* Canadian HR Reporter, 2010. **23**(16): p. 27.

51. Fischer, M., *Can institutional networks mitigate labor market disadvantages? Evidence from college summer job searches.* Social Science Quarterly, 2010. **91**(5): p. 1264.

52. Light, J., *Start-ups tag Facebook for career networking,* Wall Street Journal, 31 May 2011: p. B11.

53. Olson, A., *Long-term networking: A strategy for career success.* Management Review, 1994. **83**(4): p. 33.

54. O'Leary, M., *Stumble Upon, Yelp Expand Social Networks' Range.* Information Today, 2011. **28**(4): p. 22.

55. Strehlke, C., *Social network sites: A starting point for career development practitioners.* Journal of Employment Counseling, 2010. **47**(1): p. 38.

56. Keeton, L., *Careers (a special report): Starting out: Net-Working: Students are starting to travel the information highway in search of a job,* Wall Street Journal, 27 February 1995: p. R9.

57. May, C.S., *Globalisation and job search strategies: The use of "Guanxi" among Chinese business students.* Management Research News, 2000. **23**(2–4): p. 69.

58. Osberg, L., *Fishing in different pools: Job-search strategies and job-finding success in Canada in the early 1980s.* Journal of Labor Economics, 1993. **11**(2): p. 348.

59. Pissarides, C.A. and J. Wadsworth, *On-the-job search: Some empirical evidence from Britain.* European Economic Review, 1994. **38**(2): p. 385.

60. Wieczorkowska, G. and E. Burnstein, *Hunting for a job: How individual differences in foraging strategies influence the length of unemployment.* Group Processes & Intergroup Relations, 2004. **7**(4): p. 305.

61. Sverre, T., *The use of job search strategies among university graduates.* Journal of Socio-Economics, 2005. **34**(2): p. 223.

62. Wasmer, E., *General versus specific skills in labor markets with search frictions and firing costs.* The American Economic Review, 2006. **96**(3): p. 811.

63. Wilson, D., *Landing on your feet in the current job market: Strategies based on personal experience.* Business Perspectives, 2004. **16**(2): p. 38.

64. McKeown, T. and M. Lindorff, *The graduate job search process: A lesson in persistence rather than good career management?* Education & Training, 2011. **53**(4): p. 310.

65. Van Horn, C. and A. Fichtner, *An evaluation of state-subsidized, firm-based training: The workforce development partnership program.* International Journal of Manpower, 2003. **24**(1): p. 97.

66. Van Ours, J. and G. Ridder, *Vacancies and the recruitment of new employees.* Journal of Labor Economics, 1992. **10**(2): p. 138.

PART IV

GUIDELINES FOR WORKING & MANAGING YOUR CAREER ACROSS BORDERS

9 PRACTICAL GUIDELINES & STRATEGIES FOR WORKING IN ASIA & EUROPE

LEARNING OBJECTIVES

- Introduction to working in Asia and Europe

- Strategies for working in China

- Strategies for working in Japan

- Strategies for working in South Korea

- Strategies for working in India

- Strategies for working in Germany

- Strategies for working in Italy

- Strategies for working in France

- Strategies for working in the United Kingdom

THE ROADMAP

In Chapter 8, you were presented with practical strategies for launching your international business career. The suggested activities were all linked to four strategic areas: market research, networking, job search, and competence projection. You were shown the market research grid which presented evaluation factors, tools, and measures for investigating country, sector, and company level developments. Networking was mentioned as a key career management strategy, and four different types of networks were discussed. It was pointed out that each type of network has its advantages. Job search was broken down into the preparation, targeting, and search phases. Each phases had a range of activities that could potentially boost your chances of finding employment. The short-term aspects of a competence projection strategy were also presented. This strategic area was linked to the management of your personal brand, as well as to the effective use of business cards, résumés, cover letters, recommendations, portfolios, and interviews. The overall assertion was that if you coordinate and execute all four strategic areas effectively, you will greatly increase your short and long-term employability within and across borders.

Chapter 9 is mainly about practical strategies and guidelines for choosing and finding employment in Asia and Europe. In addition to talking about general developments in both regions, you will get a more detailed look at four countries in each of the regions. In Asia, the focus will be on China, Japan, South Korea, and India. These four economies are central to the dynamic economic activities we are witnessing in Asia. In addition, these countries have growing or well established markets that are open to foreign knowledge workers. In Europe, the four countries covered are Germany, Italy, France, and the United Kingdom. Here, again, we have economies that are very important to the European Union (EU) and general international competitiveness. Although, it might be more difficult for non-EU members to get access to employment opportunities, there are still many opportunities for skilled individuals from around the world. Moreover, these countries have established expatriate communities that can help with networking and career management decisions.

WORKING IN ASIA

The Asia region has had tremendous economic growth over the last 30 years. This chapter will focus on strategies and guidelines for working in China, Japan, South Korea, and India. These four countries account for a significant portion of the economic growth and market size in Asia. From major technological advances, to the mass production and assembly of a wide range of products, these countries have become world class competitors. These four Asian countries offer numerous working opportunities for foreign workers. Consequently, we have seen a significant increase in interest in the cultural, social, and business activities of these nations. This chapter will highlight key factors for understanding employment opportunities in these countries.

Working in China

China has emerged as an economic powerhouse, with the largest population and the second largest GDP in the world. For many years, China has been a center of manufacturing and assembly activities for many parts of the world. Although the economy still benefits from massive exports, there is now a concerted push by the government to develop the domestic market across most sectors. China sees a strong domestic economy as crucial to its long-term economic competitiveness. This combination of an active export market and a growing domestic market creates many opportunities for jobs and career development. [1, 2]

The working environment in China
In many ways, the working environment in China is very different from that of the United States. We have a situation where a country is transitioning rapidly from a communist system to a more capitalist environment. The country is also growing rapidly, and new wealth is being created regularly. This situation leads to many contradictions, which can be very confusing to foreigners visiting or working in China. From a political perspective, China is a closed country with the Communist Party dominating the power structure. However, from an economic perspective, China is relatively open, with intense interaction and competition between domestic and foreign firms. You have to be able to move beyond these contradictions in order to make sense of what could be called a "Chinese management style." [3, 4]

China's long history has indirectly had an impact on its management style. The Chinese generally have a greater respect for people in positions of authority and power. This includes their elders, as well as managers and other leaders. Confucianism also works to support many of those attitudes. It is, therefore, not uncommon for managers to give direct and detailed instructions, expecting subordinates to perform without too much questioning. This type of respect for the hierarchical separation of power and influence affects behaviors in business and many areas of life in China. Another important social phenomenon is Guanxi, which is often described as the importance of personal relationships, connections, and relational networks. This factor underlies the nature of business and social activities in China. In essence, who you know is often more important than what you know. In effect, gaining the trust of the Chinese people is considered one of the most important aspects of doing business in China. Foreigners need to be aware of, and adapt to, all these factors if they desire to work in China. [3-5]

The attitude towards foreign workers in China has changed significantly over the years. Initially, there was some resentment because of the perceived special treatment and differences in behavior of foreigners. Those attitudes have started to change, as China opens up and more Chinese travel abroad. Moreover, although China is facing a growing problem with an increasing number of illegal workers from neighboring countries, the government is supportive of skilled foreign workers getting certain jobs in China. The government sees this as a way of bringing in important skills, and as a way of improving the overall quality of the workforce in certain industries. Consequently, the employment of highly skilled foreigners in certain areas is seen as important for the long-term growth of the country. [1, 6]

Despite the general support for skilled foreign workers, the attitude towards them and the need for them vary significantly by region. Partly because of living and working conditions, foreign workers tend to be concentrated in the highly industrialized and international cities like Beijing, Shanghai, Guangzhou, and Hong Kong. The compensation for foreigners will depend on whether they were hired elsewhere as an expatriate or as a local hire. Benefits, perks, and salaries are much better for expatriates. Benefits for expatriates often include bonuses, housing allowance, paid vacation, a round trip air ticket once a year, full healthcare, evacuation insurance, tax coverage, and coverage of shipping fees. [2, 7]

A popular career choice for many westerners who are not sent by foreign firms is becoming an English teacher in China. However, it appears that the majority of skilled foreign workers are either employed by foreign firms or by Chinese firms dealing directly with foreigner clients. The sought-after occupations are mainly in areas such as sales, marketing, engineering, business management, and information technology. As can be expected, having good personal connections or being fluent in Mandarin Chinese are clearly advantages for foreigners seeking work in China. [7]

Legal guidelines for working in China

China is known for having very strict immigration and visa-related policies, and the number of foreign workers is relatively low compared to the overall population. In order to work in China, one must first have a letter of support from an employer or a sponsoring organization. This invitation must then be approved by the Chinese authorities. The Chinese visa authorities can issue a diplomatic, courtesy, service, or ordinary visa to foreigners, according to their identity, purpose of visit, and passport type. The ordinary visas consist of eight sub-categories, which are marked with the letters D, Z, X, F, L, G, C, J-1, and J-2, respectively. [2, 6, 7]

Visa D is issued to permanent resident aliens in China. Visa Z is issued to foreigners (and their family members) who will work and live in China. Visa X is issued to foreigners to go to China for study or job training. Visa F is issued to those who are invited to China for visit, study, lecture, a business tour, or scientific, technological, and cultural exchanges for periods of no more than six months. Visa L is issued to those who go for sightseeing, visiting relatives, or other private purposes. Visa G is issued to foreigners who will transit through China. Visa C is issued to train attendants, air crew members, and seamen, operating international services, and to their accompanying family members. Visa J-1 is issued to foreign resident correspondents in China. Visa J-2 is issued to foreign correspondents that make short trips to China on reporting tasks. [2, 7]

Working in Japan

Although Japan has undergone a deep recession and has had relatively slower economic growth since the early 1990s, the country is still the third largest economy in the world. Japanese companies are still strong world class competitors in sectors such as consumer electronics, automobiles, mobile technology, machine tools, and video gaming. Japanese companies also have a reputation for applied research and the commercialization of new developments. In recent years, the increasing success of activities linked to Japanese popular culture has also created new consumers worldwide, in areas such as manga, animation, video games, movies, TV shows, music, and Japanese food. Moreover, certain parts of Japan are still popular tourist destinations, and the domestic economy now has a stronger service sector. The job market has had its ups and downs, but many foreigners continue to seek job opportunities in Japan. [8, 9]

The work environment in Japan

The importance of work is central in the Japanese environment. There are also many dimensions to the important role that work plays in people's lives. In a country where there are still many single-income families, having and keeping a job is crucial for income generation and also social identity. Another aspect is how hard and how long individuals are expected to work to help their companies stay competitive. Japanese workers often leave home early and return home late. An additional aspect is the impact of a strong corporate culture that reinforces the idea of the company as a family. After-work socializing and living in company dormitories are just two examples of practices that support the strong corporate culture approach. [10, 11]

The lifetime employment practice that people associate with Japan has changed drastically over the last 20 years. Although companies do a lot to hold onto core employees, a series of restructurings and downsizings have made it difficult for workers to have a guaranteed long-term position in most companies. Some companies have also started emphasizing merit and ability and have down played long term tenure. Despite these changes, it remains a society with strong hierarchical awareness and a collective approach to interaction and problem solving. The main work unit in many organizations is usually the team or work group. In many organizations, everyone works together to complete the group assignments and the focus is not usually on individual task completion. The core employees do not usually go home immediately after their daily tasks are completed. After the regular work is done, the groups often have meetings or socializing situations where they can exchange information and solve problems informally. [10, 12]

In the post-war era, the Japanese have generally had a welcome attitude towards foreign visitors. People often speak of the courteous, helpful, and honest treatment they get from the Japanese. However, the attitude towards foreign workers is more complex. It is probably best to separate the view of foreigners in the workforce into three groups: skilled expatriates working for foreign firms, skilled foreigners working for Japanese firms, and unskilled foreigners working for Japanese firms or in the informal economy. The first group tends to be in the best position, since they are generally highly paid and have a lot of support and benefits from the foreign firms for which they work. This group has been in Japan for a long time, and the Japanese are generally welcoming. Skilled foreigners in Japanese firms represent a growing category, as they are recently more aggressively sought-after by firms actively engaged in international business activities. These foreigners are generally expected to speak Japanese and behave in ways that don't disrupt the Japanese management style. This group is generally more accepted since they are usually committed to adapting to the Japanese environment and are more willing to stay in Japan for the longterm. The third category includes foreigners who are willing to do many of the "dirty, dangerous and dreary" jobs that the Japanese are avoiding. This group usually has a more difficult time, and there are many accounts of mistreatment and outright discrimination in certain areas. However, overall, knowing the language and being willing to adapt to Japanese customs and behavior generally makes interaction and acceptance by the Japanese much easier. [8, 13]

Despite a growing acceptance of skilled foreigner workers, there is still much anxiety in Japan about having a large influx of foreigners. Some fear that crime and other problems will escalate if there are too many foreigners in the country. For many westerners, the easiest way to start working in Japan is to teach English or another foreign language. Another entry level area of opportunity for foreigners is to participate in a "trainee program," which often last up to 12 months. After graduating these programs, individuals can land a technical internship which can last up to three years. Finally, there are a growing number of foreign students who, after graduating from a Japanese university, find positions with Japanese or foreign firms in Japan. Overall, there are many positions available in business, services, manufacturing, and entertainment. The key concern for most foreigners is the cost of living, since a number of Japanese cities rank as some of the most expensive places to live in the world. [9, 13, 14]

Legal guidelines for working in Japan

If one is just visiting Japan, there a number of visa-exempt countries whose citizens are allowed to enter Japan with a valid passport for up to 90 days. Americans are allowed to visit Japan without a visa. Visitors from a variety of other countries need to go through the visa application process before going to Japan. A complete list of current visa-exempt countries and their permitted lengths of stay can be found through the website of the Japanese Ministry of Foreign Affairs.

To work legally in Japan, it is necessary to have a valid passport and the proper visa. As part of the visa application process, an individual must receive a "Certificate of Eligibility" from the proper authorities in Japan. The Certificate of Eligibility proves that the foreign applicant meets the conditions necessary for living and working in Japan. Once the Certificate of Eligibility is received, a visa can quickly be issued at a nearby embassy or consulate. After you arrive in Japan, you need to pick up an Alien Registration Card, which the police may ask you for at any time. Not having this is illegal if you are in the country longer than a tourist visa allows. There are many types of visas and they can be classified into 27 categories. Below are some examples of visas that are available for living and working in Japan. [12, 15]

The Professor Working Visa allows work as a researcher at a college or educational institution. The Artist Working Visa is issued to those who can generate income while working in the arts. The Investor/Business Manager Visa is offered for the purposes of international trade, investment in a Japanese business, or managing any business-related activities in Japan. The Legal/Accounting Services Work Visa is issued to foreign law or accounting specialists. The Medical Services Work Visa allows individuals to work as a physician, dentist, or in other related medical areas. The Researcher Working Visa permits one to work as a researcher in a Japanese company. The Instructor Japan Working Visa is issued to language teachers and instructors at elementary school, high school, vocational school, and other related educational institutions. The Engineer Work Visa is intended for specialists within the physical science, engineering, and other related fields. The Humanities/International Services Visa is given to specialists in jurisprudence, economics, sociology, and other related human science fields. The Intra-Company Transferee Working Visa permits international business employees to work at a Japanese branch. The Entertainer Work Visa is given to theatrical and musical performers, sports people, and other related fields. A Student Visa is offered to college students, pre-college students, and trainees not affiliated with any instructional institution. A Family Visa is offered to the spouse and children of Japanese national, and allows them to stay from one to three years. [8, 15]

Finally, a Working Holiday Visa is also available for 18–30 year-olds, and it allows them to live, work, and travel within Japan for a 12 month period. There are no working holiday agreements between the US and Japan. However, information on the conditions and a list of select countries that allow working holiday visa arrangements with Japan can be found at the website of the Ministry of Foreign Affairs.

Working in South Korea

Despite facing many challenges and constraints, South Korea continues to have a strong and vibrant economy and remains a powerhouse in Asia. Over the years, the country has been a significant competitor in shipbuilding, automobiles, construction and, more recently, consumer electronics and mobile technology. Economic reforms and South Korea's move away from the centrally planned, government-directed investment model towards a more market-oriented system have unleashed a tremendous entrepreneurial spirit and allowed some sectors to become globally competitive. With almost no natural resources, and bordering on overpopulation in some areas, South Korea has adopted an export-oriented economic strategy. In 2010, South Korea was the sixth largest exporter and tenth largest importer in the world. With a growing economy and numerous alliances with foreign firms, there has been a jump in the number of foreigners working in South Korea. [16, 17]

The work environment in South Korea

South Korea is another country where the influence of Confucianism is strong. There is tremendous respect for parents, family, elders, and people with authority. There is also lot of emphasis placed on, and admiration for, education and occupational success. It is not unusual for South Koreans to ask one's age and occupation when they first meet. This type of information is important in a society that respects hierarchy and professional achievement. Although they often appear reserved, South Koreans are known to have an intense and competitive spirit. They will work intensively to achieve their business and occupational goals. Although education and achievements are crucial for respect, the importance of relationships and trust can never be overlooked. [18]

The South Korean work ethic is something of which foreigners need to be aware. South Korea has one of the highest average working hours and overtime hours per week in the world. This can be a challenge for foreigners who are unwilling to work long hours and show the effort and commitment to satisfy a South Korean company. Although there is legislation which limits the maximum work-week hours, the law is not strictly enforced. There are many strategies to which employees resort in order to complete their work beyond working hours. On the other hand, some Korean companies are known for offering good bonuses and vacation time for employees who perform well. In addition to the work ethic, working in South Korea also requires individuals to put a lot of time into building relationships inside and outside the firm. [19, 20]

In general, South Koreans have had a cautious attitude towards foreigners working in their country. However, as their companies become more global, and as they seek out more highly skilled employees, foreign workers are seen as necessary for building a competitive advantage in some areas. The result is that the population is become more tolerant of different nationalities working in South Korea. Aside from language teachers, there is a lot of stress being placed on hiring highly skilled foreign professionals. Workers who enter the country illegally have a much tougher time finding a place in society. These workers are paid low wages and are subject to poor living and working conditions. Overall, the most desired foreign employees are corporate executives, scientists, engineers, professors, and others in banking, finance, architecture, design, and information technology. [13, 18]

Legal guidelines for working in South Korea

If you are not sent by your foreign employer to South Korea, the best way to find work is to take advantage of personal networks, or by promoting your English language teaching ability. Other locally-hired skilled jobs are available for foreigners, but a good knowledge of Korean is generally required, unless you are a high profile foreign executive, researcher, or professor. As for visiting South Korea, citizens from a number of countries are allowed for no longer than 90 days without a visa. These are usually citizens from those countries or regions with which Korea has signed a visa waiver. To work in South Korea, you must obtain a work permit, which is a valid proof of employment from a sponsoring employer. Below is a short list of the types of visas that are available. [16, 21]

The Short Term Employment Visa (C4) is for those who plan on working in Korea for 90 days or less. The Professional Employment Visa (E5) is issued to those who wish to work in South Korea on a more permanent basis. The Foreign Language Instructor Visa (E2 visa) is awarded to language teachers accepted for work in educational establishments. The Working Holiday Visa can be given if you are between the ages of 18 and 25, and are from a country which has signed the Tourism Employment Agreement. The Student Visa (D2 visa) is issued to college students that have been invited by an educational institution; it is also available for those undergoing industrial training. The Intra-Company Transfer Visa (D7) is issued to company employees who have been transferred to South Korea. [21]

Working in India

India is a country with a rich history, and it is increasingly playing an important strategic role in international business and politics. The country has had an average annual GDP growth of over 5 percent for many years, and is now the tenth largest economy in the world. Besides having one of the fastest growing economies in the world, India has been at the center of the global outsourcing boom of the last decade. This has not always been the case, and much of the change is due to a shift from a closed economy to a more open one since the early 1990s. Although India still has many infrastructure problems, the country has been learning to take advantage of its cheap labor and a constant flow of engineers and computer-savvy graduates. India is now a major player in the steel, automotive, information technology, and pharmaceuticals industries. The country has a growing upper and middle class and numerous market opportunities for a variety of products and services. The country's large base of English speakers also gives it an advantage, as it does business with firms from around the world. It is no wonder, then, that many individuals have gone to India either on assignment or to find new opportunities to expand their business careers. [22, 23]

The work environment in India

Working in India can pose challenges on many levels. There is a stunning mixture of wealth and poverty in close proximity. There are many bustling urban centers with inadequate infrastructure, often leading to a sometimes uncomfortable mixture of people, vehicles, and animals competing for space. In addition to the diversity of regions and cultures, work behaviors will differ, depending on whether an individual works for a small, medium-sized or large company. Business practices also vary between regions. In addition, the caste system continues to have an impact on the nature of interaction between groups in India. Moreover, as in other Asian countries, India is a country where relationships play a paramount role in how business in conducted. There are strong family, community, and regional ties that dominate the level of trust in business relationships. [23, 24]

Hierarchy is important in business relationships and the daily work environment. We see different behaviors and treatment of people at different management levels. This is especially true in the behavior of superiors towards subordinates. Indian bosses can at times appear bossy and even rude. From an American perspective, management in India involves a lot of micro-managing. Superiors often give out detailed instructions on how and when they want tasks to be completed. In general, decisions are made at the top and the responsibility of those on the bottom is to get the job done. This does not stop Indians from working very hard at all levels. Given the large number of Indians that have to deal with companies in other time zones, many Indians work long days and nights to make the adjustments necessary. [25, 26]

The attitude of Indians towards foreign workers is generally good. Indians generally show a lot of hospitality towards expatriates working in India. Since English is widely used, it is not absolutely necessary to learn the local language. However, it does help if one understands the culture and typical business behaviors. As the number of multinationals in India increases, the demand for both local and foreign workers has gone up. Many foreign firms generally fill the top executive positions and training roles with foreign employees. The most popular sectors and jobs for expatriates are in technical fields, information technology, medical services, and construction. Teaching English is another option for those looking for jobs in high schools, language schools, universities, and call centers. Overall, the government is supportive of giving visas to skilled foreign workers, but is clearly not supportive of any increase in the number of unskilled foreign workers. [23, 26, 27]

Legal guidelines for working in India

All foreigners going to India are required to have a passport and a visa. There are no visas issued on arrival and, therefore, it is necessary to apply for a visa at an embassy or consulate in one's home country. The only exceptions are citizens of Bhutan, Nepal, and the Maldives, if the purpose is for tourism or a stay up for up to 90 days. Other groups that only need passports are Persons of Indian Origin (PIOs) and Overseas Citizen[s] of India (OCI). Since the application process is often very time-consuming, individuals should apply for a visa well in advance. To obtain a visa, a letter of invitation is required from a sponsor. The letter must provide contact information and explain the purpose and length of the intended stay in India. [22, 28]

India has separate classifications of visas for tourism, business, and employment. A Tourist Visa is generally valid for six months. A Business Visa is issued for one year, or more with multiple entries. An Employment Visa (E visa) is issued for a year but can be extended up to five years. These visas can also be used for intra-company transfers on a case-by-case basis. (Multiple-Entry Visas require that the visa holder leave the country for two months between entries to the country.) A Transit Visa is issued to for the purpose of allowing visitors to enter India for up to 15days, while travelling to another country. A Student Visa is issued to students who have received an invitation from an Indian educational institution, and it allows them a stay up to five years. A Medical Visa (M visa) allows individuals into the country to seek medical treatment. M visas allow a stay of up to one year, but can be extended if necessary. [24, 28]

The Employment Visa (E-visa) is given to foreigners who desire to work for a foreign or Indian firm in India. This is the same visa that is required for an internship in India. The application process for employment visas can be complicated and time consuming. However, the Employment Visa automatically serves as a work permit for India. Consequently, once it is received, it is not necessary to apply for additional permits to work in India. [28]

WORKING IN EUROPE

Western Europe has always played an important role in the modern world economy. The major countries in western Europe continue to have the economic and political clout that sometimes goes far beyond their actual size. Moreover, the creation of the European Union (EU) has given additional influence to this region of the world. The 27 member states coordinate many economic activities and the combined market makes the EU an economic force. The purpose of the EU is to create an economic and political partnership among the member states in ways that allow it to create a larger market and compete with the strong economies of the US and a number of countries in Asia. The partnership allows citizens of the member states to travel and work freely within each other's countries. Germany, Italy, France, and United Kingdom are western Europe's richest and most populous nations. These four countries create many job opportunities and attract workers from a variety of countries. Although they all give preference to workers from EU countries, they have varying attitudes towards non-EU individuals working within their borders. The sections below will provide more detailed information on the working environment and employment guidelines for these four major EU countries.

Working in Germany

Germany has the largest economy in Europe. The workforce numbers over 40 million and it has the highest level of education in Europe. A unique partnership between labor, business, and the government since World War II has created a relatively stable labor environment. In addition, the awareness of, and focus on, improving environmental, health, and safety conditions has led to generally good working conditions in Germany. By law, German workers receive six weeks of vacation as well as 14 public holidays off. There are also generous sick leave policies in place. However, the German economy has been troubled for a long time with a persistent high average unemployment rate of over 8 percent. Structural unemployment is estimated at around 80 percent of the total unemployment. Despite this situation, the country continues to attract individuals looking for a chance to benefit from this powerful economy. [29, 30]

The working environment in Germany

Being the most populous member of the European Union, Germany carries a lot of political and economic clout in Europe. Germany continues to be one the world's largest exporting countries. However, although the Germany economy has historically been based on manufacturing, the service sector has grown tremendously in recent years. Yet, despite having a large labor force and a strong economy, there is a significant shortage of skilled workers in certain important areas. Many German firms in information technology, services, and marketing are searching in earnest for qualified employees. [30, 31]

The working environment in Germany is substantially different from the one in the US. Germany has implemented greater use of flexible working hours and it is unusual to have employees working past 7pm. However, management executives and highly paid senior staff are expected to work overtime without additional compensation. Overall, it can be said that there is a greater emphasis placed on a work-life balance in Germany. As mentioned previously, sick leave and pregnancy leave can be generous, while health insurance is mandatory and accessible to all. The emphasis in Germany is often on how efficiently work is done and not the length of time during the work-week. This could be partly due to the setting of the legal maximum work-week at around 48 hours. In addition, workers in Germany have many protected rights, and this is one of the most highly regulated labor markets in the world. Consequently, the combination of a strong economy and strong labor regulations result in salaries which are some of the highest in the world. [32-34]

As for their approach to the work, Germans are known for being detail-oriented, and they spend a lot of time in meetings gathering information and deciding on process and strategy. This is a low context culture and individuals can be very direct in their comments. They often come across as rude to cultures that use more indirect communication strategies. In general, German management and company structures are also more hierarchical and formal than their American counterparts. Finally, it is important to be punctual, since lateness projects irresponsibility. [29, 35]

As for the attitude towards foreign workers, Germans are somewhat ambivalent. In the past, the government eased restrictions and passed a bill allowing German companies to find skilled workers abroad to make up for domestic skill shortages. The professions experiencing the most shortages are scientists, engineers, professors, and specialists in high technology. However, despite the relaxation, it is still easier to find a job in Germany if you are from an EU nation. The process is much more difficult for non-EU workers. Because of the chronic high unemployment, some sectors of the German population have been very wary of foreigners, and attitudes have bordered on racist from time to time. Illegal immigrants and foreigners from Turkey, the Middle East, and Africa have experienced the most negative reactions. [29, 36]

Another approach to developing a career in Germany is to attend a German university. Foreign graduates of German universities are given a year to find a position if they wish to stay in the country. This is a shift, because it was quite difficult in the past for foreign students to remain in the country after finishing their studies. Germany also offers a working holiday option for certain individuals from countries such as Australia, New Zealand, Canada, and Japan. Citizens from these countries can stay in Germany for up to 12 months with this visa. Below are more guidelines when considering working in Germany. [29]

Legal guidelines for working in Germany

Except for foreigners from the European Union, the United States, Australia, Canada, New Zealand, Japan, South Korea, and Israel, all foreigners are required to have a visa to enter Germany. As for working in Germany, EU citizens do not need a work permit but they need to go through the simple procedure of obtaining a residence permit. On the other hand, there is no work visa or permit restrictions in Germany for voluntary work. It is generally recommended that individuals obtain the necessary visas or permits in their own country before departure. [32, 33]

The visa approval process can take up to three months. Once in Germany, it is necessary to register with the local authorities. Individuals need to show proof of residence at that time, and non-EU residents need to take a German medical exam also. If an individual's country is party to the Schengen agreement, they are eligible for a Schengen visa. The 15 Schengen countries are Austria, Belgium, Denmark, Finland, France, Germany, Iceland, Italy, Greece, Luxembourg, the Netherlands, Norway, Portugal, Spain, and Sweden. With a Schengen visa, an individual may enter and travel freely throughout the Schengen zone. [29, 33]

Working in Italy

Italy has the fourth largest economy in Europe, and the country's firms are active in many different sectors. It is also a major exporting nation. Although the country has had a long history of ineffective governments, its companies continue to be innovators and competitors in many international industries. Italy is one of the world's largest wine producers and continues to have a significant impact in automobiles and fashion. With numerous small and medium-sized firms, the country is also known for its entrepreneurial capabilities. Despite all these positive factors, the country has experienced a slowdown in its long-term growth rate and has debt, unemployment and illegal immigration problems to tackle. Nevertheless, Italy remains a primary tourist destination and its major cities also attract job seekers from around the world. [37-39]

The work environment in Italy

Italy suffers from a serious gap in economic conditions between the northern and southern parts of the country. The northern part is highly industrialized, economically active, and has lower unemployment levels. The southern part of the country is less economically active, and has very high unemployment levels. Unemployment is particularly high among the young people. These conditions give even greater importance to the underground or informal economy in Italy. Unfortunately, the people who control the informal economy often ignore safety regulations, demand excessive working hours, offer no job security, and provide no pensions or severance pay. Some have estimated that over one-fifth of work activity in Italy is done secretly and without paying taxes. To avoid having the burden of full-time workers with benefits, many firms will hire people on short-term contracts or a succession of short-term contracts. Even when individuals do find full-time employment, Italian salaries are among the lowest in Europe. [40, 41]

When it comes to finding a position in Italy, it often depends more on who you know and not on what you know. Family ties, community relationships, and personal networks dominate employment and social activities in Italy. Nepotism is very common across the country. As for business behavior, the small and medium-sized firms are agile and influenced by the founder or by local families. On the other hand, the larger Italian firms are more bureaucratic and rigid. A major cultural value of Italians is their collectivism. They have a strong group orientation and value family and community to a high degree. The Italian business culture reflects a very high context culture orientation. Context, non-verbal behavior, and repeated interactions are often necessary to fully understand the dynamics of a situation. [42, 43]

The daily business work flow in Italy is vastly different from that in the US. Most businesses in Italy open from 9am to 1pm and 3.30pm to 7.30pm Monday to Saturday. Some firms close on Saturday or some other afternoon during the week. The main exception would be department stores, supermarkets, and tourism-related activities. In essence, work centrality is lower in Italy. People clearly prefer to focus on a balance between work and non-work areas of their lives. The regulatory environment also supports this approach. The maximum allowable number of working hours is 48 and all workers are entitled to a minimum of four weeks' annual leave. [40-42]

Working in Italy can be difficult if you do not know the language, since English is not widely spoken. In general, Italians are very friendly when dealing with tourists. They are more ambivalent when it comes to dealing with foreign workers in Italy. This is despite the fact that certain types of foreign workers have been in high demand for many years. Italians have a strong sense of cultural identity and they are sometimes wary of foreign cultural practices. By some estimates, there are almost-five million immigrants living in Italy and a significant percentage is there to work. The foreigners with skills generally go after jobs in media, tourism, technology, finance, fashion design, and English teaching. [37, 41]

Legal guidelines for working in Italy

European Union nationals do not require a visa for stays of up to 90 days in Italy. Usually, a visa is not needed for United States citizens who desire to visit Italy for up to 90 days. However, if you are from a non-EU country and you desire to work in Italy, you will need a visa and a work permit. In order to get a work permit, you must have a job offer from an Italian employer who is willing to sponsor you. It is important to note that the process can be time consuming and varies significantly among different regions. Attitudes towards foreign workers have turned more negative of late, since it has become even harder for native Italians to find jobs. There is push by some to make it harder to obtain or renew work permits. Work permits are granted for a maximum of one year, with an option to extend it as necessary.

EU citizens are allowed to work in Italy, but they are required to have a tax-file number. An easier route for non-EU individuals is the Working Holiday Visa. However, Italy only offers Working Holiday Visas to citizens of Australia, New Zealand, and Canada. Finally, since Italy is also a member of the Schengen Agreement, citizens from Austria, Belgium, Denmark, Finland, France, Germany, Iceland, Italy, Greece, Luxembourg, the Netherlands, Norway, Portugal, Spain, and Sweden may enter and travel freely throughout the country. [37, 39, 41, 42]

Working in France

France has Europe's second largest economy and plays a vital economic and political role in the European Union. Although there many internationally competitive firms and sectors in France, the government does still have significant influence in many areas of the economy. However, privatization has continued steadily, as the government continues to sell off its holdings in many firms. France has a very active economy with a high level of inward foreign direct investment. France is also one of the world's major importers and exporters of manufactured goods. Due to both its economic and cultural influence, France continues to attract individuals for tourism, and for employment from around the world. [44]

The working environment in France

France has one of the most highly educated workforces in Europe. France is third in productivity and fourth in labor costs in Europe. However, France is known for having strong regulations and institutional arrangements that affect the work environment and work process. Everything from working hours per week to the length of vacations is impacted by institutional arrangements. In larger organizations, the work culture is relatively formal, with clear distinctions between lower, middle, and upper management. The hierarchical structure makes it harder to operate across levels quickly. However, in smaller and medium-sized organizations, the work style is more relaxed. Finally, France is infamous for its formal and informal regulations that make everything from getting a license to renting an apartment a bureaucratic nightmare. [45, 46]

A little more than a decade ago, the French government introduced a 35 hour week to ease unemployment. The logic was that it would bring more people into the workforce. Only workers in certain categories were exempt. There has been continued debate over the effectiveness of the shorter work hours per week limitations in France. In practice, the average number of working hours is 35 to 48 hours per week, and holidays can be up to 37 days a year. If we consider the shorter working hours and the holidays and leaves that are available, France appears to be a great place to work. However, some individuals find it difficult to generate as much income as they would like under these restrictions, and some say it even makes it harder to find full-time work. Nevertheless, with generally high salaries and good health and education benefits, the French have a high standard of living. [47–49]

France is known for having high taxation, which supports a generous social security system. Although union membership is lower than in the past, unions continue to have significant power and regular strikes that affect the public sector are not unusual. There is clearly a rigid labor market in certain sectors, and we see constant battles to protect or change employment arrangements. The level of unemployment is relatively high, and it is difficult to fire individuals once they are hired. Moreover, full-time workers are guaranteed at least five weeks' vacation a year. Despite the rigidity, the economy has undergone significant changes. The majority of the workforce is now employed in the service sector, while about 27 percent is employed in industry. Only about 5 percent of the workforce is now in agriculture. [44]

The attitude towards foreign workers may even be considered hostile at times. The government has made it difficult for non-French citizens to get jobs. Even if EU members have the right to work freely in France, the government still gives priority to French citizens. Everyone else needs to show proof that they are more qualified than French alternatives for the positions. Many bureaucratic hurdles stand in the way of firms wishing to recruit foreign workers. Overall, this makes it very difficult for foreigners to find jobs in France. Some say that France's attitude towards foreign workers turned more hostile when Nicolas Sarkozy became president. Many laws limit immigration, and the focus is now on attracting mainly highly skilled immigrants that could be a benefit to the French economy. Moreover, the French have a strong sense of their national culture and expect foreign nationals to do their best to adopt the language and cultural practices. Despite the restrictions and barriers, many people continue to go to France from poorer countries to find work. Many of those come from former colonies. [50, 51]

Legal guidelines for working in France

It is clear that France has one of the most protected labor markets in Europe. EU nationals can work in France without having to obtain a work permit or a visa. This excludes members who joined the EU after 2004. EU nationals have up to three months to apply for an EU Resident Permit at the closest government authority to where they live. If the individual desires to stay on a permanent basis, a renewable five year permit is usually issued. Non-EU nationals are generally not encouraged to look for employment in France. Permits are usually issued only after there is sponsorship by an employer and the local market has been notified and tested for the position. It is a little easier for highly qualified workers that belong to foreign firms operating in France. [44, 51]

There are only two types work permits in France: Temporary Secondment and Full Work Permit. The Temporary Secondment is used for non-French companies that need to place their employees in their branches or operations in France. The maximum duration for this permit is usually 18 months, but it can be extended. A Full Work Permit is issued on behalf of a French company that wants to directly hire a non-EU national. [44, 51]

Working in the United Kingdom (UK)

The United Kingdom (UK) is a nation that results from the combination of four countries (England, Northern Ireland, Scotland and Wales) that are governed under a constitutional monarchy and a parliamentary system. The capital city is London. The service sector in the UK accounts for over 70 percent of GDP and the capital city of London is one the world's largest financial centers. Tourism plays a major role in the UK, since it is ranked as the sixth major tourist destination in the world. A lot of its influence can be linked to its history. The industrial revolution originated in the UK and the empire that was created later served as the market for the products and services produced. Even though the empire is long gone, the UK still has extensive business and institutional ties with numerous countries around the world. In addition to international trade, the country continues to be a major competitor in the finance, aerospace, and automotive sectors. Given that the UK is the world's sixth largest economy and the third largest in Europe, it continues to be a magnet for those seeking employment from around the world. The population of many areas in the UK shows extreme ethnic diversity. The wide variety of ethnic groups represents both strengths and challenges for the communities and the government. [52, 53]

The working environment in the U.K.

On the surface, one would assume that the work climate and business practices would be extremely similar to the US. Yet, even though English is spoken in both countries, there are enough differences that make it necessary to study the country more in depth before jumping to conclusions. In general, the British are more restrained and polite in their daily business interactions. This sometimes makes it a little harder to get a quick read of their intentions in certain situations. This is a low context culture, but there are clear class distinctions which still govern perceptions and behaviors between certain groups. [54, 55]

Legislation in the late 1990s established a 48-hour maximum work-week. However, there are many situations whereby individuals are working much longer hours. Workers are also supposed to receive rest periods after four hours of work, and at least one day off per week. Workers are also supposed to receive a 4-week paid vacation per year. Work centrality is high in the UK, since the work ethic is firmly established. Although unemployment has tended to be lower than in continental Europe, serious debt issues and the after-effects of the financial crisis have put serious pressure on employment arrangements and employee benefits in the UK. [56–58]

With the jump in unemployment and drastic steps to curb spending, British workers are under tremendous pressure. Similar to other European nations, we see a growing anti-immigration movement in the UK. The acts of terrorism that they have experienced have also exacerbated this anti-immigrant attitude. This new attitude is also making it harder for skilled foreign workers to find employment. Legal steps have already been taken to ban the movement of unskilled economic migrants from non-European countries. The global economic downturn and higher unemployment are behind steps to reduce the categories of jobs usually made available to even skilled workers from outside the European Union. Nevertheless, it has been reported that currently foreign workers from outside the European Union hold more than 3.5 million jobs and account for 13 percent of total jobs. This indicates that historically the UK has been much more open than other European countries to foreign workers. The harshness of future employment limitations will depend on how long the economic downturn lasts and how persistently immigrants continue trying to find work in the UK. [52, 55, 57]

Legal guidelines for working in the UK

Citizens of full European Member countries can live and work in the UK. Non-EU nationals who want to live and work in the UK must apply for a Work Visa, Work Permit, Working Holiday or Youth Mobility Visa. Americans visiting the UK do not need a visa but, if they wish to work, they will need to get a Work Permit. In order to get a Work Permit, an individual must be sponsored by an employer for a specific high-skill job. In general, the job should have been offered to a British or an EU national before it can be offered to another foreign worker. [56, 57]

The UK completely re-did its immigration system in 2008, and implemented a points-based approach. This was done to address the issue of non-EU migrants wishing to work, study, or train in the UK. The new immigration system is broken into a five tiers. Each tier has different conditions, entitlements, and entry requirements. Tier 1 is for highly skilled migrants, entrepreneurs, investors, and graduate students. Tier 2 is for skilled workers who have a job offer. Tier 3 is for a limited number of lower skilled workers to fill temporary shortages in the labor market. Tier 4 is for students wishing to study in the UK. Tier 5 is for youth mobility and temporary workers, such as those who come under working holiday agreements with other countries. Each tier has a requirement that applicants score a sufficient number of points to gain entry clearance or to extend their leave to remain in the UK. [57]

CHAPTER SUMMARY & OBSERVATIONS

This chapter reviewed the general economic conditions, the working environment, and legal guidelines for working in a number of Asian and European countries. This type of information is very important for those seeking employment in these regions. The chapter also tried to give you an idea of the attitude towards foreigner workers in these countries. In most cases, we can say that governments and local citizens tend to have varying attitudes towards highly skilled expatriates and lower skilled immigrants. In general, the most prestigious situation for a foreign worker is when you have been sent by a multinational firm to manage or support their operations or interests in that local environment. Another category of foreign workers are those that have been hired by well-known local firms for their knowledge and capabilities. There are, however, many foreign workers who go directly to the different countries to seek employment under a variety of conditions. They are generally treated as local hires and their compensation and treatment by locals will vary by the prestige of their occupation as well as by their country of origin. China, Japan, South Korea, and India are countries that continue to attract foreign workers, and these countries have a wide range of sectors where skilled foreign workers can contribute.

If you are interested in working in Asia, there are many other countries that also offer interesting employment opportunities. There are vibrant employment environments in places such as Singapore, Hong Kong, Taiwan, Thailand, Vietnam, Indonesia, and the Philippines. In all cases, you will need to do your traditional and career market research to find out which sectors and which occupations offer the best opportunities for career development. In many of these countries, the international development sector is very active, and is one area you might consider using to develop important international business skills. One country and continent that is close to Asia in economic activity is Australia. It also has an excellent program for attracting and working with skilled workers from abroad (immi.gov.au/asri). Overall, the forecast for economic growth in Asia and Australia is very good, and that bodes well for the creation and expansion of many international careers.

In Chapter 10, you will examine practical strategies and guidelines for choosing and finding employment in Latin America and Africa. In addition to talking about general developments in both regions, you will get a more detailed look at a selection of countries in each of the regions. In Latin America, the focus will be on Brazil, Argentina, Mexico, and Chile. These four economies are important to the dynamic economic activities in Latin America. In Africa, you will examine developments in Ghana, Nigeria, and South Africa. The African continent is going through an important phase as economic activity in emerging markets takes center stage. South Africa is leading the way, but many countries are making it easier for foreign direct investment to take place and, consequently, there has been a major influx of funds from a variety of countries. China has become a major player in Africa, and we expect that tendency to increase as countries compete for energy and natural resources.

REFERENCES

1. Torres, J., *Market strategies, analysis, competitive intelligence and challenges in entering the Chinese market.* Journal of American Academy of Business, Cambridge, 2011. **16**(2): p. 39.
2. Guerin, T., *An assessment and ranking of barriers to doing environmental business with China.* Business Strategy and the Environment, 2009. **18**(6): p. 380.
3. Dong, K. and Y. Liu, *Cross-cultural management in China.* Cross Cultural Management, 2010. **17**(3): p. 223.
4. Wilson, J. and R. Brennan, *Doing business in China: Is the importance of guanxi diminishing?* European Business Review, 2010. **22**(6): p. 652.
5. Kriz, A. and B. Keating, *Business relationships in China: Lessons about deep trust.* Asia Pacific Business Review, 2010. **16**(3): p. 299.
6. China1. *Chinese work culture: My observations.*2008 [cited 2011, April 4]. Available from: http://3gen.experience.com/2008/09/chinese-work-culture-my-observations.html.
7. Kohnen, J., *An American's guide to doing business in China: Negotiating contracts and agreements. Understanding culture and customs. Marketing products and services.* The Quality Management Journal, 2009. **16**(3): p. 61.
8. Tezuka, K.,*Foreign workers in Japan.*2005 [cited 2011, April 3]. Available from: http://idb-docs.iadb.org/wsdocs/getdocument.aspx?docnum=556652.
9. Nakamura, M., *Adoption and policy implications of Japan's new corporate governance practices after the reform.* Asia Pacific Journal of Management, 2011. **28**(1): p. 187.
10. Kobayashi, Y., *Key challenges for Japanese managers.* Management Japan, 1997. **30**(2): p. 2.
11. Suchan, J., *Drinking parties and learning: A tale from Japan.* Business Communication Quarterly, 2007. **70**(2): p. 194.
12. Honda, H.*Themodernworkenvironmentin Japan.*1992[cited2011,April3].Availablefrom:http://www.allbusiness.com/human-resources/employee-development/280926-1.html.
13. Lee, Y.-I. and P. Trim, *The link between cultural value systems and strategic marketing.* Cross Cultural Management, 2008. **15**(1): p. 62.
14. Lai, G.M.-H., *Knowing who you are doing business with in Japan: A managerial view of keiretsu and keiretsu business groups.* Journal of World Business, 1999. **34**(4): p. 423.
15. Japan1. *Japan work visa.* 2011 [cited 2011, April 4]. Available from: http://www.globalvisas.com/japan_visa/japan_work_visa.html.
16. Wollmann, G., *South Korea: A complex but worthwhile market.* The International Executive (1986-1998), 1990. **32**(2): p. 36.
17. Rodrik, D., *Home-grown growth.* Harvard International Review, 2006. **27**(4): p. 74.
18. Thomas, J., *Contexting Koreans: Does the high/low model work?* Business Communication Quarterly, 1998. **61**(4): p. 9.
19. Chnag, J., *Samsung founding chairman Lee Byung-Chull's place in Korean business management.* SERI Quarterly, 2010. **3**(2): p. 58.
20. Dong-Hun, L., *Korean consumer and society: Growing popularity of social media and business strategy.* SERI Quarterly, 2010. **3**(4): p. 112.
21. South_Korea1. *South Korea visa requirements.*2011 [cited 2011, April 6]. Available from: http://www.globalvisas.com/south_korea_visa/south_korea_visa_requirements.html.
22. Kumar, R., *Doing business in India: Caveat Venditor.* Ivey Business Journal Online, 2007.
23. Lees, A. and S. Khatri, *Made in India: Are you ready for outsourced contract manufacturing?* Journal of Commercial Biotechnology, 2010. **16**(3): p. 258.
24. Pawan, B., *Doing business in India.* Thunderbird International Business Review, 2001. **43**(4): p. 549.
25. Quer, D., E. Claver and L. Rienda, *Doing business in China and India: A comparative approach.* Asia-Pacific Journal of Business Administration, 2010. **2**(2): p. 153.

26. Velrajan, S. *Work environment in India: Then andNow.*2010 [cited 2011, April 5]. Available from: http://r2i.saroscorner.com/2010/01/work-environment-in-india-then-now.html.

27. Saini, D. and P. Budhwar, *Managing the human resource in Indian SMEs: The role of indigenous realities.* Journal of World Business, 2008. **43**(4): p. 417.

28. India1. *India visas.*2011 [cited 2011, April 5]. Available from: http://www.globalvisas.com/countries/india_visas.html.

29. Germany2. *Working in Germany.*2011 [cited 2011, April 3]. Available from: http://germany-explorer.com/german-culture/working-in-germany.html.

30. Tamasy, C., *Determinants of regional entrepreneurship dynamics in contemporary Germany: A conceptual and empirical analysis.* Regional Studies, 2006. **40**(4): p. 365.

31. Silberhorn, D. and R. Warren, *Defining corporate social responsibility.* European Business Review, 2007. **19**(5): p. 352.

32. Chizema, A., *Early and late adoption of American-style executive pay in Germany: Governance and institutions.* Journal of World Business, 2010. **45**(1): p. 9.

33. Germany1. *The labour market in Germany.*2011 [cited 2011, March 29]. Available from: http://www.expat-blog.com/en/guide/europe/germany/915-the-labour-market-in-germany.html.

34. Horst, A., *German experiences with codes and their enforcement.* Journal of Communication Management, 2007. **11**(2): p. 99.

35. Ehrenreich, S., *English as a business lingua franca in a German multinational corporation.* The Journal of Business Communication, 2010. **47**(4): p. 408.

36. Tuselmann, H.-J., F. McDonaldand R. Thorpe, *The emerging approach to employee relations in German overseas affiliates: A role model for international operation?* Journal of World Business, 2006. **41**(1): p. 66.

37. Italy1. *Italy: Work and study.* 2011 [cited 2011, March 29]. Available from: http://www.lonelyplanet.com/italy/work-study-volunteering/work.

38. Lazzarotti, V., R. Manzini and L. Pellegrini, *Open innovation models adopted in practice: An extensive study in Italy.* Measuring Business Excellence, 2010. **14**(4): p. 11.

39. Mengoli, S., F. Pazzaglia and E. Sapienza, *Effect of governance reforms on corporate ownership in Italy: Is it still pizza, spaghetti, and mandolino?* Corporate Governance : An International Review, 2009. **17**(5): p. 629.

40. Calabrese, G., *Best performance, best practices: The case of Italian manufacturing companies.* International Journal of Business Performance Management, 2009. **11**(3): p. 203.

41. Italy2. *Italy : Living and working conditions.*2011 [cited 2011, April 1]. Available from: http://www.ajob.cz/en/about-countries-at5/italy-living-and-working-conditions-a563.

42. Comunian, R., *Culture Italian style: Business and the arts.* The Journal of Business Strategy, 2008. **29**(3): p. 37.

43. Mazzanti, M., S. Montresorand P. Pini, *Outsourcing and innovation: Evidence for a local production system of Emilia-Romagna.* Innovation : Management, Policy & Practice, 2007. **9**(3/4): p. 324.

44. France1. *France: Living and Working Conditions.*2011 [cited 2011, April 1]. Available from: http://www.ajob.cz/en/about-countries-at5/france-living-and-working-conditions-a568.

45. Kontinen, T., *Succeeding in the French market: Recommendations for small businesses.* The Journal of Business Strategy, 2011. **32**(1): p. 15.

46. Smith, J., S. Wrightand D. Pickton, *Competitive intelligence programmes for SMEs in France: Evidence of changing attitudes.* Journal of Strategic Marketing, 2010. **18**(7): p. 523.

47. Maux, J., *La « coalition de contrôle ».* Revue Française de Gestion, 2008. **34**(181): p. 15.

48. Paucar-Caceres, A., *Pragmatism and rationalism in the development of management science methodologies in the UK and France.* Systems Research and Behavioral Science, 2009. **26**(4): p. 429.

49. Tanner, J. F., et al., *Executives' perspectives of the changing role of the sales profession: Views from France, the United States, and Mexico.* The Journal of Business & Industrial Marketing, 2008. **23**(3): p. 193.

50. Carayol, V., *PR professionals in France: An overview of the sector.* Journal of Communication Management, 2010. **14**(2): p. 167.

51. France2. *Foreign workers* .1998 [cited 2011, April 2]. Available from: http://migration. ucdavis.edu/mn/more.php?id=1438_0_3_0.

52. Millward, R., *Business and public management in the UK, 1900-2003.* Business History Review, 2006. **80**(4): p. 809.

53. Phillips, S., *London to host the best in licensing.* License! Global, 2010. **13**(7): p. 42.

54. Daneshfar, A., et al., *Motives for employee profit sharing schemes in the US, UK and Canada.* The International Business & Economics Research Journal, 2010. **9**(10): p. 1.

55. Macfarlane, B. and R. Ottewill, *Business ethics in the curriculum: Assessing the evidence from UK subject review.* Journal of Business Ethics, 2004. **54**(4): p. 339.

56. Blackburn, R. and D. Smallbone, *Researching small firms and entrepreneurship in the UK: Developments and distinctiveness.* Entrepreneurship Theory and Practice, 2008. **32**(2): p. 267.

57. Britain1. *UK immigration and UK visa services.* 2011 [cited 2011, March 29]. Available from: http://www.workpermit.com/uk/uk.htm.

58. Richards, M., P. Palmer and M. Bogdanova, *Irresponsible lending? A case study of a UKcredit industry reform initiative.* Journal of Business Ethics, 2008. **81**(3): p. 499.

10 PRACTICAL GUIDELINES & STRATEGIES FOR WORKING IN LATIN AMERICA & AFRICA

LEARNING OBJECTIVES

- Introduction to working in Latin America and Africa

- Strategies for working in Brazil

- Strategies for working in Argentina

- Strategies for working in Mexico

- Strategies for working in Chile

- Strategies for working in Ghana

- Strategies for working in Nigeria

- Strategies for working in South Africa

- Strategies for working in Dubai (UAE)

THE ROADMAP

Chapter 9 presented practical strategies and guidelines for choosing and finding employment in Asia and Europe. The chapter also reviewed the general economic conditions, working environment, and legal guidelines for working in a number of Asian and European countries. In Asia, the four countries covered were China, Japan, South Korea, and India. In Europe, the countries presented were Germany, Italy, France, and the United Kingdom. These countries were chosen because they play a central role in the dynamic activities of the respective regions. In addition, these countries have growing or well-established markets that are open to knowledge workers. Some of these countries also have well-established expatriate communities that can support your networking and career management decisions. It was pointed out that this type of information is very important for those seeking employment in these regions. Chapter 9 also talked about the attitude towards foreigner workers in these countries. It was emphasized that, in general, the most prestigious situation for foreign workers is when they have been sent by a multinational firm to manage or support the firm's operations or interests in that local environment.

Chapter 10 will highlight practical strategies and guidelines for developing and expanding your career in Latin America, Africa, and the Middle East. Although the main focus will be on Latin America and Africa, there will be a discussion of the importance of the Middle East and an in-depth review of conditions in Dubai. The countries covered in Latin America will be Brazil, Argentina, Mexico, and Chile. The ones reviewed for Africa will be Nigeria, Ghana, and South Africa. For all the countries, there will be background social and economic information presented. There will also be a review of the working environment, attitude towards foreign workers, and general guidelines for getting permission to work in these countries. As emerging markets gain more prominence, these countries are becoming interesting locations for career development and expansion.

WORKING IN LATIN AMERICA

Latin America represents an area of the Americas where mainly Spanish and Portuguese are spoken. The area has a combined population of over 590 million and total GDP of over $5 trillion dollars. The region encompasses a wide range of ethnic groups and cultures. It is not surprising that there is also a wide diversity of social, political, and economic policies that are characteristic of the countries in the region. Despite all the differences, there are number of areas of similarity across the region. Poverty is still a major issue, and the level of social, economic, and gender inequality tends to be very high. This situation has an impact on most of the strategies being taken to make the region more economically competitive. From a social perspective, people are more collectivist in behavior. Friends, family, community, and region are very important to people's identity. [1–3]

The approach to communication is definitely a high context orientation. Verbal and non-verbal signals, as well the value of context and repeated interactions, are crucial for getting at the real meaning when communicating with others in Latin America. In terms of economic conditions, the region has had its ups and downs. However, over the last decade we have seen many positive developments in a variety of countries and Brazil has become an economic powerhouse behind the new-found influence of the region. In the sections below, the conditions in four influential Latin American countries will be examined. The four countries are Brazil, Argentina, Chile, and Mexico. There are also other important countries in the region, but the insights gained from looking at these four can be very instructive for anyone wishing to work with or in Latin America. [4–6]

Working in Brazil

Brazil is the fifth largest country in the world, with a total area of 8.5 million sq km and a population of around 200 million people. The official language in Brazil is Portuguese. This is in contrast to most of Latin America, which speaks Spanish. Brazil is easily the largest country in Latin America and the eighth largest economy in the world. With abundant natural resources and a vibrant economy, Brazil has the potential of becoming one of the top five economies in the world in a few decades. Although the country has a huge population, the majority of the people are located along the Atlantic coastal regions. Besides its new-found economic and political clout, Brazil is known for its beautiful beaches, word famous carnivals, and famous soccer teams. Now that the country has been chosen to be the host of the 2014 World Cup and 2016 Olympic Games, we can expect that greater attention will be paid to its role as a leading economy in Latin America and the world. [3, 7]

The working environment in Brazil

Except for the temporary impact of the world financial crisis, Brazil's economic growth rate has been increasing steadily in recent years. A lot of the growth is due to increased demand for Brazil's commodities. The discovery of new oil fields will only boost its influence in world energy markets. Brazil's major trading partners include China, the United States, and Argentina. With the rapid growth of the economy there is a huge demand for skilled professionals in a variety of sectors. However, despite the rosy economic forecasts, Brazil does suffer from a number of issues that could impact its long-term potential. Brazil ranks in the middle of the pack in areas such as corruption, regulations, the index of economic freedom, and political risk. The country has taken many steps to improve in these areas, but still lags far behind in the "ease of doing business" rankings. Brazil ranks 124th out of 183 countries in this area. [7–9]

Unions play a major role in business in Brazil. They are represented in all major industries. Unions are legal and they are financed by payments deducted from workers' pay checks and by membership dues. Approximately 20 to 30 percent of the workforce is unionized. In the late 1990s, strikes were very common in Brazil. However, they have worked to improve labor management relations in recent years. [10, 11]

Finding a job can be difficult in Brazil. One reason is that hiring is primarily done by referrals or personal contacts. In the competitive work environment, Brazilians prefer to work with someone they know or someone who is close to others in their group. This highlights the importance of trust and relationships in that environment. Nevertheless, there is a lot of hierarchy in the workplace in Brazil. Titles are very important. This might seem unusual, since the communication style is very high context and can seem chaotic at times. It is possible to hear a lot of debates and disagreements during the decision-making process in Brazil. The society is also very collective, and group meetings and group work are important in most organizations. [11–13]

Brazil has generally been known to have a positive attitude towards foreigners. In the past, they have welcomed foreigners through tourism, immigration, and business activities. Brazil generally sees skilled workers as a benefit, since they bring knowledge and ideas into a fast growing country. However, the job market is very competitive, and foreign workers continue to show up for new career opportunities. This recent situation has caused some resentment from local Brazilians seeking jobs. Nevertheless, there are many institutions and professional associations in Brazil that can help highly skilled foreigners find positions. Yet, even with this kind of assistance, it is difficult for foreigners who do not have well-established friendships and networks to find a job. Other difficulties for most foreigners include the language barrier, job regulations, and the generally low compensation levels. [7, 10, 14]

Legal guidelines for working in Brazil

The nationals of certain countries can visit Brazil for up to three months without a visa. However, if they intend to work, they are required to get a Work Permit. Brazil requires US citizens to carry a valid US passport and a visa when traveling to Brazil. If you have visited other countries previously, you may be required to present a vaccination card showing that you have received a yellow fever immunization shot. As for Work Permits, they are only issued to organizations that are registered in Brazil. A company or organization needs to sponsor most visa applications. There is a Working Holiday Visa available for citizens of New Zealand. New Zealand and

Brazil have signed a reciprocal working holiday scheme allowing New Zealanders aged between 18 and 30 years to work, study, or travel for a year. Apart from this arrangement, there are a number of different kinds of visas that a person who is looking to work in Brazil is able to obtain. Most fall under the category of Business Visa, Temporary Visa or Work Permit. [13, 15]

Overall, there are ten different types of visa one can obtain from Brazilian authorities: (1) The Tourist Visa is issued to foreigners who visit for tourism or family visits. It is usually a 90 day single or multiple entry visa. (2) The Temporary Visa I (VITEM-I) is issued to people who participate in technical or athletic training programs. In addition to unpaid trainees, interns, and exchange students, the same visa is given to people who participate in cultural, technological, or scientific missions. (3) The Temporary Visa II (VITEM-II) is generally known as the Brazilian Business Visa. It is issued to foreigners who enter Brazil as members of a foreign company and are paid overseas. This visa is also given out to journalists and crew members. (4) The Temporary Visa III (VITEM-III) is issued to paid athletes or performing artists. (5) The Temporary Visa IV (VITEM-IV) is issued to students pursuing graduate or postgraduate studies in Brazil. (6) The Temporary Visa V (VITEM-V) serves the purpose of a work permit and is given to foreigners who work for a Brazilian-based company or the Brazilian government. (7) The Temporary Visa VI (Vitem-VI) is given to media correspondents. (8) The Temporary Visa VII (VITEM-VII) is issued to foreigners who go to Brazil for religious or missionary purposes. (9) A Permanent Visa is given to foreigners who wish to live in Brazil permanently. However, the reasons must be linked to investments, family reunification, or retirement. This visa can also be given to managers or directors of Brazilian companies or organizations. (10) Finally, there are diplomatic and official visas given to people who travel on diplomatic or official missions. [16]

Working in Argentina

In terms of land area, Argentina is the second largest country in South America and eighth largest in the world. It also has the fourth largest population of Spanish speakers in the world. The country is bordered by Paraguay, Bolivia, Brazil, Uruguay, and Chile. Argentina is Latin America's third largest economy and it has significant natural resources. In order of their size, the largest sectors in the economy are service, manufacturing, agriculture, construction, mining, and public utilities. [1, 17]

Argentina has a very educated population and a very competitive agricultural sector. The country went through very difficult times because of the 2001–2002 financial crisis, but its move to a more flexible exchange rate system, economic reforms and the boost in the international demand for its commodities have put the country on a strong recovery path. The country has maintained good economic growth for several years now. Although there are many different ethnic groups in the country, the most dominant ones are the descendants of Italian and Spanish immigrants. In recent years, the country has had to deal with a steady influx of people from neighboring countries, such as Paraguay, Bolivia, and Peru. In fact, Argentina has one of the highest rates of foreign workers entering of all the Latin American countries. [4, 18]

The working environment in Argentina

Argentina has a lot of natural beauty and its cultural and culinary activities attract large number of visitors each year. Similar to Brazil, Argentina is a nation of fanatic soccer lovers. If there is an important international soccer match, a lot of business comes to a halt while people watch. Argentina's workforce is not as unionized as in Brazil. However, there is a high level of gender bias, with about 60 percent of the workforce being male, and women are often hindered from reaching higher level positions. Argentina is also another Latin American country where relationships dominate the employment landscape. Once good relationships are established, people tend to be very loyal and dependable. [18–20]

In terms of doing business, Argentinians prefer to meet in person rather than speak on the phone. Although relationships dominate the job search dynamics, a significant role is being played by some internet search firms, online sites and other media. The four major online sites in this area are Execuzone, Portal RH, Zona Jobs, and Bumeran. The newspapers that are the most helpful for finding jobs are La Nación and El Clarín. When relationships are not sufficient to find qualified applicants, companies in Argentina have been known to use these sources to find suitable employees. This makes the external labor market a little more flexible in Argentina, and individuals can benefit by using these intermediaries effectively. As for the management style, it is hierarchical in nature. Decision-making is usually top down, and the attitude towards employees is generally paternalistic. Nevertheless, Argentinians are friendly people who like to socialize inside and outside of the workplace. [4, 17, 21]

Except for the inflow of illegal immigrants from neighboring countries, the attitude towards skilled foreign workers is somewhat open in Argentina. Much will depend on your level of education, the way you carry yourself and nature of your personal networks in Argentina. It is also crucial that you are able to speak Spanish and willing to adapt to local business practices. The main downside for highly skilled foreign workers is the extremely low wages in Argentina. [18, 19, 22]

Legal guidelines for working in Argentina

Foreigners from certain countries can visit Argentina for up to 90 days without a visa. However, in order to work in the country, a Work Permit is required. A valid passport is required for US citizens to enter Argentina; however, US citizens do not need a visa for visits of up to 90 days for tourism or business. For paid employment, you must be sponsored by the hiring organization. An extended Working Holiday Visa is available to citizens of New Zealand between the ages of 18 and 30. The period for this visa usually ranges from six months to one year. [23]

The application process for a visa can be lengthy and should be started well ahead of time. There are basically three types of visa that Argentina issues: (1) The Article 29 (E) Visa is a short-term visa and it is issued for short-term work in Argentina. It is usually issued for 15 days but can be extended for another 15 once in Argentina. (2) An Article 15 (E) Visa is a labor contract or temporary residence visa. This visa is issued to employees and people on internships or projects contracted by companies in Argentina. It usually is valid for 6–12 months. A formal labor contract between the company in Argentina and the employee is required in order to obtain the visa. (3) An Article 15 (E) Visa is a temporary residence visa, and it is issued to employees sent abroad by their company for at least 6–12 months. A labor contract is not required for this visa. Once foreign employees arrive in Argentina, they need to apply for a DNI (National Identity Document) and a CUIL (Unique Work Identification Code). The DNI is similar to a social security number in its function. When entering into any type of contract, your DNI will be required. [24]

Working in Mexico

Mexico, which is bordered by the United States, is the fifth largest country in the Americas and the 11th largest by population in the world. Mexico is an important economic power and was the first Latin American member of the OECD. In terms of nominal GDP, it is 14th in the world. Because of NAFTA (the North American Free Trade Agreement), its economy has strong ties to those of the United States and Canada. Mexico is a large Spanish-speaking country with a very active tourism industry. The country also has rapidly developing industrial and service sectors. The country has an export-oriented economy and trades with over 40 countries. However, trade with the NAFTA partners dominates a significant portion of the economic activities. [25–27]

The working environment in Mexico

Mexico's proximity to the United States has greatly influenced its economy. This is due to both NAFTA and the geographical proximity. However, under NAFTA, the United States petitioned that the free flow of labor should not be part of the agreement. Despite that, millions of Mexicans have immigrated to the United States, a lot of them through illegal means. Many other immigrants from other Latin American countries also try to cross into the USA from Mexico. Most of them are seeking better opportunities in the USA. The recent war against drugs in Mexico has put a lot of pressure on the stability of the country and made the illegal border crossings a deadly affair in many cases. Since a large portion of the anti-immigrant sentiments in the USA has been focused on Mexico, it has made relations between the two countries quite tense. [28, 29]

Although Mexico is the closest Latin American country to the US, the cultural distance between them is quite large. Despite the fact that there are numerous agencies and online job sites, the best way of finding a job in Mexico is still through one's personal network. A job referral by an insider is still the best way of getting employed. The working conditions in the country depend on whether you are part of the formal or the informal economy. Salaries, worker protections, and working conditions are much worse for those in the informal economy. However, workers in the formal economy are protected by a variety of labor laws. If we just look at the formal economy, Mexico is highly unionized. The unions are represented in the vast majority of the labor force in manufacturing. In addition, employees receive a number of government-mandated benefits. However, salaries can vary widely depending on one's education and social class. This contributes to the very wide income inequality in the country. [26, 30, 31]

Work centrality is lower in Mexico, since people place a greater emphasis on family, friends, and personal relationships over business and work. There are also very clear gender role distinctions in Mexico, and women are somewhat at a disadvantage. Your social position in Mexico is very important in how you are treated. Very often people will use titles and address you in ways that show clearly your social status. For this reason, the work environment is somewhat hierarchical. We see a lot of top-down decision-making in Mexican firms. The high context culture also affects the nature of business communication and work flow. There is a lot of social interaction inside and outside firms. Lunch breaks in Mexico are longer than in any other Latin American country. [27, 29, 32]

Highly skilled foreigners can find employment in Mexico, and they are even treated with respect. However, the government does have rules in place that make sure that jobs held by foreigners are not being taken away from capable Mexican nationals. One way of gaining entry into the country as a business person is to be sent by a well-established foreign firm doing business in Mexico. Another way is to set up a business as an entrepreneur. Other foreigners are active in development and social projects that benefit Mexican communities. [29, 30]

Legal guidelines for working in Mexico

Foreigners from some countries can visit Mexico without a visa for up to three months. However, a Work Permit is needed if they wish to work in Mexico. There is a Working Holiday Visa arrangement between Mexico and New Zealand. Citizens of New Zealand between the ages of 18 and 30 years can apply for this type of visa. For an American citizen with a valid US passport, no visa is necessary to visit Mexico for a maximum period of 90 days.

There are several different types of visas available to foreigners wishing to visit or work in Mexico. There are three main types of visas issued by Mexico. The FMM Visa (Tourist Visa) is a short-term non-immigrant visa aimed at visitors who will stay 6 months or less in the country. The FM3 (Residency Visa) is a long-term non-immigrant visa, which is renewable for longer terms. The visa also allows one the right to work. The FM3 can be renewed for an additional four years at the appropriate time. However, the FM3 doesn't help the applicant to get a citizenship or permanent residency visa in Mexico. The FM2 is known as the Immigrant Visa. It is issued to people who are seeking permanent residency in Mexico and who could eventually seek Mexican citizenship, such as investors, professionals, retirees, artists, and sports people. The visa itself does not grant permanent residency or citizenship but can be converted to it. The FM2 can also be used for a company-sponsored job, scientific research-related job, or for investment activity in Mexico. [25, 33]

Working in Chile

Chile is a Spanish-speaking country that is located along a narrow coastal strip between the Andes mountains in the east and the Pacific Ocean to the west. It is also bordered by Peru, Bolivia, and Argentina. Chile has extreme variety in its climates, from dry desert to rainy weather, and even a Mediterranean type environment. The country has significant copper deposits and other minerals. The center of the country contains most of the population and the agricultural resources. Chile is one of Latin America's most stable and productive nations. It has one of the highest GDP per capita, much economic freedom, and relatively low corruption levels. However, as in many Latin American countries, income inequality is quite high. The three major sectors that drive the economy are agriculture, industry, and services. Recently, Chile has attracted many immigrants from neighboring countries such as Argentina, Bolivia, and Peru. [34, 35]

The working environment in Chile

Partly because of its stunning natural beauty, Chile has well developed tourism-related facilities. The country attracts tourists, investors, and people seeking employment opportunities. Chile has a large educated middle class and a robust economy. Although Chile went through a big recession in the late 1990s, it has steadily recovered. The country has a relaxed attitude towards work but has one of the highest working hours per week in the world. There are various competing explanations for this paradox. [36, 37]

Chileans are generally polite people, and can be somewhat formal with people with whom they are unacquainted, or those in higher positions of authority. Although they may work long hours, they socialize a lot before, during, and after work with their colleagues. However, this is another Latin American country where the workplace is very hierarchical. There is more top-down decision-making and not as much socializing across corporate authority levels. [38, 39]

Chile has well developed labor laws that are aimed at protecting workers. The government allows workers to join or form labor unions without needing to request any kind of government authorization. Moreover, legislation passed in the 1990s gave workers many of the same rights that union workers have. Currently, about 12 percent of the workforce that is unionized in Chile. Although Chile is performing better than most countries in the region, some claim that restrictive labor regulations and an inefficient bureaucracy are holding back growth. Another dimension to consider is the situation in the informal economy. Workers in that part of the economy face poor working conditions and have few protections. This may partially explain why income inequality is still a major problem in Chile. [34, 36, 37]

The attitude towards foreign workers depends greatly on their status, education, and the type of work being done. Foreigners who do low wage jobs or those in the informal economy are not treated very nicely. However, highly skilled expatriates or those investing money in Chile are generally welcomed. In terms of finding employment in Chile, relationships and networks play a major role. If you do need to use the media for job search, newspapers and weekly publications such as El Mercurio, Empleos and Economia y Negocios, El Rastro, Mercado Laboral, Anuntis and Ene Avisos contain a lot of classified listings. [36, 37, 39]

Legal guidelines for working in Chile

Citizens from certain countries do not need to apply for a visa to visit Chile for up to three months. However, people seeking paid employment need to have the proper visa or a Work Permit. A Working Holiday Visa arrangement is available to citizens of New Zealand, Canada, and Australia. This visa allows nationals between the ages of 18 and 30 from those countries to work temporarily, either part-time or full-time in Chile. This type of visa can be valid for up to 12 months. American citizens traveling to Chile for recreation, tourism, business, or academic conferences do not need to obtain a visa prior to their arrival in Chile. Temporary Work Permits can be issued in exceptional cases, mainly to artists. [40]

Generally speaking, Chile offers a Tourist Visa, a Temporary Residence Visa, a Permanent Residence Visa, a Student Visa, and a Work Visa or Work Permit. It is usually illegal for a person to work in Chile with a Tourist Visa. However, some have suggested going to the country on a Tourist Visa and then going through the process of changing your status after you arrive. In that way, you can take advantage of local connections or specific job offers that you have received in your location. [41]

As for Work Visas or Permits in Chile, there are 3 main types: (1) A Special Work Card; (2) A Subject-to-Contract Visa; and (3) A Temporary Residence Visa for Freelance Workers. The Special Work Card Visa is a 90 day visa which allows you to work in Chile while being a tourist. The Subject-to-Contract Visa is the most common type of visa, and it is often used by businesses that hire foreigners under contract. The Temporary Residence Visa for Freelance Workers is issued to individuals who are self-employed entrepreneurs or local investors. After obtaining this type of visa it is usually necessary to get a Chilean identification card. [40, 41]

WORKING IN AFRICA

Africa is the second largest continent in the world and the also the second most populated. It covers about 6 percent of the Earth's surface and has just over one-billion people in 54 sovereign states. Although the continent has abundant natural resources, it remains the world's poorest overall. Some of the major problems include ineffective governments, corruption, disease control, poor healthcare systems, ethnic conflicts, and poverty. Despite all these obstacles and challenges, Africa still holds much promise, and there are signs that the global economy is taking notice. The competition for energy and natural resources among the industrialized and rapidly growing countries have given African governments new leverage and greater access to external capital. Although international development institutions and aid programs still dominate economic development efforts, there is growing hope that an investment model can energize African economies and lift many regions out of poverty. [42–44]

In the sections below, there will be a review of activities in three exciting African countries: Ghana, Nigeria, and South Africa. Each of these countries has different challenges and opportunities but they all have growing influence in the politics and economics of Africa. We have included one country from the Middle East in this section, because of the increasing importance of that region. That country is the UAE (Dubai focus). Working in Africa and the Middle East can seem completely foreign to most westerners. However, as emerging markets play a greater role in the global economy, a deeper understanding of these regions will be necessary. [45–47]

Working in Ghana

Ghana has a population of over 24 million people. The country is located in west Africa and is bordered by Ivory Coast, Burkina Faso, and Togo. Ghana has a lot of natural resources, and its GDP is much higher than its neighbors. However, four of every ten Ghanaians still live in poverty. Ghana has great potential since it is a major gold producer and exports cocoa, oil, timber, diamonds, bauxite, and manganese. Major oil discoveries in 2007 and 2010 have greatly boosted the long-term economic potential of the country. Unlike what has occurred in Nigeria, the government has promised to avoid the mismanagement of this major resource. The most active industries in Ghana are mining, light manufacturing, aluminum smelting, food processing, cement, and small commercial ship-building. Mobile communications has exploded in Ghana, and cell phone usage is transforming many business and social activities in the country. Ghana is an attractive place to do business for many types of firms, but there is clearly a shortage of skilled labor. [48, 49]

The working environment in Ghana

Ghana is a stable and rapidly improving economy in Africa. It is generally open to foreign direct investment, and has managed to avoid some of the nasty political and ethnic conflicts that have plagued some African nations. Of the over four million people in the labor force, about 60 percent are in agriculture, 15 percent in industry and 25 percent in services. As in many African countries, there is tremendous gender bias in Ghana. Although harassment and discrimination are prohibited by law, working women see greater wage disparity, limited promotions, and little maternity support. [50–52]

There is a lot of respect for elders and people in authority in Ghana. Titles are considered to be very important, so honorific, professional, and educational titles are often used before surnames. This is a more collectivist society, and so family, community, and regions impact their approach to business and social relations. Communication is dynamic and people spend a lot of time building trust and getting to know the people with whom they have to work. [53, 54]

People work very hard to survive in Ghana. Those working in agriculture are mainly food crop and subsistence farmers. A growing number of groups and individuals are involved in micro-enterprises. However, there is an informal economy and some people have to resort to daily labor situations to generate income to survive. Over the years, the unemployment rate has generally been between 10 and 20 percent depending on the level of economic activity. There are no social security provisions, and those without work or support from families or charities have a difficult time. On the positive side, economic conditions have steadily improved since 2000 and new-found resources should give a boost to long-term development goals.

Most Ghanaians are very welcoming to foreign visitors. They are also generally friendly to foreign workers who are supported by their national firms. The attitude is a little more complicated when we talk about the competition for local jobs that might go to Ghanaian nationals. Most foreigners work with development projects, manage company activities, or work in activities related to the vast mining operations in the country. [42, 49, 50]

Legal guidelines for working in Ghana

Citizens of some countries do not need to apply for a visa to visit Ghana for up to three months. However, Ghana currently does not provide Working Holiday Visas to any foreign countries. If foreigners desire to work in Ghana, they need to be issued Work Permits. Overall, there are six types of visas that Ghana offers: Diplomatic, Official, Business, Tourist, Student, and Special Cases. However, the two main categories for a Ghanaian entry visa are Diplomatic and Ordinary Visas. Diplomatic Visas are issued to members of the diplomatic or consular services of a foreign country. Ordinary Visas are issued to visitors on business, tourism or holidays, temporary employment, or in transit. If you plan to move to Ghana to work, you would need to apply for an Official Visa (Visa-B). However, if you will only be in Ghana for a shorter term, you only need to apply for a Work Visa (Visa-C). Residence and Work Permits are issued to expatriates employed by companies and churches. Dependants of expatriate employees are also granted Residence Permits but not Work Permits. [55, 56]

Working in Nigeria

Nigeria is located in west Africa, and is comprised of 36 states, with its capital in Abuja. The country shares borders with Benin, Chad, Cameroon, and Niger. The three largest ethnic groups in the country are the Hausa, Igbo, and Yoruba. Nigeria has the largest population in Africa and is the seventh most populated country in the world. Nigeria has abundant natural resources and is also a major oil exporting nation. The country has satisfactory financial, legal, and transportation sectors, but has been plagued by government inefficiency and corruption for many years. Nigeria ranks 37th in GDP in the world and is a major trading partner of the US. The US and other nations are actively engaged in foreign direct investment in Nigeria.

The country has survived military rule and years of mismanagement. Although some regional conflict and high unemployment remain major issues, Nigeria is now the second largest economy in Africa after South Africa, and its growth rate seems to be accelerating. [43, 57, 58]

The working environment in Nigeria

While Nigeria holds vast reserves of oil, the domestic infrastructure to support rapid expansion is still lagging. The business landscape is also very tricky due, to a history of corruption and government inefficiency. Nigeria has an estimated labor force of over 42 million. Women account for about 36 percent of it. Generating enough jobs has been a long-term problem for the country. The unemployment rate has stayed above 18 percent for many years. Between 40 to 50 percent of the unemployed are urban youth. Very often, even college graduates go through long periods without finding employment. [45, 59]

The government in Nigeria is the largest employer outside the agricultural sector. Nevertheless, there are many unions in Nigeria. They have the right to strike to obtain improved working conditions and can bargain collectively for higher wages. Although there are restrictions on child labor in industry and certain areas of agriculture, you can see many children working alone or with their parents in the informal economy. This is because the informal economy is essential for huge sections of the population. Overall, conditions for workers vary widely in Nigeria. Civil servants and employees of leading foreign and domestic companies have relatively good offices, facilities, health care, and wages. That is not the case for workers in other areas of the economy. [58, 60, 61]

Another problem in Nigeria is inequality. As the economy generates more wealth, certain groups are getting richer. As in many African countries, income inequality is linked to uneven access to resources and the dominance of certain social and ethnic groups. Despite all the challenges in the social and work environments, Nigerians are very hard workers. Eight hour days are the norm. Many people work beyond the standard 40 hour week. However, most Nigerian organizations operate with a family-like atmosphere. There is a lot of communication inside the workplace and personal relationships matter a great deal outside. There is also a formal side to social behavior in Nigeria. There is a lot of respect for elders and people with status or authority. The use of professional titles in written and verbal form is very common in Nigeria. As we can see, there are many sides to Nigeria, but in the long run it will be the health of the economy that affects its role in the world economy. Being a major economic force in Africa makes Nigeria a magnet for individuals seeking employment and foreign firms seeking business opportunities. [43, 57, 58, 60]

Legal guidelines for working in Nigeria

All foreign nationals are required to have visas before travelling to Nigeria. At present, the only exceptions are nationals from the ECOWAS (Economic Community of West African States) countries. They do not need a visa for entry. If you plan on working in Nigeria, you must obtain a Work Permit. Those individuals who will work for more than three months need to get a Subject-to-Regularization (STR) Visa, which is valid for 90 days upon entry into Nigeria. The individual then asks to be "regularized" after arriving in the country. There are three general categories of visas that are offered: (1) Visitor, Tourist, and Transit visas; (2) Business, Education, and Religious Visas; and (3) Temporary Work Permits. It may seem confusing, but it is helpful to focus specifically on work-related visas. There are three different types of work-related visas offered. The first is a Business Visa, which permits foreign firms to send their employees or agents to carry out business in Nigeria. The second is a Work Permit that is given to individuals sponsored by Nigerian-based firms. The third type is a Temporary Work Permit that allows foreigners to work and live in Nigeria for up to three months. This visa can later be converted into a regular Work Permit. The regular Work Permit allows foreigners to live and work in the country for much longer periods. [42, 62]

Working in South Africa

South Africa consists of nine provinces, and is located at the southern end of the continent of Africa. It is bordered by Namibia, Botswana, Zimbabwe, Mozambique, and Swaziland. In terms of biological diversity, South Africa ranks third in the world. The country also has substantial amounts of natural resources. The country is a leading supplier of a range of minerals and mineral products that are exported to numerous countries. Each year, approximately 55 different minerals are produced from more than 700 mines, with gold, platinum, coal, and diamonds dominating exports and revenue earnings. There are also important deposits of iron and copper. It should be no surprise that, originally, the whole economy was built on mining. South Africa has well developed financial, communications, energy, and transportation sectors. The country's infrastructure is one of the most modern in sub-Saharan Africa. It has the highest GDP in Africa, and is ranked 25th in the world. [63–65]

South Africa is a multi-ethnic country with many official languages. However, English is commonly used in public and international commercial interactions. About 79 percent of the population are Black African and the rest include people of European, Asian, and mixed ancestry. The most developed parts of the country are around four areas: Cape Town, Port Elizabeth, Durban, and Pretoria-Johannesburg. Economic development lags significantly in other areas.

South Africa is, economically and politically, a powerhouse in Africa. However, South Africa has had to deal with a consistently high unemployment rate of over 20 percent. Nevertheless, it has one of the fastest growing telecommunications industries, and tourism has improved steadily. The global recession has affected some sectors, but the country has tremendous potential. The government continues to struggle with economic inequality and has used certain affirmative action strategies to help some segments of the population. Overall, South Africa continues to play a vital political and economic role in the global economy. Their successful hosting of the 2010 Soccer World Cup was a clear signal that they were determined to be a major political player and a significant emerging market country. [44, 66]

The working environment in South Africa

In post-apartheid South Africa, a lot has been done to try to eliminate racism based on skin color or language background. There has been success in some areas, but there is still a feeling that inequalities persist and some groups are doing better than others. Promotion, wage, and gender discrimination are some of the major concerns of South African workers. Among the rights listed in the Bill of Rights in the 1996 Constitution were provisions guaranteeing workers the right to fair labor practices, the right to collective bargaining, the right to strike, and other labor friendly practices. The government has since then established a number of other worker friendly laws. [47, 64, 67]

The labor market in South Africa is unfortunately flush with unskilled workers, while there is a persistent shortage of skilled workers. The high population growth continually puts pressure on economic productivity and job creation efforts. Add to this is the fact that finding a job in South Africa can be difficult since South Africansrely a lot on personal networks or referrals. However, there are some positive signs in the direction the government is taking. The political environment is relatively stable and the government will focus a lot more on privatization and deregulation in the coming years. Sectors such as information technology, telecommunications, healthcare, e-commerce, tourism, and finance could benefit tremendously from more effective business strategies. [46, 63, 64]

One problem which does not seem to be going away is that of refugees. There has been a steady influx of people seeking work from poorer countries such as the Democratic Republic of the Congo, Mozambique, Zimbabwe, and Malawi. Most of them depend on activities in the informal sector for work. Since unemployment remains high, many poorer South Africans have developed very negative attitudes towards these immigrants. This attitude has become even harsher as South African employers have hired migrants from other countries for lower pay than South African citizens, especially in the construction, tourism, agriculture, and domestic services. This is despite the fact that Work Permits are usually not issued for occupations for which there are sufficient local South African workers. However, the government is more flexible when it comes to the hiring of highly skilled foreigners that can help the company bolster its economic competitiveness. Most of the positions available for highly skilled foreigners are in finance, accounting, marketing, information technology, and sales. [47, 65, 66]

Legal guidelines for working in South Africa

South Africa only provides Working Holiday and Temporary Working Visas to individuals with student status or to people who are citizens of Australia, Canada, and the United Kingdom. A Working Holiday Visa permits applicants to work in South Africa for up to a 12-month period. The general visas available to foreigners are the Work Visa, Study Visa, Retirement Visa, Permanent Residence Visa, and Visitor/Tourist Visa. The Retirement Visa is popular for people who wish to live in South Africa on a seasonal basis while still maintaining their main country of residence. [68, 69]

If you wish to work in South Africa, you will need to obtain a Quota Work Permit or a Work Permit (Extraordinary Quota). The former is given to a set number of employees in a certain occupational categories. The latter is given to a number of foreigners with extraordinary skills or qualifications; this is judged on a case-by-case basis, since there are no set rules to cover all situations. This type of permit includes academics, sport professionals, or other famous professionals. Corporate Work Permits are usually requested by organizations that need to recruit a number of foreign staff over a set period of time. The General Work Permit is given to individuals who do not meet the criteria for the two preceding work permits and must be accompanied by an offer of employment from a South Africa-based organization. [69]

Working in Africa: Some Observations

There are many more countries than the three discussed above that might be of interest to those interested in working in, or doing business with, Africa. The diversity of this continent is astounding. One of the main geographic divisions to consider is that between the north and sub-Saharan Africa. Another issue to consider is the extent of ethnic diversity within the borders of most African countries. Some of these ethnic divisions have led to ongoing tension, and serious conflicts have erupted. Understanding how the various ethnic groups are connected to the power structure of a country is crucial for getting an insight into the politics of a country or region.

There seems to be a constant discussion of the mismanagement of resources and aid in many African countries. This has an impact on the level of corruption, as well as the distribution of wealth. Understanding corruption, income inequality, and their link to government politics, is also important for getting at the dynamics of the political processes in many African countries. [44, 47]

In recent years, the role of China has loomed large in Africa. As the competition for energy sources and valuable minerals has intensified around the world, China has become very aggressive in its dealings with African countries. China has presented many African nations with alternative funding sources and put western nations on the defensive. Some African nations see this as an opportunity to boost investment and develop infrastructure without the use of traditional aid funds from the West. Others see China's push as another kind of Eastern imperialism. Whatever the perspective, the reality is that Africa has gained new-found political and economic clout, and many countries are taking advantage of the competition for resources.

We see, now, many development projects in Africa, as the focus has shifted to emerging markets. Micro-finance projects have been expanded in many African countries, and there is a push to energize the entrepreneurial capabilities of many regions. Another development in many parts of Africa is the push by many non-African countries to actively develop agriculture, energy, and communications projects that benefit their own countries, and the local economies as well. This is because there has been a steady liberalization of FDI regulatory regimes and international investments are being encouraged on a grand scale. [45, 46]

All this economic activity and new found entrepreneurial focus bodes well for career opportunities in Africa. However, there is a shortage of skilled workers and entrepreneurs in most countries in Africa. Whether one wishes to work for a non-profit organization, a governmental entity or a multinational firm, there are now numerous pathways for developing and expanding an international career in Africa. [43, 44, 47]

WORKING IN THE MIDDLE EAST

The Middle East is a diverse, challenging, and fascinating region of the world. For some individuals, it is hard to adjust to the cultural, religious, and social issues. However, there is a lot of wealth in the Middle East, and many opportunities for career development and expansion. For those who are able to adjust to the various demands of the region, there are a number of advantages to pursuing a career there. The first and most obvious is the financial incentive. Many skilled positions earn much more than in similar positions in many western countries. If you add certain tax benefits, it is easy to see why even a short-term assignment can be very profitable.

Another benefit is working in locations that have important links to some parts of Europe, Africa, central and east Asia. In addition, countries like UAE, Turkey, Jordan, Kuwait, Saudi Arabia, Lebanon, and Israel have dynamic economies with interesting opportunities for skilled foreign and local workers. Logistically speaking, it is also easy to get to a wide range of destinations within seven hours of many capitals in the Middle East.

This is an excellent region in which to build up your professional network across a variety of sectors. Financial, oil, and gas resources are very important in the world economy, and having good local contacts here can make you a valuable individual for many different international corporations. Moreover, since many expatriates work in the region, it is also another way of expanding your connections with international executives who have a global mindset. It goes without saying that having extensive business experience, in a part of world that is considered challenging by many, can boost your personal brand significantly. If you can perform well and distinguish yourself in the Middle East, you will undoubtedly have established an enviable international track record.

One country that has received a lot of attention over the years is the UAE, especially the development strategies of Dubai. In the section below, some of the economic reorganization and modernization activities of this important emirate will be examined. This region has attracted large numbers of foreign workers over the years and, for those considering an international career with a link to the Middle East, it is a good place to start.

Dubai (UAE)

Dubai is an emirate within the United Arab Emirates (UAE), which is located south of the Persian Gulf on the Arabian Peninsula. Dubai is one of the seven emirates of the UAE and is also the most populous. In the past, the petroleum industry provided the UAE with most of its GDP. However, that focus changed when the emirates discovered that their oil supply would dwindle in the coming years. To become less dependent on oil and to create new industries, UAE officials and Dubai implemented a massive transformation of Dubai into a global business and tourism center. Numerous massive construction projects were undertaken and foreign direct investments also increased significantly. This economic restructuring and modernization have had very good results for Dubai, and the UAE in general. In recent years, the UAE's revenues from oil and gas account for less than 30 percent of the economy. In Dubai's case, most of the economic activity is linked to developments in the real estate, construction, trade, tourism, and financial services sectors. Unfortunately, the global financial crisis tightened credit and forced the economy to contract in 2009 and 2010. The economy is now slowly recovering, and Dubai is focusing on more economic diversification and a push to develop more employment opportunities for its citizens. [70–73]

A very distinct characteristic of the workforce in Dubai is its diversity, and this is coupled with certain employment patterns. Over 80 percent of the population is made up of expatriates from around the world. However, in general, westerners and Asians fill most of the managerial and hospitality positions in Dubai. Workers from India, Pakistan, Sri Lanka, Bangladesh, the Philippines, and other Asian countries supply most of the large number of manual laborers employed in Dubai's massive construction projects. That is a distinct shift from the past, when laborers came from the surrounding poor Arab countries, such as Egypt, Yemen, Syria, and Jordan. On the other hand, Dubai nationals work mainly in government jobs. The women work mainly in education and healthcare. In recent years, the government has been pushing aggressively to educate and train more nationals for more jobs in the private sector. However, overall, the citizens of Dubai generally enjoy a high standard of living and economic diversification has dampened the shocks of oil price fluctuations. [74, 75]

The working environment in Dubai

There has been a tremendous jump in the population since the country modernized, and that has necessitated a considerable investment in education. Dubai now offers comprehensive education to all male and female students from kindergarten to university. This education is provided free of charge at all levels for the country's citizens. There is also an extensive private education sector, and many students are able to pursue courses of higher education abroad at government expense. Moreover, a number of top schools in several western countries have branches or jointly-operated graduate programs in Dubai. Education programs based in Dubai are popular with students from the Middle East and other parts of the world. [70]

For many years, the economy in Dubai was growing across several sectors. The most active were construction, finance, banking, IT, and hospitality. The country was very effective at using a number of free trade zones to expand activities in various sectors. However, the sector that really got the world's attention was construction. Large scale projects such as the world's largest tower, an underwater hotel, large man-made islands, the largest airport, and many others, underscored Dubai's bold push to be a major economic and recreation hub in the Middle East. One of the mega projects was Dubai Internet City. This is an information technology park created as a free trade economic zone and a strategic base for companies targeting regional emerging markets. Many global information technology firms have located their regional bases there. Another project, Dubai Media City, is also a free trade zone which aims to become a regional hub for media organizations from around the world. Overall, fancy hotels and skyscrapers are now backdrops to a cosmopolitan lifestyle. All this activity has attracted workers from around the world. The financial crisis has slowed down many activities, but the country has not abandoned its goal of being an influential business and social hub in the Middle East. [73, 74, 76, 77]

In Dubai, as in other hierarchical societies, managers have a somewhat paternalistic attitude to their employees. In general, employees do not publicly question the decisions that managers have made. However, the relationship between management and labor can vary drastically by sector in Dubai. Expatriates and those who work with large foreign firms tend to have more globally-oriented managers. However, unskilled workers tend to get exploited and their relationship with management is very bad. Many unskilled workers have large debts, live in cramped conditions, and work very long shifts for low wages and no job security. Moreover, trade unions and workers associations are banned. The situation for highly skilled workers is very different. They tend to have very nice living conditions and are highly paid for their services. This is extremely beneficial, since individuals who live in Dubai pay no tax on income, property, or capital gains. In effect, this boosts an individual's real income to much higher levels than if they were in their home countries. [70, 75]

Work centrality and the importance of careers are very high in Dubai. Part of the reason for the large expatriate community is that individuals move there to cash in on rewarding employment opportunities. As for local citizens, the men are usually the main income earners for the family. However, an increasing number of women in Dubai are finding important and well paying positions in education, healthcare and even the financial services. For skilled workers, finding and changing jobs is not that difficult in Dubai, since there are many different sectors that need knowledge workers. There are also many employment agencies that specialize in the Dubai region. Some of these include Clarend on Parker, Michael Page, Nadia-me, Kershaw Leonard, BAC Middle East, Jobs at The Emirates Network, Morgan Mckinley, and SOS Recruitment. These agencies operate all over the country to find employment positions. Besides employment agencies, there are English language newspapers, such as Gulf News and the Khaleej Times, that feature job classified sections. Aside from agencies and newspapers, there are also online job search sites such as bayt.com, uaejobfinder.com, and dubaidonkey.com. Finally, all the major western recruitment agencies have offices located in Dubai. The western agencies tend to specialize in particular areas of work, mainly medical and nursing staff, computer personnel, accountants, construction managers, executive and office staff, engineering, and the technical trades. The Middle Eastern agencies provide focus mainly on low-skill or manual laborer positions. [76–79]

Legal guidelines for working in Dubai

In general, most expatriates are either sent directly or recruited through agencies or other media organizations. Contracts are then worked out that detail the length of employment, compensation, and other benefits. In order to work in Dubai, all expatriates must have a sponsor which can be an individual, company, or institution that serves as a guardian or guarantor. Compensation is increasingly just a salary, but many organizations receive remuneration packages that often include health benefits, and allowances for housing, transportation, and schooling. This is especially true if you are sent by your organization to work in Dubai. [70, 71]

Since working hours in Dubai are not that strictly regulated, people often end up working for long hours on a regular basis. In addition to working hours, some people spend a few hours in traffic each day getting to and from work. The work day typically starts around 8.30am and goes on until 5.30pm or later. During the month of Ramadan, working hours are generally reduced to six hours. However, it is not unusual to find companies that only give that benefit to their Muslim employees. Since Friday is a day of rest for Muslims, it is a regular day off from work. Depending on the situation, the other day off is usually Thursday or Saturday.

There are several different types of visas that can be obtained, depending on how long you want to stay. There are Visit Visas (for more than 14-days stay), Transit Visas (96 hours), Entry Service Permits (14-day visit), Multiple-Entry Visas (continuous visits to UAE) and Residence Visas (if you want to reside and become employed in the UAE). Recently, new guidelines for Temporary Work Permits have been issued. Temporary Work Permits are now open to all work categories. This new law allows foreign workers to acquire Work Permits twice within three years. It is an improvement from the previous law that required foreign temporary workers to acquire their Work Permits every six months. However, the Work Permit in Dubai is not the same as a Residence Visa. The Residence Visa allows any qualified foreign national to live in Dubai. To work in Dubai, a foreigner must also apply for a Labor Card or Work Permit. [70, 71]

CHAPTER SUMMARY & OBSERVATIONS

Chapter 10 focused on strategies and guidelines for working in Latin America and Africa. There was also a section which covered the situation in the Middle East, and Dubai was presented as an interesting location for expanding your international career. The countries discussed in Latin America were Brazil, Argentina, Mexico, and Chile. These countries were chosen because they are important economic engines for their region and they hold significant promise of becoming dynamic leaders among emerging market countries. Brazil has already become a major player in global politics and economics and the Latin American region will benefit from its political clout, abundance of resources, and economic strategies. In Africa, Nigeria, Ghana, and South Africa were covered. All three countries have significant resources and tremendous economic potential. The competition for energy resources and minerals has given these countries new influence, and foreign direct investments are pouring in at very high levels. For all the countries covered in Latin America and Africa, this chapter presented information on the general working environment and attitude towards foreign workers. This information is important because these countries are increasingly being seen as potential locations to develop or expand an international business career.

There was also a section of Chapter 10 which briefly covered the Middle East. The Emirate of Dubai (in the UAE) was singled out as an expatriate-friendly environment. Because of the massive economic restructuring, large construction projects, and aggressive push to become a regional business center, foreigners have poured into Dubai and many have managed to develop significant international business credentials working in that region. The Middle East is generally viewed as a difficult region of the world, for some. This chapter pointed out that, by working in the Middle East, you can significantly boost your personal brand as a business professional who can work with, and in, difficult business areas. Despite the challenges, the chapter also pointed out that the compensation and networking potential of employment in the Middle East was well worth the risks.

Chapter 11 is the final chapter of the book, and it will be presented in the form of a free flowing discussion on strategies that individuals can use to develop, manage, and expand their international business careers over their working lives. This book sees career management success as being generally linked to an individual's expectations, as well as medium and long-term career goals and strategies. This is because career goals give individuals targets of achievement. However, the ways in which these career goals can be achieved vary widely. There are a number of different educational, training, and occupational paths that an individual can take to accumulate their targeted capabilities and experiences. For this reason, Chapter 11 will separate career strategies and activities into three different phases. Each phase will presents a different set of opportunities and challenges. In phase I, individuals are preparing for, and starting to work with, foreign markets. In phase II, individuals are working with, and finding positions in, foreign markets. In phase III, individuals have had longer-term experiences abroad and need to leverage their experiences for greater success at the top of the managerial ladder. More details on significant activities in each phase will be presented in the final chapter.

REFERENCES

1. Aiolfi, M., L. Catao and A. Timmermann, *Common factors in Latin America's business cycles.* Journal of Development Economics, 2011. **95**(2): p. 212.
2. Becker, T.H., *Doing business in the new Latin America,* 2005, Westport, CT: Praeger.
3. McCue, D., *The hottest emerging markets.* World Trade, WT 100, 2011. **24**(7): p. 18.
4. Parnell, J., *Strategic capabilities, competitive strategy, and performance among retailers in Argentina, Peru and the United States.* Management Decision, 2011. **49**(1): p. 139.
5. Reid, M., *Forgotten continent: The battle for Latin America's soul,* 2007, New Haven, CT: Yale University Press.
6. Tuller, L., *An American's guide to doing business in Latin America,* 2008, Avon, MA: Adam Business.

7. Kalette, D., *Brazil's churning economy beckons investors.* National Real Estate Investor, 2007. **49**(11): p. 79.

8. Doyle, A., *Bountiful Brazil.* Successful Meetings, 2009. **58**(7): p. 76.

9. Klonowski, D., *Private equity in emerging markets: Stacking up the BRICs.* The Journal of Private Equity, 2011. **14**(3): p. 24.

10. de Azevedo, A.F.Z. and P.R.S. Terra, *Building resilience to international financial crises: Lessons from Brazil.* Critical Perspectives on International Business, 2009. **5**(1/2): p. 141.

11. Simoes, P., *Introduction: Brazilian workers as national and international actors.* Latin American Perspectives, 2006. **33**(3): p. 5.

12. De Guzman, D., *Oil firms expand in Brazilian ethanol.* ICIS Chemical Business, 2011. **279**(22): p. 22.

13. Going Global, *Brazil career guide 2006: Work permits and visas.* Going Global Career Guides. Brazil, 2006: p. 1.

14. Tu, Y., S. Lin and Y. Chang, *A cross-cultural comparison by individualism/collectivism among Brazil, Russia, India and China.* International Business Research, 2011. **4**(2): p. 175.

15. Brazil1. *Brazil working conditions: Information about working conditions in Brazil.* 2011 [cited 2011, April 14]. Available from: <http://www.nationsencyclopedia.com/economies/Americas/Brazil-WORKING-CONDITIONS.html>.

16. Brazil2. *Brazil visa and application requirements: Apply for Brazilian visas online.* 2011 [cited 2011, April 14]. Available from: <http://www.travelvisapro.com/visa/brazil?gclid=CN63lN3xk6gCFUoZQgod9jltCQ>.

17. Connolly, J., *Insurers view "new" Argentina as virgin territory.* National Underwriter, 1994. **98**(26): p. 45.

18. Dwyer, R., *Argentine credit: Argentina tempers optimism with uncertainty.* Euromoney, 2011.

19. Dwyer, R., *Argentina: Domestic capital markets rebound after liquidity crash.* Euromoney, 2011.

20. Schoeff, M., *Multinationals taking notice of Argentine talent.* Workforce Management, 2007. **86**(6): p. 10.

21. Mitchell, J., *Argentina: Managers prepare for private equity boom.* Euromoney, 2011.

22. Keaveny, J., *Argentina's corporate beef.* Institutional Investor, 2002. **36**(3): p. 89.

23. Argentina1. *Argentinian Visa.* 2011 [cited 2011, April 14]. Available from: <http://www.mapsofworld.com/argentina/argentina-tourism/argentina-visa.html>.

24. Argentina2. *Argentina working holiday and visa information.* 2011 [cited 2011, April 14]. Available from: <http://www.anyworkanywhere.com/whv_ar.html>.

25. Masterson, B. *The people's guide to Mexico.* 2011 [cited 2011, April 14]. Available from: <http://www.peoplesguide.com/1pages/retire/work/bil-maste/starting-business.html>.

26. Anonymous1, *Ministry of the Economy of Mexico: Mexican telecom industry expected to grow ten times by 2015.* Economics Week, 2011: p. 572.

27. Anonymous4, *Development in individual OECD countries: Mexico.* Organisation for Economic Cooperation and Development. OECD Economic Outlook, 2011(89): p. 164.

28. Squires, A., *The North American Free Trade Agreement (NAFTA) and Mexican nursing.* Health Policy and Planning, 2011. **26**(2): p. 124.

29. Anonymous 2, *The Americas: A turning tide: Crime and politics in Mexico.* The Economist, 2011. **400**(8740): p. 29.

30. Chong, A. and F. Lopez-de-Silanes, *Privatization in Mexico.* SSRN Working Paper Series, 2011.

31. Mityakov, S., *Special interests and financial liberalization: The case of Mexico.* Economics & Politics, 2011. **23**(1): p. 1.

32. Anonymous 3, *Fiscal reform for a stronger fairer and cleaner Mexican economy.* OECD Economic Surveys, 2011. **2011**(8): p. 75.

33. Mexico1. *Mexico travel and Mexico lifestyle.* 2011 [cited 2011, April 14]. Available from: <http://www.mexperience.com/living/immigration-mexico.php>.

34. Aninat, C., et al., *The political economy of productivity: The case of Chile.* SSRN Working Paper Series, 2011.

35. Anonymous, *Chile's Piñera: Seeking to bring back the Chilean miracle.* Institutional Investor, 2010.

36. Farchy, J., *China tightening threatens copper,* Financial Times, 6 April 2011: p. 32.

37. Pavoni, S., *Chile on course to realise its lofty ambitions.* The Banker, 2011.

38. Platt, G., *Brazilians develop taste for Chilean wines.* Global Finance, 2010. **24**(9): p. 28.

39. Tarziján, J. and C. Ramirez, *Firm, industry and corporation effects revisited: A mixed multilevel analysis for Chilean companies.* Applied Economics Letters, 2011. **18**(1): p. 95.

40. Chile1. *Business in Chile. South America travel guide.* 2011 [cited 2011, April 14]. Available from: <http://www.southamerica.cl/Chile/Business.htm>.

41. Chile2. *Chilean Visas. Spencer Global Chile and South America.* 2011 [cited 2011, April 14]. Available from: <http://www.spencerglobal.com/chile-immigration-law/32-chile-visas-and-immigration/114-chile-visas.html>.

42. Abor, J. and N. Biekpe, *How do we explain the capital structure of SMEs in sub-Saharan Africa?* Journal of Economic Studies, 2009. **36**(1): p. 83.

43. Adegbie, F. and A. Adeniji, *The competitive advantage of outsourcing the products and services of the Nigerian service industry.* Interdisciplinary Journal of Contemporary Research In Business, 2011. **3**(2): p. 77.

44. Chironga, M., et al., *Cracking the next growth market: Africa.* Harvard Business Review, 2011. **89**(5).

45. Connors, W., *Africa rising: In Nigeria, "lace" market reflects rising middle class: Africa's middle class embraces the fabric as an underground economy expands,* Wall Street Journal, 28 June 2011: p. B1.

46. Narayan, P., S. Narayan and R. Smyth, *Does democracy facilitate economic growth or does economic growth facilitate democracy? An empirical study of sub-Saharan Africa.* Economic Modelling, 2011. **28**(3): p. 900.

47. Noury, V., *What BRICS membership means to Africa.* African Business, 2011(376): p. 37.

48. Robson, P. and M. Freel, *Small firm exporters in a developing economy context: Evidence from Ghana.* Entrepreneurship and Regional Development, 2008. **20**(5): p. 431.

49. Yartey, C.A., *Small business finance in sub-Saharan Africa: The case of Ghana.* Management Research Review, 2011. **34**(2): p. 172.

50. Ghanaian Economy, *Ghana.* Oxford Analytica Country Profiles, 2010.

51. Gottschalk, J. and J. Dagher, *Oil windfalls in Ghana: A DSGE approach.* SSRN Working Paper Series, 2010.

52. Osei-Tutu, E., E. Badu and D. Owusu-Manu, *Exploring corruption practices in public procurement of infrastructural projects in Ghana.* International Journal of Managing Projects in Business, 2010. **3**(2): p. 236.

53. Dzisi, S., *Entrepreneurial activities of indigenous African women: A case of Ghana.* Journal of Enterprising Communities, 2008. **2**(3): p. 254.

54. Elijah-Mensah, A. and K. Saffu, *An empirical study of the role of motivation and government support among self-employed women in Ghana's tourism industry.* International Council for Small Business (ICSB). World Conference Proceedings, 2010: p. 1.

55. Ghana 1. *Ghana Immigration Service.* 2011 [cited 2011, April 7]. Available from: <http://www.ghanaimmigration.org/procedure_workpermit.html>.

56. Ghana 2. *Jobs portal for Ghana.* 2011 [cited 2011, April 7]. Available from: <http://www.ghanaweb.com/GhanaHomePage/jobs/>.

57. Adeleye, I., *The diffusion of employment flexibility in Nigeria's banking industry: Its nature, extent and causes.* International Journal of Business and Management, 2011. **6**(4): p. 150.

58. Nwaobi, G., *The economics of politics vs. the politics of economics: Nigerian case.* SSRN Working Paper Series, 2011.

59. Chuku, C., et al., *Oil price shocks and the dynamics of current account balances in Nigeria.* OPEC Energy Review, 2011. **35**(2): p. 119.

60. Anonymous, *A man and a morass: Nigeria's prospects.* The Economist, 2011. **399**(8735): p. 26.

61. Connors, W., *In Nigeria, "Lace" market reflects rising middle class: Africa's middle class embraces the fabric as an underground economy expands,* Wall Street Journal, 28 June 2011: p. B1.

62. Nigeria1. *Jobs in Nigeria.* 2011 [cited 2011, April 7]. Available from: <http://www.jobs-in-nigeria.net/>.

63. EIU, *South Africa economy: Clash over labour policy*. EIU Views Wire, 2011.

64. Ford, N., *South Africa targets stronger growth*. African Business, 2011(375): p. 41.

65. Ford, N., *South African firms look north*. African Business, 2011(375): p. 53.

66. Anonymous, *International: No jobs, boys: South Africa's economy*. The Economist, 2011. **398**(8722): p. 54.

67. Seekings, J. and N. Nattrass, *State-business relations and pro-poor growth in South Africa*. Journal of International Development, 2011. **23**(3): p. 338.

68. South Africa1. *South Africa: Visas and immigration*. 2011 [cited 2011, April 7]. Available from: <http://www.globalvisas.com/countries/south_africa.html>.

69. South Africa2. *Working abroad career guide for South Africa*. 2011 [cited 2011, April 7]. Available from: <http://www.overseasdigest.com/country/southafrica.htm>.

70. Dubai1. *Living and working in Dubai*. 2007 [cited 2007, May 6]; Available from: http://www.shelteroffshore.com/index.php/living/more/living_and_working_in_dubai/.

71. Dubai2. *UAE: Info at a glance*. 2007 [cited 2007]. Available from: www.datadubai.com.

72. Renaud, B., *Dubai's real estate boom and bust of 2002–2008: Dynamics and policy responses*. Housing Finance International (Online), 2010. **24**(4): p. 6.

73. Vora, N., *United Arab Emirates: Dubai: The city as corporation*. The Middle East Journal, 2012. **66**(1): p. 188.

74. Dubai3. *Top UAE job growth sectors*. 2012 [cited 2012]. Available from: <http://www.emirates247.com/business/top-uae-job-growth-sectors-2011-12-15-1.432908>.

75. Vora, N., *Unofficial citizens: Indian entrepreneurs and the state: Effect in Dubai, United Arab Emirates*. International Labor and Working Class History, 2011. **79**(1): p. 122.

76. Coombe, W. and J. Melki, *Global media and brand Dubai*. Place Branding and Public Diplomacy, 2012. **8**(1): p. 58.

77. Madichie, N. and J. Blythe, *The "bold and the beautiful" of the UAE retail environment*. Marketing Intelligence & Planning, 2011. **29**(6): p. 593.

78. Gallant, M., S. Majumdar and D. Varadarajan, *Outlook of female students towards entrepreneurship*. Education, Business and Society: Contemporary Middle Eastern Issues, 2010. **3**(3): p. 218.

79. Govers, R., *Brand Dubai and its competitors in the Middle East: An image and reputation analysis*. Place Branding and Public Diplomacy, 2012. **8**(1): p. 48.

11 MANAGING YOUR INTERNATIONAL BUSINESS CAREER

LEARNING OBJECTIVES

• Review challenges to international career development

• Examine strategies for capabilities development

• Understand how to maximize capability, mobility, and transferability

• Leverage international experience for long-term career success

THE ROADMAP

Chapter 10 highlighted the practical strategies and guidelines for developing and expanding your international career in Latin America, Africa, and parts of the Middle East. Although the main focus of the chapter was on Latin America and Africa, there was a brief discussion of conditions in the Middle East and a more in-depth analysis of the working environment in Dubai. The countries covered in Latin America were Brazil, Argentina, Mexico, and Chile. The countries reviewed in Africa were Nigeria, Ghana, and South Africa. For all of the countries, there was an examination of the working environment, attitude towards foreigners, and general legal guidelines for entry and work. As the importance of emerging markets grows, these countries are creating employment environments that have a great demand for knowledge workers and entrepreneurs from around the world. In effect, these countries are becoming interesting locations for career development and expansion.

In this final chapter, you will be presented with a general discussion on strategies and challenges you might face at different phases of your career development and expansion. The chapter focuses on three main phases of international career management. In phase I, individuals are preparing for, and starting to work with, foreign markets. In phase II, individuals are working with, and finding positions in, foreign markets. In phase III, individuals have had longer-term experiences abroad and need to leverage their experiences for greater success as they move up the managerial ladder.

Overall, the chapter is structured in the form of a free flowing discussion on strategies that individuals can use to develop, manage, and expand their international business careers over their working lives. Career management success is generally linked to an individual's expectations, as well as to medium and long-term career goals and strategies. This is because career goals give individuals targets of achievement. However, the ways in which these career goals can be achieved vary widely. There are a number of different educational, training, and occupational paths that can be taken to help individual accumulate their targeted capabilities and experiences. For this reason, this chapter will separate career strategies and activities into three different phases. Each phase presents a different set of opportunities and challenges.

TOPIC FOCUS

In phase I, individuals are preparing for and starting to work with foreign markets. This is a developmental phase when individuals are acquiring the necessary education, experiences, and skills that will allow them to analyze and work with foreign markets. This phase usually occurs during the early periods of one's career. However, it is during this time that a number of fundamental experiences and skills are acquired. Work with foreign firms and markets usually occur in the local environment, and the individual has not yet attainted a managerial role. In phase II, individuals are working with, and finding positions in, foreign markets. Some have even had management positions in foreign environments. During this period, individuals may have to deal with expatriate issues and how they impact longer-term career success. The main career goal is to perform effectively abroad in ways that boost one's status with an organization or boost general employability. In phase III, individuals have had longer-term experiences abroad and need to leverage their experiences for greater success at the top of the managerial ladder. Some individuals choose to use their accumulated experiences to change sectors or professions as they get to the latter stages of their career. More details on significant activities in each phase are included below.

PHASE I: PREPARING FOR & WORKING WITH FOREIGN MARKETS

The role of education in international business career preparation

Going to a college or university is very important for most careers in the international business arena. There are some situations where an associate degree or a business certificate are enough to get an entry level position but, in the long run, it is important to have at least a four year undergraduate degree. There are a number of different undergraduate majors that can be helpful in preparing you for a career in the international environment. An *international business degree* can be quite helpful. In this major, students usually learn how to do comparative market research, cross-border industry analysis, and how to evaluate management styles and the impact of different cultures on business activities. An *international relations degree* is appropriate for those who want to work with international policy institutions or even with international business firms. This degree covers mainly international politics, international institutions, and the dynamics behind international policy processes. The role of governments and national stakeholders in economic, social, and political arenas are also stressed. *An international economics degree* is more technical and usually relies on more quantitative methods for analyzing domestic and international economic activities. Besides the fundamentals of micro and macro economics, students learn how to forecast and build economic models. This degree can be helpful in the consulting, financial, or government arenas. However, to work as an economist, it is usually necessary to have a Ph.D. in economics. *An international development degree* focuses squarely on economic and social development in countries around the world. Students usually learn some aspects of economics, international affairs, project management, and community development. The vast majority of graduates have a desire to work in, or with, developing nations. Recently, sustainable development has become a key aspect of this major. *A general or functional business degree* in areas such as marketing, finance, management, entrepreneurship, hospitality, and accounting can also lead to successful careers in the international business arena. Majoring in a foreign language can also be helpful, but it is best to link that degree with a minor in some business function. All of the degrees mentioned above have both undergraduate and graduate versions. The graduate degrees are usually recognized as professional degrees worldwide. Beyond these typical majors for those in business, it is possible to use other majors and experiences to get to work with and in foreign markets, but that usually involves more targeted proactive strategies. [1–4]

The importance of travel/study abroad programs in building cross-cultural skills

The study abroad experience is the most effective way to get significantly acquainted with a different culture. Beyond learning the language and culture, one can develop many friendships that will last a lifetime. For some countries where it is difficult to gain entry for employment, the study abroad programs can give you the chance to establish local contacts that can help you get interviews for possible positions in the future. Some nations even allow foreign students to work while attending school. This type of program not only provides you with living abroad experiences, but gives you the opportunity to build your reputation. It is advisable that students take advantage of these programs during their junior or senior year at a university. Some programs last for one semester and others for a full year. The longer the experience in the foreign environment, the better it is for accumulating valuable cross-cultural skills. For those who cannot afford a full semester abroad, even a short-term visit or study tour of a foreign country can provide valuable insights that might guide future career decisions. [5–7]

The use of internships to develop skills and experiences

Students are often faced with the "catch 22" situation whereby you need work experience to get a job and you also need a job to get work experience. Well, domestic and foreign internships remain the most significant ways for inexperienced individuals to gain the valuable skills and experiences they need to break into a particular sector. It is always easier to get an unpaid internship, but there are many that also compensate you. The crucial factors in choosing an internship are whether it helps with your planned career trajectory, or whether it gets you access to an organization or sector that would otherwise be beyond reach. Having internships on your résumé also shows commitment to a particular sector or profession. If you are lucky enough to be able to arrange an internship in a foreign country, you have signaled both your interest in, and commitment to, work in foreign markets. [8, 9]

The role of job fairs, career forums, & school career centers in career development

Many schools have very well-established career centers to assist students with career development. Unfortunately, most individuals wait until they are just about to graduate to enquire about career assistance. These career centers often provide résumé-writing help, interviewing practice, alumni connections, internship opportunities, and even full-time employment situations. There a number of career forums that target international employment. These forums are normally held once or twice a year in some major city. For individuals who are looking to change careers or for those who are about to graduate, these career forums can expose you to a wide range of organizations. Job fairs occur more frequently. They are also referred to as career fairs. They usually bring together employers, recruiters, and schools in a particular location. Individuals often present their résumés and talk with employers as they move from one booth to the next. Most of the positions are usually entry level, at this type of event. Recently, online job fairs have also become popular. [9–11]

Using relationships and social networks to maximize employability

Using relationships and networks to improve employment opportunities is considered essential in present and future job markets. Organizations know that they can avoid significant screening and recruiting costs if they get internal referrals. Job seekers also avoid the intense competition for publicly announced positions. Friends, family, and community members represent the closest circle of trust and they tend to know you best. However, the areas where you need to be the most proactive are your links to your schools, professional associations, and online social media. It is also important to manage the image you project in all these interactions. Consistent, trustworthy and reliable behaviors should underlie all network relations. It is important to remember not to wait until there is a crisis in your career to build and expand your network relations. Updating your professional achievements, taking part in network events, and keeping up with occasional correspondence are some of the basic steps necessary to keep in touch with your network. Having people from diverse regions, backgrounds, and professions also can boost the effectiveness of your network. The more diverse a network, the more resilient, flexible, and information-rich that network tends to be. Finally, try to remain on good terms with everyone with whom you have had significant long-term interactions. During challenging or traumatic periods of your career, positive support from your network can speed up the adjustment to new employment situations. [12–15]

Working for foreign firms in the domestic environment

Given the extensive use, and importance, of foreign direct investment in the global economy, many individuals find themselves working for foreign firms in their home market. There are many challenges and opportunities for those individuals who work for foreign firms. The working conditions may be better or worse than the situation in domestic firms, and the compensation can be higher or lower than with local firms. However, foreign firms provide badly needed employment opportunities and they can also expose you to new cultural behaviors, new management styles and new business strategies. It may also be the easiest way to build your international connections and experiences by working with foreign markets.

If you manage to perform well and establish your reputation of working well with foreign firms, this can translate into improved employment opportunities with local or other international firms. There are many American executives who first established their reputation by working for foreign firms, and later parlayed that situation into more lucrative positions with American or other multinational organizations. [16–19]

Researching international oriented business sector & firms in the US

Given the global nature of business activities, most firms and sectors have a part of their activity that is significantly influenced by international business developments. However, the operations of some sectors and firms are more significantly influenced by foreign clients or foreign markets. If you are seeking to develop and maintain your career in international business, you should be targeting sectors and firms that are actively operating abroad or intensively interacting with foreign clients. There are many sources for researching firms operating in international markets. However, the key is to know the indicators and factors that would help you pick out the firms that are very active internationally. Below are some indicators or factors that you should consider to find internationally active firms:

1. The percentage of total sales or total revenue that can be attributed to international operations.

2. The number of branch offices or plants that a firm has in foreign countries.

3. The percentage of home country employees that work abroad or go abroad because of the firm's business activities.

4. The percentage of the firm's employees that do not come from the home country.

5. The number of alliances that the firm has with international partners.

6. The importance of foreign markets to future strategies and operations.

There are many other questions and factors that one can consider, but these questions should provide significant insight into a firm's international operations. Earlier in the book we talked about sectors that have generally had a major exposure to international markets. Sectors such as finance, banking, insurance, logistics, consulting, hospitality, information technology, and wine provide numerous positions for those wishing to work in international business. Within these sectors, there are many occupations and many employment paths that one can choose to have a successful career in international business. [1, 4, 10, 11, 20]

PHASE II: WORKING & MANAGING IN FOREIGN ENVIRONMENTS

Finding employment positions abroad before you leave

If you are determined to work and live abroad, there are many different approaches you can take. Working for a non-profit organization abroad is one way of getting experience and sometimes contributing to the development of communities and nations elsewhere. The Peace Corps has had a well established program for over 50 years, and places volunteers in a wide variety of jobs and projects around the world. There are many other non-profit organizations that are active around the world, and they seek individuals that are committed and willing to contribute while they learn. Many people who got their initial experiences abroad in one of these programs have gone on to develop respectable careers in international business and international development. Another approach is to be a language teacher in countries where resources are being put into developing foreign language skills. The advantage of this approach is that you are connected to an organization and earn a salary while you learn to adapt to the local culture. Many language teachers have used their experiences abroad to develop new careers in the international arena. Employment positions in the areas mentioned can often be found in your home country through employment intermediaries, on websites, or even through international agencies. [21–24]

Convincing your organization to send you to work for them abroad

There are many individuals who want to work abroad but they don't have access to the kind of jobs that would send them there. There are also firms which seek individuals to work in their foreign operations, but find it hard to get home country workers to volunteer. In many firms, there are also individuals who have a strong interest in going abroad, but have difficulty getting internal support for a foreign posting. A lot of this is due to a mismatch of skills and aspirations. Sometimes, it is also because the organization is not really aware of how serious an employee is about working abroad. Being an expatriate can be a demanding assignment, but it can also be exciting and can really open up long-term career opportunities. The best situation is always to have your organization send you to work abroad with all the benefits and compensation that goes with being an expatriate. The main difficulty is that you generally have to have special capabilities before an organization is willing to cover all the expenses of an expatriate employee. If you are lucky enough to be hired by a firm with international operations, it is important that you start a quiet campaign from the beginning to show that you have the interest and the skills necessary to be sent abroad. It may sometimes be necessary to transfer from one division to another in order to increase your chances of being sent abroad. From your perspective, the main issues you have to worry about are: (1) Can you adapt and perform successfully in the foreign environment? (2) During your time abroad, can you acquire skills and relationships that will boost your capabilities and career advancement potential? and (3) Upon returning home, will you be able to successfully re-integrate into the firm's management structure or find a fitting position in another organization? [21, 25–27]

Finding employment as a local hire abroad

Many individuals who want to work abroad do not have the patience to work their way up in an organization with the hope of being sent abroad. Others have a strong desire to start working as soon as possible in a particular foreign environment, or wish to have more control over the specific location where they work in a certain country. There are also others who, for personal or other reasons, wish to immigrate into, or live for a long time in, a certain foreign country. For all these individuals, one solution is to go directly to the chosen country and attempt to find employment on their own. The major issues here are sponsorship and visa-related difficulties. In some cases, family connections can lead to some type of sponsorship. However, the typical goal should be to find either a local firm or a foreign firm that is willing to sponsor you and assist with a work visa. Many multinationals will hire some of their own nationals who are living locally in the country where they are doing business. This, sometimes, has a trust element to it, and sometimes it is an easy way to pay less for capable workers who can help with their foreign operations. These positions are not usually top management but, since you have certain skills and a general knowledge of the foreign country, you can be valuable to a firm. This would make you a local hire for the foreign firm. Local hires do not usually get the same compensation and benefits as expatriates who are sent from the home country. It is also difficult to move up the management chain when you are hired locally by a foreign firm. The exception, of course, is if you are a highly skilled individual who has an established reputation for working with foreign firms and in foreign countries. In those situations, you might find a technical or management position by going through local channels. The other approach is to find a job working for a local company in the chosen country. You would be a foreign employee to them, but your compensation and benefits would be more in line with their local employees. However, there are situation where you might receive more, and some cases where you might receive less than local citizens. Despite the drawbacks to the approach of going directly to a foreign country to seek employment, it is a much faster way of working in areas that you have targeted as essential for your international career development. [27–30]

What are the skills & competences of a global manager?

Global managers are usually comfortable working in uncertain environments and have a wide range of problem-solving skills. They can be country, business, or functional managers but their duties and roles span a number of domains. Despite the different definitions of global managers, everyone agrees that they need to have a "global mindset" and have capabilities which are a good fit for cross border activities. Below are six qualities or capabilities that are generally put forward as essential for global managers:

1. Having general international and country-specific knowledge.

2. Cross-cultural awareness and adaptability.

3. Expertise in functional business or technical knowledge.

4. Excellent communication with cross-cultural negotiation skills.

5. Diversity management experience.

6. Honesty and open mindedness.

Individuals who develop a combination of these skills are very valuable. Very often, they become specialists at handling a variety of international business issues and spend their careers moving from one foreign country to another. Some individuals become experts at doing business in one specific country or region. The most difficult issue for global managers is whether one organization can give them the flexibility to expand their career into a number of domains, or if it is more rewarding to be a boundary-spanning professional who mainly focuses on loyalty to their own career advancement. [31–34]

Succeeding in international assignments

Being able to perform successfully in international environments requires a range of different strategies. The first is the *preparation* for the assignment. This can include cultural training, operational training, moving logistics, and even a preliminary visit to clear away up some uncertainties. Good preparation will help to make the transition to the new environment less troublesome. The second strategy is *setting up good headquarters or home country support*. It is crucial to know ahead of time which home country resources and contacts are available to help you in your new assignment. Understanding how this assignment fits into to the overall strategy of the firm is also important. A third strategy is extensive *networking* at home and in the new location. This includes finding out about employees and family members who might have lived and worked in the same environment. There might also be other employees still in the new environment, and they will have a lot of useful information for you and any family members who might accompany you. The other type of networking is expanding your local contacts after you have started your new assignment abroad. Once your assignment is underway, a key strategy is to *build trust with local colleagues and other business contacts*. In many international environments, trust is the key element for successful business relationships. A fifth strategy is *focusing on achievable goals*. Very often, foreign managers overextend themselves or try to micro-manage too many areas of operations. This not only increases the level of stress, but takes away from the focus necessary for success. Finally, the strategy that is essential for long-term international career success is continuous learning and adaptation. Circumstances abroad will continue to change, and the skills and information necessary to succeed will sometimes change as well. Those individuals who can continue learning and adapting will be the ones that can successfully build and expand their international careers. [29, 30, 35–37]

PHASE III: LEVERAGING INTERNATIONAL EXPERIENCES FOR CAREER MOBILITY & SUCCESS

Challenges of the long-term expatriate lifestyle

If you end up living and working abroad for extended periods, there are a number of challenges with which you need to deal. The first challenge is that of being disconnected from structural and power changes in your company in your home country. As time goes by, firms go through strategic reorganizations, and that often results in shifts in power and new priorities. The result could be the feeling of being left on an island far away without significant support for your career goals. Another challenge is your family's ability to adapt to the demands of long-term residence abroad. This could occur with your spouse or with your children, as they adjust to different educational systems and different cultural expectations. Another challenge that some expatriates have faced is the unusual situation whereby you and your family actually end up liking your posting abroad and are reluctant to return home. Some individuals may end up leaving the organization that posted them in their foreign location in order to work for another foreign firm or a local firm that would support their continued stay in the country. In situations where individuals decide to continue their career for the long-term in a foreign country, the difficulty becomes how to advance their career without the formal connection to a home country firm. However, this may be an acceptable situation if an individuals has built up an excellent reputation and an extensive local network that can be used to expand their career options. [29, 38–40]

Networking abroad while being based mainly in your home country

There are some careers in international business where individuals travel frequently to foreign countries while maintaining strong links to their home county firms. Some of these individuals are flexpatriates, project managers, auditors, or those just on short-term assignments. Although these situations are physically demanding and sometimes psychologically stressful, they do highlight your problem-solving abilities and give you the opportunity to build relationships across borders without giving up on the strong support of the home country headquarters. The drawback to this kind of career is the stress it places on families. It is usually easier for a single person to be traveling frequently, than for someone with family demands. [29, 40, 41]

Keeping up with employment opportunities across borders

It is now much easier to keep track of employment opportunities in different countries. If you know any foreign languages, that will make it even easier to carry out extensive job searchers in other languages. There are numerous websites dedicated to posting job offerings in different countries. The process can sometimes be cumbersome, but it is possible to narrow down your options to realistic choices and then take an exploratory trip to the target country. There are also many executive search and specialized headhunters that will explore and select opportunities abroad for experienced individuals. If one is lacking in work experience, a master's degree is considered a professional degree in most countries, and it increases the chances of being considered. Finally, building and keeping a network of friends across many countries is a way of finding out about various employment opportunities. The building of such networks should start from one's experiences in a university or study abroad program. Company assignments abroad also present another opportunity to build international friendship networks. [23, 42–44]

Volunteering or giving-back projects that get you working abroad

There are numerous non-profit organizations and international institutions that have opportunities for individuals who want to volunteer to work abroad. The types of positions range from entry level to highly skilled executives and technicians. For individuals who are at the beginning of their career, volunteering represents one strategy for getting the opportunity to live and work in foreign environments. For more experienced individuals who have mainly worked in the domestic market, volunteering gives them opportunities to use their capabilities to help others and build their international experience at the same time. Even if individuals have completed their main careers, volunteering abroad presents the opportunity to give back and gain satisfaction in new ways. This type of behavior can be considered an *encore career* for some. For those who wish to work throughout their careers in areas like development, corporate social responsibility, governance, and international health, there are many career paths available that can take them from entry level to a high level management executive or policy-maker position. [43–46]

Consulting as a way of levering your international experience

If your international expertise is linked to very good technical, functional, geographic, linguistic, or cross-cultural skills, you might be able to make an impact in consulting. Consulting firms operate in fields such as technology management, business strategy, human resources, negotiation, market research, and policy development. Your international experience coupled with your accumulated capabilities can make you an attractive candidate. If your expertise and networks are excellent, you might even consider starting up your own consulting venture. In a business world that is increasingly global, international expertise, a good reputation, and relationship networks can go a long way in making your career strong and vibrant. [41, 47–50]

CHAPTER SUMMARY & OBSERVATIONS

What all the comments above have in common is the concept of employability. Employability can be considered as the core characteristic of a successful modern day career. Now that organizational loyalty, job security, and mutual commitment are no longer dominant attributes of a career, employability has taken center stage as the most effective strategy for individuals as they strive to create meaningful careers. Throughout this book, careers have been treated as vehicles for taking individuals through different employment landscapes. Employability is the fuel for such vehicles. Consequently, the more employable individuals remain, the better the potential journey to some form of career success. The personalized resource management (PRM) approach has identified three main factors behind the phenomenon of employability: capability, mobility, and transferability.

"Capability," again, refers to the developing, expanding, and accumulating of skills and relationships that enhance individuals' ability to solve the problems they encounter throughout their career. In terms of business-related problems, capability focuses on problem-solving abilities across functional areas. In terms of leadership issues, capability is tied to communication and negation skills that can inspire others to perform more effectively. As for the international business environment, capability is linked closely to cross-cultural understanding, as well as knowledge of international markets and the ability to adapt to changing and uncertain environments. The keys to keeping your capability at a high level are continuous learning, and adaptation as you overcome business and career challenges.

"Mobility" refers to the ability to change jobs and locations with relative ease in order to advance your career. There are three main types of mobility: psychological mobility, location mobility, and job-search mobility. "Psychological mobility" refers to the motivation, as well as the readiness and commitment, to change your work environment. "Location mobility" indicates your ability to move and adapt to different work environments. "Job-search mobility" relates to your ability to conduct meaningful searches in different national environments. This type of search involves your connection to intermediaries, colleagues, and informational networks in different environments. One aspect of mobility that has not been mentioned is timing. You have to develop a sense of timing. It is important to know when it is better to stay or leave. Overall, you need to remain aware of your working environment, sector, and firm performance, so that you can proactively prepare for significant career changes.

Over the long term, transferability is probably the most difficult of the three employability factors. "Transferability" refers to the ability to use your capabilities in different national environments, sectors, and occupations. Maximizing your transferability requires a modular approach to the acquisition and use of your capabilities. Your transferability will depend greatly on your ability to combine and package capabilities in ways which project expertise across firms and sectors. Informational and relational networks are also crucial to maximizing your transferability. The transferability factor really comes into play during the transition periods of your career. It is important to realize that, to stay employed, it might be necessary to change locations, sectors, or even occupations. Being able to evaluate the status of your career management is something of which you should continually be aware. The career evaluation chart at Figure 11.1 gives you a good overview of how various factors are linked to your career trajectory.

Figure 11.1 Personalized career strategy chart

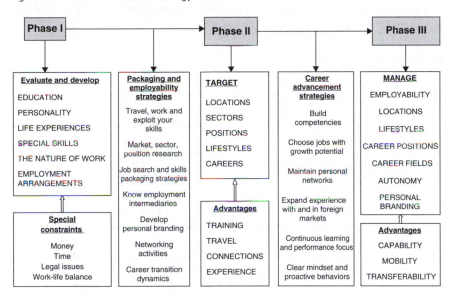

Developed by Roblyn Simeon.

Looking back at the information presented in this and previous chapters, we can see that there are several aspects to managing your international business career. It goes without saying that knowing the social, cultural, and business developments in various national environments is the first step in searching for and building an international career. Clarifying and fortifying your motivations, skill development, and employment goals are also constant requirements of good career management. Finally, regularly assessing, packaging, and mobilizing your capabilities and relationships represent the core strategies of the personalized resource management approach. Figure 11.1 shows the range of career management strategies that underlie the personalized resource management approach. It is also an effective tool for evaluating your overall approach to career development and success.

At the end of each chapter, there is an extensive list of references related to the main themes of the chapter. The articles, books, and other materials referenced represent a rich source of information for more in-depth investigations. This field of international career management is supported by many theoretical and practical insights that can guide you to develop your own effective strategies for long-term career success. After this final chapter, you will find an Appendix. The materials in the Appendix are linked to the first eight chapters of the book. These are the more theoretical chapters, and many different concepts and career management strategies are covered. There are also many links to organizations that can help with the career management process.

The main reason for including this supplementary material in the Appendix is the conviction that it can be very helpful to those interested in various aspects of career management in the international environment. Although the material in the Appendix is generally very detailed, it does expand on the major themes and ideas covered in the main chapters. Some of the material can also serve as a reference for further investigations. Overall, the Appendix really highlights the fact that international career development and management is an endeavor which draws on many different fields and insights. If, by reading the chapters and exploring the Appendix, you gain a greater understanding of your international career development potential, then this book will have served its purpose.

REFERENCES

1. Baruch, Y., *To MBA or not to MBA.* Career Development International, 2009. **14**(4): p. 388.
2. Eisner, S., *E-employment? College grad career building in a changing and electronic age.* American Journal of Business Education, 2010. **3**(7): p. 25.
3. Hirschi, A., *The role of chance events in the school-to-work transition: The influence of demographic, personality and career development variables.* Journal of Vocational Behavior, 2010. **77**(1): p. 39.
4. Schermerhorn, J., *Learning by going? The management educator as expatriate.* Journal of Management Inquiry, 1999. **8**(3): p. 246.
5. Broughton, P., *Why it can pay to study abroad.* Management Today, June 2010: p. 68.
6. Mills, L., D. Deviney and B. Ball, *Short-term study abroad programs: A diversity of options.* The Journal of Human Resources and Adult Learning, 2010. **6**(2): p. 1.
7. Timiraos, N., *Map widens for studies abroad: American students seeking a leg up step outside comfort zone.* Wall Street Journal, December 19 2006: p. B8.
8. Grensing-Pophal, L., *Hiring interns.* Credit Union Management, 2010. **33**(12): p. 44.
9. Light, J., *Managing and careers: Interns get a head start in competition for jobs,* Wall Street Journal, May 16 2011: p. B9.
10. Petriglieri, G. and J. Petriglieri, *Identity workspaces: The case of business schools.* Academy of Management Learning & Education, 2010. **9**(1): p. 44.
11. Saumya, B., *The talent catchers.* Business Today, 2009.
12. Gerstner, L., *Use social media to retool your career.* Kiplinger's Personal Finance, 2011. **65**(7): p. 1.
13. Nelson, J., *Mastering the art of the social-web CV.* Canadian Business, 2011. **84**(5): p. 55.
14. Walker, K., *Getting the most out of LinkedIn.* Paralegal Today, 2011. **28**(2): p. 12.
15. Woo, S. and L. Cowan, *LinkedIn IPO sizzles: Career website's 30% increase signals demand for social-networking stocks,* Wall Street Journal (online), May 18 2011: p. B1.
16. Capell, P., *Careers Q & A: Being an expatriate in the US doesn't give one the upper hand,* Wall Street Journal, October 18 2005: p. B10.
17. Krisher, B., *Outsiders inside Japanese companies.* Fortune, 1982. **106**(1): p. 114.

18. Lancaster, H., *Managing your career: How you can learn to feel at home in foreign-based firm*, in *Wall Street Journal*, June 4 1996: p. B1.
19. Rochman, B., *American twenty somethings land in Vietnam*. Fortune, 1996. **133**(12): p. 114.
20. Rousseau, G. and D. Venter, *Investigating the importance of factors related to career choice*. Management Dynamics, 2009. **18**(3): p. 2.
21. Bleakley, F.R., *US firms shift more office jobs abroad*, Wall Street Journal, April 22 1996: p. A2.
22. Güngör, N.D. and A. Tansel, *Brain drain from Turkey: The case of professionals abroad*. International Journal of Manpower, 2008. **29**(4): p. 323.
23. Lacey, J., *Working abroad: Finding international internships and entry-level jobs*. Occupational Outlook Quarterly, 2006. **50**(3): p. 2.
24. Morella, M., *How to find a job abroad*. U.S. News & World Report, 2010: p. 1.
25. Prystay, C. and T. Herman, *Tax hike hits home for Americans abroad: Higher levy on expatriates spurs employers to rethink hiring policies, especially in Asia*, Wall Street Journal, July 19 2006: p. D1.
26. Rakesh, S. and B. Jyotsna, *Talent management: competency development: key to global leadership*. Industrial and Commercial Training, 2009. **41**(3): p. 118.
27. Shankaran, G., R. Murray and P. Miller, *Short-term international assignments: Maximizing effectiveness, minimizing cost and risk*. International Tax Journal, 2011. **37**(1): p. 41.
28. Garretson, R., *The perils of overseas jobs*. Network World, 2006. **23**(45): p. 55.
29. Stroppa, C. and E. Spiess, *International assignments: The role of social support and personal initiative*. International Journal of Intercultural Relations: IJIR, 2011. **35**(2): p. 234.
30. van Bakel, M., M. Gerritsen and J. van Oudenhoven, *Impact of a local host on the success of an international assignment*. Thunderbird International Business Review, 2011. **53**(3): p. 391.
31. Bowen, D. and A. Inkpen, *Exploring the role of "global mindset" in leading change in international contexts*. The Journal of Applied Behavioral Science, 2009. **45**(2): p. 239.
32. Kjar, R., *Global mindset: Characteristics and contributing factors*, 2007, Lisle, IL: Benedictine University. p. 225.
33. Nardon, L. and R. Steers, *The new global manager: Learning cultures on the fly*. Organizational Dynamics, 2008. **37**(1): p. 47.
34. Ramalu, S., et al., *Personality and cross-cultural adjustment among expatriate assignees in Malaysia*. International Business Research, 2010. **3**(4): p. 96.
35. Brookes, M. and N. Becket, *Internationalising hospitality management degree programmes*. International Journal of Contemporary Hospitality Management, 2011. **23**(2): p. 241.
36. Collings, D., et al., *Understanding and supporting the career implications of international assignments*. Journal of Vocational Behavior, 2011. **78**(3): p. 361.
37. Lublin, J., *Grappling with the expatriate issue: Companies try to cut subsidies for employees*, Wall Street Journal, December 11 1989: p. 1.
38. Okpara, J. and J. Kabongo, *Cross-cultural training and expatriate adjustment: A study of western expatriates in Nigeria*. Journal of World Business, 2011. **46**(1): p. 22.
39. Stroppa, C. and E. Spiess, *Expatriates social networks: the role of company size*. The International Journal of Human Resource Management, 2010. **21**(13): p. 2306.
40. Wagner, G. and U. Vormbusch, *Informal networks as "global microstructures": The case of German expatriates in Russia*. Critical Perspectives on International Business, 2010. **6**(4): p. 216.
41. Yette, M., *How to go global*. Black Enterprise, 2008. **39**(2): p. 62.
42. Banjo, S., *Help wanted: "Voluntour" at home and abroad*, Wall Street Journal, June 27 2010: p. 1.
43. Liebesman, S., *Bridging the gap between the classroom and real world*. Quality Progress, 2006. **39**(5): p. 60.
44. Ocal, A., *Lending more than a helping hand*. CMA Management, 2010. **83**(9): p. 24.
45. Hudson, S. and K. Inkson, *Volunteer overseas development workers: The hero's adventure and personal transformation*. Career Development International, 2006. **11**(4): p. 304.
46. Shellenbarger, S., *Delaying college to fill in the gaps: More students take year off to travel, study and volunteer: Top reason cited is high school burnout*, Wall Street Journal, December 29 2010: p. D1.
47. Kittler, M. and T. Schuster, *The impact of human and social capital on the internationalisation of German consulting firms*. International Journal of Entrepreneurship and Innovation Management, 2010. **12**(2): p. 138.

48. Schwartzmann, M., *Steps on road to developing a global mindset*, Financial Times, March 14 2011: p. 6.
49. Thurston, T. and V. Singh, *Disrupting the consultants: Could the advisers use some advice?* Thunderbird International Business Review, 2010. **52**(1): p. 61.
50. Yen, D., B. Barnes and C. Wang, *The measurement of guanxi: Introducing the GRX scale.* Industrial Marketing Management, 2011. **40**(1): p. 97.

APPENDIX

CHAPTER I

Context dimensions of the concept of work

Although discussions about the context of work abound, they generally emphasize the three aspects below.

Context dimension	Explanations
The technical activity aspect	This is a focus on the formal and informal tasks, routines, technical, and knowledge factors that are needed to do work or create a product or service.
The socio-institutional aspect	The focus here is on how work connects individuals to groups and society as well as the formal and informal institutional recognition that is needed for certain types of work.
The economic aspect	This highlights the financial compensation, non-wage benefits, and the wealth-producing potential of work.

Types of Work-Related Psychological Attachments

Given all the research done on work goals, it should come as no surprise that work-related attitudes continue to be of major interest to organizational psychologists, human resource specialists, and consultants. What they all hope is that, depending on an individual's psychological attachment to different aspects of the world of work, it might be possible to explain or influence their work behaviors. However, attitudes of attachment to task, job, project, work unit, organization, and profession can vary significantly across individuals. Many theorists and consultants point out that an understanding of work-related attitudes could help individuals or organizations decide which skill development, work environment, and career management strategies they should choose. Three types of psychological attachments that continue to be studied are job satisfaction, organizational commitment, and professional commitment (Herzberg and Mausner, 1959; Sladek and Hollander, 2009).

Job satisfaction

Job satisfaction is a concept which reflects how content individuals are with their jobs. The assumption has generally been that, the more satisfied workers are, the more likely it is that their work performance will improve. Over the years, organizations have spent a lot of time and resources measuring job satisfaction and then designing jobs or work environments which might boost the level of worker satisfaction. Many practices such as job rotation, job enlargement, job enrichment, employee involvement, and autonomous work groups were implemented to maximize job satisfaction and worker performance.

Organizational commitment

Organizational commitment is a work-related attitude which indicates the level of psychological attachment or sense of loyalty that an individual has for an organization. The general finding has been that the higher the level of organizational commitment, the more likely it is that an individual will work harder than obligated, and even sacrifice to accomplish the goals of the organization. It is important to point out that it is possible for workers to be dissatisfied with their jobs and still maintain high levels of organizational commitment. This usually occurs when the worker understands that a particular job is only temporary, or that other benefits from belonging to that organization greatly outweigh current discomforts.

Professional Commitment

Professional commitment can be considered a complicated occupation-related attitude. Professional commitment generally refers to the extent to which working professionals feel a strong attachment to their particular occupation. This can be further broken down into (a) how attached or loyal these individuals are to the ideals and fundamental practices of the profession; and (b) how determined individuals are to maintaining their association with this profession even in times of difficulty. There have been many studies of how professional commitment attitudes affect the behaviors and decisions of professionals such as nurses, doctors, accountants, and lawyers.

Types of Non-traditional Employment Arrangements

Moderated traditional employment arrangements

Worker-lending or worker-transfers: This can be a temporary or permanent lending or transfer of main company employees to an affiliated company. If the lending or transfer is short-term, the main company usually covers all the employees' wages and benefits. If the lending or transfer is longer-term or permanent, then the main firm either pays a portion of the costs or all the employee costs shift to the receiving company. The reasons for this practice include strategies for training, supporting joint development projects, knowledge sharing, cultivating inter-firm cooperation, downsizing, and reducing payroll costs. This employment arrangement is mainly associated with Japanese firms.

Piece work: The services of the workers are compensated based on the completion of specific tasks which can be measured or counted. Under certain conditions, the person can be considered an employee of the organization and be eligible for benefits. The expectation of longer-term continued employment can also exist.

Fixed-term: Employees that are hired to substitute for workers on leave, or to complete a task or project during a fixed period. They receive a salary and are eligible for some benefits, but do not have an expectation of continued employment beyond their contracted term.

Commission-based: Individuals are hired to complete certain tasks or promote the products or services of an organization, and are compensated completely by commission or by a percentage reward. They may or may not have a base salary, depending on the agreement, and can sometimes be considered an employee of the firm with expectations of longer-term employment. Those considered employees can be eligible for certain benefits.

Apprentice or trainee: Individuals are conditionally hired for fixed-term training programs that can last from a few months to a few years. After successfully completing the training program or apprenticeship, the organization can then include them in their regular workforce. During the training program, the organization usually provides a partial or full salary to these individuals. Until the training programs are successfully completed, there is no certain expectation of continued long-term employment with the organization. However, many organizations provide partial or full non-wage benefits.

Probation: Individuals are hired by the organization with the understanding that their work performance during a fixed period of time has to be judged acceptable before they can considered a permanent hire. The employees receive a salary during this period and are generally entitled to benefits. The expectation of continued long-term employment is linked to one's performance evaluations.

Internships or volunteering: Individuals are hired by the organization to complete certain projects, assist with ongoing operations or even undergo training. The period of employment can vary significantly, since organizations often use this arrangement as a screening mechanism or to engage the community or educational institutions in mutually beneficial endeavors. These positions may be paid or unpaid. The paid positions are generally at a lower level than that of a full-time employee in a similar position. There is generally no expectation of continued long-term employment with the organization, but the interaction allows both sides to develop a better understanding of the benefits of a more permanent employment relationship.

Alternative employment arrangements

Independent contractors: This group of workers can include "sub-contractors," independent consultants, or freelance workers. They are generally not considered employees of the organization, since they have greater control over where, when, or for whom they work. They generally provide their own expertise and tools, and are usually paid when the work or project is completed. There are no expectations of receiving benefits or a continued long-term employment relationship.

On-call agreements: Workers are called to work only when they are needed. They can be scheduled to work for only a few days, or for several weeks each time. Depending on the agreement, they may be considered as part-time employees of the firm with some partial benefits. However, their salaries tend to be low, and there is no expectation of long-term permanent employment.

Temporary help agency workers: The salaries of these workers are paid by a temporary help agency. However, the duration of their job at the organization can vary widely. There is no expectation of benefits or continued long-term employment from the organization. However, there are many cases where an organization makes an offer to an employee and they are able to become a full-time member of that workforce. Depending on the length of the relationship with the temporary help agency, benefits are sometimes provided by the agency.

Contract-firm workers: Workers are hired by an organization and then asked to work for another organization under contracted conditions. They usually work for one customer at a time, and carry out their assignments at the worksite of the customer. Depending on the agreement, the contract firm can provide some benefits and there can be expectations of continued employment with the contract firm. On some rare occasions, the customer can pay the contract firm a fee to release the worker and allow them to become a full-time member of their organization.

Contingent employment arrangements

Casual or contingent work arrangements occur when individuals are hired for short-term or irregular periods of employment. They can be hired on a daily, hourly, or weekly basis. There is no expectation of ongoing work, and the individuals are not required to be available for work. Overall, contingent work arrangements do not provide a full-time wage; they have short employment agreements, have no access to benefits and have higher risks of termination. In essence, they are conditional and transitory work arrangements. We sometimes hear the term "on-demand employment" for this type of arrangement.

The concept of contingency work has been used extensively by various writers to cover many work situations. Much of the confusion stems from the fact that there is a narrow definition and expanded definition of the concept. The narrow definition of contingency focuses on two conditions: (a) no expectation of continued employment; and (b) the unpredictability or variability of working hours. The expanded definition focuses more on the poor qualities of the jobs. So, even for jobs that have stable hours and longer tenures, they can be considered contingent if some of these other conditions exist: (a) they are part-time jobs that require little skill, responsibility, or training; (b) they offer low pay and no benefits; and (c) they generally involve high rates of turnover (Tilly, 1996; Polivka & Nardone, 1989).

Type of Flexible Work Arrangements

Arrangements	Explanations
Flextime	This is a work arrangement where employees work a full day but can vary their working hours. A range of start and finish times are usually pre-arranged with the company or supervisor in such a way that the total number of hours worked are not affected. Employees maintain their flextimes in conjunction with the flexible shifts of other employees, so that the overall work flows are not affected.
Reduced hours	This is an arrangement where employers and employees agree on a temporary or permanent reduction of working hours below the standard 35 or 40 hour work-week. This could be due to health or disability issues. It is also possible that working hours are set to match workloads that change because of seasonality or the type of business.
Compressed work week	This refers to a situation where employees work for longer times per day or per shift. This allows the employee to have more days off, or makes it easier for the firm to manage crucial operations without interruptions. A typical situation could have an employee working ten hours per day for four days and getting an extra day off.
Telecommuting	This arrangement allows employees to do part of their regular work from home instead of going to the office. This is usually coordinated with the work group and firm, so that important meetings and client interactions are not missed.

Job sharing	This occurs when two or more workers share one or more positions or occupational responsibilities. In essence, it is a team approach to work organization, and this has evaluation and compensation implications.
Annualized hours (or banking of hours)	This is a negotiated arrangement whereby the employees choose the maximum hours they can work for different periods (weekly, monthly, or yearly). This is another form of a compressed work schedule. Employees are usually guaranteed a certain number of working hours per period and, in exchange, the employers can adjust work schedules to meet seasonal or project demands.
Gradual retirement	This arrangement gives employees the opportunity to gradually reduce their workload over a period of time to avoid the drastic change to full retirement. Organizations often use this approach to provide the opportunity for training new employees or redistributing work tasks, or to help with major corporate restructurings.
Leaves and sabbaticals	This situation allows employees to take time off from work without losing their employment rights or compensation status. These periods away from work can be paid or unpaid depending on the agreement with the organization. These situations are usually granted for educational, health or leisure reasons. These arrangements can occur on a regular, competitive, or negotiated basis.

Definitions of good jobs, bad jobs and dead-end jobs

Good Jobs

These jobs are those that generally pay higher salaries, require more skills, and give individuals more flexibility, autonomy, and chances for promotion and occupational growth. These jobs can be found in larger or smaller organizations, but they tend to be challenging and rewarding. There is usually an expectation of longer-term employment, and they come with a range of additional non-wage benefits.

Bad Jobs

These are the jobs that generally pay lower salaries, require less education, and don't give individuals the opportunity for significant advancement or occupational growth. Many of them include the three D jobs: dirty, demanding, and dangerous jobs. These jobs can be found in either the formal or the informal economy, and they have few non-wage benefits. Working hours tend to be irregular and, for many of these jobs, there is not a strong expectation of continued longer-term employment.

Dead-End Jobs

These jobs can also be considered bad jobs, but they have the additional stigma of not really holding any promise of imparting any potentially valuable skills to the individuals holding them. They tend to be terminal jobs, with no prospect of promotion. Since there are few pay raises and no significant responsibility attached to the job, the job position itself has a bad reputation. These jobs can exist in large or small organizations in areas that are not of key importance to operations. Individuals often comment that this type of employment situation appears to lead to nowhere, because they can't see any link to an acceptable career trajectory.

Key concepts to review in Chapter 1

Human resource management	Personalized resource management	Employment opportunity landscapes
Personal employability strategies	Work transition management	Personal capital
Work as contextual	Work as metaphoric	Work as evolutionary
Work centrality	Work goals	Intrinsic motivation
Extrinsic motivation	Flextime	Participative management
Job design	Job enrichment	Goal setting
Psychological attachment	Job satisfaction	Job rotation
Employee involvement	Autonomous work groups	Professional commitment
Employment structures	Primary sector	Secondary sector
Tertiary sector	Primary markets	Secondary markets
Public sector	Private sector	Non-profit sector
Employment arrangements	Traditional employment	Moderated-traditional employment
Alternative employment	Contingent employment	Flexible work arrangements
Internal labor market	External labor market	Restructuring
Downsizing	Mergers and acquisitions	Outsourcing
Off-shoring	Externalizing employment	Career forms
Bureaucratic career form	Boundary-switching career form	Portfolio career form
Entrepreneurial career form	Peripheral career form	Portable skills
Professional career type	Protean career type	Boundary-less career type
Behavioral style	Intra-preneurship	Entrepreneurship
Corporate venturing	Spin-offs	Entrepreneurs-in-residence
Goal orientation	Novice entrepreneur	Serial entrepreneur
Parallel entrepreneur	Portfolio entrepreneur	Good jobs/bad jobs debate

Appendix Chapter 1 References

Herzberg, F. and D. Mausner, *The motivation to Work*, 1959, New York: Wiley.

Sladek, C. and E. Hollander, *Where is everyone? The rise of workplace flexibility*. Benefits Quarterly, 2009. 25(2): p. 17.

Tilly, C., *Half a job: Bad and good part-time jobs in a changing labor market*, 1996, Philadelphia, PA: Temple University Press.

Polivka, A. and T. Nardone, *On the definition of "contingent work'"*. Monthly Labor Review, 1989. December: p. 9–14.

CHAPTER 2

Examples of Employment Intermediaries

Appendix Table 2.1 Examples of employment intermediaries

Type of EMI	Country	Name	Link	Comments
Private Sector	USA/Gobal	Vault	http://www.vault.com/wps/portal/usa	Career Consulting & Job search firm
Private Sector	USA/Gobal	DBM	http://www.dbm.com	Global career transitions management firm
Private	USA/Gobal	Career	http://www.careerconsultantscorp.com	A global Career

Sector		Consultants Corp.		consuting organization
Private Sector	USA/Gobal	Michael Page International	http://www.michaelpage.com	Multi-sector & global recruiting firm
Private Sector	USA/Gobal	Robert Half International	http://www.roberthalf.com	International staffing & recruiting firm
Private Sector	USA	Career Consulting international	http://www.thedegreepeople.com/	Foreign credential evaluating Service
Private Sector	USA	Kelly Employment Services	http://kellyservices.com	Workforce solutions organization
Private Sector	USA	Apple One	http://www.appleone.com/	Career assistance organization
Private Sector	USA	The Balanced Scorecard Institute	http://www.balancedscorecard.org/	Consulting & Management services group
Private Sector	USA	Manpower	http://us.manpower.com/us/en/default.jsp	Employment and career development
Private Sector	USA	Career Consulting Staffing Services	http://www.careeraustin.com/public/pag1.aspx	Career services & temp. agency
Private Sector	USA	Kforce	http://www.kforce.com	Financial, Technology & health care jobs focus
Private Sector	USA	Momentum Career Consulting	http://momentumcareers.com/	Career evaluation & consulting organization
Private Sector	USA	eFinancial Careers	http://www.efinancialcareers.com/	Organization focusing on jobs in financial services
Private Sector	USA	Adminstaff	http://www.administaff.com/	Large professional employer organization
Private Sector	USA	Career Consulting Services	http://www.careerconsultmd.com/	Jobs or Career Services
Private Sector	UK/Global	Antal International	http://www.antal.com	Global recruiting and placement company
Private Sector	UK/Europe	European Recruitment Agency	http://www.recruitment-agency.eu	Employment solutions throughout Europe
Private Sector	UK/Europe	French Selection	https://www.french-selection.co.uk/index.php	Multi-lingual job search site for Europe

Private Sector	UK	Joslin Rowe	http://www.joslinrowe.com/	Financial Services Recruitment
Private Sector	UK	Eden Brown	http://www.edenbrown.com/	Training & recruitment consulting services
Private Sector	UK	Templine Recruitment	http://www.templinerecruitment.co.uk	Temporary staffing and recruiting firm
Private Sector	Spain	Recruit Spain	http://www.recruitspain.com/index.asp	Multi-sector recruiting firm
Private Sector	Japan	East–West Consulting	http://www.ewc.co.jp/en/default.htm	Executive search and career consulting firm
Private Sector	Japan	Disco Internationa	http://www.discointer.com/	Japanese-English bilingual recruitment firm
Private Sector	Japan	Recruite Consulting	http://www.recruit-cc.co.jp/index.html	Career consulting firm in Japan
Private Sector	Ireland/Europe	Grafton Employment Group	http://www.grafton.hu/	Multi-county recuruiment and placement firm
Private Sector	Hong Kong	JobMarket	http://www.jobmarket.com.hk	Job search & career assistance organization
Private Sector	France	JobMultipass.com	http://www.jobmultipass.com/	Jobs search and skill matching site in France
Private Sector	China	Oasis Training Center	http://www.oasistrainingcenter.com/	Language and & Job Training in China

Type of EMI	Country	Name	Link	Comments
Public Sector	USA	CA. Employment Development Department	http://www.edd.ca.gov/	California jobs & training organization
Public Sector	USA	California State Association of Counties	http://www.counties.org	Public Sector California jobs organization
Public Sector	USA	USA-Jobs	http://www.usajobs.gov	Federal, State & Local Jobs Processing Organization
Public Sector	USA	AmeriCorps	http://www.americorps.gov/	National & governmental service organization
Public Sector	UK	Department for Works & Pensions	http://www.dwp.gov.uk/about-dwp/	Jobs & pension services organization

Public Sector	UAE/Dubai	Tanmia	http://www.tanmia.ae/tanmia/general/contactus.aspx	National human resource development site
Public Sector	Japan	HelloWork_Japan	https://www.hellowork.go.jp/	Career advice & job matching govt. organization
Public Sector	India	NVTIS_India	http://dget.nic.in/lisdapp/nvtis/nvtis.htm	Training & service to help unemployed in India
Public Sector	Hong Kong	GovHK	http://www.gov.hk/en/residents/employment/	Hong Kong govt. funded jobs site
Public Sector	Hong Kong	Employees Retraining Board of Hong Kong	http://www.erb.org	Retraining services public organization
Public Sector	France	ANPE (agence national pour l'emploi)	http://www.pole-emploi.fr/accueil/	Career advising & job matching organization

Type of EMI	Country	Name	Link	Comments
Member Based	USA/Gobal	French Tuesdays	http://www.frenchtuesdays.com	Career and networking site for French speakers
Member Based	USA	Calcpa Education Foundation	http://www.calcpa.org/Content/home.aspx	California Based Accountants Group
Member Based	USA	CFA Institute	https://www.cfainstitute.org/Pages/index.aspx	Global Association of CFA Members
Member Based	USA	GymJOB.com	http://www.gymjob.com/	Sports oriented member based organization
Member Based	USA	The Intermediary Network (INet)	http://www.intermediarynetwork.org/	Workforce & youth development organization
Member Based	USA	The Ladders	https://www.theladders.com	High earning job matching membership group
Member Based	USA	Banker's compliance group	http://www.bankerscompliancegroup.com/viewjobs.php	Employment & Training Opportunity Group
Member Based	USA	Intermediary Network	http://www.intermediarynetwork.org/	Youth and workfoce development Group
Member Based	USA	United Association of Plumbers	http://www.ua.org	Training programs & apprenticeships for members

Member Based	USA	Amer. Society of Training & Development	http://www.astd.org	Training & development activities nationwide
Member Based	USA	Latinos for Hire	http://www.latinosforhire.com/	Networking & career advice organization
Member Based	USA	AIGA (Design Focus)	http://www.aiga.org	Professional association for the design field
Member Based	USA	NAPO (Organizers)	http://www.napo.net/	National association for professional organizers
Member Based	USA	ASIS (Security Professionals)	http://www.asisonline.org/	National association of security professionals
Member Based	UK/Global	The International Bar Association	http://www.ibanet.org/Default.aspx	International legal practitioners group
Member Based	UK	Recruitment and Employment Confederation	http://www.rec.uk.com	Recruitment industry professionals
Member Based	UK	The Synergy Group	http://www.synergygroup.co.uk	Recruitment & training services organization
Member Based	UK	The Art Workers Guild	http://www.artworkersguild.org	Training & support for members
Member Based	UK	ViewCreatives.com	http://www.viewcreatives.com/	Networking for the creative industry
Member Based	Japan	RENGO	http://www.jtuc-rengo.org/about/index.html	Trade Union Based Member Site
Member Based	Japan	SBI Business Japan	http://www.sbibusiness.com/	Social networking for entrepreneurs
Member Based	Ireland	The Irish Congress of Trade Unions	http://www.ictu.ie/	Govenental-Union related organization
Member Based	India	Self Employed Women's Association	http://www.sewa.org/	Member based union
Member Based	Global	AIESEC	http://www.aiesec.org/	Global student run study, travel & job advising
Member Based	Europe	EuroCHRIE_Hospitality	http://www.eurochrie.org/	Hospitaly career advice & membership site

Member Based	China	ACFTU (China Trade Union Federation)	http://www.acftu.org.cn/template/10002/index.jsp	Working class trade union member organization
Member Based	Belgium/Europe	Airports Council International (ACI)	http://www.aci-europe.org/	Worldwide airport professionals association
Member Based	Belgium/Europe	European Projects Association	http://www.europeanprojects.org	Projects and training assistance for members

Type of EMI	Country	Name	Link	Comments
Web & Media	Vietnam	UNGVIEN.com	http://ungvien.com.vn/employee/contact.html	Job seeking & career development site in Vietnam
Web & Media	Vietnam	Career Link Vietnam	http://www.careerlink.vn/index.php?language=en	Multi-lingual job search site in Vietnam
Web & Media	USA/Gobal	Craigslist.org	www.craigslist.org:	Job listings website sections
Web & Media	USA/Gobal	Jobs Abroad	http://www.jobsabroad.com/	International jobs opportunity web site
Web & Media	USA/Gobal	Sing Tao Newspaper	http://www.singtao.com/	Chinese related jobs & info. worldwide
Web & Media	USA	Monster.com	http://www.monster.com/	Job resources web-site
Web & Media	USA	Women in Sports Careers	http://www.wiscfoundation.org	Sports related careers information
Web & Media	USA	Careerbuilder.com	http://www.careerbuilder.com	Job Search web site
Web & Media	USA	ExecuJobs	http://www.execujobs.net/webportfolios.html	Careers & Porfolio management site
Web & Media	USA	SFKorean.com	http://sfkorean.com	Korean Immigrant focuses job site
Web & Media	USA	CV Tips	www.cvtips.com	Resume writing & career advising site
Web & Media	USA	Yahoojobs	http://jobs.com/yahoo_jobs_14?co=xyahoox	Multi-sector job search site
Web & Media	USA	Jobmonkey.com	http://www.jobmonkey.com	Nation-wide job & int'l work search site
Web & Media	USA	Hotjobs.com	http://www.hotjobs.com	A major online-recruiting site
Web & Media	USA	BAJobs.com	http://www.bajobs.com/	Job opportunities and career networking site

Web & Media	USA	Recruit Tube	http://www.recruittube.com/Home.aspx	Interactive web site for jobs & career preparation
Web & Media	UK/Global	Global Careers.com	http://www.globalcareercompany.com/	Jobs & Careers in Africa, Asia and Europe
Web & Media	UK	Jobsite	http://www.jobsite.co.uk	Multi-sector jobs search & career training site
Web & Media	UK	1Job UK	http://www.1job.co.uk/	Job matching site for UK & Ireland
Web & Media	Singapore	Singapore IT Jobs	http://www.singaporeitjobs.com/	IT employment & recruitment site
Web & Media	Japan	CareerForum.net	http://www.careerforum.net/?lang=E	Career site for Japanese-English bilinguals
Web & Media	Hong Kong	JobsDB	http://www.jobsdb.com	Online recruitment database for Asia
Web & Media	Hong Kong	GeoExpat	http://www.geoexpat.com/	Multi-purpose and job search site
Web & Media	France	Cadre Emploi	http://www.cadremploi.fr/emploi/recherche_offres	Job matching & career advice site in France
Web & Media	Europe	Eurojobs	http://www.eurojobs.com	Multi-country job search site
Web & Media	Europe	Academic Jobs EU	http://www.academicjobseu.com	Site for Academic & research jobs in the EU
Web & Media	China	China Job	http://www.chinajob.com/	Job search & country adjustment site in China
Web & Media	China	Zhong Shan International Job Market Site	http://zs.job001.cn/	Multi-sector job site in China
Web & Media	Australia	Seek	http://www.seek.com.au	Major job site in Australia
Web & Media	Australia	Careerone.com	http://www.careerone.com.au/	Job Search & Career Management Site

Type of EMI	Country	Name	Link	Comments
Social Networking	Vietnam	360 Plus Vietnam	http://vn.360plus.yahoo.com/	Student centered social networking site
Social Networking	USA/Gobal	LinkedIn	http://www.linkedin.com	Professional networking site
Social Networking	USA/Gobal	Latpro Network	http://network.latpro.com/	Multi-country hispanic career networking site

Social Networking	USA	Doostang.com	http://www.doostang.com	High Earning Jobs & Social Networking Site
Social Networking	USA	Bebo	http://www.bebo.com/	Social networking site
Social Networking	USA	Hub Culture	http://www.hubculture.com/	Sharing business related expertise & advice
Social Networking	USA	Twitter	http://www.twitter.com	Social networking medium
Social Networking	Spain	Tuenti	http://www.tuenti.com/?m=login	A Spanish social networking site
Social Networking	Japan	MIXI	http://mixi.jp/about.pl	Social networking site in Japan
Social Networking	Hong Kong	Hong Kong Discussion Forum	http://careers.discuss.com.hk	Personal & career related discussions
Social networking	Global	Skyrock	http://www.skyrock.com/	Social networking site in many languages
Social networking	Global	Two Lingos	http://www.twolingos.com/jobs/index.php	Social networking for multilingual job seekers
Social networking	Germany/Global	XING	http://www.xing.com	Professional networking and career Site
Social networking	Germany	StudiVZ	http://www.studivz.net	Student-oriented German social networking site
Social networking	France/Global	Viadeo	http://www.viadeo.com	Business-oriented social networking site
Social networking	China/Asia	QQ (ICQ)	http://www.qq.com/	China and Asia social networking site
Social networking	China	Italki.com	http://www.italki.com/static/about.htm	Language learning and social networking site
Social networking	China	Renren (Xiaonei Network)	http://www.renren.com/	Chinese university social networking site
Social networking	China	kaixin001.com	www.kaixin001.com	Social networking site in China
Social networking	Brazil	Orkut	http://www.orkut.com	Social networking site in Brazil

Key concepts to review in Chapter 2

Job transition dynamics	Non-diversification of skills	Related diversification of skills
Unrelated diversification of Skills	Employability	Employability management
Up-skilling	Employment intermediaries	Labor market intermediaries
Labor market adjustment	Private sector intermediary	Member-based intermediary
Public sector intermediary	Web-based intermediary	Social networks
Secondary sourcing arrangement	On-site management	Sub-contractor management
Joint-employment	Co-employment	Employment environment
Employment opportunity landscape	Internal labor market	External labor market
Political economy	Educating function	Enhancing function
Protecting function	Regulating function	Funding function
Networking function	Brokering function	Credentialing function
Employing function	Dynamic sectors	Competence transferability

CHAPTER 3

Certifications to Boost Mobility and Capability

Professional certifications are institutional recognitions that a person is qualified to perform certain jobs or tasks. The argument of these local or international institutions is that these certifications represent a level of quality or accomplishment that will safeguard the public interest or the reputation of a particular profession. In most cases, these certifications must either be renewed or updated through supplemental service or educational activities. Some of these certifications act as enhancements to degrees received at educational institutions, while others are stand alone achievements that can also give access to more lucrative positions in their fields. Overall, the certifications represent an important aspect of personalized resource management, since they boost the capability, mobility, and transferability factors that drive careers. The table below presents a sample of some well-recognized certifications.

Type of certification	Conferring institutions
ACA, FCA or CA (Chartered Accountant)	Institute of Chartered Accountants in England and Wales (ICAEW), the Institute of Chartered Accountants of Scotland (ICAS), and the Institute of Chartered Accountants in Ireland (ICAI).
CPA (Certified Public Accountant)	American Institute of Certified Public Accountants (AICPA).
CIA (Certified Internal Auditor)	Institute of Internal Auditors (IIA).
CMA (Certified Management Accountant)	Institute of Certified Management Accountants (ICMA in Australia), Institute of Management Accountants (IMA in US).
CFA (Chartered Financial Analyst)	CFA Institute (CFAI).
CFP (Certified Financial Planner)	Certified Financial Planner Board of Standards and Financial Planning Standards Board.
CFM (Chartered Financial Manager)	Chartered Institute of Professional Financial Managers (CIPFM in the USA).
CPM (Chartered Portfolio Manager)	USA Board of Standards American Academy of Financial Management (AAFM).
PPL (Private Pilot License)	FAA (Federal Aviation Administration) or JAA (Joint Aviation Authorities).
CPL (Commercial Pilot License)	FAA (Federal Aviation Administration) or JAA (Joint Aviation Authorities.

ATP (Airline Transport Pilot)	FAA (Federal Aviation Administration) or JAA (Joint Aviation Authorities).
CPCL (Certified Professional in Learning and Performance)	The American Society for Training and Development.
TESOL (Teaching English as a Second Language)	The appropriate colleges and universities in various countries.
MILT (Member Institute of Logistics and Transport)	The Chartered Institute of Logistics and Transport (CILT).
Certified Associate in Project Management (CAPM)	Project Management Institute (PMI).
Project Management Professional (PMP)	Project Management Institute (PMI).
Physical Security Professional, Board-Certified (PSP)	AISIS: The American Society for Industrial Security.
Certified Protection Professional: Board-Certified in Security Management (CPP)	AISIS: The American Society for Industrial Security.

Areas of professional certification

Key concepts to review in Chapter 3

Entry and participation Strategies	Sector capability focus	Management capability
Administrative capability	Operations capability	Technical capability
Business development capability	Financial capability	Logistics capability
Regulatory capability	Cultural barrier	Institutional barrier
Technical barrier	Psychological carrier	Country-specific competence
Company-specific competence	Profession-specific competence	Modes of knowing
Knowing what	Knowing why	Knowing how
Knowing where	Knowing when	Knowing whom
Modes of doing	Modes of entering	Modes of participation
Entry and access strategies	Capability	Mobility
Transferability	Continuous employability	Personal career capital

CHAPTER 4

Studying in Tokyo

Studying in Tokyo	Background information
1. **The Institute for the International Education of Students** (iesabroad.org)	**IES** is a non-profit organization that provides students and universities with academic study abroad opportunities.
2. **Council on International Educational Exchange** (ciee.org)	**CIEE** is a non-profit international exchange organization for students, faculty, and administrators.
3. **Japan Times** (japantimes.co.jp/universities)	**The Japan Times** provides a guide to Japanese colleges and universities, most of which accept foreign students.
4. **Wapedia** (wa-pedia.com)	**Wapedia** provides information on language schools in Japan and information on living in and traveling in the country.
5. **The School of International Liberal Studies at Waseda** (waseda.jp.sils)	**SILS at Waseda** has extensive international exchange ties with universities around the world.
6. **Temple UniversityJapan Campus** (tuj.ac.jp)	**Temple University** in Japan has excellent undergraduate and graduate programs in English.

Studying in New York City

Studying in New York City	Background information
1. **New York City Colleges** (newyorkcitycolleges.com)	**New York City Colleges** is a site which provides links and information on colleges in the NYC area.
2. **The New School** (newschool.edu)	**The New School** is a famous NYC university providing undergraduate and graduate programs for bringing about positive change.
3. **NY.com** (ny.com/academia/)	**NY.com** is a comprehensive site with information on NYC and on colleges, language schools, libraries, and medical institutions in NYC.
4. **EnglishUSA** (englishinusa.com/NY1)	**EnglishUSA.com** provides information on language schools in New York and other states in the USA.

Studying in London

Studying in London	Background information
1. **Study London** (studylondon.ac.uk)	**Study London** is the official website for universities in the London area. Many language versions available on the site.
2. **City University London** (city.ac.uk/study)	**City University London** is a centrally located internationally-oriented school for business and other professions.
3. **Studies and Careers** (studiesandcareers.com)	**Studies and Careers** is a global company that helps students with admission and enrollment to schools in the UK and Europe.
4. **International Student House (ISH)** (ish.org.uk)	**ISH** is a well-knowm accommodation, social, and cultural center for British and international students.
5. **London School of Economics & Political Science** (lse.ac.uk)	**LSE** is a leading social science institution with many excellent undergraduate and post graduate programs.

Studying in Shanghai

Studying in Shanghai	Background information
1. **Study in Shanghai** (shmec.gov.cn)	**Study in Shanghai** provides information on colleges in Shanghai. The site is hosted by the Municipal Education Commission.
2. **Imandarin** (imandarin.net)	**I-Mandarin** is an institute that offers an extensive selection of Mandarin language courses, as well as an internship program.
3. **China Study Abroad** (chinastudyabroad.org)	**China Study Abroad** is an organization which sponsors study abroad program and support activities in China.
4. **Go Abroad** (goabroad.com)	**Go Abroad** is a global site providing information on language schools and study abroad programs in China and other countries.

Studying in Mumbai

Studying in Mumbai	Background information
1. **Mumbai Education** (mumbaieducation.net)	**Mumbai Education** has links to institutes and most educational institutions in Mumbai.
2. **Mumbai Schools** (mumbaischools.net)	**Mumbai Schools** lists education information and info on the best schools in the city.
3. **Coaching Indians** (coachingindians.com)	**Coaching Indians** is an online coaching center with info on schools, education, and careers.
4. **India Study Abroad** (indiastudyabroad.org)	**India Study Abroad** is an organization based in Mumbai which offers experiential learning programs.

Studying in Sao Paulo

Studying in Sao Paulo	Background Information
1. **The American Institute for Foreign Study** (AIFS:aifsabroad.com/brazil/saopaulo)	**AIFS Sao Paulo** has short and longer term educational and experiential programs in Brazil.
2. **Easy Go Languages Sao Paulo** (easygolanguages.com/study-abroad)	**Easy Go Languages Sao Paulo** offers small classes for Portuguese study in a scenic part of the city.
3. **CIEE Sao Paulo** (ciee.org/study-abroad/brazil/sao-paulo)	**CIEE Sao Paulo** has liberal arts study programs for students with some experience with Portuguese.
4. **Time Out Sao Paulo** (timeout.com/sao-paulo)	**Time Out Sao Paulo** gives links and an overview of a wide range of activities in Sao Paulo.

Studying in Moscow

Studying in Moscow	Background Information
1. **Globus International** (globusworldwide.com/Moscow)	**Globus International** has information on learning Russian in Moscow, and also advice on living in the city.
2. **MGU Russian** (mgu-russian.com)	**MGU** is the Russian language center of Moscow University. They have online, group, and individual classes.
3. **The International School of Moscow** (ISM: internationalschool.ru)	**ISM** is an international school with classes and activities at the early, lower, and middle school levels.
4. **International Schools** (evans.ru/rent/school)	**International Schools** is a site by Evans Property Services which list many schools in Moscow, and info on living there.
5. **The Anglo American School** (AAS: aas.ru)	**AAS** follows an international program, and is chartered by the American, British, and Canadian embassies in Moscow.

Studying in Dubai

Studying in Dubai	Background information
1. **Arabian Campus** (arabiancampus.com)	**Arabian Campus** has extensive lists of colleges and universities in Dubai and throughout the Middle East.
2. **Heriot-Watt University Dubai** (hw.ac.uk/dubai)	**Heriot-Watt University Dubai** is the first overseas university to set up in Dubai and offers British-style education programs.
3. **Dubai Education Guide** (dubaieducationguide.com)	**Dubai Education Guide** presents links and information on studying and training programs in Dubai.
4. **Study in Dubai** (studyindubai.info)	**Study in Dubai** gives information on visas and all types of schools at all levels in Dubai.
5. **Allo Expat Dubai** (dubai.alloexpat.com)	**Allo Expat Dubai** has information on international schools in Dubai and other links for expatriates.

Studying in Johannesburg

Studying in Johannesburg	Background information
1. **The University of Johannesburg** (uj.ac.za/EN)	**The University of Johannesburg** is a large multi campus university with a good higher education reputation.
2. **SA Private Schools** (saprivateschools.co.za)	**SA Private Schools** list private schools in Johannesburg and the rest of South Africa.
3. **SA Schools** (saschools.co.za)	**SA Schools** is massive directory of schools of all types in Johannesburg and other cities in South Africa.
4. **Sacred Heart College** (sacredheart.co.za)	**Sacred Heart College**, founded in 1889, provides quality education from pre-primary to high school in Johannesburg.

CHAPTER 5

Key Websites for the Information Technology Sector

Organization	Content
1. **Computer World** (computerworld.com)	**Computer World** is a comprehensive online magazine with news and information on the IT sector.
2. **InfoWorld** (infoworld.com)	**Info World** is a website with extensive information on trends and developments in the IT sector.
3. **Indeed** (indeed.com)	**Indeed** provides a wide variety of job listing for all areas of IT and other sectors throughout the US.
4. **ITjobs** (itjobs.com)	**IT Jobs** is a site created specifically for IT professionals and list numerous jobs by categories.
5. **DICE** (dice.com)	**Dice** is a well-known IT-centric site which lists available positions in many areas of IT.

Key Websites for the Financial Sector

Organization	Content
1. **eFinancialcareers** (efinancialcareer.com)	1. Jobs in the financial sector.
2. **Worldsalaries** (worldsalaries.org)	2. Financial sector salaries.
3. **CFA Institute** (cfainstitute.org)	3. CFA certification information.
4. **Jobs in Finance** (jobsinfinance.org)	4. Jobs in finance.
5. **Financial Executives** (financialexecutives.org)	5. Executive positions in the financial sector.
6. **World Bank** (worldbank.org)	6. World Bank information.
7. **Economy Watch** (economywatch.com)	7. Information on the major US banks.
8. **IMF** (imf.org)	8. International Monetary Fund information.

Key Websites for the Wine Sector

Links	Content
1. Wine Pro Recruiters (wineprorecruiters.com)	1. Wine jobs recruiter.
2. Wine Institute (wineinstitute.org)	2. Wine Institute of California.
3. Wine Business (winebusiness.com)	3. Wine business information.
4. Wine and Hospitality Jobs (wineandhospitablityjobs.com)	4. Wine and hospitality job site.
5. Wine Industry (wineindustryjobs.jobamatic.com)	5. Wine industry jobs.
6. Crushpad Wine (crushpadwine.com)	6. Learning about wine making.

7. International Wine Guild (internationalwineguild.com)
8. Wine Industry Sales Education (wineindustrysaleseducation.com)
9. Wine schools (education-portal.com/)
10. Wine business management (gsb.uct.ac.za)
11. Wine business in France (bsbu.eu)
12. Graduate wine program (masters.inseec-france.com)

7. International wine sector information.
8. Wine industry education and certification site.
9. Wine sector education and schools.
10. Wine business management in South Africa.
11. Wine business management in France.
12. Graduate program in wine business.

Key Websites for the Logistics Sector

Organization	Content
1. Jobs in Logistics (jobsinlogistics.com)	1. Jobs in logistics.
2. CSMP (cscmp.org)	2. Council of Supply Chain Management.
3. About Logistics (logistics.about.com)	3. Information on logistics.
4. World Bid (worldbid.com)	4. International trade marketplace.
5. APICS (apics.org)	5. Association of Operations Management.
6. Commerce Department (commerce.gov)	6. Commerce Department information.
7. Exporting (export.gov)	7. Government site for exporting activities.
8. International Export (fita.org)	8. International import-export site.
9. ITA (ita.doc.gov)	9. The International Trade Association.
10. IWLA (iwla.com)	10. International Warehouse Logistics Association.
11. Logistics Directory (logisticsworld.com)	11. Directory of logistics resources.
12. Open Entry (openentry.com)	12. Social network for buyers and sellers.

CHAPTER 6

Links to Important Development Organizations and Activities

www.aah-usa.org | www.worldbank.org | www.cgdev.org/
www.amnesty.org | www.rti.org/ | www.infodev.org/
www.care.org | www.usaid.gov/ | www.un.org/
www.caritas.org | iddsummit.org/ | www.un.org/millenniumgoals/
www.crs.org | www.cgdev.org | ran.org/
www.devdir.org | www.imf.org | www.sourcewatch.org/
www.devex.com | jobs.undp.org/ | www.finca.org/
www.dwb.org | www.IFC.org | water.org/
www.hrw.org | www.peacecorps.gov | www.internationaljobs.org/
www.imf.org | www.wto.org | www.cssp.org.pk/home
www.oired.vt.edu | www.un.org/esa | www.unesco.org

Information on American and Foreign Educational Institutions

Country: **USA**
Program: San Francisco State University (SFSU)
Department of International Business: BS in International Business.
Link: cob.sfsu.edu

The Department of International Business is one of the oldest and largest international business programs in the United States. The professors are committed to providing quality education to SFSU students. Upon the completion of the program, students will have acquired the knowledge and skills necessary to perform successfully in domestic and international business environments. More importantly, the program aims to develop a global mindset that will enable the students to overcome the numerous ethical, social, cultural, political, economic, geographic, and technology challenges to come. The program has over 600 students engaging in concentrated studies of international business at both the graduate and undergraduate levels. The program is also designed to help students develop a better understanding of potential career paths and strategies for successful career development.

Country: **USA**
Program: Haas School of Business: BA in Global Management
Link: haas.berkeley.edu

The Haas School of Business is a famous in the USA and abroad. It is part of the University of California, Berkeley, one of the best public universities in the US. The Haas Global Management Bachelors is an international business program that promises to provide a high level of knowledge and skills to prepare students for an international business career. In addition to interesting coursework, the program provides business students with opportunities to study abroad and improve their fluency in a foreign language. Students can take complete the course work at UC Berkeley or abroad. This program is designed for students who are truly dedicated to pursuing an international business career.

Country: **USA**
Program: Temple University, Philadelphia: BA in International Business
Link: sbm.temple.edu

This is an undergraduate program at Temple University, Philadelphia. The International Business major (IBUS) at Temple University is rated as one of the top 10 in the US by US News and World reports. The IBUS major combines international business coursework with language studies. This builds the students competence to work in the international business arena. Because of the emphasis on cross-cultural and language experience, a study aboard program is recommended and students usually spend a semester or a year abroad. The program also exposes students to coursework in areas such as economics, finance, and marketing. This educational experience is designed to equip students with the knowledge and global perspectives required to thrive in the global workforce of the twenty-first century.

Country: **USA**
Program: Kellogg School of Management, Northwestern University:BA inInternational Business and Markets
Link: kellogg.northwestern.edu

The International Business and Markets Program is a bachelor's degree program that is centered around a strong discipline-based international business curriculum focused on providing students with the specialized tools in accounting, finance, marketing, organizations management, and management strategy necessary to understand the international dimension of business. The major also allows students to apply what they have learned in the classroom about international business strategy with real-world research experience abroad, through the popular Global Initiatives in Management (GIM) course. By participating in GIM, students gain valuable leadership skills and enhance their awareness of the global business environment. The students select their destination and target industries, plan the logistics, finances, and public relations tactics for their two-week visit to their chosen country, making corporate, cultural, and media contacts.

Country: **USA**
Program: Pepperdine University: International MBA Program
Link: bschool.pepperdine.edu

Pepperdine University's Graziadio School of Business and Management offers multiple MBA programs including a full time accelerated one-year program an international program and an Executive MBA. The main campus is located in Malibu, California, but the school also has multiple satellite campuses throughout the greater Los Angeles area. Pepperdine's International MBA (IMBA) program has partnerships and opportunities in countries across Europe, Latin America and Asia. The IMBA program provides a concentration of international business electives as well as a trimester abroad.

Country: **USA**
Program: San Diego State University: B.A. in International Business
Link: sdsu.edu

This program results in a BA in International Business. The international business program at San Diego State University is ranked as one of the top 15 international business programs in the United States. The program offers classes such as business administration and foreign languages, and places a great emphasis on regional culture studies. One aspect of the program that differentiates it from others is the fact that it requires one semester abroad. This program also requires students to complete an internship that prepares them for future employment.

Country: **USA**
Program: Thunderbird School of Global Management: MBA in Global
                    Management
Link: thunderbird.edu

Thunderbird offers two options for students pursuing an MBA in Global Management: a traditional program and an accelerated program. The accelerated program differs from the traditional program in terms of length and scope. The accelerated program does not offer a section abroad within the program. The courses offered center around five core values: global learning network, global entrepreneurship, global mindset, global citizenship, and global thought leadership. In addition, the courses focus on business analysis, leadership skills, analytical skills, and understanding key emerging business areas. Upon graduation, students should not only learn the global concepts of the different business areas, but also have the ability to converse in another language. If taking the traditional program, students are sent to take courses abroad for six weeks.

Country: **USA**
Program: Johns Hopkins University: MA in International Affairs
Source: sais-jhu.edu

The MA at the Johns Hopkins University SAIS (School of Advanced International Studies) requires two years of study, during which candidates take four courses each semester and study a modern foreign language. SAIS offers an interdisciplinary program in which students can concentrate in either a functional area of international relations (general international relations; conflict management; energy, resources and environment; global theory and history; international law and organizations; strategic studies or international development) or a region of the world (African studies; American foreign policy; China studies; Japan studies; Korea studies; south Asia studies; southeast Asia studies; European studies; Middle East studies; Russia and Eurasian studies; Canadian studies, or Latin American studies). Additionally, MA students must complete a concentration in international economics; pass a foreign language proficiency exam; pass core exams; and complete a capstone. SAIS stands out among the top graduate programs for these unique aspects of its curriculum. SAIS also has the unique option of dual degree programs. The formal dual-degree programs lead to an MA in international relations from SAIS, combined with another graduate degree in business, law, public health, or public administration.

Country: **Japan**
Program: Rikkyo University: MIB in International Business
Link: cob.rikkyo.ac.jp

The College of Business at Rikkyo University offers a full-time, two-year Master of International Business (MIB) degree program. All courses are taught in English, and the program prepares graduates to achieve their goals and boost their careers in the global market. The program offers a wide array of Asia-focused electives, ranging from Japanese human resource management to strategic technological innovation in Asia.

Country:	**Singapore**
Program:	Institution: Singapore Polytechnic (SP): DIP in International Business
Link:	sp.edu.sg

Singapore Polytechnic offers a Diploma in International Business. In this program, they prepare students to succeed in the global marketplace. They state that, by teaching core international business competencies, students will be graduating "world-ready." Students are also required to work in a relevant business position as an intern, an experience which helps them with their careers after graduation. The program allows for travel to foreign countries in order to immerse students in another country's business practices and culture. It also gives students the chance to learn new foreign languages and take special seminars in other parts of the world.

Country:	**Hong Kong S.A.R. China**
Program:	The University of Hong Kong: BBA in International Business and Global Management.
Link:	hku.hk

The International Business and Global Management Program integrates two major academic areas, business and economics, and social sciences. The program not only teaches international business and global management, it also offers opportunities to participate in overseas exchange, international field trips, internships, and a global analysis team project the aim of which is to help students develop global perspectives while they adapt to real-world business environments.

Country:	**New Zealand**
Program:	Victoria University of Wellington: School of Marketing and International Business: BA, MA in International Business
Link:	victoria.ac.nz

The school of Marketing and International Business offers an undergraduate International Business major. The program teaches how to apply business principles in an ever more competitive and cooperative global business environment. The course structure offers basic business principles, language, and culture study in the first year, international marketing, human resource management, and dynamic strategy and structure in international business in the second year, and concludes the program with simulation courses in cross-cultural management, business research, and international logistics. The school also offers an international business emphasis in their Master of Commerce and Administration program.

Country: **France**
Program: The American Business School in Paris: BA, MBA
Link: absparis.org

The BA program is accredited through the International Assembly for Collegiate Business Education (IACBE). It is also recognized in France (titre certifié niveau II). The program consists of core courses in business, general education, and liberal arts, with specialized courses for the chosen majors. It is the same structure as a regular American university. ABS Paris also offers a specialized Master's degree program in International Business Development. The Master of Arts program is a two-year program.

Country: **France**
Program: SKEMA Business School: MSc in International Business.
Link: skema.edu

This International Business Program is a one-year graduate program available to international students. SKEMA's International Business Program is taught in English and was ranked 29th globally by the Financial Times. The program consists of a range of highly experienced international professors, who not only offer their academic knowledge, but also practical experience to the students. The school has also partnered with large companies such as IBM, Orange, Amadeus and Groupe Accord, as well as non-profit organizations such as the EU and Chambers of Commerce.

Country: **Switzerland**
Program: SBS Swiss Business School: MBA
Link: sbs.edu

The Master of Business Administration program is designed to provide the knowledge and skills needed to become an effective manager in a variety of organizational settings. It is a broad-based career-advancement degree, rather than a technical training for a particular job within an organization. The broad goal of the program is to provide students with in-depth knowledge and competencies that support their further career development.

Country: **Turkey**
Program: KOÇ University: Master of Science in International Management
Link: ku.edu.tr

This program consists of one year in the classroom with highly renowned faculty from around the world, and a second year obtaining experience via internships or research abroad. This is the only Turkish university that is a member of the Community of European Management Schools (CEMS). The program has emerged as the number one program for combined international results (international faculty, student and board diversity, alumni mobility, and international course experience).

CHAPTER 7

Name: **Career Direct Online**
Source: Careerdirectonline.org
Description: This site offers a variety of tests. They analyze four area: personality, interests, skills, and values. This is more than a typical aptitude test. The personality ID test component is free. The survey consists of 16 questions. After you complete the survey, they will inform you of your strengths and give you suggestions of areas that would be beneficial to your career. They email the results to you.

Name: **Human Metrics, Jung Typology Test**
Source: Humanmetrics.com
Description: This assessment tool is based on a test created by researcher Carl Jung to identify the specific traits of an individual according to three separate categories. This test also includes a fourth category which is used in a Myers-Briggs assessment. The four main categories are as follows: Extraversion–Introversion; Sensing–Intuition; Thinking–Feeling; and Judging-Perceiving. This test is free at this website. However, for a fee, but for a more complete career development profile based on the same categories, you can go to Personalityexplorer.com.

Name: **Quest Career**
Source: Questcareer.com
Description: If you are interested in taking a career aptitude test that shows for which jobs you might be a good match, then you can try this free test. There are about 71 questions and, after you are done, they will give you an overview of your strengths, job aptitude, and workplace attitudes.

Name:	**CareerLink Inventory**
Source:	Mpcfaculty.net
Description:	The CareerLink Inventory was designed to provide the information necessary to begin a career search. The survey tool will assess you in five categories: your aptitudes, interests, temperaments, physical capacities/working conditions, and career preparation time. It will then match you to careers accordingly. The test appears to be free at this website location.

Name:	**Keirsey Temperament Sorter**
Source:	Advisorteam.com
Description:	The Keirsey Temperament Sorter (KTS®-II) is a widely used personality instrument. It asks 70 question that help to uncover your personality type. The KTS-II is based on Keirsey Temperament Theory™, published in the books, Please Understand Me® and Please Understand Me® II, by Dr. David Keirsey. This test appears to be free of charge.

Name:	**Careerpath.com**
Source:	Careerpath.com
Description:	The site provides a variety of career tests that help with career decisions. It claims to help you assess your options as you begin a career or look for a career change. One of the career test has 24 pairs of statements and you pick the one most appealing to you. You are then give an analysis of the results. This test appears to be free of charge.

Name:	**Job Diagnosis**
Source:	Jobdiagnosis.com
Description:	This site provides free career testing. They use their survey instrument to analyze your skills and aptitude in terms of a sector, as well as a job position and career for which you might be best suited. The whole test questionnaire requires approximately 5–10 minutes.

Name:	**The Princeton Review Career Quiz**
Source:	Princetonreview.com
Description:	This assessment quiz examines four behavioral categories: interests, style, needs, and stress behavior. Each of the four behavioral categories is then generalized into four colors.

After you complete the Princeton Review Career Quiz, the site will show you careers that match the "style, needs, interest and stress" colors you created. The colors have the following meanings: red = expediting; green = communicating; blue = planning; and yellow = administrating. The test appears to be free of charge.

Imagined Career Biography #1

Ten years from now, I will be 32 years old and hopefully well-established in my career as an international executive specializing in global business development. My career trajectory will show many positions that gave me the chance to develop my extensive market research and negotiations skills. I used those skills to become very good at developing new business ventures across national borders. However, I mainly focused on working in, and with, emerging markets, in order to take advantage of the numerous opportunities in various sectors in those regions. I am especially experienced at positions in the hospitality and tourism sector.

To attain these goals, I had to switch jobs a number of times to gain the professional expertise required to become a successful international executive. I began working towards my career goals by getting a position with a consultant firm as a junior consultant. I was lucky to get the junior consultant position without having an MBA. However, I had to work very hard and quickly learned many things about various industries. I even got the chance to travel to a number of countries. I believe that the consultant position allowed me to gain invaluable experience in the business world and exposed me to the various challenges that firms face when doing business across borders.

Besides the work experience, I was lucky enough to get my company to sponsor my MBA studies. I guess the firm saw my dedication and wanted me to expand my areas of expertise. After going to school and working at the same time, I finished my MBA in three years. I used that opportunity to move up from junior consultant to consultant manager and finally a senior consultant. As a senior consultant, I spoke directly speak with the CEO and prospective clients. I was put in charge of developing competitive strategies for our clients. The senior consultant's position also involved overseeing a group of junior consultants and working with other managers.

After being in the consulting industry for about five years, I took a position with a multinational firm that had me working overseas as an expatriate. I worked in three different countries and helped the firm manage its global workforce, as well as develop more competitive international strategies. I learned many things from those assignments, and was especially proud of my ability to work with many different cultures and negotiating styles. I am now very confident in my ability to adapt to, and work effectively in, different national environments. I worked as a global strategy manager for about three years. At that point in my career, I had acquired an MBA and worked for eight years in international business. For the next two years, I worked very hard to become part of the executive team at this multinational firm. I feel confident that I can continue to contribute to their success and hope they recognize my leadership and strategic capabilities. Someday, I hope to be a CEO of this or another large company in the hospitality and tourism industry.

Imagined Career Biography #2

James Doe is now 34 years old, and has had a successful business career to date. As a director of corporate strategy, James Doe has identified and implemented growth strategies to help his company enter and expand into different markets around the world. Throughout his career so far, he has had a strong commitment to quality market research, expanding the customer base and adapting to cultural and institutional barriers abroad. He effectively coordinated the sales and marketing channels to strengthen his company's competitive advantage.

From early in his career, James Doe had a passion for working with people and solving difficult problems. As a student at California State University, he was actively involved in coordinating events to bring students together with business practitioners. Later, after completing his degree in international business, he began his career as a marketing analyst at a medium-sized e-tailer in San Francisco. This was a crucial phase of his development, and he gathered much-needed business experience. He was also very active in gaining and maintaining various certifications. He got a certificate in Business Process Management and then was successful at becoming a Certified Associate Project Manager through the Project Management Institute. He got these certifications during a three-year span while he worked as a marketing analyst.

After about three years in the e-commerce sector, James Doe became a project manager's assistant at a leading IT firm. His job was to assist with implementing B2B cloud-based computing projects. While holding this position, he went back to school and earned a Master's degree in e-commerce. These activities and experiences allowed him to accomplish his five-year goal of becoming a Certified Project Manager and taking on a lead role as a project manager at Yahoo. He was happy to work with a talented group of international IT professionals in the online shopping sector.

After two years in that position as a project manager, James Doe became a leading member of the International Sales Division of Dell Computers, in their Tokyo-Japan office. Using all of his past experiences, he was able to find creative and innovative ways to improve their online sales and marketing channels and increase brand loyalty at the same time. During this time, James Doe worked on and led cross-functional teams while reporting directly to top management. He gained invaluable experience in completing projects and working closely with colleagues, top executives, and programmers at all levels of the company. These experiences were crucial to his success in his current role as a director of corporate strategy. His knowledge and professional experiences are helping him every day in getting the best from his people and in building new relationships in international markets.

CHAPTER 8

Doing Research on (the Strategic Behavior of) Top Management

An important aspect of market research is finding out the importance of upper management to the success of a company. How the top executives got their positions can be very revealing. Are appointments generally made from within, or do we see a situation whereby an outsider usually comes in to run the show? The educational background and previous accomplishments of the executive team can signal the strategic capabilities of the firm. Compensation and bonuses are often mentioned, but more often it is more helpful to evaluate the leadership ability and strategic approach of a company's executive team. The factors and tools presented below should give significant insight into the strategic behavior and capabilities of top management.

Management structure (evaluation factor)

Management structure refers to the organization of business units and the distribution of authority within an organization. These structural factors have a significant impact on how top management, mid and lower level staff, departments, divisions, and affiliates interact to achieve organizational goals.

In terms of the organizations of business units, the main forms that we find are the functional, multi-divisional, or hybrid structures. In terms of the distribution of authority, we can see a range from a high distribution of authority and responsibility to one in which we have centralized decision making and authority. These factors, together, then determine if we see a flat or very hierarchical management structure in an organization. Depending on how the firm and top management decide to organize activities within, we can see very different approaches to decision making, communication, and coordination. Overall, the choice of management structure is a crucial element in the potential performance of a company. In general, we expect to see that a firm's structure should match its strategy.

McKinsey 7-S (evaluation tool)

The McKinsey 7-S framework emerged from the idea that the key internal aspects of a firm needs to be alinged for it to be successful. The seven key aspects put forth are strategy, structure, systems, shared values, staff, style, and skills. The first three are considered "hard elements"; the remaining four are the "soft elements" that firms need to consider. The McKinsey 7-S framework is a valuable tool for assessing the internal environment of a company, as well as top management strategy. Some have even used this to to evaluate the elements of a team or project.

The balanced scorecard (BSC) (evaluation tool)

The balanced scorecard is a strategic planning and management tool used to align business activities with the vision and goals of the organization. It is a semi-standard structured report format that helps executives evaluate, score, and keeptrack of key firm activities. It supposedly gives executives a more balanced view of the organization. This tool can also give us insights into how well the top management team is leading the organization.

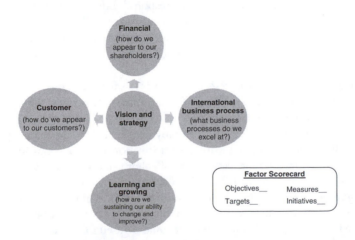

Management turnover rate (evaluation measure)

Turnover refers to the rate at which an organization gains and lose employees. Employees join because they are recruited to benefit the organization. Employees leave either voluntarily or because they have been let go. Looking at the turnover history of the top management team can give us some insights as to the stability of the firm or the consistency of the firm's strategic direction. If more employees are joining than leaving, that is usually a good thing. However, we also have to examine the quality and the importance of those executives who have left the organization. Losing one or two powerful leaders can be just as devastating as losing many generally capable executives.

Price/Earnings ratio (P/E ratio) (evaluation measure)

Whether or not it's justifiable, investors, the board of directors, and the market in general often look at the P/E ratios of a firm during a certain period as an indirect way of evaluating the performance of top management. Very often, the bonuses of those executives are linked to the stock performance of the firm for that period. The P/E ratio is obtained by dividing the market value per share of a company by its earnings per share (EPS). According to agency theory, the managers' interests should be aligned with those of the shareholders. Consequently, actions or strategies that reward the shareholders are a good sign that top management is performing well.

Level of international experience-exposition (evaluation factor)

As competition becomes more global, it is imperative that organizations have executives who are familiar with the international environment. The level of international experience of top management can be ascertained from the history of their job assignments abroad. It can also be evaluated based on their education or living experience in foreign environments. In addition to work experience, the strong multi-lingual or multicultural experiences of top management can make it easier for the firm to navigate the difficult international environment.

Doing Research on Occupations

The ability to do extensive research on jobs and occupations is essential for effective long-term career management. Whether individuals are looking for a position at the entry, mid, or upper level of an organization, it is important that they have a clear picture of the compensation, skills, responsibilities, working conditions, and potential job trajectories that a particular occupation entails. Since the fundamental factors surrounding an occupation will vary significantly depending on the sector in which it is located, it is also important to understand how a particular sector can affect job content and career trajectories.

In many ways, this type of research involves less formal strategies. A lot of information often can be obtained from informal sources such as friendship networks, blogs, websites, and popular magazines. Another source of information about jobs would be career centers, job forums, employment agencies, and company websites. One invaluable source of occupational information is the Occupational Outlook Handbook developed by the Department of Labor. An online version is available at http://www.bls.gov/oco/. This handbook provides information on job outlook, earnings potential, education, training, duties, and working conditions. This handbook is also kept up to date with the latest information on occupations. Below is a list of some factors, tools, and measures that could be used to evaluate occupations.

Occupational demand (evaluation factor)

This refers to the level of demand for a specific occupation. Many factors can affect the occupational demand. The greatest impact is probably the general level of economic growth in a region or country. However, the next factors would definitely be the outlook for continued growth in a particular sector and the importance of that occupation to the capabilities needed in a sector. The third important factor would be the demand for those occupations from the most dynamic firms in a sector. Finally, certain product or service trends can indicate the potential for new careers. When a new technology or new type of service takes hold and grows, we also see new careers develop and grow. With globalization affecting human resource developments, we can expect that individuals will start taking advantage of opportunities in different environments around the globe. Consequently, an evaluation of occupational demand should include local, regional, national, and international factors as well as demand conditions in the industry.

Job evaluation point method (evaluation tool)

The job evaluation point method is a technique used to determine the relative worth of a job. By using this method, a company can evaluate the importance of an occupation compared to others in the organization. This kind of information allows companies to set internal compensation levels that are both equitable and competitive. The job evaluation point method is based on a quantitative process that breaks jobs down into key elements that are then rated. The key elements in the point method are skill, effort, responsibility, and working conditions. Table A8.2 further breaks down the job qualities that are linked to those elements.

Table A8.2 Compensable factors in a point factor method of job evaluation

Compensable factor	Rating criteria
Skill/know-how	Education, experience, knowledge
Effort	Physical effort, mental effort
Responsibility	Judgment, decision-making, international business contacts, consequence of error, degree of influence, supervisory responsibilities, independent action responsibility, fiscal responsibility, confidential information responsibility, machinery and equipment responsibility
Working conditions	Risks, comfort, physical demands, personal demands

Career assessment surveys (evaluation tool)

There are many job and career assessment surveys that individuals can take online to get a clearer picture of their skills, aptitude, and preference for certain occupations. These surveys will ask a battery of questions that capture personal attributes and capabilities. The ultimate objective of these surveys is to help individuals make better career decisions.

Compensation level (evaluation measure)

Compensation levels often reflect how attractive a particular position is in a sector. However, determining the correct compensation level for a position can often be very difficult. Compensation for the same occupation will often vary significantly by sector, region, and country. The best approach to getting a fair idea of the right compensation level is to compare jobs within the same sector and in the same region. Fortunately, there are websites such as www.glassdoor.com and www.salary.com that have tools to enable individuals to get the appropriate salary range. Beyond the appropriate level, individuals have to depend on their negotiation skills and their sense of how much a firm needs their particular skill set.

Doing Research on Products and Services

Knowing about a company's products and services is crucial when interviewing for a new position. A good understanding of basic product or service research should also be helpful to most employees of a firm. The methods used for this type of research can vary significantly, depending on the specific product or service being evaluated. However, it is important to note that the evaluation process looks very different if one is carrying out the research from inside or outside the firm. Inside the firm, managers have access to surveys, customer feedback, history of returns, and other concrete measures. Outside the firm, one often has to rely on word of mouth, feedback websites, and other written materials. Very often, the company will provide detailed information about their products and services on their websites or in their annual reports. Below is a list of some items that an individual can use to get a better idea of the nature of a company's products and services.

Brand loyalty (evaluation factor)

Brand loyalty is a reflection of how committed consumers are to using, purchasing, or repurchasing the same product or service in a particular market. Brand loyalty usually stems from the level of satisfaction that the customer feels from using the product or service. This sense of satisfaction could be based on higher levels of the perceived quality, usefulness, innovation, or exclusiveness that is attached to the product or service. Ultimately, companies that have high levels of brand loyalty can usually charge more, and can be more confident that they will maintain or grow their market share.

Market share (evaluation measure)

Market share is an important factor to consider when researching products and services. The market share of the product or service is determined by the percentage of total sales that it commands in a particular market segment. Products or services with high market shares tend to either generate excess cash or give the firm a competitive advantage in certain markets. Evaluating the market share movement over time can give an even better picture of how competitive a product or service is.

Product life cycle (evaluation tool)

The product life cycle framework illustrates the different stages of a product in the marketplace, and the various strategies that are usually necessary to make the product successful at that stage. By being aware of a product's stage in the lifecycle, marketers can often gauge demand and develop marketing and distribution strategies. Table A8.3 shows the division of the product life into the introduction, growth, maturity, and decline stages.

Customer and employee feedback (evaluation factor)

Consumer feedback refers to the information from consumers, posted on websites or transmitted by word of mouth, about their perceptions of a product, service, or

Table A8.3 Stages of the product life cycle

	Introduction	Growth	Maturity	Decline
Marketing objective	Gain awareness	Stress differentiation	Maintain brand loyalty	Harvesting or disposal
Competition	Few	More	Many	Reduced
Product	One	More version	Full product line	Best sellers
Price	Skimming or penetration	Gain market share, deals	Defend market share, profit	Stay profitable
Promotion	Inform, educate	Stress competitive differences	Reminder-oriented	Minimal promotion
Place	Limited	More outlets	Maximum outlets	Fewer outlets

organization. These can come in the form of a quantitative rating or in the form of qualitative comments. Websites such a www.yelp.comprovide a mechanism for transmitting extensive feedback about organizations, products and services. Some websites, such as www.glassdoor.com and www.feedbackmetrics.com, even provide employee feedback about working conditions at various organizations. The information provided by all these sites can be invaluable for individuals making crucial career decisions.

The 4Ps (marketing mix) (evaluation tool)

The "4Ps" refers to a well-established tool that shows the combination of marketing strategies that can be used make a product or service successful. The name "4Ps" is short for product, price, place, and promotion. "Product" refers to the functional, process, or visual aspects of a product or service. "Price" refers to the pricing and other financial aspects of the product or service. "Place" refers to the distribution decisions that impact how effectively a product or service is delivered. "Promotion" refers to the communication and selling activities that attract customers and develop their loyalty. The Summary of Marketing Mix Decisions table shows some of the strategic decisions that are linked to each of the 4Ps.

Summary of marketing mix decisions

Product	Price	Place	Promotion
Functionality	List price	Channel members	Advertising
Appearance	Discounts	Channel motivation	Personal selling
Quality	Allowances	Market coverage	Public relations
Packaging	Financing	Locations	Message
Brand	Leasing options	Logistics	Media
Warranty		Service levels	Budget
Service and support			

Source: http://www.quickmba.com/marketing/mix/

INDEX